THE
HOLOCAUST
AND THE
CHRISTIAN
WORLD

THE
HOLOCAUST
AND THE
CHRISTIAN
WORLD

REFLECTIONS ON THE PAST

CHALLENGES FOR THE FUTURE

Edited by

Carol Rittner, Stephen D. Smith and Irena Steinfeldt

Consulting Editor: Yehuda Bauer

Beth Shalom Holocaust Memorial Centre
Yad Vashem International School for Holocaust Studies

Continuum • New York

2000
Continuum International Publishing Group Inc
370 Lexington Avenue, New York, NY 10017

First published in Great Britain 2000 by Kuperard

Printed in Great Britain

Library of Congress Cataloging-in-Publication Data

The Holocaust and the Christian world: reflections on the past,
challenges for the future/edited by Carol Rittner, Stephen D. Smith,
and Irena Steinfeldt; consulting editor: Yehuda Bauer.
     p. cm.
    Includes bibliographical references and index.
    ISBN 0-8264-1298-X (alk. paper)—ISBN 0-8264-1299-8 (pbk.: alk. paper)
      1. Christianity and antisemitism—History. 2. Holocaust, Jewish
(1939–1945)—Influence. 5. Judaism—Relations—Christianity. 6.
Christianity and other religions—Judaism. I. Rittner, Carol Ann, 1943–
II. Smith, Stephen D. (Stephen David), 1967– III. Steinfeldt, Irena. IV.
Bauer, Yehuda.
BM535.H615 2000
261.2'6'0904—dc21   00-034034

All photographs courtesy of Yad Vashem, with the exception of:
United States Holocaust Memorial Museum: pp. 5, 44, 105, 111, 163
Auschwitz State Museum Archives: pp. 49, 71, 108, 111
Topham Photos: pp. 224, 231, 233
Breit Lohamei Haghetaot: pp. 69
Evangelisches Zentralarchiv: pp. 52, 54
Stephen D. Smith: pp. 198, 199, 200, 202, 239

Design and production by CDA Creative Communications
Mansfield, Nottinghamshire, UK

To the Minority

Who did more than the call of duty

And to all with the courage

To be like them

Comprehension does not mean denying the outrageous, deducing the unprecedented from precedents, or explaining phenomena by such analogies and generalities that the impact of reality and the shock of experience are no longer felt. It means, rather, examining and bearing consciously the burden which our century has placed on us – neither denying its existence nor submitting weakly to its weight. Comprehension, in short, means the unpremeditated, attentive facing up to, and resisting of, reality – whatever it may be.

Hannah Arendt

CONTENTS

CONTENTS

PART FIVE: THE REACTION OF THE CHURCHES IN NAZI-OCCUPIED EUROPE

PART SIX: THE VATICAN, THE POPE, AND THE PERSECUTION OF THE JEWS

CONTENTS

CONTENTS

ISSUES

PART NINE: AFTERWORD

FOR FURTHER STUDY

ACKNOWLEDGMENTS

First of all, I have to thank all of you, the authors, who produced to such a high standard this amazing collection of essays. Thank you for giving time in your busy schedules to reflect on these difficult issues. Once again, each one of you has demonstrated your commitment and dedication to helping people – Christians and Jews – understand the challenge the Holocaust poses to the Christian world. Thank you.

I particularly want to thank my co-editor, Dr. Carol Rittner, R.S.M., who came to this project late and dedicated an enormous amount of personal time, energy and resources to make this collection of essays possible. Without her experience, her commitment and personal expertise, this book would not, and could not, be all that it is.

Many thanks also to our co-editor, Irena Steinfeldt and her colleague, Efrat Balberg and staff members of the International School for Holocaust Studies at Yad Vashem, who brought all the expertise, care and concern which one would expect from such a significant institution. Her personal experience and eye for detail has ensured the balance, the variety and the accuracy of the essays so that readers will be both challenged and informed.

To so many others who assisted in this project, in particular, Amy Kettler and Henry Klos, students at The Richard Stockton College of New Jersey (USA) who have demonstrated their professional abilities as research assistants. And, of course, to Dr. James Smith, Marina Smith and the team at Beth Shalom Holocaust Memorial Centre, Steve, Claire, David and John, who have worked to their usual high standards and short deadlines, our thanks as well.

Finally, to my publishing partner at Yad Vashem, Dr. Motti Shalem, Director of the International School for Holocaust Studies, for his vision in suggesting our partnership and for the trust he put in me to make it happen, thank you. Thanks, as always, to Dr. Yehuda Bauer, our Consulting Editor, a consummate scholar and friend.

Finally, to all who contributed their time, energy, dedication, and resources to this project, sincere thanks.

Stephen D. Smith
February 2000

Papal envoy greets Hitler in Berlin, 1935.
USHMM

FOREWORD

Dorothee Sölle

I am a German citizen who grew up after World War II, with all the questions coming out of the darkest years in the history of my people. "Where were you when this happened? What did you do about it?" we asked our parents, relatives, teachers, neighbors, and later our textbooks, our songbooks, our history novels and our families' memories. And the longer we did so, the more often we asked about our own religion in all of this. We cannot avoid searching for the roots.

What does the *Shoah* have to do with Christianity? Was the Holocaust prepared in Christendom? Was antisemitism prepared in the New Testament? What are the roots for lying about Christ's death, as if the Jews had killed him and not imperial power and the law of the Roman Empire?

I studied theology and for a long time I asked myself why God didn't intervene on behalf of his people. Quite a number of people have lost their faith over this, both Jews and Christians. Today I would say, God was very weak at that time, because he had no friends in Germany. According to the tradition, God has no other hands than ours, and during the *Shoah*, God was very alone. Because of the lack of friends, God is indeed "in need of humans", as the Jewish teacher, Abraham Joshua Heschel, phrased it.

The quest for faith after its greatest catastrophe turned out to be a lifelong path of struggling and putting into question many of the classical Christian traditions. It made us more critical about the institutional side of the Christian faith – the churches. It led me into a radical criticism of obedience towards the leaders of the State. In the last twenty years, many people in the churches started questioning even some parts of the New Testament tradition because of its latent anti-Judaism. The same learning experience moved us into a better understanding of the Jewish man from Nazareth by the name of Jesus. He never gave up his faithfulness to his own Jewish tradition. We should follow him instead of pitting the 'Old' Testament against the 'New' Testament.

> 'Today I would say, God was very weak at that time, because he had no friends in Germany.'

Two Jewish pupils being humiliated before their classmates. The writing on the board reads, 'The Jew is our enemy! Beware of the Jews!'

Personal interest in the role Christianity played during the *Shoah* was not so much in the criminal evildoers, the guards in the concentration camps and their Nazi leaders, but in the majority of my people who claimed later not to have known what was going on. I became suspicious about this denial of reality. Wasn't it rather that they did not want to know what happened in their own country? We do not live alone. Some things are not understandable when we set our eyes only on the innermost life of the individual. There are a few things in the world which are not 'private property' – and God is among them.

Following liberation, civilians are forced to enter the camps and view the atrocities committed by the Nazis.

When I sing on Good Friday the moving song from the Afro-American tradition, *'Were you there when they crucified my Lord? Were you there when they nailed him to the cross?'* I always think then about those children who were humiliated in their school classes, deported in trains, and finally gassed. Were you there, then? I ask myself.

> *'I always think about those children who were humiliated in their school classes, deported in trains, and finally gassed. Were you there, then? I ask myself.'*

We can learn that the role of the spectator, the bystander, is not acceptable. Christians who love this Jewish man who was crucified in Jerusalem are to remain close to him. The whole story of the passion of Jesus teaches us to side with the victims. To become a Christian means to ask in any given situation: Who are the winners? Who are the losers? Where is our place? Where is Christ in all of this?

Dorothee Sölle (Germany) is a well-known German Protestant Christian theologian who for many years was the Harry Emerson Fosdick Professor of Theology at Union Theological Seminary in New York. She is the author of many books and essays, her most recent book, forthcoming in English soon, is her life's theme, *Mysticism and Resistance*.

If we are serious in our wish to know, it is not enough to visit Gethsemane or the Church of the Holy Sepulchre. We need to go to Yad Vashem and see and listen and learn. Yad Vashem is a place not only for Jewish people to visit; it is a place for Christians to visit as well. There is no salvation without remembering. Remembrance is for all of us the secret of salvation.

BEFORE YOU START

'The Holocaust and the Christian World' seems an unlikely combination of ideas. Surely nothing could be further removed from the principles, ethics and aspirations of well-intentioned Christians than to have Christianity linked to one of the greatest episodes of human hatred in history. And yet, that is exactly what this book does.

During the Nazi era (1933-1945) and the Holocaust - or, Shoah - some Christians spoke out against the persecution of the Jews, others collaborated with the Nazis, still others remained silent, 'neither for nor against', as Elie Wiesel, himself a survivor of the Holocaust, put it. Those Christians who risked their lives to help Jews during the Holocaust were very few indeed.

What Christians did and failed to do during the Holocaust continues to haunt and challenge the Christian world even in the twenty-first century, which is why we have prepared this volume.

Those who wrote essays for this book include scholars and educators - Christians and Jews, Europeans, Israelis, and North Americans. They responded to our request to address some of the questions and issues about the Holocaust and the Christian world they think we Christians and Jews should be thinking about and discussing today, at the beginning of the twenty-first century and more than fifty years after the liberation of the last Nazi death camp. Each of our writers has thought about these issues and questions for many years. Some are theologians - Catholic, Protestant, and Jewish - others are historians or sociologists, a few are survivors. Most have dedicated their professional lives to teaching, writing, and lecturing about the Holocaust.

The essays they have written are intended to inform, inspire, and challenge as you read and reflect on the subject. Included with the essays - in what we have called 'sidebars' - are quotations from within the essays themselves, or from other sources; questions for reflection and discussion, as well as suggestions for further reading. We have also included, toward the back of the book, texts - or excerpts from texts - of documents issued by the Christian churches after 1945, videos related to the topic, and a few selected sites from the world wide web (www) we thought might be helpful to the reader who wants more information about this subject. We hope you will make use of these as you study and think about issues and questions you may not have thought about before.

This book is only a beginning. It is intended to raise questions, not give answers. We hope reading it will encourage you to think about, study, and reflect on 'the Holocaust and the Christian world.' While we do not invite you to enjoy this book, we do encourage you to engage with it, and to encourage others to do so as well.

CONFRONTING THE HOLOCAUST

1

A CHRISTIAN PASSES THROUGH YAD VASHEM

Michael McGarry

May [We Remember: A Reflection of the Shoah] enable memory to play its necessary part in the process of shaping a future in which the unspeakable iniquity of the Shoah will never again be possible.[1]

What Pope John Paul II said of his Church's official consideration on the *Shoah* might well be said of a Christian's walking through Yad Vashem. The *Shoah* happened and it happened in a Christian country. For those of us who are Christian, coming to realize that some of our relatives or forerunners in the faith took part in the grotesquely single-minded effort to destroy European Jewry is a discomforting and sobering moment of truth. How do we react to this?

Many Christians, when confronted with the *Shoah*, gaze on it as if some aliens landed on the earth, took on the name 'Nazi', and proceeded to torture and kill Jews. They regard the perpetrators of these monstrous acts as from another planet, as people who otherwise did not hug their children, weep at the death of a parent, bleed when they were wounded – in other words, non-human creatures without a conscience, automatons of some mad and evil creator. But the *Shoah* is not the story about a group of alien people, rather about human beings. And they, we must admit, were primarily Christian – from the great Lutheran and Catholic traditions. Somehow they had lost that which made them followers of Jesus or they had chosen to suppress it in their horrid pursuit of killing Jews.

For some, to think of Christian participation in the *Shoah* is so horrific that it must be immediately denied. They protest quickly that the perpetrators were not Christian, for, they reason, a Christian by definition could not have committed such barbarity, such obscenity.

> 'We must begin our agonizing self-assessment and reappraisal with the fact that in a season of betrayal and faithlessness the vast majority of the martyrs for the Lord of history were Jews.'
>
> Franklin H. Littell,
> *Crucifixion of the Jews*

> 'The Shoah is a part of Christian history. It is part of our history, if we are Christian. This is frightening, this is sickening, this is, for many, unbelievable. But the first thing we Christians need to recognize is that we study the Shoah because it is part of our history, as well as part of Jewish history. Not only do we study what happened to them but what happened to us Christians.'

Indeed, some Christians simply define Christians out of the *Shoah*: if someone did such horrendous acts, they cannot be called Christian. They have forsaken their right to be called Christian.

But then there were all those who were bystanders. True, they didn't pull the triggers or herd Jews into boxcars. Rather they were on the sidelines, knowing or half-suspecting what was happening to their Jewish neighbors. And the bystanders were Christians.

> 'We must embrace the biblical insight that our God loves the Jewish people as Jews and not simply as potential Christians.'

Or perhaps our response is filtered through the fact that we are Christians who come from countries totally unrelated to events of mid-Twentieth Century Europe. We come from Bolivia, the Philippines, Ghana, or India. And we pass through Yad Vashem, curious about the events depicted here, and wonder how other human beings could have been so cruel, so unfeeling, so godless. And our heart is softened for the Jewish people.

Yet, emerging from Yad Vashem, we Christians need to go deeper even as we would desperately like to escape our own thoughts and feelings. We need to ask ourselves not only the obvious questions (What would I have done? What was it like to be a Jew in Nazi Germany or Nazi-controlled Poland?). We need to ask how Christians could have allowed themselves to become perpetrators or bystanders. While we might even humbly glory in the deeds of holy and admirable Christians through the ages, we need also to recall those appalling sins committed by other Christians – those times in history when they departed from the spirit of Christ and his Gospel and, instead of offering to the world the witness of a life inspired by the values of faith, indulged in ways of thinking and acting which were truly forms of counter-witness and scandal.[2]

For Reflection

How do you feel when someone asserts that the *Shoah* is a tragedy in Christian history?

How do you understand the meaning of Jewish survival?

What can you do to prevent the conditions which caused, or allowed, the *Shoah*?

Furthermore, we need to ask how the *Shoah* relates to us Christians – no matter what our age, our background, or our nationality. For we Christians, no matter what our age or country of birth, claim to be uniquely related to the Jewish people as our dearly beloved brothers, 'indeed our elder brothers [and sisters]' in the faith.[3]

And so, what is the meaning of the *Shoah* for us Christians as we slowly, thoughtfully stumble away from the horrific displays at Yad Vashem? I suggest five directions for thoughtful Christians to ponder, no matter what their physical, generational, or geographical relation to European events of the 1930s and 40s.

First, we Christians need to remember that studying the *Shoah* is not simply reading about 'what happened to the Jews', but what some Christians – some still worshiping, others long drop-outs from the Church – did to the Jews. The *Shoah* is a part of Christian history. It is part of our history, if we are Christian. This is frightening; this is sickening;, this is, for many, unbelievable. But the first thing we Christians need to recognize is that we study the *Shoah* because it is part of our history, as well as part

Warsaw Ghetto Uprising Monument. Yad Vashem, Jerusalem. Sculptor: Nathan Rappaport

of Jewish history. Not only do we study what happened to them but what happened to us Christians.

Second, when we come to this reflection – which causes some to go either numb with denial or frozen with horror – we begin to ask some of the same questions of ourselves that Jewish survivors have asked of themselves: what kind of God can we believe in after the *Shoah*? How can we pray after such a moment in our history? Some will say, 'No problem: that was then, this is now.' Others will say, 'God had nothing to do with this. It was a fluke in our history, indeed, a severe aberration, but it doesn't affect my faith.' To both these answers let me suggest another way, and I believe a more authentic way, to respond to the *Shoah* as a Christian: that is, our faith in God has to make sense in a world where the *Shoah* can happen . . . because it did happen. And so in our prayer we meditate on what conditions allowed, and caused, those events to happen. And we pray for the guidance and courage to make sure that these conditions never arise again, for the Jews or anyone.

Thirdly, some will say, 'Well the *Shoah* is one tragedy among many: look at Hiroshima, or some recent earthquakes, or the Armenian genocide. It's just one more of a series of human tragedies and it need not affect my faith in God.' Understandably one may place the *Shoah* amid other tragedies, but its uniqueness, if one is now reflecting after walking through Yad Vashem, is that it was perpetrated by followers of Jesus in the face of the Christians' claim that God chose them to be his people. And in the face of such a dreadful realization, Christians must then ponder the mystery of Jewish survival. For centuries Christian teachers have suggested that the Jews endured, sometimes in miserable conditions, so as to be a living proof of Christian truth. After the *Shoah*, we can no longer hold such a position. And so, the third direction for Christians to consider is that God wishes the Jews to survive as Jews. We must embrace the biblical insight that our God loves the Jewish people as Jews and not simply as potential Christians. Of course, this does not mean that everything a Jew does is good, or that a corporate representation of the Jewish people is immune from criticism. Rather, it means that Christians, in a committed way, explore ways of solidarity with the Jews. We believe that God, in a marvelously imaginative and creative way, has chosen to be faithful to his covenant with the Jewish people and that our Gracious God loves people as a people.

Fourthly, as we have seen in the Yad Vashem memorial, reflection on the *Shoah* must move us Christians to examine the behavior of the good Christians of the *Shoah*. We need to study the stories of those Christians who stepped out from the sidelines and rescued Jews from the Nazi assault. As we study those too few Christians of whom we can be proud, we ask ourselves difficult questions: What would we have done? What can we do in our own religious and prayer life to develop those qualities that will help us to work for human rights when we see them violated? How can we teach our children that sometimes the Christian is called to speak out in the face of injustice, to risk even one's own life for the life of another? This connection of the *Shoah,* for us Christians, I call its ethical

For Further Reading

Elisabeth Schüssler Fiorenza and David Tracy. *The Holocaust as Interruption.* Edinburgh: T. & T. Clark, 1984.

Steven L. Jacobs, ed. *Contemporary Christian Religious Responses to the Shoah.* Lanham, MD: University Press, 1993.

Marcia Sachs Littell, Richard Libowitz and Evelyn Bodek Rosen, eds. *The Holocaust: Forty Years After.* Lewiston, NY: The Edwin Mellon Press, 1989.

Abraham J. Peck, ed. *Jews and Christians After the Holocaust.* Philadelphia: Fortress Press, 1982.

Simon Wiesenthal. *The Sunflower: On the Possibilities and Limits of Forgiveness.* New York: Schocken Press, 1997.

Box car as used for transporting Jews during the Holocaust. Yad Vashem, Jerusalem.

Avenue of The Righteous, Yad Vashem. Trees planted in honor of those recognized for risking their lives to save Jews by Yad Vashem.

Michael McGarry C.S.P. (USA / Israel), a Roman Catholic Paulist priest, is the Rector of Tantur Ecumenical Institute in Jerusalem. He is the author of *Christology After the Holocaust*, as well as numerous essays on the *Shoah* and Christian-Jewish Relations after the Holocaust.

Notes:

1 Pope John Paul II, letter introducing 'We Remember: A Reflection on the *Shoah*', in *Catholics Remember the Holocaust* (Washington, DC: United States Catholic Conference, 1998), 43.

2 *'We Remember'*, quotation from *Tertio Mellennio Adveniente*, 47.

3 Pope John Paul II, Address to the Jewish People, Rome Synagogue, 1986, in Eugene Fisher and Leon Klenicki, eds., *Spiritual Pilgrimage: Texts on Jews and Judaism 1979-1995*. NY: Crossroad, 1995.

relevance. That is, the *Shoah* must affect our conscience, our usual way of doing things, our priorities regarding that for which we will give our life.

Here I must digress for a moment. Perhaps our overwhelming reaction to passing through Yad Vashem is a numbing sense of 'I can't take any more tragedy!' Recent social commentators have named this 'compassion fatigue'. Surely many dreadful things assault our sensibilities: racism, natural disasters, the disparity between the rich and poor, childhood disease, and so on. One may understandably say, 'I can't take on one more issue.' But we must be honest here: have we seriously taken on any issue? The point is not to add one more unbearable burden to a world already broken by pain and tragedy. Rather it is to ask, have I allowed the many issues in the world to deaden me, or have I allowed the goodness in them discovered there – here, the 'Righteous Gentiles' of the *Shoah* – to make me more tender, more compassionate, and more actively committed to making the world a better place?

The final direction to ponder, as we Christians ponder on what we saw at Yad Vashem, is our own self-understanding. Just as we Christians rightly take pride in some of our best ancestors (calling some of them 'saints'), so we must humbly grant that many of our ancestors did horrifying things during the *Shoah*. Consequently, we realize that, since God continues to love and cherish the Jewish people, our Christian claim on God is not an exclusive one. In humility, we see that our God chooses us Christians along with the Jewish people, as well as the other peoples of the earth. In our love of Christ, we love the Jewish people. The *Shoah* should not make us retreat to our Christian particularism. Rather our Christianity, in the wake of the *Shoah*, should make us compassionate in identifying across the spectrum all peoples as our brothers and sisters. We need to pray that the sometimes unpleasant experience of reflecting on the *Shoah* – both in terms of what happened to the Jews and in terms of the fact that baptized persons were, for the most part, its perpetrators – will make us more courageously kindhearted in responding to all persons in need.

Finally, however much we may feel guilt about what some of our forebears did to the Jewish people, we need to let that go in favor of a newly gained sense of responsibility for the world where our God has placed us. While nothing on the scale of what happened in Europe in the 1930s is happening now, nonetheless, our God beckons us to a new commitment to reflect humbly on our attitudes towards the Jewish people. And this should lead us to reflect on our attitudes about all peoples. Our sense of responsibility, perhaps encouraged and emboldened by our study of the rescuers, may move us Christians to make sure that not only does something like the *Shoah* never happen to the Jewish people, but that something like the *Shoah* never happens to any people.

WHAT DOES THE HOLOCAUST HAVE TO DO WITH CHRISTIANITY?

John K. Roth

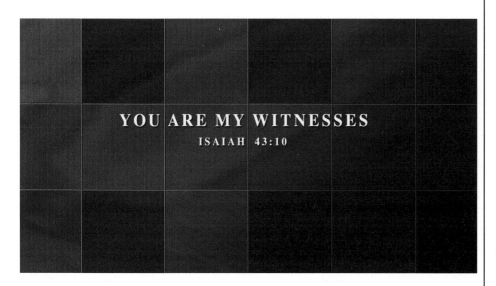

YOU ARE MY WITNESSES
ISAIAH 43:10

You are my Witnesses: Inscription in black marble/granite at the United States Holocaust Memorial Museum, Washington, D.C.

At the United States Holocaust Memorial Museum in Washington, D.C., biblical words from the prophet Isaiah – 'You are my witnesses' – are inscribed on a wall where it is difficult for visitors to miss them. Whenever I visit the Museum, I stop for a moment to read that ancient text, which expresses an expectation, a commandment, and a fact all at once. Those simple but immensely challenging words make me think about my Christian identity. Specifically, Isaiah's words require me to reflect on Christianity's relationship to the Holocaust, Nazi Germany's attempt to destroy the European Jews, and to wrestle with the implications of that event for my religious tradition.

Most of my academic life has been devoted to studying the Holocaust. Frequently I am asked how I became involved in that work, which has been my passion for more than twenty-five years. Sometimes people ask, 'Are you Jewish?' perhaps assuming, mistakenly, that dedicated attention to Holocaust history is something that only Jews are likely to pursue. To the question 'Are you Jewish?'

'The post-Holocaust condition that is most necessary for us Christians is a soul-searching that leads us to ask: What should it mean for me, for us, to be Christian after Auschwitz?'

I would be glad and proud to answer yes, but my identity is different. I have immersed myself in a study of the Holocaust, or the *Shoah* as it is called in Hebrew, because my Christian identity (indeed, I believe anyone's identity as a Christian) is linked to that catastrophe. As I explain what I mean, I also want to suggest how we Christians might re-identify ourselves in a post-Holocaust situation and how we might do so in ways that would give our tradition greater integrity, an integrity that depends in so many ways on solidarity with Jewish tradition, Israel, and the Jewish people.

To develop those ideas, follow me from the entry hall in the Holocaust Museum, where Isaiah's words are inscribed, to a smaller but even more solemn place within the Museum, a circular space called the Hall of Remembrance. The names of places can be found around the perimeter of this hall. Auschwitz, Treblinka, and Majdanek – three of the Nazi killing centers on Polish soil where Jews were gassed – are among them. The Hall of Remembrance also includes places for memorial candles to be lit. They honor the six million Jewish children, women, and men who were killed, one by one, in camps of death and destruction. Opposite the entry of the circular Hall of Remembrance, an eternal flame burns where soil from camps in Poland, Germany, and other countries has been deposited.

Biblical words appear on the circular walls of the Hall of Remembrance. Shared by Jews and Christians, the three passages from the Hebrew Bible can be read in different sequences, depending on how one's eyes follow the arc that contains them. Consider those three passages (one from Genesis, the other two from Deuteronomy) as guideposts for deepening our thinking about identity, integrity, and being a witness, especially as those ideas relate to post-Holocaust Christian life.

The first biblical quotation says this: 'And the Lord said, 'What have you done? Listen, your brother's blood is crying out to me from the ground.'' Those words remind us that witnesses are those who have seen or heard something. They are people who are called to testify. They furnish evidence. Often, they sign their names to documents to certify an event's occurrence or a statement's truth. So when one reads that verse from the Genesis story of Cain and Abel, God's question calls for testimony and for bearing witness.

A Christian who contemplates those words ('What have you done?') in the United States Holocaust Memorial Museum setting must do some soul-searching about identity and integrity, for the Holocaust's history testifies to a disturbing fact, namely, that while Christianity was not a sufficient condition for the Holocaust, nevertheless, it was a necessary condition for that disaster. That statement does not mean that Christianity caused the Holocaust. Nevertheless, apart from Christianity, the *Shoah* is scarcely imaginable because Nazi Germany's targeting cannot be explained apart from the anti-Jewish images ('Christ-killers,' willfull blasphemers, unrepentant sons and daughters of the Devil, to name only a few) that have been deeply rooted in Christian practices.

'The discovery that our traditions have sanctioned contempt for the other and that the inheritance lives on in us delivers a jolt to the system. The convulsion shakes the foundations of the faith. A world which once appeared certain and dependable is rocked by doubt and distrust. A dreadful sense of loss is almost inevitable. Some people respond to this disruption by withdrawing into familiar patterns and tightening their defensive positions. Others yield to despair and abandon the tradition. The challenge is to navigate a path through the uncertainty, to hold onto the questions as the old answers flag, and finally to risk and adventure into uncharted theological terrain.'

Christopher Leighton, 'Strategies for the Jewish-Christian Encounter: The Baltimore Experiment' in *Visions of the Other: Jewish and Christian Theologians Assess the Dialogue*, ed. Fisher.

Existing centuries before Nazism, Christianity's negative images of Jews and Judaism – supported by the institutions and social relationships that promoted those stereotypes – played key parts in bolstering the racial and genocidal antisemitism of Adolf Hitler and his Third Reich.

There can be no doubt about it: Christianity's anti-Jewish elements provided essential background, preparation, and motivation for the Holocaust that happened when Germans and their collaborators carried out the 'Final Solution' of the so-called Jewish question. 'What have you done?' God's question to Cain challenges post-Holocaust Christians, too.

The second biblical quotation in the Hall of Remembrance at the United States Holocaust Memorial Museum says this: 'Keep these words

A debate between Jewish rabbis and clergymen who had converted from Judaism about the validity of the Jewish Talmud. Woodcut by Johann von Armssheim. Printed by Konrad Dinckmut. Ulm, Germany, 1483.

that I am commanding you today in your heart. Recite them to your children and talk about them when you are at home and when you are away, when you lie down and when you rise.' Those words from the Hebrew Bible are inscribed above the eternal flame that burns in the Hall of Remembrance near the spot where soil from the Nazi death camps has been deposited. In that place, standing before those words can and should make deep impressions upon a Christian. Those impressions involve, once again, identity, integrity, and being a witness.

The words inscribed from Deuteronomy are calls to remember. Such calls are crucial because the Jewish saying is true when it proclaims that in memory lies the redemption of the world. That outlook, of course, is not referring to just any kind of memory. In this case, memory should lead to repentance, to what the Jewish tradition calls *teshuvah*, a return to God and to a right path. To explain further what I mean, I want to acknowledge two feelings that are important for both Christians and Jews to grasp.

First, some contemporary Christians – those of us who live in the United States, for example – may wonder why we need to remember Christianity's role in the Holocaust. That involvement, it might be argued, took place long ago and far away. It was part of Europe's 'Old World' corruption. In our country, we Twenty-first Century Americans may be tempted to say, things have been different; we

For Further Reading

Marcia Sachs Littell and Sharon Weissman Gutman, eds. *Liturgies on the Holocaust: An Interfaith Anthology.* Revised edition. Harrisburg, PA: Trinity Press International, 1996.

John K. Roth and Michael Berenbaum, eds. *Holocaust: Religious and Philosophical Implications.* St. Paul, MN: Paragon House, 1989.

Richard L. Rubenstein and John K. Roth. *Approaches to Auschwitz: The Holocaust and Its Legacy.* Louisville: Westminster/John Knox Press, 1987.

Ekkehard Schuste, and Reinhold Boschert-Kimmig. *Hope Against Hope: Johann Baptist Metz and Elie Wiesel Speak Out on the Holocaust.* Translated by J. Matthew Ashley. Mahwah, NJ: Paulist Press, 1999.

Michael Shermis and Arthur E. Zannoni, eds. *Introduction to Jewish-Christian Relations.* Mahwah, NJ: Paulist Press, 1991.

made a new beginning, breaking away from fallen European ways. The Holocaust was not, could not have been, any responsibility of ours, especially if – like me – we live in California, which is about as far away from Auschwitz as one can get in the United States.

Fortunately, I would say, history will not let such shallow analysis stand. In the Twenty-first Century, very few people anywhere – American or not – would be among the world's two billion Christians if it were not for a centuries-old Christian tradition whose history includes Holocaust-related hostility to Jews and Judaism, even if many Christians are not as aware of this fact as we ought to be.

Remembering can be hard, often painful work, but it can also remind us of other qualities. So the second point is that remembering can take us post-Holocaust Christians back to our roots in ways that remind us about who we are, and who we ought to be, when we are at our best. Here I can clarify my meaning by emphasizing that I was drawn to study the Holocaust more and more because of a collision between two features of my experience. On the one hand, I have personally experienced Christianity as something basically good. On the other hand, I know that Christianity, my tradition, has not been good to or for everyone; the Holocaust bears witness to that. I found myself wanting to know where things had gone wrong, especially insofar as Christians and Jews were concerned. In the process of self-definition, I discovered, Christians had lost sight of their close and essential ties to Jewish tradition. How different history would have been if that result had not happened; how much better life would be even now if those gaps could be closed.

These feelings take me back to the words from Deuteronomy that are inscribed above the eternal flame in the Hall of Remembrance at the Museum in Washington, D.C. The commandment to remember contained in the words from Deuteronomy refers to other words that say: 'Hear, O Israel: The Lord is our God, the Lord is One. You shall love the Lord your God with all your heart and with all your might.' When the Christian New Testament reports that Jesus was asked which commandment was the first of all, he gave those words in reply, adding in true Jewish fashion that the second commandment is to love your neighbor as yourself. Then, when Jesus was asked to define who is one's neighbor, he told the parable of the Good Samaritan, which summarizes about as well as any part of Christian scripture what it ought to mean to be a Christian. The key point here, however, is that we Christians have our identity because the workings of history put before us a relationship with God that can be understood neither apart from Jewish history nor (and this is very important) apart from the ongoing vitality of Jewish life.

We Christians came to know God through the Jewish tradition as Jesus and his followers made that tradition accessible to us and grafted us into it. As time passed, changes distorted those connections, and, tragically, the full price of those distortions would not be known until the Holocaust

> 'On the one hand, I have personally experienced Christianity as something basically good. On the other hand, I know that Christianity, my tradition, has not been good to or for everyone, the Holocaust bears witness to that.'

For Reflection

Why has Christian history involved negative views about Jews and Judaism?

How does Christianity need to change to remove these elements in Christian tradition?

What should Christians do to remember the Holocaust?

What should it mean – and not mean – to be a post-Holocaust Christian?

scarred the earth. Nevertheless, the basic point was there to be recognized all along: if Christians are essentially the followers of Jesus, a faithful Jew, then our responsibility is to love God and to love our neighbors as ourselves. As we Christians interpret the identity of Jesus, the bottom line comes back to those words from Deuteronomy that are inscribed above the eternal flame in the Hall of Remembrance, including the way in which they point to God.

Christian re-identification after the Holocaust, I believe, can lead to a deepened integrity for Christian life just to the extent that there is a Christian *teshuvah*, a returning to a love of our rootedness in Jewish tradition. This returning should underscore an awareness that Jews are not indebted to Christians as we are to them. As Clark Williamson, a thoughtful Christian thinker, has put it, we Christians should think of ourselves as 'guests in the house of Israel' and behave accordingly.

As one's eyes follow the Hall of Remembrance's arc from left to right, from words that question 'What have you done?' to words, underscored by an eternal flame, that encourage one to remember, a third inscription requires attention as well. Its words, attributed to Moses, say this: 'I have set before you life and death . . . Choose life so that you and your descendants may live.'

Traditional etching of The Good Samaritan from a Nineteenth Century illustrated Bible.
William Collins, Glasgow, 1865

A few years ago (on April 7, 1994, to be exact), Pope John Paul II hosted a special concert at the Vatican. The concert was held to commemorate the Holocaust. It was a night of 'firsts,' which was not entirely a cause for celebration, because the 'firsts' were so late in coming. For example, on that occasion the Chief Rabbi of Rome was invited for the first time to co-officiate at a public function in the Vatican. For the first time, a Jewish cantor sang in the Vatican. For the first time, a 500-year-old Vatican choir sang a Hebrew text in performance. Late though these 'firsts' turned out to be, the music at the Vatican's interfaith concert was moving, and the Pope's concluding words went to the heart of the matter when he asked the concert's listeners to observe silence and to "hear once more the plea, 'Do not forget us,'" a plea rising from the Holocaust's victims, the dead and the living. Rightly, John Paul II described that plea as "powerful, agonizing, heartrending." The Pope's remarks also suggested that no memory can be worthy of that plea unless remembering leads people to check what he called 'the specter of racism, exclusion, alienation, slavery and xenophobia' and to act so that 'evil does not prevail over good' as it did for millions of Jews during the Holocaust.

Destruction after the *Kristallnacht* pogrom. November 9-10, 1938.

The Papal Concert closed with Leonard Bernstein's *Chichester Psalms*. Sung on that occasion by a Vatican choir, the Hebrew text included these words from Psalm 133:

> 'Behold how good
> And how pleasant it is
> For brothers to dwell
> Together in unity.'

The music, the Pope's words, and particularly the *Chichester Psalms* accented a very important point: the value of beliefs (Christian or Jewish) must be measured by the justice or injustice, the good or evil, that they inspire. The Holocaust was unjust and evil, or nothing ever could be. At least in part, the value of specifically Christian beliefs needs to be tested by their contributions to the Holocaust. Such a test leaves Christianity wanting in ways that should make my religious tradition much less triumphal than it has been in the past. Far from being an occasion for regret, however, such changes ought to be welcomed because they reflect needed honesty and candor, and they could encourage atoning work that protests against injustice and that tries its best to protect those who become evil's prey.

In Psalm 51, another text that Jews and Christians share, we find these words: 'O Lord, open my lips, and my mouth will declare your praise. For you have no delight in sacrifice; if I were to give a burnt offering, you would not be pleased. The sacrifice acceptable to God is a broken spirit; a broken and contrite heart, O God, you will not despise.' The post-Holocaust condition that is most necessary for us Christians is a spiritual and ethical 'turning,' a soul-searching (personal and communal) that leads us to ask: What should it mean for me, for us, to be Christian after Auschwitz?

Responses to that question will still take time to form. Just to the extent that they are formed well, I believe, will Christianity have the identity and integrity that it ought to have. Those responses, I also believe, will be formed well just to the extent that they focus on three points: (1) the question that asks 'What have you done?'; (2) the necessity to remember that Christians are followers of the Jew named Jesus; (3) the responsibility to choose life. Doing those things will help us post-Holocaust Christians to respond authentically to the charge from Isaiah's text, 'You are my witnesses,' by saying 'Yes, we are your witnesses indeed.' Only to the extent that we post-Holocaust Christians make that response an honest one will our identity and integrity become what it ought to be.

'Christianity was not a sufficient condition for the Holocaust, nevertheless, it was a necessary condition for that disaster.'

John K. Roth (USA) is the Russell K. Pitzer Professor of Philosophy at Claremont McKenna College California, where he has taught since 1966. Many of his twenty-five books are Holocaust-related, including, most recently, *Ethics after the Holocaust*. Roth has served on the United States Holocaust Memorial Council, which oversees the United States Holocaust Memorial Museum in Washington, D.C. In 1988, Roth was named U.S. National Professor of the Year by the Council for Advancement and Support of Education and the Carnegie Foundation for the Advancement of Teaching.

HARD QUESTIONS ASKED BY THE HOLOCAUST

David A. Rausch

How do we explain the apathy of the general population of Europe (not just the German citizenry) and the ready compliance of a select number eager to help the Nazi regime in any way possible? Ukrainians, Lithuanians, Poles and Hungarians all helped. Even in France, Nazi leaders were astounded by the eagerness Frenchmen displayed in trying to please their conquerors . . .

The historian is overwhelmed with the question, What made the difference? What made the difference between the few who helped the Jewish people during their dreadful persecution and the multitude who turned their backs on them? Why did a few put themselves, their families, their possessions, and their careers on the line for a persecuted people, while most did not? What is that moral kernel within our psychological, mental, or religious makeup that makes some react differently from the multitude in the face of prejudice, scapegoating, caricature, oppression, and outright physical violence to a race or religious group different from their own?

That is a difficult question in light of the Holocaust, as its study reveals that only a few Evangelicals, a few Protestants, a few Catholics, a few Orthodox, a few agnostics, and a few atheists (and not necessarily in that order) helped the Jewish people during their persecution. Varian Fry, a bespectacled, frail, moody intellectual; a man who would seem to be a most unlikely candidate to stand against the Gestapo, succeeded in organizing the escape of approximately fifteen hundred men and women from Nazi occupied France in 1940-1941. A man who appeared to have no religious motivation, Fry explained to his mother that he stayed because it took courage and 'courage is a quality I hadn't previously been sure I possessed.' To his wife he wrote: 'Now I think I can say that I possess an ordinary amount of courage.' (Donald Carroll, 'Escaped from Vichy,' *American Heritage* 34 (June/July 1983), p 91.

Are Christians really different from the rest of society? Some Christians throughout Europe not only opposed the Nazis but also helped and defended the Jewish people. They met the challenge that was suddenly thrust upon them. However, they were relatively few in number – a fact that perplexed Richard Gutteridge as he studied German evangelical response to Nazi racist propaganda. In his book, *Open Thy Mouth for the Dumb: The German Evangelical Church and the Jews, 1879-1950,*

> '. . . how did human beings who had previously lived unexceptional and inoffensive lives end up watching, condoning, or inflicting continuous acts of intense cruelty and unprecedented genocidal destruction against the aged, women, children, and generally helpless people who engaged in no acts of provocation and committed no crimes, as crime is defined by advanced societies?'
>
> John K. Roth, 'Ethics after Auschwitz' in Ethics after the Holocaust: Perspectives, Critiques, and Responses, p.xv.

'Some Christians did choose to stand with suffering Jews in the Holocaust. Many more Christians, however, chose to stare silently away from the flames while embracing twenty centuries of anti-Jewish theology.'

Sidney G Hall, *Christian Anti-Semitism and Paul's Theology*

Varian Fry, European director of the Emergency Rescue Committee in the United States. Through the use of false documents and underground resistance, Fry organised the escape of more than a thousand Jews from occupied France.

'Let us remember: What hurts the victim most is not the cruelty of the oppressor, but the silence of the bystander.'

Elie Wiesel in *The Courage to Care: Rescuers of Jews During the Holocaust,* eds. Carol Rittner and Sondra Myers. New York: New York University Press, 1986, p. x..

For Reflection

Why do you think that ordinary people come to do extraordinary evil?

Why were the Churches not able to 'innoculate' Christians against hatred?

Gutteridge concluded: 'Most tragically of all, what was missing was a spontaneous outburst at any point by ordinary decent Christian folk, who certainly existed in considerable numbers.' Even after the war, when the call for a national Christian repentance for such neglect was made in the Stuttgart Declaration, Catholic and Protestant German church leaders developed what John Conway in his essay, 'The German Church Struggle and Its Aftermath' has termed 'collective amnesia' about their role in the Nazi era. They explained that the majority of the German people did not know about the Nazi excesses or that their cries had been quickly silenced by the all-powerful German police state. Hitler and his minions, they said, were to take full blame for that dark period in German church history. The church, in another failure to meet the challenge, shirked her responsibility by seeking to lay the blame on others.

Modern psychology has much to say about the capacity within man to commit atrocities. Stanley Milgram has spent decades studying this phenomenon, and in his book *Obedience to Authority* he stresses that we all have something to worry about when hate, distrust, or dislike of other racial or religious groups permeates our society. He emphasizes:

'This is, perhaps, the most fundamental lesson of our study; ordinary people simply doing their jobs, and without any particular hostility on their part, can become agents in a terrible destructive process. Moreover, even when the destructive effects of their work become patently clear, and they are asked to carry out actions incompatible with fundamental standards of morality, relatively few people have the resources needed to resist authority. A variety of inhibitions against disobeying authority come into play and successfully keep the person in his place.'

To understand such societal pressures one has only to recall how difficult it is to speak out when a member of one's family, a boss, or a friend tells a joke about an ethnic or religious group. Even those who dislike such jokes are hard pressed to overcome peer pressure, and they give in with a half-hearted laugh. An awareness of the Holocaust experience makes such jokes ring hollow, because the student is suddenly aware that even 'innocent' caricatures and stereotypes shape attitudes and behavior.

Self-examination is certainly an important result of Holocaust study. We learn that those who believe that such collaboration with the forces of evil is beyond their potential are sometimes the first to succumb to genocidal impulses; and we see that we might do the same.

Without an understanding of the Holocaust, we would fail to understand that racists will devour their own people. Once unleashed, racial theory begins its own pecking order even among the 'white races.' Hitler had plans to weed out the human race in favor of the purest of the pure Aryan. Slavs, Ukrainians, and Poles who helped him had no idea he planned either to enslave or exterminate them. In discussing the 'mastering' of the plague of racial impurity, Hitler noted in *Mein Kampf*: 'This also is only a touchstone for the value of a race, and that race which does not pass the test will die and make room for races healthier or at least tougher and of greater resistance.' As the German people found, this could extend to individuals even among their own people – individuals who were not Jews, blacks or Gypsies.

Excerpted from David A. Rausch. *A Legacy of Hatred: Why Christians Must Not Forget the Holocaust*. Chicago: Moody Press, 1984, pp. 4, 5-6. By permission of the author.

Hitler with a young boy in SA uniform.

For Further Reading

Yehuda Bauer. *A History of the Holocaust*. New York: Franklin Watts, 1982.

Douglas K. Huneke. *The Stones Will Cry Out: Pastoral Reflections on the Shoah (With Liturgical Resources)*. London: Greenwood Press, 1995.

David A. Rausch. *A Legacy of Hatred: Why Christians Must Not Forget the Holocaust*. Chicago: Moody Press, 1984.

Corrie ten Boom. *The Hiding Place*. New York: Bantam, 1971.

Clark Williamson, ed. *A Mutual Witness: Toward Critical Solidarity Between Jews & Christians*. St. Louis, MO: Chalice Press, 1992.

David A. Rausch (USA) is Professor of History at Ashland University, Ashland, Ohio.

'The principle that governs the biblical vision of society is, 'Thou shall not stand idly by when your fellow man is hurting, suffering, or being victimized.' It is because that injunction was ignored or violated that the catastrophe involving such multitudes occurred.'

Elie Wiesel in *The Courage to Care: Rescuers of Jews During the Holocaust*, p.125.

CHRONOLOGY 2

CHRONOLOGY

Carol Rittner   Stephen Smith

With the Assistance of Amy Kettler and Henry Klos

In addition to noting major events during the Third Reich, World War II, and the Holocaust, this chronology pays attention to those events that are particularly relevant to the subject of the Holocaust and the Christian World. While this is not an exhaustive chronology, we have tried to include some of the major events of the period as well as actions of major Church figures, institutions, and individuals from the beginning of the Third Reich in the 1930s to post-Holocaust period, up to and including events such as the recently published *We Remember: A Reflection on the Shoah*. The chronology is divided into general events of the period, specific events relating to the Holocaust, and Christian reactions to some of the unfolding historical scenario happening around them.

	GENERAL	HOLOCAUST	CHRISTIAN
1932			
Summer			Summer: Politicians, pastors, and lay people meet in Berlin to discuss how to capture the energies of Germany's Protestant Churches for the National Socialist cause. Wilhelm Kube, Gauleiter of Brandenburg and chairman of the National Socialist group in the Prussian Lantag, initiated the effort. Kube's circle planned to call themselves the Protestant National Socialists, but Adolf Hitler vetoed this and suggested 'German Christians' instead.
1933			
January 30	Adolf Hitler becomes Chancellor of Germany.		
March 22	Dachau concentration camp established about 10 miles from Munich.		
March 23	The Reichstag passes the Enabling Act, which becomes the basis for Hitler's dictatorship.		
April 1		German boycott of Jewish businesses. It is the first major test on a national scale of the attitude of the Christian Churches toward the situation of the Jews under the new government.	
April 7	Nazi Germany enacts the Law for the Restoration of the Professional Civil Service, authorizing the dismissal of 'non-Aryans' – Jews – from government and public positions.		
May 10		The Nazis instigate public burnings of books by Jewish authors as well as non-Jewish authors opposed to Nazism.	
July 14	The Nazi Party is proclaimed by law to be the one and only legal political party in Germany. People holding non-Nazi political meetings are subject to arrest and imprisonment in a concentration camp.		
July 20			Pope Pius XI signs a Concordat [an agreement between a Pope and a sovereign or government regulating ecclesiastical matters] with Hitler.
September 27			Former naval chaplain Ludwig Müller is elected Germany's first and last Protestant Reich Bishop (*Reichsbishof*).
December 25			The [Protestant] Pastors' Emergency League (*Pfarrernotbund*) is established by Martin Niemöller and Dietrich Bonhoeffer.

	GENERAL	HOLOCAUST	CHRISTIAN
1934			
May			First meeting of the Confessing Church *(Bekennende Kirche)*, a network of Protestants under the slogan 'church must remain church' is held in Barman, Germany. The Barman Declaration is issued.
June 30	'Night of the Long Knives' – Hitler orders the SS, under Heinrich Himmler, to purge SA leadership. Many are murdered, including Ernst Röhm, chief of staff of the SA.		
August 3	With the death of President von Hindenburg, Hitler declares himself Chancellor and President *(Reichsführer)*.		
1935			
September 15	The Nuremberg Laws are decreed at a Nazi party rally. They contain two especially important provisions: (1) The Reich Citizenship Law states that German citizenship belongs only to those of 'German or related blood'; (2) The Law for the Protection of German Blood and German Honor prohibits marriage and extramarital intercourse between Jews and persons of 'German or related blood'.	The First Ordinance to the Reich Citizenship Law specifies that 'a Jew cannot be a Reich citizen'. It also enacts a classification system to define various degrees of Jewishness. One is defined as a full Jew if 'descended from at least three grandparents who are fully Jewish by race', or if 'descended from two fully Jewish grandparents' and subject to other conditions specified by the ordinance. A grandparent is defined as fully Jewish if he or she 'belonged to the Jewish religious community'.	
November 14			
1936			
August	The Olympic Games are held in Berlin; they afford the Nazis an opportunity to impress the world with 'the achievements' of the Third Reich.		
1937			
March 14			Pope Pius XI issues the encyclical, *Mit Brennender Sorge*. It is read from the pulpit of all Catholic Churches in Nazi Germany on Palm Sunday, March 21, 1937.
July 1			In Germany, The Confessing Church *(Bekennende Kirche)* is banned; Martin Niemöller is arrested and sent to Sachsenhausen; he is later sent to Dachau where he remains imprisoned until Dachau is liberated, April 29, 1945.
July 16	The concentration camp at Buchenwald is established.		
1938			
March 12-13	*Anschluss* – Nazi Germany annexes Austria.		
May 27	Declaration of Neutrality with regard to German aggression is signed by the governments of Denmark, Norway, Finland, Iceland, and Sweden.		Pope Pius XI instructs John LeFarge, an American Jesuit priest, and two other Jesuits, Gustave Desbuquois and Gustav Gundlach, to draft an encyclical letter denouncing racism and antisemitism. Entitled *Humani Generis Unitas* (The Unity of the Human Race), it is never published.
June 22			
July 6-15	Representatives from thirty-two nations attend the Evian Conference in France to discuss the German refugee problem; no significant action is taken.		
August 17		Jewish women in Nazi Germany are required to add 'Sarah' to their names, and all Jewish men 'Israel' to theirs.	
September 2-3		The Italian government announces that foreign Jews can no longer establish residence in Italy, Libya, or the Dodecanese Islands. Jews who have been nationalized after January 1, 1919 lose their citizenship and are considered foreigners.	
September 29-30	Munich Conference, attended by the heads of state of Great Britain (Chamberlain), France (Daladier), Italy (Mussolini) and Germany (Hitler). Britain and France agree to Germany's annexing part of Czechoslovakia. No Czech representative is present.		
October 5		The passports of German Jews are marked with a large red J, for *Jude* as requested by the Swiss gov't.	

1938	HOLOCAUST	JEWISH	CHRISTIAN
October 28		Some 17,000 Polish Jews are expelled from Germany to Zbaszyn on the Polish border.	
November 9-10		Following the assassination of Ernst vom Rath, a minor German diplomat in Paris, by a Jewish youth named Herschel Grynszpan (whose parents were expelled from Germany on October 28th), the Kristallnacht pogrom – instigated by Josef Goebbels, the Nazi Minister of Propaganda – erupts in Germany and Austria. Synagogues are burned, Jewish businesses looted, and Jews are beaten by Nazi thugs. Some 30,000 Jews are interned in concentration camps.	
November 15		Jewish children are excluded from German schools.	
1939			
February 10			Pope Pius XI dies.
March 2			Cardinal Eugenio Pacelli (1876-1958) is elected Pope (1939-1958); he takes the name Pius XII.
March 15	Hitler takes over the Czechoslovak Republic. One day earlier (March 14th), under the protection of the Nazis, the Slovak leadership had proclaimed an independent state. The new rulers of Slovakia – Msgr. Jozef Tiso, head of the clericalist-nationalist *Hlinka* Party, and his deputy, Professor Vöjtech Tuka – copy from their benefactors a number of measures against the Jews.		
April 4			The 'German Christians' establish the Institute for Research into and Elimination of Jewish Influence in German Church Life.
April 18		The first anti-Jewish decree is enacted in Slovakia. It defines who is a Jew.	
August 23	Nazi-Soviet Non-Aggression Pact is signed.		
September 1	Nazi Germany invades Poland. On September 3rd, France and Great Britain declare war on Germany; World War II begins.		
September 4		The first *Judenrat* (Jewish Council) is established in Piotrkow, Poland, which is in the Radom District, immediately after the German army enters the city.	
September 8		A regulation ordering Jews to mark their businesses with a Star of David is issued in Poland.	
September 27	Warsaw surrenders; Polish military opposition crumbles.		
September 28	Russia and Germany divide Poland.		
October	The order for the 'Euthanasia' program, code name T4, is given by Hitler. The order is backdated to September 1, 1939, to coincide with the beginning of the war.		
October	Msgr. Jozef Tiso is elected President of Slovakia; pro-Nazi Vöytech Tuka becomes Prime Minister.		
October 9		Westerbork, an internment and transit camp, opens in north eastern Holland near Assen. The camp is built for 750 German Jews who flee to Holland illegally.	
October-November			214 Catholic priests are executed in Poland. By the end of 1939, 1,000 Polish clergymen are imprisoned.
November 20	Heinrich Himmler, head of the SS, orders the arrest and incarceration of all Gypsy women, astrologers, and fortune-tellers in areas controlled by the Germans.		
November 23		The order is given that whenever they are in public, Polish Jews must wear armbands imprinted with the Star of David.	

1939	**GENERAL**	**HOLOCAUST**	**CHRISTIAN**
November 28		A decree is issued in Poland ordering every Jewish community with a population of up to 10,000 to elect a *Judenrat* (Jewish Council) of twelve members; Jewish communities with more than 10,000 people must elect twenty-four members.	

1940			
Early January	The first experimental gassing of mental patients as part of the 'Euthanasia' program occurs in German asylums. More than 70,000 persons perish before protests, spurred by a few church leaders, bring about the program's official termination on September 1, 1941. However, the operation continues until the end of World War II.		
February 8		Lodz ghetto is established; the ghetto is sealed on May 1, 1940.	
April 9	Nazi Germany invades and occupies Denmark and Norway.		
April 27	Himmler orders the establishment of a concentration camp at Oswiecim (Auschwitz), Poland. The camp has major railway lines nearby, a key factor in making Auschwitz the main killing center in the Nazi system.		A 'Council of Churches' is established in Holland. It consists of The Reformed Churches in the Netherlands, the Christian Reformed Church, the Re-united Reformed Churches, the Evangelical Lutheran Church, the Re-united Evangelical Lutheran Church, the Brotherhood of Remonstrants and the Society of Mennonites. This later becomes known as the 'Inter-Church Consultation'. Most future public protests are issued by this Council.
May 10	Germany invades Holland, Belgium and France.		
May 18	Artur Seyss-Inquart is appointed Reich Commissioner of Holland.		
June 15			
August 22			The 'Circle of Lunteren,' a group of ministers belonging mostly to the Dutch Reformed Church, meets for the first time. This group is sympathetic to the Confessing Church of Germany and many are influenced by the teachings of Karl Barth. A letter is sent to the Synodal Committee of the Dutch Reformed Church urging the Church to give advice to local churches and the nation, especially regarding increased antisemitic propaganda. The reply to this letter is evasive and reserved.
September 1	On the first anniversary of the outbreak of war, the Poles in Warsaw boycott all cafes and restaurants between 2:00 and 4:00 p.m., and they refuse to buy German newspapers. Instead, Poles go to church.		
September 5			Msgr. Giuseppe Burzio writes a dispatch concerning regulations against Slovak Jews to Cardinal Luigi Maglione, Vatican Secretariat of State. On October 5 Maglione replies and instructs Burzio to keep him informed of the attitude of the Slovak Bishops.
October		The first anti-Jewish decrees are promulgated in Holland.	
Mid October		The Jews of Warsaw are ghettoized. By November 15, the ghetto is sealed by a brick wall which the Jews themselves are forced to build.	
October 24			Protestant Churches in Holland send a letter to the Reich Commissioner for occupied Holland, Artur Seyss-Inquart, protesting against the discriminatory regulations against Jewish officials. The Boards of the Lutheran Churches refuse to associate their Churches with this protest. It is submitted on behalf of six of the eight Protestant Churches.
October 27			The text of the protest against 'Aryan attestation' is made public in most churches in the Netherlands. The Reformed Churches in the Netherlands and the Christian Reformed Church do not make the protest public to their congregations.
November 15			Even before Bulgaria joins the Tripartite Pact, the 'Holy Synod of the Bulgarian Church' sends a letter of protest to Prime Minister Filov, with a copy to the Speaker of the Parliament. The letter is signed by the Deputy Chairman of the Holy Synod, Metropolitan Neophit, and states that the Church disapproves of any measure taken against the Jews as a national minority.

1941	GENERAL	HOLOCAUST	CHRISTIAN
February 9		The first raid on the Jewish quarter of Amsterdam is made by the Germans.	
February 25	A general anti-Nazi strike that paralyzes transport and industry is held in Amsterdam; it spreads to other districts. Within three days, it is suppressed by force.		
February			Pastoral letter written by the Bishops of the Lutheran Church of Norway states, 'Can the church sit quietly on the sidelines while the commandments of God are being set aside and while many other events are taking place which dissolve law and order?'
March 1	Bulgaria officially joins the Tripartite Pact (Germany, Italy, and Japan). German army is admitted to Bulgaria.		
March 5			A letter of protest from the Protestant churches of Holland is sent to the Assembly of General Secretaries. The Evangelical Lutheran Church also signs this protest; thus seven Protestant Churches participate in this action. A declaration of this letter is planned for all the congregations on March 23.
March 30	Hitler tells his military leaders that the forthcoming war against Russia will be one of 'extermination.'		
March		Cracow Jewish ghetto is established.	
April 6	Greece is invaded by Nazi Germany.		
April 8		Salonika, Greece is occupied by the Germans. Almost immediately a discriminatory policy against the Jews of the city is implemented.	
April 15		All the members of the Jewish Community Council of Salonika are arrested; they are subsequently released.	
April 17	The kingdom of Yugoslavia capitulates to the invading German army and its Italian, Bulgarian, and Hungarian allies.		
April 23	Greece signs an armistice with Germany.		
April 29		Jews in Greece are ordered to surrender their radios.	
April		Lublin ghetto is established.	
June 22		Germany attacks the USSR. The *Einsatzgruppen* engage in mass killing. All of Poland falls under German domination. Einsatzgruppen continue killing behind the German armies until December 1942. Using guns and gas vans, they murder an estimated 1.4 million Jews.	
July 21		Hermann Goering signs an order giving Reinhard Heydrich the authorization to prepare a 'final solution' to the 'Jewish question' in Europe.	
August 3			Count Clemens August Graf von Galen, the Catholic Bishop of Münster, Germany, publicly protests the Nazi 'Euthanasia' program.
August 15		The Kovno Ghetto is sealed.	
August 29			Provost Bernard Lichtenberg of Berlin's St. Hedwig Cathedral publicly declares that he will include Jews in his daily prayers. On October 23, 1941, he is arrested and sent to Dachau but he dies on the way.
September 3	Six hundred Soviet POWs are gassed with Zyklon B in Auschwitz as the Nazis experiment to find efficient methods of mass extermination.		
September 9		The 'Jewish Codex' is promulgated in Slovakia. It consists of 270 articles and comprises all laws promulgated to this point against the Jews, in addition to several new edicts.	
September 19		German Jews are required to wear the Star of David in public.	
September 29-30		More than 32,000 Jews from Kiev are murdered by *Einsatzkommando* 4a at the Babi Yar ravine.	
October			Lutheran Church leaders in Saxony order their churches not to permit 'star-wearers' into worship services.
October 23		Emigration – but not deportation – of Jews from Germany is prohibited.	
November 6			In a letter, Msgr. Dr. Karol Kmetko of Slovakia appeals to the Slovakian Minister of the Interior, Sano Mach, on behalf of baptized Jews, protesting the requirement that they must wear the Star of David.
November 8		The establishment of a ghetto in Lvov is ordered.	

1941	GENERAL	HOLOCAUST	CHRISTIAN
November 12			In a note to Charles Sidor, the Slovak Minister to the Holy See, Vatican Secretary of State, Luigi Cardinal Maglione, intervenes on behalf of baptized Jews and the rights of the Roman Catholic Church in Slovakia. The note is ignored.
December 7	Japan attacks Pearl Harbor; The United States enters World War II.		
December 8		Gas vans are introduced at Chelmno extermination camp.	
December 11	Germany declares war on the United States.		

1942			
January 5			Delegates of Holland's Protestant and Roman Catholic Churches apply to the General Secretary of the Ministry of Justice for an interview with the Reich Commissioner, Seyss-Inquart. This is the first time in Dutch History that the Protestant and Roman Catholic Churches act together and sign a letter of protest.
January 20		Reinhard Heydrich convenes the Wannsee Conference in a suburb of Berlin to discuss the measures and inter-ministerial coordination needed to implement the 'Final Solution' of the Jewish problem. Officials from the SS, the civil service, the diplomatic service, the railroads and the military are present.	
January		Escapees from the first extermination camp, Chelmno, reach Warsaw and bring eyewitness testimony of the horrors being committed there.	The Apostolic Nuncio to Slovakia declares to Prime Minister Vojtech Tuka that 'it is incorrect to believe that the Jews are being sent to Poland to work; in reality they are being exterminated there.'
February			
March 1		Construction of the Sobibor killing center begins in Poland. Jews are first killed there in early May, 1942.	
March 13			Archbishop Angelo Rotta, Vatican Nuncio in Budapest, passes on an appeal from the World Jewish Congress requesting that the Pope attempt to persuade Msgr. Tiso to cancel the deportation of Slovakian Jews. This is followed on March 14 by a note of protest to the Slovak Government from Vatican Secretary of State Maglione. The note is ignored.
March 26		The first deportation train of Jews leaves from Poprad, Slovakia to Auschwitz.	
March 28		The first transport of French Jews is sent to Auschwitz.	
April 9	American forces surrender to the Japanese at Bataan.		
April 19			A short message regarding an interview between Reich Commissioner Seyss-Inquart, and delegates from Netherlands' Protestant and Roman Catholic Churches is read from the pulpits of the Dutch Reformed Church. The message states: '...The Church has protested against the lawlessness and cruelty to which those of Jewish faith in our nation are being subjected and against the attempt to enforce a national-socialist philosophy of life which stands in direct contradiction to the Gospel'.
April 26			The Catholic Bishops of Slovakia issue a pastoral letter to the faithful. The Bishops have mixed beliefs regarding the actions that are being taken against the Jews.
April 27	The first transport of female Polish political prisoners arrives at Auschwitz.		
April 29		The order is issued for Dutch Jews to begin wearing the yellow star.	
May 2		First mass killing in Sobibor extermination camp.	The Slovak Parliament passes post hoc authorization for deportations. Not one Catholic priest who is a representative to the Slovak Parliament votes against this measure.
May 15			
May 20			The General Presbytery of the Lutheran Bishops in Slovakia, under the leadership of Vladimir Cobdra and Dr. Samuel Stefan Osusky, issues a pastoral letter condemning the excesses accompanying the deportation of Slovakian Jews.
May 21	Operated by I.G. Farben, a synthetic rubber and petroleum plant opens at Monowitz (also known as Buna or Auschwitz III).		
May 27		Jews in Belgium are ordered to wear the Star of David.	
June		Mass deportations of Jews from Holland begin.	

1942	GENERAL	HOLOCAUST	CHRISTIAN
July 1	German *Sicherheitspolizei* (Security Police) take over control of Westerbork camp.		
July 4		For the first time, the camp administration at Auschwitz carries out a 'selection' at the railroad unloading platform. The transport involved contains Jews from Slovakia.	
July 6		The 400 year old Jewish graveyard in Salonika is destroyed.	
July 15-16		Dutch Jews are deported from Westerbork to Auschwitz.	
July 17-18		Himmler inspects the Auschwitz camp complex, takes part in the killing of a transport of Jews, attends roll-call in the women's camp, and approves the flogging of female prisoners. He orders Rudolf Höss, the commandant of Auschwitz, to proceed faster with construction of the Birkenau camp (Auschwitz II).	
July 19		Himmler orders the extermination of the Jews of Poland completed by the end of 1942.	
July 22		The killing center at Treblinka is operational. By August 1943, some 870,000 Jews perish there.	Protest of the French Assembly of Cardinals and Archbishops against the mass arrests and cruel
July 22			treatment of the French Jews is sent to Marshal Henri-Philippe Pétain, leader of the Vichy government.
July 26			Protest against the persecution of Dutch Jews is read from the pulpits of all Churches in Holland, except the Dutch Reformed Church. In retaliation, Roman Catholics of Jewish origin are arrested.
August 8			Edith Stein (Sister Theresa Benedicta of the Cross), a German Jewish philosopher who converted to
August 8	In Geneva, Gerhart Riegner cables Rabbi Stephen S. Wise in New York and Sidney Silverman in London about Nazi plans for the extermination of European Jewry. Rabbi Wise releases the information contained in the Riegner cable to the press on November 24.		Catholicism and became a Carmelite nun, arrives in Auschwitz after deportation from Westerbork. After a 'selection,' she is murdered in the gas chambers with other Jews. In 1987, she is beatified by Pope John Paul II.
August		Jews in Bulgaria are ordered to wear the yellow star.	The Minister of the Interior in Romania announces that all Jews will be deported. The Papal Nuncio in
Mid August			Bucharest, Archbishop Andrea Cassulo, together with Swiss minister Rene de Week, protests to the Romanian government.
Summer			Belgium's Cardinal Jozef-Ernest Van Roey, Archbishop of Malines, tells the Vatican that 'the persecution of the Jews was provoking a feeling of revolt among the general population of Belgium.'
September 6			In a pastoral letter, Cardinal Pierre Gerlier, the Archbishop of Lyon condemns the deportation of Jews from France.
September 9			Bulgarian Orthodox Metropolitan Stephan of Sophia, gives a sermon protesting actions taken against the Jews.
September			Two Belgian Catholic newspapers, *La Libre-Belgique – Peter Pan* and *De Vrijschutter*, print 'the first editorial
September		In Poland the Provisional Committee for Assistance to the Jews is formed. Three months later (December 1942) it is replaced by the Council for Aid to Jews, or *Zegota*.	protests against the deportation of Jews in Belgium'.
October 3			The Polish Embassy at the Vatican sends two reports to Vatican Secretary of State, Luigi Maglione, describing the German atrocities against the Jews in Poland. The embassy speaks of mass killings of Jews by asphyxiation, the depopulation of the ghettos of Vilna and Warsaw, and camps where Jews are gathered and killed.

	GENERAL	HOLOCAUST	CHRISTIAN
1942			
November 11			Norwegian Lutheran bishops, in cooperation with clergy from several other Protestant denominations, send a letter of protest to Minister-President of Norway, Vidkun Quisling, against the confiscation of Jewish property and the arrest of Jewish men. In December the protest was twice read from the pulpit and it was published as the Church's New Year's message for 1943.
November 19	Soviet troops launch a key counter-attack against German forces near Stalingrad.		
December 12			Archbishop Anthony Springovics of Riga, Latvia, sends the Pope information that most of the Jews of Riga have been murdered and only a few thousand remain in the ghetto.
December 17	An Allied declaration is made condemning the Nazis' "bestial policy of cold-blooded extermination."		
December 23			Pope Pius XII's Christmas message contains only veiled references to the hundreds of thousands of men, women, and children being murdered by the Nazis and their collaborators because of their race.
December		The Council for Aid to the Jews, *Zegota*, an organization uniting members of Polish democratic parties and Jews representing the Jewish Coordinating Committee, is formed after the Provisional Committee for Assistance to the Jews, initiated by Catholics of conscience who protest the murder of Jews, refuses to accept the Jewish representatives.	
1943			
January 2			The President of Poland, Wladislas Raczkiewicz, 'recalls for the Pope, in a letter from London, the three years of terror experienced by Poland under the Nazis. He bluntly reminds Pius XII of statements made by his predecessors on behalf of Poland and begs him to break his silence. Among other crimes, he [refers] to the scientifically planned mass killing of Jews and of baptized Jews.'
January 18		The first Warsaw ghetto uprising occurs.	
January			The Lutheran Bishop of Copenhagen, Denmark, Hans Fuglsang-Damgaard, issues a public warning against racial hatred.
February 2	Soviet forces defeat the German army at Stalingrad.		
February 12		Orders are given for the wearing of the Star of David by Greek Jews.	
February 26	First transport of Gypsies (Sinti and Roma) reaches Auschwitz.		
March 3		Jews from Thrace, Greece, are dragged from their beds during the night and arrested. On March 6, they are brought to the town of Drama, then taken to the old Greek-Bulgarian border and transported to concentration camps in Dunpnistsa and Gorna Dzhumaya.	
March 14			Archbishop Aloysius Stepinac (1898-1960), the highest Roman Catholic prelate in Croatia, publicly denounces racial dogma in a sermon in which he also affirms 'the worth of the hunting peoples of Africa.'
March 15		The first transport of Jews is sent from Salonika to Auschwitz.	
March 22			Slovakian Catholic Bishops publicly protest the deportation of Jews in a pastoral letter read in Latin from the pulpits. The German minister in Bratislava reports that many priests have refused to read the letter or have interjected their own comments negating its contents. Clerical opposition to the message is so strong that the Slovak Church has not published it with the official seal.
March 22- June 25	Construction is completed on four crematoria and gas chambers at Auschwitz-Birkenau, and they are made operational.		
March 23			Archbishop Damaskinos Papandreou, Archbishop of Athens and Primate of all Greece, sends a letter of protest to Prime Minister Logotheropoulos concerning the persecution of the Jews of Greece and on March 24, he sends a memorandum to Guenther Altenburg, Representative of the Reich for Greece, concerning the treatment and persecution of the Jews of Greece.
March 29		The order is issued to deport all Dutch Gypsies to Auschwitz.	
March		The Cracow Jewish ghetto is liquidated.	

	GENERAL	HOLOCAUST	CHRISTIAN
1943			

April 2 — Metropolitan Stefan of Bulgaria holds a plenary session of the Orthodox Holy Synod. He informs all the Metropolitans of the dangers threatening Bulgarian Jewry. The Metropolitans unanimously agree to send a letter of protest to the Prime Minister, the Minister of the Interior, and the Minister of Religions.

April 5 — Dietrich Bonhoeffer is arrested by the Gestapo. On October 5, 1944, he is transferred from Tegel prison to the main Gestapo prison in the Prinz Albrechtstrasse in Berlin. On April 9, 1945, he is executed by special order of Heinrich Himmler at the concentration camp at Flossenburg, just a few days before it was liberated.

April 19 — The British and the Americans hold a conference on the island of Bermuda to discuss the possibility of helping to rescue Jews in Europe. The conference concludes with no significant plan and is deemed a dismal failure by the press and public alike.

— The Warsaw Ghetto uprising begins. On May 16, General Jürgen Stroop writes: 'One hundred and eighty Jews, thugs, and the scum of humanity were killed. The 'Grand *Aktion*' ended at 20:15 [8:15pm] with the demolition of the Warsaw synagogue'.

April 19 —

May 4 — The Vatican writes to the government of Slovakia expressing its concern at the rumors that they were about to expel 'the Jews who live in Slovakia without discrimination for women and children and without excepting even those who have entered the Catholic religion.'

May 12 — End of all Axis resistance in Tunisia.

May 15 — The Belgian Catholic Bishops issue an open letter expressing 'their disapproval of people [Jews] being rounded up for compulsory labor.'

May 19 — In Holland representatives of the Dutch Reformed Church, the Roman Catholic Church, the New Reformed Church, the Christian Reformed Church, the Lutheran Evangelical Church, the Reformed Lutheran Evangelical Church, The Remonstrant Brotherhood, the Baptist Union and the Old Catholic Church lodge an official protest with Artur Seyss-Inquart, Reich Commissioner of Holland, against the sterilization of Jews in mixed marriages.

May 19 — Berlin declared *Judenfrei* (cleansed of Jews).

May 24 — In a note to Cardinal Luigi Maglione, Vatican Secretary of State, Archbishop Aloysius Stepinac denies charges that Croatia has committed any crimes, although he admits that 'irresponsible' persons, in the name of the state, might have done so in 1941. He 'praises' the actions of the government to rectify past evils which had been committed by Jews and Orthodox Serbs.

May — King Boris orders the resettlement of the Sofia Jews in provincial towns, despite protests by Jews and Bulgarians.

June 1 — A transport leaves Salonika, with 880 passengers, 'the cream of the Jewish community.' They are sent to Auschwitz – not to Theresienstadt as promised. On June 8, more than 500 are sent straight to the gas chamber.

June 1 — The final liquidation of the Lvov Jewish ghetto begins.

June 8 — A transport of 3,000 children and their mothers leaves Holland for Sobibor. All are gassed on arrival.

June 21 — Himmler orders the liquidation of all Jewish ghettos in occupied Soviet territories.

July 10 — The Allies invade Sicily.

July 11 — Hitler bans public reference to the 'Final Solution of the Jewish question.'

August 28 — King Boris of Bulgaria dies. A new cabinet is formed under Dobri Boshilov.

September 3 — Belgian Jews are arrested for deportation to Auschwitz.

September 10 — General Jürgen Stroop, the 'Conqueror of the Warsaw Ghetto,' arrives in Athens to assume the position of Higher SS leader.

Georg F. Duckwitz, a German naval attaché, alerts the leader of the Danish Social Democratic Party about an impending *aktion* against Jews in Denmark, scheduled for October 1-2. The non-Jewish Danish community spontaneously organizes efforts to rescue the Jews.

September 28 —

1943	GENERAL	HOLOCAUST	CHRISTIAN
September 29			The Danish Lutheran Church sends a protest against the Jewish persecution to Nazi authorities. The protest is read from all pulpits of the Danish Lutheran State Church on Sunday, October 3, 1943.
October 3		In Greece, General Jürgen Stroop issues a general anti-Jewish regulation, defining who is a Jew. Jews in Athens and Southern Greece are ordered to register.	
October 18		In Italy, the Jews of Rome are arrested and deported to Auschwitz. No protest is issued from the Vatican.	
October 25			In Croatia, Archbishop Aloysius Stepinac asserts from the pulpit that 'one cannot efface from the earth Gypsies or Jews because one considers them inferior races.'
October–November		Round-ups and raids on Jews such as those that occurred in Rome and other large cities in Italy are repeated on a smaller scale in many Italian cities and towns. Sometimes arrests are accompanied by violence and murder.	
November 11			A New Year's message protesting the persecution of Jews is read from Norwegian church pulpits. It is also read over the Norwegian language BBC.

1944	GENERAL	HOLOCAUST	CHRISTIAN
January 1			Kaj Munk, an ordained Lutheran minister, delivers a speech in Copenhagen urging resistance to the Nazis. On January 4, he is found shot to death.
March 19	Nazi Germany occupies Hungary.	Beginning of mass deportations of Hungarian Jews to Auschwitz-Birkenau. From the first deportation on May 15, until the transports are halted on July 7, 437,000 Jews are deported; a large majority of them meet their deaths in the gas chambers of Auschwitz-Birkenau.	
May 15			
June 6 D-Day	Allied forces land in Normandy.		Jusztinian Cardinal Seredi, head of the Hungarian Catholic Church, refuses the request of Budapest Jewish leaders that he appeal to the Regent, Admiral Horthy, to stop deportation of the Jews. However, Seredi intervenes on behalf of baptized Jews.
June 23			
July 20	German officers attempt to assassinate Hitler.		
August 4		Anne Frank and her family are betrayed, arrested in Amsterdam and sent to Westerbork.	
August 29	The Bulgarian Cabinet under Dobri Boshilov votes to abolish all anti-Jewish legislation.		
August		The Lodz ghetto is liquidated.	
October 7		Revolt by the Jewish *Sonderkommando* in Auschwitz-Birkenau. With explosives smuggled by women prisoners, the men in the *Sonderkommando* wreck Crematorium IV before the uprising is crushed.	
October	Salonika is recaptured by the Greek and Allied forces.		
November 8		Deportations from Budapest resume in a collaboration between the Germans and the Hungarian Arrow Cross Party. The Swedish diplomat Raoul Wallenberg, who has already managed to issue thousands of Jews in Budapest with diplomatic protection papers, saves about 20,000 people, whom he houses in special buildings under Swedish protection.	
November 8	John Pehle, Director of the American War Refugee Board, requests the bombing of the Auschwitz gas chambers; however, the Allies never bomb the main Auschwitz camp.		
November 25	Nazis discontinue gassings at Auschwitz.		

1945	GENERAL	HOLOCAUST	CHRISTIAN
January 18	Auschwitz is abandoned; the forced evacuation – death march – of prisoners begins, sending 58,000 prisoners, mostly Jews, out of the camp in the direction of concentration and labor camps in Germany.		

	GENERAL	HOLOCAUST	CHRISTIAN

1945

January 27 — The Red Army liberates Auschwitz.

April 9 — Dietrich Bonhoeffer is hanged.

April 15 — Bergen-Belsen concentration camp is liberated by British forces.

April 30 — Adolf Hitler and Eva Braun commit suicide in Hitler's Berlin bunker.

May 6 — Holland is liberated by the Allies; Queen Wilhelmina returns to her throne.

May 7-8 — Germany surrenders; V.E. Day, the war in Europe ends.

Sept 17-Nov 17 — Bergen-Belsen War Crimes Trials are held.

October 19 — The Stuttgart Declaration of Guilt is issued by the Evangelical Church in Germany. It states, in part, "We accuse ourselves that we didn't witness more courageously, pray more faithfully, believe more joyously, love more ardently".

November 20 — The Nuremberg War Crimes Trials begins. An International Military Tribunal convenes in Nuremberg, Germany. With Allied judges presiding, it brings accusations of war crimes and crimes against humanity against twenty-four defendants. Twelve are found guilty and sentenced to death; seven are found guilty and sentenced to variable terms of imprisonment; three are acquitted.

1946

The very first international gathering of Christian and Jews was held in Oxford in 1946. The subject of the conference is "Faith, Responsibility, Justice". A joint document was agreed upon, including a denunciation of antisemitism. But the conference did not deal with the two issues that were to become paramount in Jewish-Christian relations in the post-war world: the role of Christian teaching in creating an atmosphere in which a Holocaust was possible, and the struggle for the Jewish State then in full swing.

March — Following his arrest at the conclusion of the war, Ludwig Müller, Germany's *Reichsbishof*, commits suicide in a Berlin prison, although his family denies it is suicide.

Oct 25 1946-Aug 20 1947 — The Nuremberg Doctors' Trial is held. Twenty-three German physicians and scientists are accused of inflicting a range of vile and lethal procedures on vulnerable populations and inmates of concentration camps between 1933 and 1945.

1947

April — Msgr. Jozef Tiso, former President of Slovakia, is condemned and executed.

August — At a conference in Seeligsberg, Switzerland, the International Conference of Christians and Jews draws up a document that has a historic impact as the initial institutional assault on antisemitism. The "Ten Points of Seeligsberg" becomes the stimulus for ensuring dialogue between Christians and Jews. It outlines steps Christianity needs to take if it is to strip future Christian teaching of negative images of Jews and Judaism and replace them with new positive theological understandings. The document becomes known as the Ten Points of Seeligsberg.

	GENERAL	HOLOCAUST	CHRISTIAN
1948			
May 14	The establishment of the State of Israel.		The first Assembly of the Protestant World Council of Churches is held in Amsterdam. While the Assembly shows its awareness of Jewish suffering during the Holocaust - "We cannot forget that we meet in a land [Holland] from which 110,000 Jews were taken to be murdered" - there is no hint of Christians being at least partially responsible for these sufferings. A document, however, is produced on the Christian Approach to the Jews; it condemns antisemitism.
1953			Protestant theologian Paul Tillich propounds a program to review Church publications to purge them of dangerous anti-Jewish stereotypes; to emphasize the Old Testament in the Church; to abandon missionary movement to the Jews; to foster theological dialogue and joint activities in the struggle for social justice; and to accept the continuity and authenticity of the Jewish faith.
1958			
October 9			Pope Pius XII (Eugenio Pacelli) dies.
October 28			Cardinal Angelo Roncalli is elected Supreme Pontiff of the Roman Catholic Church. He takes the name, Pope John XXIII.
1959			
January 25			Pope John XXIII announces plans for an Ecumenical Council, which will become known as Vatican Council II.
1962			
October 11			Vatican Council II is opened by Pope John XXIII. More than 2200 Roman Catholic bishops from around the world meet in sessions held in St. Peter's Basilica, Rome. Protestant and Jewish scholars are invited as official observers.
1963			
June 3			Pope John XXIII dies.
June 21			Cardinal Giovanni Battista Montini is elected Supreme Pontiff of the Roman Catholic Church. He takes the name Pope Paul VI.
1965			Pope Paul VI and 2221 Roman Catholic bishops from around the world overwhelmingly approve the document, *Nostra Aetate* ("In Our Time"), the key statement with regard to Catholic-Jewish Relations. The document revolutionizes Catholic thinking and theology about Jews and Judaism and has a significant impact on Christian thinking and theology.
October 28			
1978			
August 6			Pope Paul VI dies.
August 26			Cardinal Albino Luciani is elected Supreme Pontiff of the Roman Catholic Church - Pope John Paul I.
September 28			Pope John Paul I dies.
October 16			Cardinal Karol Wojtyla is elected Supreme Pontiff of the Roman Catholic Churchm, taking the name Pope John Paul II. He is the first Polish Pope.
1998			
March 16			*We Remember: A Reflection on the Shoah* is issued by the Vatican's Commission for Religious Relations with the Jewish People.

ANTISEMITISM

3

TWO THOUSAND YEARS OF JEWISH LIFE IN EUROPE

Following the destruction of the Temple in 70 CE, Jews settled throughout the European continent. For nearly two millennia, Christians and Jews lived together, worked alongside each other, and shared the same geographical space and cultural environment. During this time, Jewish communities experienced both good times and bad. Through it all, they created the rich textures of European Jewish history as we know it today.

The Golden Age of Spanish Jewry in the early Middle Ages, the spontaneity of East European Hasidism, the cultural beauty of the Amsterdam community and the proud achievements of German Jewry have all formed part of a rich history. The ability to adapt to new and changing situations, such as expulsion, inquisition, enlightenment and emancipation, have all facilitated the development of its rich heritage. European culture owes a debt of gratitude to European Jewish communities for the consistently valuable dimension they have brought to the overall cultural and intellectual life of Europe. The

This illustration is taken from Martin Gilbert's useful collection of maps on the Holocaust. It shows approximately the number of Jews that resided in Europe at the time of the Nazis rise to power. London, JM Dent, 1993.

legacy of hatred and perpetual cycle of victimization that Jewish communities have experienced over the centuries within the European Christian environment is important to understand, but it should always be understood within the historical context of the life of individuals and communities.

This illustration is taken from Martin Gilbert's useful collection of maps on the Holocaust. It shows the approximate number of Jews that resided in Europe at the time of the Nazis' rise to power. London: JM Dent, 1993.

WHAT IS ANTISEMITISM?

Carol Rittner   John K. Roth

'Antisemitism' is such a common term that one might suppose it has been around a long time. In fact, it was first popularized in the late 1870s by a German journalist and racist ideologue named Wilhelm Marr. He employed it in speaking about the largely secular anti-Jewish political campaigns that were widespread in Europe at the time. The word derives from an 18th-Century etymological analysis that differentiated between languages with 'Aryan' roots and those with 'Semitic' ones. This distinction led to the assumption – a false one – that there are corresponding racial groups. Under this rubric, Jews became 'Semites', thus paving the way for Marr's usage. Marr could have used the conventional German term *Judenhass*, but that way of referring to Jew-hatred carried religious connotations that Marr wanted to de-emphasize in favor of racial ones. Apparently more 'scientific,' the term *antisemitismus* caught on and eventually became a way of speaking about all forms of hostility directed at and experienced by Jews throughout history.

What is Antisemitism? According to the French Jewish scholar Jules Isaac, in his book *The Teaching of Contempt*, antisemitism refers 'to anti-Jewish prejudice, to feelings of suspicion, contempt, hostility, and hatred towards Jews, both those who follow the religion of Israel and those who are merely of Jewish parentage.' It ranges from quiet contempt to bullying, persecution and racist violence directed against Jewish people. Its distinguishing mark is hatred or contempt for Jews. It goes beyond normal political conflict, beyond even the normal hostilities and prejudices that arise between different peoples. Antisemitism attributes to Jews some quality of cosmic and diabolic evil.

After the defeat of Nazi Germany in 1945, many people thought antisemitism was dead and buried, but they were wrong. It went into hibernation, but in the last decade or so it has once again stirred to life, cloaking itself in disguises old and new. Once again Jews are singled out by international terrorists, Jewish old age homes and schools are defaced, synagogues and cemeteries are desecrated. 'Revisionist historians' hold 'scholarly' meetings and publish books denying the Holocaust ever happened. Radical right-wing political organizations contend that economic woes are the fault of rich and powerful Jews who control money markets, banks, newspapers, radio and television. Social clubs and country clubs, fraternities and sororities, city neighborhoods and suburban sub-divisions still find 'polite' but firm ways to exclude people with names like Stein, Goldberg, and Fried.

For Reflection

What is the difference between racial and religious antisemitism?

Why is antisemitism refered to as the longest hatred of human history?

How can we help people to develop faith without prejudice?

Many Christians are appallingly ignorant about Jews and Judaism. They are unaware of the suffering Christians have inflicted on Jews across two millennia. It is just such historical ignorance that contributes to the extraordinary durability of what has been called the 'longest hatred' of human history. Prejudice against Jews may have predated Christianity, but nothing in history can match Christian enmity toward Jews and Judaism.

In his book, *The World Must Know*, Michael Berenbaum writes: 'Historians agree that the break between Judaism and Christianity followed the Roman destruction of Jerusalem in the year 70 C.E. In the aftermath of this devastating defeat, which was interpreted by Jew and Christian alike as a sign of divine punishment, the Gospels were recast to diminish Roman responsibility and emphasize Jewish culpability in the death of Jesus.' One result of that emphasis was that for nearly two thousand years, Jews were 'depicted as killers of the Son of God' (the deicide charge). Christian 'teaching of contempt' for Jews and Judaism became embedded in the formation of the Christian Scriptures (New Testament). It also found its way into the writing and preaching of some of the early Church Fathers – St. Augustine and St. John Chrysostom, for example. And through the centuries, some of the most eloquent and influential Christian preachers, teachers, and theologians – from St. Bernard of Clairvaux to Martin Luther, and others – excoriated Jews as 'stiff-necked' and 'blind', a 'brood of vipers', 'companions of the devil'.

From the late Middle Ages on, antisemitism was expressed in many ways. In Christian worship and art, preaching and teaching, Jews were blamed for the death of Jesus, accused of kidnapping and murdering Christian children, then using their blood to make matza for the Passover seder (the blood libel), Jews were expelled from cities, forced to live in restricted areas, compelled to wear distinctive clothing, prohibited from occupying various professions, denied citizenship, even expelled from countries, like England in 1290 and Spain in 1492. While the 18th-Century Enlightenment saw the emancipation of Jews in some European countries, economic and social restrictions persisted, as did antisemitic myths, superstitions, feelings and beliefs.

By the 19th Century, European society, particularly western society, had become more secular, less religious. As a result, so did prejudice against Jews. As Carrie Supple writes in *From Prejudice to Genocide*, '. . . anti-Jewishness became secular and antisemitism took a racial form. . . This important change coincided with the spread of ideas of Social Darwinism, taken from the ideas of Charles Darwin in his book *Origin of Species* (1859). . . Although Darwin had not intended his evolution principles to be applied to humans, it was soon extended by others to a notional 'ladder' of races with white, 'Aryan', Anglo-Saxons at the top and blacks, Slavs and Jews at the bottom. This fitted in well with Christian antisemitism and racism.' Antisemites began to call Jews a genetically inferior 'race'.

For Further Reading

Mary C. Boys. *Jewish-Christian Dialogue: One Woman's Experience.* New York: Paulist Press, 1997.

Rabbi Yechiel Eckstein. *What Christians Should Know about Jews and Judaism.* Waco, TX: Word Books, 1984.

Edward H. Flannery. *The Anguish of the Jews: Twenty-Three Centuries of Antisemitism* (rev. and updated). Mahwah, NJ: Paulist Press, 1985.

Eugene Fisher and Rabbi Leon Klenicki. *Antisemitism is a Sin.* New York: Anti-Defamation League of B'nai B'rith, 1990.

Rosemary Ruether. *Faith and Fratricide: The Theological Roots of Anti-Semitism.* New York: The Seabury Press, 1979.

'Antisemitism is easy to analyse, to dissect, to condemn. It is infinitely more difficult to fight it effectively.'

Jules Isaac, *The Christian Roots of Antisemitism*, p. 1.

A Jewish woman wearing the obligatory Jew-badge on her outer garment, which Jews were required to wear when leaving the Jewish quarter. Worms, Germany, 16th century.

Carol Rittner R.S.M. (USA), Distinguished Professor Of Holocaust Studies at The Richard Stockton College of New Jersey, is the co-editor of *The Holocaust and the Christian World: Reflections on the Past, Challenges for the Future.*

John K. Roth (USA), Russell Pitzer Professor of Philosophy at Claremont McKenna College in California, has written, co-authored, or edited more than twenty-five books, many of them about the Holocaust, including *Approaches to Auschwitz: The Holocaust and Its Legacy* and *Ethics After the Holocaust.*

Because many Jews never assimilated into the surrounding dominant Christian society, they were easy targets in societies undergoing rapid industrialization and change. They were easily identifiable – they went to synagogue on Saturday, not church on Sunday, they celebrated *Hanukkah* and Passover, not Christmas and Easter, and they often observed special dietary regulations. Jews became 'the other' – marginalized, persecuted, blamed for every woe, from unemployment and slums, to military defeats and unsolved murders. By the 1920s and 1930s, Hitler and the Nazis had a fertile seedbed to exploit for their own vicious purposes. As Raul Hilberg said in his book, *The Destruction of the European Jews,* 'The Nazi destruction process did not come out of a void; it was the culmination of a cyclical trend. . . The missionaries of Christianity said in effect: You have no right to live among us as Jews. The secular rulers who followed proclaimed: You have no right to live among us. The Nazis at last decreed: You have no right to live.'

Not until Vatican II and its declaration, *Nostra Aetate* (1965) did the mainstream Christian Churches, Catholic as well as Protestant, seriously begin to critique their negative preaching and teaching about Jews and Judaism. While we Christians cannot change the facts of history, we can put back into our books the 'pages of history' we have torn out but that Jews 'have committed to memory'. If we begin to do that, perhaps, we shall finally be able to develop faith without prejudice.

When Jews were no longer useful to rulers or when hatred toward them became overwhelming, expulsion often followed.

Between the 15th Century and 1722, the Jews were not allowed in Russia. The Ottoman Empire and Polish Galicia were two of the countries where Jews were allowed in after these expulsions. The Ottoman Empire, founded in the early 14th Century, was Muslim and accepted Jews.

Carrie Supple. *From Prejudice to Genocide: Learning about the Holocaust.* Stoke-on-Trent, UK: Trentham, 1993, p. 20.

Country	Year Expelled
England	1290
France	1306
Hungary	1349
Spain	1492
Portugal	1497
Germany	Different times in 14th, 15th, 16th centuries

Table of Canonical Law and Nazi Anti-Jewish Measures

The comparison below of Canonical Law and Nazi measures clearly demonstrates that anti-Judaism had long been a visible part of Christian society. The Final Solution was an unprecedented event; unfortunately, many Jews had precedents in Christian history.

Canonical Law	Nazi Measure
Prohibition of intermarriage and of sexual intercourse between Christians and Jews, Synod of Elvira, 306	Law for the Protection of German Blood and Honor, September 15, 1935
Jews not allowed to employ Christian servants or possess Christian slaves, 3rd Synod of Orléans, 538	Law for the Protection of German Blood and Honor, September 15, 1935
Jews not permitted to show themselves in the streets during Passion Week, 3rd Synod of Orléans, 538	Decree authorizing local authorities to bar Jews from the streets on certain days (i.e. Nazi holidays), December 3, 1938
Burning of the Talmud and other books, 12th Synod of Toledo, 681	Book burnings in Nazi Germany
Christians not permitted to patronize Jewish doctors, Trulanic Synod, 692	Decree of July 25, 1938
Jews not permitted to be plaintiffs, or witnesses against Christians in the Courts, 3rd Lateran Council, 1179, Canon 26	Proposal by the Party Chancellery that Jews not be permitted to institute civil suits, September 9, 1942
Jews not permitted to withhold inheritance from descendants who had accepted Christianity, 3rd Lateran Council, 1179, Canon 26	Decree empowering the Justice Ministry to void wills offending the 'sound judgment of the people,' July 31, 1938
The marking of Jewish clothes with a badge, 4th Lateran Council, 1215, Canon 68 (Copied from the legislation by Caliph Omar II [634-644], who had decreed that Christians wear blue belts and Jews, yellow belts	Decree of September 1, 1941 – the Yellow Star
Construction of new synagogues prohibited, Council of Oxford, 1222	Destruction of synagogues in entire Reich, November 10, 1938
Compulsory ghettos, Synod of Breslau, 1267	Order by Heydrich, September 21, 1939
Christians not permitted to sell or rent real estate to Jews, Synod of Ofen, 1279	Decree providing for compulsory sale of Jewish real estate, December 3, 1938
Adoption by a Christian of the Jewish religion or return by a baptized Jew to the Jewish religion defined as a heresy, Synod of Mainz, 1310	Adoption of the Jewish religion by a Christian places him in jeopardy of being treated as a Jew. June 26, 1942
Jews not permitted to obtain academic degrees, Council of Basel, 1434, Sessio XIX	Law against Overcrowding of German Schools and Universities, April 25, 1933

Adapted with permission from: Raul Hilberg; *The Destruction of European Jewry*. New York: Holmes and Meier, 1985

INDIFFERENCE TO THE PLIGHT OF THE JEWS DURING THE HOLOCAUST

Carol Rittner   John K. Roth

The Holocaust was not just an unfortunate event in human history unrelated to the religious, moral, intellectual, and cultural traditions of western civilization. The Holocaust cannot be reduced to a monstrous criminal act, then forgotten. In remembering the Holocaust, we Christians must ask ourselves how it could have happened in the 20th Century in the epicenter of 'Christian' Europe. We also need to ask ourselves why compassion, indignation, indeed, active 'Christian' resistance to the Nazis could be found only in exceptional instances when it came to the Jews.

While there is no simple explanation to these questions, one way of approaching them is to do so from the perspective of sociology and its important insight that thought is socially grounded, that society affects our consciousness, the way we perceive reality and think about it. Even religion, however spiritual in appearance, has a social impact that often is hidden from its adherents, including clergy and theologians. Some sociologists make this hidden dimension of religion the special object of their attention. They, in turn, have influenced some theologians, who have tried to subject Christian theology to what is known as an 'ideological critique'. For these sociologists, and the theologians influenced by them, ideology is a distortion of the truth for the sake of social interest. It is a symbolic framework of mind that legitimizes the power and the privileges of a dominant group by sanctioning the social evils inflicted on people without access to power. Through a largely unconscious process, every community of men and women generates a set of symbols that protects its position of power and affirms its identity over its competitor.

'They know only one thing, wrote St. John Chrysostom, to satisfy their stomachs, to get drunk, to kill. The synagogue, he wrote, is worse than a brothel . . . It is the den of scoundrels and the repair of wild beasts . . . the temple of demons devoted to idolatrous cults . . . the cavern of devils . . . a criminal assembly of Jews . . . a place of meetings for the assassins of Christ . . . the refuge of devils.'

Quoted in Dennis Prager and Joseph Telushkin, *Why the Jews?: The Reason for Antisemitism.* p. 94.

Gregory Baum, a Canadian Catholic theologian at McGill University in Montreal, says that behind the straightforward and obvious aims of religion and culture are hidden trends which exercise a powerful influence on society and sustain the authority of existing institutions. Often these features are closely interwoven with the true content of a religion. They have so affected the inherited consciousness of a religion that it is not easy for an adherent to see how the original message has been distorted. As Baum says in the Foreword to Charlotte Klein's book, *Anti-Judaism in Christian Theology*, 'to discover the ideological influences' in one's religion requires more than 'intelligence and good will'. Discovering these influences in one's religion becomes possible 'only when these find expression in a great and terrible historical happening where their destructive power is too obvious to go unnoticed.' While we know that 'the hatred and persecution of the Jews in Hitler's Germany, leading to the extermination camps in the east, were a terrifying racial-pagan phenomenon which had nothing directly to do with religion', it is clear that 'this terrible event, surpassing all that could be imagined, would not have been possible if hostility to the Jews had not been fostered by Christian preaching which spoke of the Jews and Judaism almost from the beginning only in terms of rejection.'

This historical anti-Jewish bias in Christian preaching and teaching is a startling example of ideological

For Reflection

What arguments could you use against the accusation that the Jews killed Jesus?

What is the connection between historical events like the Crusades and traditional anti-Jewish Christian theology?

How can we Christians purge our teaching and preaching of an anti-Jewish bias without at the same time destroying the essence of our Christian beliefs?

Statues on the façade of Strasbourg Cathedral portraying the Church - *Ecclesia* - (opposite) and the blind-folded Synagogue - *Synagoga* - holding a broken staff and the Tablets of the Law. Such images were highly influential in an age where Christian visual art played an important role in shaping the negative opinions and attitudes of the public toward the Jews. Such statues appear on many medieval cathedrals.

'. . . it is not easy to proclaim Jesus Christ without at the same time implying a negation of the Jews.'

Gregory Baum, 'Foreword' in Charlotte Klein, *Anti-Judaism in Christian Theology.* p. xi.

For Further Reading

Donald J. Dietrich. *God and Humanity in Auschwitz: Jewish-Christian Relations and Sanctioned Murder.* New Brunswick: Transaction Publications, 1995.

Harry James Cargas, ed. *Holocaust Scholars Write to the Vatican.* Westport, CT: Greenwood Press, 1998.

Jules Isaac. *The Christian Roots of Antisemitism.* London: The Council of Christian and Jews, 1960.

William Nicholls. *Christian Anti-Semitism: A History of Hate.* New York: Jason Aronson, 1995.

Richard L. Rubenstein. *After Auschwitz: History, Theology, and Contemporary Judaism,* 2nd ed. Baltimore: The Johns Hopkins University Press, 1992

deformation, the result, some scholars say, of the Christian churches' need to justify a messianic reading of the scriptures. Christian teachers and preachers – Catholic, Protestant, and Orthodox alike – accompanied the proclamation of the Gospel with a refutation of Judaism and the negation of Jewish existence before God. For centuries, they argued that the Jewish people never understood the prophetic message, that they lived in blindness and infidelity, that they rejected Jesus as the Messiah because they were hard-hearted and stubborn, and that they condemned Jesus to death. In the Christian worldview, Jews were a people excluded from grace, reprobated and condemned, preserved in history only as a sign of God's wrath.

The negation of Jewish existence was translated into social and political terms when Christianity became the official religion of the Roman Empire in 321 C.E. Jews were pushed to the margins of civil society, forced to live as social outcasts. During the Middle Ages, they were excluded from various Guilds, forbidden to engage in certain professions, denied citizenship, protection, and social interaction with the Christian population. Kings and queens expelled them from their territories. Great theologians of the time (Martin Luther, for example) excoriated the Jews, particularly when they realized they would not convert to their particular reformed version of the Christian religion. The legal oppression of the Jews in much of Europe lasted until the Enlightenment (18th Century). Even then, however, the negative theological symbols and language of contempt applied to the Jews did not disappear with the secular age.

The negation of Jewish existence, which the Christian churches had symbolized in their liturgy and doctrines, their sermons and teaching materials helped to produce an endless series of persecutions and pogroms. Monarchs and secular rulers incorporated these symbols in laws and social structures which, in turn, fuelled hatred of Jews by Christians who often were unaware of what had become a kind of compulsive hatred of Jews and Judaism. As the humanist, Erasmus of Rotterdam (1466-1536) once reportedly said, 'If it is Christian to hate the Jews, then we are all good Christians.'

For centuries, Jews were cast outside the universe of moral obligation, placed beyond the boundaries of the normal care and concern people owe each other in the human community. After so many centuries of Christian 'teaching of contempt', is it any wonder that Christians and their churches – Catholic, Protestant, and Orthodox alike – were indifferent for the most part to the fate of the Jews during the Holocaust?

As Christians, our task is to raise questions about how people in our Churches think and speak about Jews today. To quote Gregory Baum again, 'Has there been any criticism of the ideology which prevailed up to Auschwitz? Or do people speak as they always did?' Are clergy, students of theology and theologians aware that they may only speak of Jews and Judaism in a responsible fashion, that they must avoid expressions which foster contempt for the Jewish people? Do the Christian Churches – Catholic, Protestant and Orthodox – do theology with their backs to Auschwitz?

We Christians must take as our working principle this statement of Rabbi Irving Greenberg: 'No statement, theological or otherwise, should be made that would not be credible in the presence of the burning children.' If we fail to do so, we shall never overcome the anti-Jewish bias in so much of Christian theology.

'For centuries, Jews were cast outside the universe of moral obligation, placed beyond the boundaries of the normal care and concern people owe each other in the human community.'

Carol Rittner R.S.M. (USA), Distinguished Professor Of Holocaust Studies at The Richard Stockton College of New Jersey, is the co-editor of *The Holocaust and the Christian World: Reflections on the Past, Challenges for the Future.*

John K. Roth (USA), Russell Pitzer Professor of Philosophy at Claremont McKenna College in California, has written, co-authored, or edited more than twenty-five books, many of them about the Holocaust, including *Approaches to Auschwitz: The Holocaust and Its Legacy* and *Ethics After the Holocaust.*

THE CHURCHES AND NAZI PERSECUTION

THE GERMAN CHURCHES IN THE THIRD REICH

Franklin H. Littell

The established Roman Catholic and Protestant *(Evangelisch)* churches of Germany, with their tax support and civil service ideology ratings, entered crippled into confrontation with the dynamic ideology and policies of the German Third Reich. Nazism was a populist *(völkisch)* movement, potentially genocidal from its beginnings. The church leaders mistook it for a political party.

Even today some scholars outside Germany write of the Nazi Party's coming to power as a triumph of parliamentary maneuvering through which the Party took power legitimately. After the 1923 fiasco on Munich, the so called 'Beer Hall Putsch,' the NSDAP was said to have abandoned the politics of the coup *(Staatsstreich)*. In truth, however, by assassinations and bombings and beatings and other terrorist tactics, the Party showed its fundamental disloyalty to the Republic and to constitutional government. Its outward behavior, and also inward structure, was predictive of the kind of rule it would exercise if it took control.

What wonder, then, if – in the midst of the massive unemployment, street-fighting, frenzied political demagoguery and mass meetings of the early Depression years – German church leaders were unable to read the scene as clearly as some parse it seventy years later.

The church establishments were neither equipped for confrontation with the state, nor financially able to resist, nor armed with a theoretical (theological) basis for resistance. By the time any unease set in, the Nazi Party had swallowed the State, Adolf Hitler was absolute dictator, and the vibrant program of the Führer was producing economic recovery and a series of international triumphs. The ignominy and shame that had shadowed the Weimar Republic from its beginning were lifted, and one government after another was sending emissaries to deal with 'the new Germany.'

Catholic clergy give the Nazi salute with high ranking Nazis including Josef Goebbels (far right) and Wilhelm Frick. (second right) USHMM

While diplomats and corporation representatives sought understanding with the new Germany, at the lower level substantial sectors of the peoples of the 'Christian' nations, openly antisemitic, warmed to Hitler's ranting against 'the Jews.'

It is difficult today to realize how openly antisemitic political movements and leaders – strong and unembarrassed – played an important role also outside Germany and Austria. Even in the America of Franklin D. Roosevelt (and Father Charles Coughlin) antisemitism was a powerful and dangerous political force. In France, a substantial sector was still unreconciled to loss of face in the Dreyfus Case; they greeted the first Jew ever to serve as French Premier with the bitter words, 'Better Hitler than Léon Blum!' In a few short years, Marshal Pétain's Vichy regime was to give that choice its final logic.

The Roman Catholic Story

The Roman Catholic community in Germany, with a leadership consciously international and universal, responded to the Nazi movement much differently from the Protestants. During the birth of the Empire under Bismarck's chancellorship, with the overpowering position of Prussia, the citizens of several predominantly Roman Catholic provinces were made to feel second-class subjects of the German Emperor (who was also King of Prussia).

During the short-lived Weimar republic, the Center Party, predominantly Roman Catholic in membership, and the Social Democrats held the center against extremists and splinter parties. They were also the chief centers of opposition during the two and a half years of turmoil that preceded President Hindenberg's call to Hitler ('that Austrian corporal' as he called him) to form a government. Against the substantial force of the German Communist Party (KPD) – controlled by the Kremlin, the minor blocs more or less weakly organized (monarchists, liberals, sectional) and the populist appeal of the Nazis, the alliance of the Center Party (*Zentrum*) and the Social Democrats had until then held the Republic together.

Until the signing of the Concordat, which the Vatican Secretary of State (Eugenio Pacelli) negotiated with Hitler without informing them, the German Bishops regularly refused the rites of the church to Nazi officials. Until then, the major Christian resistance to Nazi ideology and political force came from the Catholic side.

The Concordat of July 8, 1933 (which governs the relations of the Vatican and Germany to this day), remains one of the debated moments in Hitler's consolidation of power. It is clear that Cardinal Pacelli (later Pope Pius XII) had long had in mind for Germany – where he served as Papal Nuncio from 1918 until called to the Vatican post in 1930 – the model of the 1929 Concordat with Mussolini. The Concordat seemed to be a means to secure the rights and privileges of the Church.

The Führer and his entourage greeted with enthusiasm the successful conclusion of negotiations. The Center Party was liquidated officially and Roman Catholics were no longer discouraged from joining the Nazi Party. Most important, the Concordat gave Hitler his first important international treaty;

'The periods of German Church Struggle were as follows:
1. 1933-1935: The struggle was understood solely as a Church Struggle, with opportunity for nonconformism.
2. 1935-1938: The Church Struggle became an unwanted political struggle, pressure being exerted toward disobedience.
3. 1938-1945: The Church Struggle disintegrated as a mismanaged political struggle; the alternatives became secret resistance or truce.
4. After 1945: Reinterpretation followed, half of it directed toward Church Struggle, half toward resistance, accompanied by confusion of interpretation as either a fight for obedience to Christ or a fight for freedom of [hu]mankind.'

Eberhard Bethge, *'Troubled Self-Interpretation and Uncertain Reception in the Church Struggle'* in Franklin H. Littell and Hubert C. Locke, eds., *The German Church Struggle and the Holocaust*, p. 168.

'The Church Struggle was the struggle of the church to be true to its Lord. And I take that to be a vital concern not only to its members but to all [hu]mankind. I am not a member, but I am passionately convinced of its importance. What gave me that conviction was precisely the experience of Hitler's millennium and the Christian response to it.'

Beate Ruhm von Oppen,*'Revisionism and Counterrevisionism in the Historiography of the Church Struggle'* in Littell and Locke, eds., *The German Church Struggle and the Holocaust,* p. 68.

For Reflection

Was a fear of Communism justification for alliance with Nazism?

Why do you think some Christians could denounce Nazism but fail to mention the plight of the Jews?

When the Church is politically weak, what powers might it still be able to use to confront oppression?

in the colorful German saying, the Concordat made the former demagogue and street fighter *salonfähig* (fit for association with decent people.)

The Protestant Story

There was no period of restraint during which the Protestant established churches *(Landeskirchen)* denied the rites of the church to Party bonzes, although the first martyr of the Confessing Church (Paul Schneider) fell foul of the Party precisely for refusing to allow the rites of the church to be used for a local functionary. Since the 16th century division of the Latin Church, the Protestants, theologians and functionaries had defined the Gospel in the vernacular and shaped Christian culture in obedience to the political authority, *Obrigkeit*. Martin Luther, the 16th Century reformer, had tied the direction of the religious establishment to the princes, and the several Protestant territorial churches never found a secure emotional footing after the Kaiser fled to Holland at the end of World War I.

Most of the Protestant leaders, including a number who like Otto Dibelius and Martin Niemöller quickly became disenchanted, at first greeted Hitler's coming to power with genuine satisfaction. Like all good Germans, they resented the unfair attribution to Germany of sole guilt for the war. Like all Germans, they recalled the bitter months of starvation and disease that followed the ceasefire, with the deaths of hundreds of thousands who perished between the Armistice of November 11, 1918 and the Versailles Treaty (January 10, 1920) because of the Allied blockade. Even though the United States refused to sign the Versailles Treaty, in their desolation the Germans remembered they had agreed to cease hostilities with specific reference to President Woodrow Wilson's Fourteen Points – and included America in their view of a hostile surrounding circle of nations.

Like the Roman Catholics, the German Protestants feared the Communist danger. But far more than was the case with the Catholics, on the boundaries between their religious identity and their patriotic loyalty few fences had been erected. Since the 16th Century, the divisions in the Latin Church of the West between those loyal to Rome and those loyal to political rulers who functioned as lay bishops had hardened in culture and style of political life.

Each of the established churches in Germany attempted, in its own way, to defend the interests of the institutional church and to 'winter through' *(durchwinter)* the volatile years of the rise and fall of the Third Reich. The early attempt of Hitler to unite them in a National Church, with a single head, was thwarted – the first significant frustration of the program of consolidation and coordination *(Gleichschaltung)* by which all dimensions of the society were to be brought under Party supervision and the dictatorial control of the Führer. However, although there were worthy individual cases of resistance during the twelve and a half years of Hitler's Thousand Year Reich, and some individual martyrdoms. The established Churches fulfilled their expected patriotic duty in support of the regime and its programs.

Although Bishop Theophil Wurm (Protestant) and Cardinal Bertram (Roman Catholic) intervened vigorously in defense of the elderly and handicapped against euthanasia (August 1940), no such firm positions had been taken in defense of the Jews. Beginning in 1935, German citizens who were Jews were systematically deprived of their civil rights and – if they had not gone into exile by 1939 – of their lives.

Neither in the Six Articles of the *Barmen Confession of Faith* 29 May 1934 issued by the Confessing Church *(Bekennende Kirche)* nor in the papal encyclical *Mit brennender Sorge* ('With Deep Anxiety,' March 21, 1937) was the plight of the Jews mentioned. The German Jews were comparatively few in number (less than 5% of the population), and many of them had the resources to flee in time. The massive Nazi genocide of the Jews ('the Holocaust') followed upon the German invasion of Poland, September 1, 1939, and fell primarily upon the Jewry of east Central Europe. By then the large number of Protestant and Roman Catholic clergy were in the chaplaincy, a few hundreds were in concentration camps, and the work of the local parishes was in the hands of lay people (chiefly older women).

Finishing Unfinished Business

The issue most important for the credibility of Christianity, the relationship to the Jewish people – is the unfinished business of the churches during the Third Reich.

The Roman Catholic change began with Vatican II (1961-65), and with intermediate steps has resulted in the fine encyclical, *We Remember* (March 12, 1998). Carrying on the Barmen tradition, the German Protestants of one territorial church (the Rhineland Churches) released in January 1980 a powerful statement, 'Toward the Renovation of Christian-Jewish Relations,' which has been followed subsequently by a dozen other territorial churches in Germany.

The Roman Catholic message transcends national boundaries, giving it the same advantage the German Catholics enjoyed in 1933-45. The World Council of Churches, which has developed into a worldwide expression of the concerns of Protestant and Orthodox churches, has issued nothing comparable to *We Remember*. Nor have other Protestant denominations besides the German Protestant *Landeskirchen* officially acted, although there is an important study document before the United Church of Canada ('Bearing Faithful Witness').

The awareness that memory of the *Shoah* remains a deep and unmastered tragedy for Christians – and not simply 'a Jewish affair' – has yet to find lodging in most Christian churches.

For Further Reading

Karl Barth. *The German Church Conflict*. Richmond, VA: John Knox Press, 1965.

Mary Alice Gallin. *Ethical and Religious Factors in the German Resistance to Hitler*. Washington, D.C.: Catholic University of America Press, 1955.

Pater Matheson. *The Third Reich and the Christian Churches*. Edinburgh: T&T Clark, 1994 (1981).

Gordon C. Zahn. *German Catholics and Hitler's Wars*. New York: Sheed and Ward, 1962.

Franklin H. Littell (USA) is Professor Emeritus at Temple University and from 1972-92 was Adjunct at the Institute of Contemporary Jewry, Hebrew University. He is the only Christian member of the International Council of Yad Vashem. He is also co-founder of the Annual Scholars' Conference on the Holocaust and the Churches, and President of the Philadelphia Center on the Holocaust, Genocide and Human Rights.

COLLUSION, RESISTANCE, SILENCE: PROTESTANTS AND THE HOLOCAUST

Doris L. Bergen

'Who were worse,' Germans often ask me when I tell them that I study the role of the Christian Churches in the Nazi era, 'the Catholics or the Protestants?' To many people that question seems almost irrelevant in the face of the terrible crimes committed by Nazi Germans and their henchmen. Does it really matter whether those who supported Hitler's regime or who tolerated its abuses of human beings called their spiritual leaders Father or Pastor? After all, it is a painful fact that the perpetrators of Nazi crimes, and those who acquiesced to Nazi policies, were overwhelmingly Christian, at least in a nominal sense. By the outbreak of World War II, despite years of anti-Christian Nazi propaganda, more than 95 per cent of Germans were still baptized, tax-paying members of an established Christian Church. They were raised in homes, schools, and churches where the Christian Bible was read and taught, where commemorations of the birth and death of Jesus marked the high points of the year, where the Lord's Prayer and Christian hymns were as familiar as Grimm's fairy tales or the ABC. Indeed, the legacy of the Nazi era belongs to the heritage of all Christians, regardless of confession.

Nevertheless, institutional, historical, and theological realities require that the Protestant Churches, like the Catholic Church, also be considered separately. Admittedly, the decentralized nature of Protestantism complicates such efforts. In Germany alone, in the Thirties and Forties, there were Lutheran, Reformed, and united Protestants, as well as small numbers of Methodists, Baptists, Mennonites, and others. Each denomination had its own hierarchy – and its own internal divisions. Protestantism outside Germany encompassed still more groups, subgroups and factions. Indeed, the complicated, amorphous structure of Protestantism may be one of the most significant reasons why today, at least outside of Germany, we hear so much less about the responses and responsibilities of Protestants for the Holocaust than we do about the role of Catholics and their Church during the Nazi era.

Another reason why the Protestant Churches tend to attract less scrutiny now for their policies before and during World War II has to do with geography. Protestants and Catholics are concentrated in different parts of Europe. The areas in which Hitler's forces wrought their most brutal

'The false teachings of the German Christians and of the present Reich Church Government are wreaking havoc in the Church and thereby disrupting the unity of the German Evangelical Church. . . Thereby it has forfeited its right to the legitimate leadership of the German Evangelical Church.'

Part of the text of the *Barmen Declaration*, 29-31 May, 1934.

havoc were predominantly Roman Catholic and Orthodox Christian. There were relatively few Protestants in Poland, Ukraine, Belorussia, Yugoslavia, Austria, Greece, France, Romania, Hungary, and Czechoslovakia; only in the Netherlands was the population fairly equally divided between Protestants and Catholics. Does this mean that Protestant Churches have no need for the kind of soul-searching about the past in which the current Pope has engaged? Absolutely not. During Hitler's reign, the majority of Germans, approximately two-thirds of the populace, was Protestant. More to the point, Protestants were involved in every aspect of mass murder, as perpetrators and bystanders, and in smaller numbers, as victims and rescuers.

Were Protestants perpetrators? Sadly, there were disturbing links between Protestants and the commission of Nazi atrocities. But it is important to distinguish between individuals and institutions. There is no denying that men raised within a Protestant tradition played key roles in Nazi crimes: Hermann Göring, for example. Others, like Wilhelm Kube, the *Generalkommissar* of 'White Ruthenia' were active in Church activities. Kube ordered and oversaw the slaughter of tens of thousands of Jews and Slavs in the Minsk area. Protestants served in the SS alongside Catholics and anti-Christian neo-pagans; they took part in mass shootings of Jewish and Slavic civilians, worked as guards in concentration camps, and, as bureaucrats, co-ordinated expulsions, imposed mass starvation, and ordered deadly labor assignments. Some of these individuals were indifferent toward, or even contemptuous of the religion they were born into; others read the Bible, attended church services, prayed and sang hymns with their families.

Hermann Göring, brought up in a Protestant home, became a leading member of the Nazi hierarchy. Seen here with Heinrich Himmler, head of the notorious SS.

Institutionally, the Protestant Churches were not direct perpetrators of the Third Reich's brutalities. In fact, top Nazis, from Hitler himself to Party leader Martin Bormann and propaganda minister Joseph Göbbels, hated Christianity and planned to destroy it once Germany won the war. In their view Christianity, whether Protestant or Catholic, was a devious extension of Judaism that ran counter to so-called Germanic values, and rendered its adherents womanly and weak.

Nevertheless, in indirect ways the German Protestant Churches, as institutions, did contribute to the execution of Nazi crimes. Centuries of Christian anti-Jewish teachings served as a precursor to Nazi antisemitism. Some German Protestants who embraced Nazism took special pride in the antisemitic pronouncements of their German hero Martin Luther. Luther's tract *Against the Jews and Their Lies* (1542), with its vicious characterizations of Jews as parasites and its calls to 'set their synagogues and schools on fire,' was widely quoted and circulated in Hitler's Germany. Some Protestants in Nazi Germany even claimed that Luther's hatred of Jews proved that Protestants were

'Even the courageous Niemöller, who spent the years 1938-45 in Nazi prisons, characterized himself during the Nazi era as an antisemite.'

more authentically German than were Catholics. Protestant Churches provided the Nazi authorities with records that facilitated the differentiation of Jews and 'Aryans'. In 1933, in the crucial early days of Nazi rule, Protestant leaders played a significant role in legitimizing Hitler's regime. During the war, Protestant (and Catholic) military chaplains served with the *Wehrmacht*. In some cases, Church-run institutions handed over for killing people deemed handicapped.

But didn't German Protestants also offer a clear voice of witness against Nazi antisemitism? The Lutheran theologian Dietrich Bonhoeffer (1906-45) is well known among North American Protestants for opposing Hitler's regime in the name of Christianity. Executed in a Nazi concentration camp in 1945 because of his role in the plot to kill Hitler, Bonhoeffer has been suggested as someone who should be included among the 'Righteous Gentiles' honoured at Yad Vashem. Bonhoeffer belonged to what was known as the Confessing Church. Many of the group's leading figures and lay adherents suffered police harassment, abuse and incarceration for their anti-Nazi activities. Would it not be accurate to describe the Confessing Church as an institutional expression of Protestant solidarity with persecuted Jews? The issue deserves close scrutiny.

In 1933, inspired by the new Nazi government's ban against Jews in the civil service, pro-Nazi churchmen tried to force so-called non-Aryan clergy (converts from Judaism to Christianity, sons or grandsons of converts) from German Protestant pulpits. In order to challenge such efforts at exclusion, Martin Niemöller (1892-1984), a popular, outspoken pastor from Berlin-Dahlem, organized the Pastors' Emergency League. Niemöller's organization evolved into the Confessing Church, a movement within established German Protestantism (rather than a completely separate Church) that aimed to protect Protestantism's ecclesiastical integrity in the Third Reich. It vied for control of Protestantism with the so-called German Christians *(Deutsche Christen)*, who championed an explicit synthesis of Protestant theology and Nazi ideology. The rivalry was bitter, but members of both camps, as well as numerous, unaffiliated Protestant 'neutrals,' tended to accept anti-Jewish dogmas. Even the courageous Niemöller, who spent the years 1938-45 in Nazi prisons, characterized himself during the Nazi era as an antisemite. He recognized the rights of converts to Christianity within his Church but remained convinced, in the Thirties and Forties, that Germany suffered from a 'Jewish problem,' and he openly described the history of Jewish suffering as punishment for crucifying Jesus. Some German Protestants, like Bonhoeffer, came to recognize that respect for Jews and Judaism was integral to genuine Christian faith. But such thinkers and activists remained a small, isolated minority, even within the Confessing Church.

'The sad truth is that Bonhoeffer was much better than his theology.'

Franklin H. Littell, *The Crucifixion of the Jews.*

'Some Christians did choose to stand with suffering Jews in the Holocaust. . . Many more Christians, however, chose to stare silently away from the flames while embracing twenty centuries of anti-Jewish theology.'

Sidney G Hall, *Christian Anti-Semitism in Paul's Theology.*

German Belief – Journal of a particular way of life, world-view and religious devotion.

Within Germany, both the Protestant Churches and the Catholic Church played a part in assisting some Nazi campaigns against Jews. For instance, Nazi ideology claimed Jewishness was a racial category. However, even Nazi scientists and lawyers could not come up with a practical definition of Jewishness based on biology or physical traits. So the Nuremberg Laws of 1935 relied on religious distinctions. It was the religion of one's grandparents that determined if one were an 'Aryan' or a 'Jew.' The Churches willingly provided documents – baptismal and marriage records – to those who wished to establish 'legitimate' bloodlines. At least within Germany, Church officials do not seem to have falsified records to help Jews or Christian converts from Judaism.

From Hitler down, the Nazi hierarchy believed (mistakenly) that Germany had lost the previous world war because the home front had crumbled. Accordingly, the Nazi leadership was intensely concerned, even obsessed, with domestic public opinion. Could the Churches – in particular the German Protestant majority – have used the government's fear of popular disapproval at home to thwart at least some of the Nazis' policies? What if the Churches' officials had refused to participate in enforcing the Nuremberg racial classification laws? Wouldn't such refusals have curbed expropriation, deportation, and eventually murder (within Germany, if not elsewhere)? Could the Churches' officials at least have protected so-called Jewish Christians (converts) by forging or withholding records so as to conceal their Jewish ancestry? These are unanswerable but suggestive questions.

Such questions highlight the blurred line that separates the familiar categories of perpetrators and bystanders. Do those who sin by omission warrant the label perpetrator? When discussing such issues my students often invoke the familiar slogan, 'If you're not part of the solution, you're part of the problem.' Using that standard, many of them argue that there was no such thing as a 'bystander'; anyone who was not a victim or rescuer in some sense became a perpetrator. I urge them to be more nuanced in their thinking, to contemplate the ambiguity that the writer Primo Levi, a survivor of Auschwitz, called the 'grey zone.'

An obvious example of the grey zone involving perpetrators and bystanders involves the so-called T-4 Euthanasia program, the murder of people the Nazis deemed handicapped. Many of the Germans killed between 1939 and 1945 under this program lived in hospitals and other institutions run by the Churches. The Protestant institutions housing the targeted individuals had a high (though not total) degree of compliance with Nazi plans. There were some administrators, doctors, nurses and attendants who refused to participate; certain pastors (like some Catholic clergymen) protested the killings from the pulpit. But the clerical leaders of the established Protestant Churches provided neither encouragement nor protection for those who objected. Nor did they discipline or censure those Protestants who co-operated. Here the record of the Catholic Church is stronger, if still less than

'Adolf Hitler died a Roman Catholic, and an annual mass is celebrated in his memory in Madrid. Hermann Goering died a Lutheran.'

Franklin H. Littell, *The Crucifixion of the Jews.*

For Reflection

To what extent are institutions culpable, even when they do not actively participate in the execution of atrocities?

When does silence become an active form of collaboration?

Can the victim of one kind of policy, such as the church, claim immunity from assisting the victims of another, such as the Jews, and still maintain its moral credibility?

ideal. In both cases, the killings implicated an enormous range of people, whose involvement ranged from indirect support to participation in cold-blooded murder. The grey zone invites some questions: Were those only marginally involved in the killings guilty of murder? What about leaders of the Churches who declined to denounce the euthanasia program and those who were involved in it?

When we talk about perpetrators or bystanders another distinction must be kept in mind: that between historical causality and moral blame. Many people who are interested in history are uneasy about playing the role of judge, assigning blame to people in the past. Although it is tempting to indulge in denunciations after the fact, most of us have no idea how we would have behaved in certain situations. Nevertheless, realistic humility need not prevent us from analyzing the factors that led to a particular outcome and identifying the men and women behind particular historical events.

Reichsbishof Ludwig Müller entering the *Sportspalast*, November 1933.

Were Protestants victims of Nazism? Again the answer is complex. There is no doubt that the Nazi regime was hostile to institutionalized Christianity. Admittedly, Catholicism, with its international hierarchy, was perceived as more of a threat than decentralized Protestantism. But Nazi authorities harassed the Protestant Churches too, imposing restrictions on some activities, and conducting negative propaganda against them. Nevertheless, the Churches survived twelve years of National Socialist rule in Germany. Indeed, within Germany, Hitler's government continued to collect Church taxes and distribute them to the established Churches. The Nazis permitted the study of theology in state universities and left the Churches' buildings in ecclesiastical hands. Nazi campaigns against Churches and clergymen outside Germany had more to do with efforts to crush resistance movements than they did with attempts to subvert Christianity. When it suited their goals, Nazi occupation authorities even presented themselves as saviours of the Christian Churches, protecting them from godless Communism. Inside and outside Germany, the Protestant Churches, institutionally, cannot accurately be numbered among the victims of Nazi tyranny.

What about Protestant individuals? There were Protestants, of course, lay and clerical, who were political dissenters in the Third Reich and who were sent to prisons and concentration camps. Some emerged alive; others, like Bonhoeffer, did not. Although fewer in number than their Catholic counterparts, Protestant dissenters also suffered terribly, and deserve to be remembered and honored. But these Christians were victims in a different way than were the Jewish and Gypsy victims of the Third Reich. Nazi authorities didn't punish Protestants or Catholics because of their religion. Rather, they persecuted them for violating laws having nothing to do with their faith, for opposing certain government policies, or for being 'secular' pariahs; Communists, homosexuals, or disabled. Protestant clergy and lay people, by and large, were incarcerated for speaking against the

'The majority of Jews avoided deportation in every state occupied by or allied with Germany in which the head of the dominant church spoke out publicly against deportation before or as soon as it began.'

government, for aiding Jews, prisoners of war, and slave laborers; or for meeting illegally. In contrast, Nazi officials tyrannized all Jews and Gypsies in their power because they were Jews and Gypsies, and regardless of their attitudes toward the state, obedience to the government's authority, and willingness to co-operate with the regime. Nazi planners marked the Jewish people and Gypsies for death and treated members of these groups as already dead, even if they remained physically alive. The only Christians regarded the same way were those deemed handicapped – 'lives unworthy of living' – and those defined under German law as Gypsies or Jews.

Distinguishing among the victims of Nazism need not mean establishing levels of suffering. It serves no constructive purpose to create, in effect, a kind of competition in agony. But those who seek to comprehend history must think clearly, make distinctions and draw comparisons. Doing so in a spirit of respect need not belittle the experiences of anyone.

Raul Hilberg, the scholar who made the study of the Holocaust an accepted academic field, identified three groups of people particularly pertinent to the subject: perpetrators, bystanders, and victims. A fourth group is also germane: rescuers. Were Protestants and the Protestant Churches significantly involved in the rescue of those targeted for destruction by the Nazis? The Churches' record appears dismal, although with some important exceptions.

There were Protestants in Germany who assisted Jews and Christians of Jewish background. Pastor Heinrich Gruber, for example, worked with members of the Confessing Church in Berlin to help converts from Judaism escape Germany. He was imprisoned in Dachau. (Even Gruber, however, considered the Holocaust God's punishment of the Jewish people.) In Nazi-occupied Europe, some individual members of Protestant minorities risked death to harbor Jews. Among these rescuers – honored by survivors of the *Shoah* – were Baptists in Ukraine as well as Calvinists in the Netherlands and France. Rescuers offer various explanations for their courage. Some say they were motivated by religious faith; most insist they only did what any decent person would have done. All were exceptions, as were their Catholic, Orthodox Christian, and Muslim counterparts from Brussels to Kiev to Sarajevo.

The decentralized nature of Protestantism makes it almost impossible to draw comprehensive conclusions about its institutional relationships to rescue. Certainly, examples of institutional failure are all too easy to find. Inside Germany the pro-Nazi German Christian movement openly endorsed anti-Jewish measures. Its members controlled the governing bodies of most of Germany's regional Protestant Churches, and they used their positions to attack Jews, Judaism, and so-called non-Aryan Christians. They also promoted efforts to purge all aspects of Judaism from Christianity. Even the Confessing Church and those regional Churches not dominated by German Christians declined to try to protect (the few) 'non-Aryan' pastors.

For Further Reading

Doris L. Bergen. *Twisted Cross: The German Christian Movement in the Third Reich.* Chapel Hill: The University of North Carolina Press, 1996.

Robert P. Erickson. *Theologians under Hitler:* Gerhard Kittel, Paul Althaus and Emanuel Hirsch. New Haven: Yale University Press, 1965.

Robert P. Erickson & Susannah Heschel, eds. *Betrayal: German Churches and the Holocaust.* Minneapolis: Fortress Press, 1999.

Ernst Christian Helmreich, *The German Churches under Hitler: Background, Struggle and Epilogue.* Detroit: Wayne State University Press, 1985.

'Adolf Hitler, the Third Reich, the Aryan paragraphs, and the Death Camps – these were not accidental appearances in the heart of Christendom.'

Franklin H. Littell, *The Crucifixion of the Jews.*

'It serves no constructive purpose to create, in effect, a kind of competition in agony.'

'I nominate as my representative for the affairs of the evangelical churches . . . the chaplain to the Königsberg military region, Herr Müller.

He also has a particular responsibility for furthering all endeavours to create an Evangelical German Reich Church.'

Adolf Hitler, 25 April 1933.

Doris L. Bergen (USA) is Associate Professor of History at the University of Notre Dame, South Bend, Indiana, and author of *Twisted Cross: The German Christian Movement in the Third Reich*. Doris Bergen writes and lectures on the Protestant churches in Germany during the Holocaust.

In her book, *Accounting for Genocide*, the sociologist Helen Fein makes a provocative claim. 'The majority of Jews evaded deportation,' she maintains, 'in every state occupied by or allied with Germany in which the head of the dominant church spoke out publicly against deportation before or as soon as it began.' In Germany the established Protestant Churches made no formal, public protests when deportations began in the fall of 1941. The deportations, once fully implemented, proved catastrophic for German Jews.

I am convinced that the Protestant Churches could have done more to assist Jews – if their leaders had shown the way – because of Hitler's sensitivity to domestic public opinion, and the moral prestige of the Churches in North America and Great Britain. It is unlikely that they could have completely prevented or halted the Final Solution. But perhaps early and strong public criticism of the Nazi regime by leading Protestant Churchmen within Germany would have weakened Hitler's hold on the population and impaired his ability to implement anti-Jewish measures. And concerted efforts by Protestants outside Germany might have succeeded in pressuring governments to accept more Jewish refugees in the crucial years before World War II.

Material in this essay appears in a slightly different form in *Dimensions: A Journal of Holocaust Studies. Vol. 12, #2 (1998)*. Used with permission of the author and the Anti-Defamation League's Braun Holocaust Institute, New York, NY.

'German Christian' clergy following their flag to the Berlin Dom Church, September 1934.

THE ROLE OF THE CHURCHES: COMPLIANCE AND CONFRONTATION

Victoria J. Barnett

The list of 'bystanders' – those who declined to challenge the Third Reich in any way – that emerges from any study of the Holocaust is long and depressing. Few organizations, in or outside Nazi Germany, did much to resist Nazism or aid its victims. Assisting European Jews was not a high priority of the Allied governments as they sought to defeat Hitler militarily. The courageous acts of individual rescuers and resistance members proved to be the exception, not the norm.

To a great extent, this inertia defined the organized Christian community as well. Churches throughout Europe were mostly silent as Jews were persecuted, deported and murdered. In Nazi Germany in September 1935, there were a few Christians in the Protestant Confessing Church who demanded that their Church take a public stand in defence of the Jews. Their efforts, however, were overruled by Church leaders who wanted to avoid any conflict with the Nazi regime.

Three main factors shaped the behavior of the Christian Churches during the Nazi reign of terror in Germany and abroad. The first was the theological and doctrinal anti-Judaism that existed in parts of the Christian tradition. Long before 1933, this anti-Judaism – ranging from latent prejudice to the virulent diatribes of people like Martin Luther – lent legitimacy to the racial antisemitism that emerged in the late Nineteenth Century.

The second factor was the Churches' historical role in creating 'Christendom' – the Western European culture that, since the era of the Roman emperor Constantine, had been explicitly and deliberately 'Christian.' The Churches' advocacy of a 'Christian culture' led to a process that theologian Miroslav Volf, in another context, has described as the 'sacralization of cultural identity': dominant, positive values were seen as 'Christian' ones, while developments viewed negatively (such as secularism and Marxism) were attributed to 'Jewish' influences. Moreover, particularly in the German Evangelical Church (the largest Protestant church in Germany), the allegiance to the concept of Christendom was linked to a strong nationalism, symbolized by German Protestantism's 'Throne and Altar' alliance with state authority.

The third factor was the Churches' understanding of their institutional role. While most Christian

For Reflection

Am I my brother's [sister's] keeper?

Who is my neighbor?

What would have happened if the Churches – Protestant and Catholic alike – had defied Hitler during the Third Reich and stood in solidarity with the Jews?

[The Holocaust] 'happened in the 'heartland' of Western Christian Europe: the land of Goethe, Beethoven, and Mozart; of Kant, Hegel, and Schelling; of the founders of modern Christian theology, Schleiermacher, Ritschl, and Troeltsch. Germany was the Center of the Christian Enlightenment, from which flowed the classics of modern European literature and music, philosophy, theology, and biblical studies. It happened with the passive acquiescence or active collaboration of most European Christians, and with no decisive protest from church leadership, Catholic or Protestant.'

Rosemary Radford Ruether, 'The Holocaust: Theological and Ethical Reflections' in *The Twentieth Century: A Theological Overview,* ed. Gregory Baum. p. 76.

religious leaders in Germany welcomed the end of the Weimar Republic and the resurgence of nationalism, they became increasingly uneasy about their institutions' future in what was clearly becoming a totalitarian state. Moreover, some leading Nazis were overtly anti-Christian. While wanting to retain their prominent place in society, the churches in Nazi Germany opposed any state control of their affairs. Thus, the Catholic Church and the Protestant churches sought to maintain some degree of independence by entering into certain arrangements with the Nazi regime. The 1933 concordat, signed by representatives of the Nazi regime and the Vatican, ostensibly secured independence for Catholic schools and other Catholic institutions in Nazi Germany. The Protestant churches behaved cautiously, avoiding public confrontation and negotiating privately with Nazi authorities, in the hope that this would ensure institutional independence from direct Nazi control. Throughout Hitler's Germany, bishops and other Christian religious leaders deliberately avoided antagonizing Nazi officials. When Christian clergymen and Christian women deplored Nazi policies, they often felt constrained to oppose those policies in a muted fashion. Even in the Protestant Confessing Church (the church group in Germany that was most critical of Nazism), there was little support for official public criticism of the Nazi regime, particularly when it came to such central and risky issues as the persecution of Jews.

The role of anti-Judaism in Germany's Churches during the Nazi era was a complicated one. Throughout the 1930s, there was ample evidence of antisemitism in many sermons and in articles that appeared in German church publications. Some church leaders proudly announced that they were antisemites. Others warned their colleagues against any public show of support for the Jewish victims of the Nazi regime. Christian antisemitism often complemented other factors – notably, the strong nationalism in the German Protestant churches. The most extreme example of this combination of antisemitism and nationalism was the so-called German Christian movement, a Protestant group that embraced Nazism and tried to Nazify Christianity by suppressing the Old Testament, revising liturgics and hymns, and promoting Jesus as an Aryan hero who embodied the ideals of the new Germany.

It must be said that the churches' theological attitudes about Jews did not always take the form of anti-Jewish diatribes or other kinds of explicit antisemitsm. Often they manifested themselves in a determination to convert Jews, and so Nazi policies confronted the Christian churches with an unresolvable theological problem: in a society that was determined to eradicate the Jews, the Christian Gospel claimed that the Jews were God's chosen people and should be the special objects of Christian proselytization. This led to deep divisions among German clergy about what they really believed and what they were supposed to do in their new situation.

During the Nazi era, these various influences essentially paralyzed the churches and prevented them from facing the challenges posed by Nazism. The German churches stumbled, and they stumbled badly. Church leaders spent a great deal of time delineating a 'viable' position: one that would conform to Christian doctrine, prevent their church from dividing into opposing factions, and avoid antagonizing the Nazi authorities. In any examination of the German churches' public statements from this era, what is most striking is their painstaking attempt to say neither too much nor too little about what is happening around them. This ruled out any consistent or firm response to the Nazis' persecution of Jews and others. This institutional inaction gave individual Christians throughout Germany an alibi for passivity. More tragically, those individual Christians who did express solidarity with the persecuted Jews – such as the Catholic priest Bernhard Lichtenberg and the Protestant deaconess Marga Meusel – received no public (and little private) support form their respective churches.

Energetic debates took place within the German churches about where to stand firm against Hitler's regime and where to compromise, when to speak out and when to remain silent. Ecumenical documents show that there were Christian leaders inside and outside Germany who agonized about what they could do to stop Nazism and help its victims. The historical complexities suggested by these factors should never lead us to condone the churches' failures during this period; they can, however, help us to understand the specific nature of those failures so that we may learn from them.

> 'Christianity in Germany bears a greater responsibility before God than the National Socialists, the SS and the Gestapo. We ought to have recognized the Lord Jesus in the brother who suffered and was persecuted despite him being a communist or a Jew.'
>
> Martin Niemöller
> *Lecture in Zurich*, Switzerland
> March 1946

Perhaps at the heart of those failures was the fact that the churches, especially in Nazi Germany, sought to act, as institutions tend to do, in their own narrowly defined 'best' interests. There was little desire on the part of the churches for self-sacrifice or heroism, and much emphasis on 'pragmatic' and 'strategic' measures that would supposedly protect their institutional autonomy. This public institutional circumspection, and a fatal lack of insight, are the aspects of the churches' behavior during the Nazi era that are so damning in retrospect. The minutes of German Protestant synodal meetings in 1942 reveal how oblivious the participants were to what was happening in the world around them. While innocent victims throughout Europe were being brutally murdered, Christian leaders were debating what points of doctrine and policy were tenable. This is especially haunting, of course, because the Christian clergy and laity never thought of their respective churches as mere institutions, but as religious bodies called to witness to certain values, including love of neighbors, the sanctity of life and the power of moral conscience.

> 'We German Christians are the first trenchline of National Socialism . . . To live, fight and die for Adolf Hitler means to say Yes to the path of Christ.'
>
> Reichsbishof Ludwig Müller

For Further Reading

Victoria J. Barnett. *For the Soul of the People: Protestant Protest Against Hitler.* New York: Oxford University Press, 1992.

John Conway. *The Nazi Persecution of the Churches.* New York: Basic Books, 1968.

Saul Friedlander. *Nazi Germany and the Jews. Volume I: The Years of Persecution.* New York: HarperCollins, 1997.

Franklin H. Littell and Hubert G. Locke, eds. *The German Church Struggle and the Holocaust.* Detroit: Wayne State University Press, 1974.

Klaus Scholder. *The Churches and the Third Reich,* Volumes One and Two. Philadelphia: Fortress Press, 1988.

Victoria J. Barnett (USA), author of *For the Soul of the People: Protestant Protest Against Hitler,* is a writer and scholar whose work examines the Protestant churches during the Holocaust. She serves as a consultant for the Church Relations Department at the United States Holocaust Memorial Museum, Washington, D. C.

Reflection on the churches' failure to challenge Nazism should prompt us to ponder all the others – individuals, governments and institutions – which passively acquiesced to the tyranny of the Third Reich. Even the wisest and most perceptive of them, it seems, failed to develop adequate moral and political responses to Nazi genocide and to recognize that the barbarism of Hitler's regime demanded something new of them. Ultimately, the churches' lapses during the Nazi era were lapses of vision and determination. Protestant and Catholic religious leaders, loyal to creeds professing that love can withstand and conquer evil, were unable or unwilling to defy one of the great evils in human history. For this reason, the Holocaust will continue to haunt the Christian churches for a very, very long time to come.

The material in this essay appears in a slightly different form in *Dimensions: A Journal of Holocaust Studies.* Vol. 12, #2 (1998). Used with permission of the author and the Anti-Defamation League's Braun Holocaust Institute, New York, NY.

THE RESPONSE OF THE GERMAN CATHOLIC CHURCH TO NATIONAL SOCIALISM

Michael Phayer

The German Catholic Church reacted in a variety of ways to Nazism during Hitler's twelve years of rule that spanned the last years of the inter-war period and the Second World War.

Before Adolf Hitler became chancellor, Catholic bishops warned the faithful about Nazi racism. In some diocese it was not even allowed for Catholics to join the National Socialist party because of the problem of racism. These warnings proved effective; very few Catholics voted for Hitler or the National Socialists during the elections between 1930 and 1933.

After Hitler came to power early in the year 1933 the church dropped its opposition to the Nazi party. Catholics were told that they were free to cooperate with the new government and even to join the party. Many Catholics did although they remained under-represented in organizations like the SS and SA. The critical mistake of the church was its failure to hold fast to the principle that Nazi racism was immoral.

The reason behind the church's unfortunate about-face concerned the Concordat, the 1933 agreement that defined relations between the German government and the Church. Concordats are accords, like treaties, between nation states and the Vatican state. Before the Concordat between the Vatican and Germany had been signed, Catholic newspapers predicted that the Church and National Socialism would be enemies. The ink had not yet dried on the agreement before the Nazi government broke it by sterilizing people on racist principles.

The main negotiator of the Concordat was the Vatican Secretary of State, Eugenio Pacelli. As a Vatican diplomat and later as Pope Pius XII, retention of the Concordat became one of the highest priorities of the Holy See. The advantage that the Vatican saw in the Concordat lay in the fact that the religious liberties that it guaranteed German Catholics and the church would persist long after Hitler's tenure in office as Chancellor of Germany was over.

But, because the Concordat defined church-state relationships, it constrained Catholics and their leaders whenever the Nazis took actions against Jews. This could not occur in a country like the

'. . .The great and overwhelming majority of . . . Christians in the world, still believe that the Jews killed Jesus, that they are . . . rejected by God, that all the beauty of the Bible belongs to the Christian Church and not to those by whom it was written; and if on this ground . . . modern anti-Semites have reared a structure of racial and economic propaganda, the final responsibility still rests with those who prepared this soil and created the deformation of the people.'

James Parkes, *The Conflict of the Church and the Synagogue*, 1934.

'. . . there is a deep-seated moral crisis in Germany . . . What previously had been naturally understood as moral has been shattered . . . the silence of the bishops is perhaps even more fearful than anything else . . . it introduces uncertainty into the ranks of the faithful'.

Waldemar Gurian, *St Ambrosius und die deutschen Bishofe*, (1934).

For Reflection

What problems did the German bishops face during the Third Reich?

What optional paths were available for German bishops when they faced conflict with Hitler and the Nazis?

In retrospect, was the Concordat an advantage or a disadvantage for the German Catholic Church?

United States where a 'wall of separation' exists between the church and the state and concordats are impossible. In Germany the Concordat meant that the church could not meddle in affairs of state that did not concern Catholics.

As the Nazis became ever more radical in their treatment of Jews, whose rights as citizens were restricted by the Nuremberg Laws in 1935 and whose very homes, synagogues and businesses were destroyed in 1938 during the national pogrom *(Kristallnacht)*, German church authorities had to keep silent or forfeit the Concordat. Even so, the Nazi government constantly harassed the church by seizing its kindergartens, attacking its members on trumped-up moral charges, removing crucifixes from schools, closing down its presses and restricting its welfare program to caring only for the racially 'unfit'.

Pope Pius XI became increasingly alarmed late in his pontificate about racism in Europe and the United States and, in particular, Germany. In 1937 he released an encyclical, *Mit Brennender Sorge* (With Burning Anxiety), that was smuggled into Germany and read in March from all church pulpits simultaneously. This infuriated Hitler and the Nazis because, although the encyclical did not denounce them personally or National Socialism, it condemned racism.

In 1939 the Nazi regime began killing German citizens whom they singled out as racially unfit. Taking individuals from hospitals and homes for the mentally disadvantaged, Nazi personnel trucked these unfortunates to specially constructed gas chambers. Here they were killed and cremated. When word of the Nazi 'euthanasia' program gradually seeped out to the public, August Graf von Galen, the Bishop of Münster, spoke out explicitly against it, accusing the government of breaking the law. Von Galen's brave sermon did not stop the Nazis from continuing their killing, but it forced the program to go underground.

By the latter part of the decade of the Thirties church officials were well aware that the ultimate aim of Hitler and other Nazis was the total elimination of Catholicism and of the Christian religion. Since the overwhelming majority of Germans were either Catholic or Protestant this goal had to be a long-term rather than a short-term Nazi objective. Before it could be achieved Germany invaded Poland in the fall of 1939 and World War II commenced.

As a result of the war an undeclared truce governed relations between the Nazi government and the church. Hitler, not wanting to distract Christians from the war effort, restrained the anti-Catholicism of some of his top lieutenants like Martin Bormann and Josef Goebbels. The bishops, on the other hand, not wishing to appear unpatriotic in the eyes of Germans, backed the war effort even though it had been launched against Catholic Poland.

Unfortunately, nationalism, along with the Concordat, also restrained the bishops from speaking out against the Holocaust. They had the opportunity to join resistance organizations like the *Kreisau* circle but refrained from doing so. Many of the bishops knew, however, about the murder of the Jews. In the middle of the war in 1943 the bishops hotly debated at their annual meeting in Fulda whether they should speak out explicitly about the Holocaust or confront Hitler with a direct accusation. Unfortunately, bound by the Concordat and their nationalistic feelings, the bishops failed to do so.

Even so, several bishops spoke out rather explicitly about the Holocaust. In November 1942, Konrad Preysing of Berlin preached on the right of all people to life, a sermon which the Gestapo said was an attack on the state. The following month Bishop Josef Frings wrote a pastoral letter, that was read at Sunday masses throughout the diocese of Cologne, cautioning the faithful not to violate the inherent rights of others to life,

> '. . . think, my Lord Cardinal . . . and discuss with other church leaders how you want to support the great task of National Socialism . . . and how you want to establish friendly relations with the state. Either National Socialism and the church will win together or they will both go under.'
>
> Hitler, speaking to Cardinal Faulhaber in Munich on November 4, 1936.

liberty and property even under wartime conditions and even if they were 'not of our blood'. In June 1943, Bishop Frings spoke out in the Cologne cathedral: 'No one may take the property or life of an innocent person just because he is a member of a foreign race.' This and other similar statements were enough to cause the Bishop to be harassed by the Gestapo.

Some years after the war and the Holocaust, German bishops, the successors of those who had lived through the Third Reich, regretted that church leaders had not spoken out more forcefully and explicitly about Nazi antisemitic policies and about the Holocaust. As the Second Vatican Council got underway the German bishops apologized publicly for the 'inhuman extermination of the Jewish people'. During council's deliberations in 1964 the German bishops issued a letter saying that they especially welcomed the council's statements on the Jews 'because we are aware of the awful injustices that were perpetrated against the Jews in the name of our people.'

In the words of the German Jesuit historian Ludwig Volk, it was a 'genuine and deplorable difference' that the Jews, unlike the 'racially unfit', mentally retarded, and handicapped, found no champion the likes of Bishop von Galen to attempt to stop their murder through a calculated appeal to the public.

For Further Reading

John S. Conway. *The Nazi Persecution of the Churches*. New York: Basic Books, 1968.

Donald J. Dietrich. *The Catholic Church and the Third Reich*. New Brunswick, NJ: Transaction Press, 1988.

Michael Phayer. *The Catholic Church and the Holocaust, 1930-1965*. Bloomington, IN.: Indiana University Press, 2000.

Klaus Scholder. *The Churches and the Third Reich*. Trans., John Bowden. London: SCM Press, 1987.

Michael Phayer (USA) is Professor of History at Marquette University in Milwaukee, Wisconsin. He is the author of several books, including *Protestant and Catholic Women in Nazi Germany* (1990).

LUDWIG MÜLLER

Ludwig Müller was born in 1883 to the family of a railroad official. He was ordained in 1908, and joined the German Navy as a chaplain. He served in the military during World War I and in the years after. Müller joined the Nazi Party and personally met Hitler while he was still a Naval chaplain.

Müller was head of the German Christian Movement which advocated an integration of Nazi ideology and Protestant religion, a purging of the Church of all Jewish components, and the introduction of the Hitler cult and romantic nationalism into the Protestant religious practices.

'We must emphasize with all decisiveness,' he said in 1934, 'that Christianity did not grow out of Judaism but developed in opposition to Judaism. When we speak of Christianity and Judaism today, the two in their most fundamental essence stand in glaring contrast to one another. There is no bond between them, rather the sharpest opposition.'

Germany's 29 regional Protestant churches were unified into the so-called Reich Church, and Müller was nominated as Reich Bishop *(Reichsbishof)*. In the summer of 1933, Hitler gave Müller full powers in the Protestant Church. His military background, loyalty to the Nazi party, and close relations with Hitler were the reasons for his appointment. An ecclesiastical constitution was to serve as a basis for the unified church. This attempt to subjugate the church to the Nazi state was opposed by the Confessing Church. The opposition peaked when in December 1933, Müller transferred the Evangelical Youth to the Hitler Youth.

The 'German Christians' rose to prominence in the summer of 1933 when they won two-thirds of the votes cast in Protestant church elections in Germany. Later that year, the Nazi party withdrew its support of the movement. The church never achieved a wide membership. Müller's position as Reich Bishop was undermined when Hitler nominated a Minister for Church Affairs, who was charged with dealing with the German churches and the Vatican.

Following his arrest at the end of the war, Müller is believed to have committed suicide in prison in 1946, although his family strongly denied it.

Reichsbishof Ludwig Müller

'It is not the purpose of the Bible to give information about the origin of evil but to witness to its character as guilt, and as the infinite burden of humanity.'

Dietrich Bonhoeffer, *Creation and Fall*

MARTIN NIEMÖLLER

The son of a Protestant pastor, Martin Niemöller entered the German Navy in 1910 and served as a submarine commander in World War I. Deeply shaken by the German defeat in the war and opposed to the creation of a German republic, he left the military service, went to study theology and was ordained as a Protestant minister. Having voted for the Nazi party in 1924, he welcomed the Nazi rise to power. However, he soon became disenchanted with National Socialism, especially with its attempts to coordinate the Church and to undermine Christian faith. He founded the Protestant Pastors' Emergency League in September 1933 and became one of the leaders of the opposition Confessing Church. In January 1934, in a meeting with Hitler, he was very outspoken in voicing his objections. From that point on he was followed by the Gestapo.

His opposition to the regime, however, was not founded on rejection of its antisemitic policy. Niemöller maintained what many have called the traditional Lutheran anti-Jewish attitude and did not challenge the discriminating legislation against the Jews. His opposition to the Aryan Paragraph, the plans to exclude non-Aryans from the clergy which were proposed by the 'German Christian' movement, reflected primarily a concern for church independence, not for those who were affected by it: 'We have to recognize the converted Jews as fully entitled members through the Holy Spirit . . . this recognition demands of us a high measure of self-discipline as a people who have had a great deal to bear under the influence of the Jewish people, so that the wish to be freed from this demand is understandable.'

Niemöller regretted such statements later. He came to realize that anti-Jewish prejudices had prevented him and others from recognizing the full impact of Nazi racial anti-Jewish policy. In a speech in 1946, Niemöller said: 'We ought to have recognized the Lord Jesus in the brother who suffered and was persecuted despite him being . . . a Jew.'

Niemöller was arrested for alleged pulpit abuse in July 1937, a fact which shocked Confessing Christians, many of whom had assumed that the Nazis would avoid attacking a man of Niemöller's stature and fame. After seven months, he was tried, fined and released, but Hitler was so angry he was let go that the Gestapo arrested and imprisoned him again. Niemöller was sent to Sachsenhausen concentration camp, and in 1941 to Dachau, where he was interned until the end of the war in 1945.

*First they came for the Communists
and I did not speak out –
because I was not a Communist.*

*Then they came for the Socialists
and I did not speak out –
because I was not a Socialist.*

*Then they came for the trade
unionists
and I did not speak out –
because I was not a trade unionist.*

*Then they came for the Jews
and I did not speak out –
because I was not a Jew.*

*Then they came for me –
and there was no one left
to speak out for me.*

Martin Niemöller

Martin Niemöller

RESPONSES OUTSIDE THE MAINSTREAM CATHOLIC AND PROTESTANT TRADITIONS

Christine King

The Challenge to Faith

All Christians living within the Germany of the Third Reich faced, whether they recognised it or not, a challenge to their faith. National Socialism was, in its aspirations and in practice, much more like a rival religious creed than a political dogma. It offered a view of history in which the new German Empire and its 'Aryan' peoples would fulfil a mystic destiny. It had its satanic enemies, the Jews, its own religious language of blood and fire and sacred liturgies and ceremonies. The language and concepts of paganism were intermingled with those of Christianity and the Nazi Party espoused a public campaign for family values and the defeat of atheism and communism. To many Christians, mainstream and minority, National Socialism appeared, at first sight, to offer Germany an opportunity for moral renewal. Nevertheless, within a short time, many would receive a direct challenge to their faith and their leaders would need either to articulate a stand or to negotiate a safe harbour. Members of the minority churches were often amongst the first to face up to this challenge.

The Other Christians

When the Nazis came to power in 1933, Germany was already home to a number of religious groups standing alongside the majority Catholic and Protestant churches, although their numbers represented a very small percentage of the population. Such groups ranged from branches of the European Evangelical Free Churches, the Baptists and Methodists, to a large number of small groups, many of them American in origin, like the Church of Jesus Christ of the Latter Day Saints, the Seventh Day Adventists, the Christian Scientists and the Jehovah's Witnesses.

The Free Churches

Whilst there were differences within the highest ranks of the Nazi party about what attitude should be taken towards the Catholic and Protestant churches, there were even more immediate questions to be asked about the Free Churches and the sects. There was some suspicion in Party ranks about the international connections of the Free Churches and their various evangelical alliances, yet

'All Christians living within the Germany of the Third Reich faced, whether they recognised it or not, a challenge to their faith'

The Holocaust was the systematic, bureaucratic extermination of six million Jews by the Nazis and their collaborators as a central act of state during the Second World War; as night descended, millions of other peoples were swept into this net of death.

Report to the President, President's Commission on the Holocaust.

members were believed to be largely loyal, patriotic and conservative in their values. Whilst, as with all sections of society, there were those who made an individual moral and practical stand against the regime, the leadership of the Free Churches managed to negotiate the survival of their institutions. By minimising their European links and by quiet allegiance they were able to escape serious attention from the Gestapo to whom they presented no particular challenges.

Minority Christian Religious Groups

There was more unanimity within the higher ranks of the Nazi Party about what should be done with the American based 'sects'. They were seen as potentially very dangerous, offering a focus for internationalism, pacifism, communism and other anti-German attitudes and actions. More importantly, many of these groups make extensive use of the language of the Hebrew Scriptures and therefore could be seen as pro-Jewish and Zionist. The Gestapo was therefore ordered to draw up a catalogue of 'dangerous sects' and to set about investigating their activities. Such investigations led, in most cases, to a ban on their activities, starting as early as 1934, and a clear policy decision was made to close down all such groups speedily and finally.

Survival Strategies

Members of these minority Christian groups therefore faced an immediate challenge to their beliefs and to the future of their religious work. Many had members, like the two major churches and the Free Churches who, as patriotic Germans, had fought in the First World War and who supported the Nazi campaign against atheism and communism. None had positioned themselves as critics of the new regime and its policies. Once the challenge came, however, they were under an intense spotlight and, having few friends and many critics from within the ranks of the major churches and the Party, were isolated and vulnerable. In the new context they had a number of stark choices.

* Members could leave Germany and continue their work in a safer
context.
* Groups could submit to the ban and cease to meet and work as a religious community.
* Beliefs and practices could be changed in line with Nazi teachings, either for reasons of survival or from conviction, or a mixture of both. Whilst this did not guarantee freedom of worship, it clearly made this more easily negotiable and ensured that there was at least a chance that the group might be able to continue its important work in German society.
* They could decide that it was important to continue their missionary work and meetings without any compromise and at whatever cost to the group and to individual members and their families.

> 'We may or may not share their beliefs, but the fact that the vast majority were willing to face imprisonment and death rather than, as they saw it, deny their God, did make a difference.'

For Reflection

If I had been a member of a Free Church or minority Christian group in Germany in 1933, could I reasonably have been expected to see that Nazism was in conflict with my beliefs?

What can we learn from the story of the Jehovah's Witnesses about the power of refusing to compromise in the face of evil?

If I had been living as a Christian in Nazi Germany, what would have been my concerns and what would I have done?

What obligation do we have to stand up for people whose beliefs we do not share?

What Happened

Many of the very small groups were simply closed down and ceased to operate within Germany. For the relatively larger organisations, however, it became essential to articulate rapidly what it meant to be a member of that group living within secular society and what the group was and was not prepared to sacrifice in order to continue in existence. The history and theology of each of the groups influenced these decisions. Responses ranged from the more sophisticated, like that of the Mormon Church which was able to point to the legality of the Nazi regime and to the positive elements of its social and welfare policies, to attempts to buy time. Christian Scientists, for example, only found themselves at serious risk after America's entry into the war. Seventh Day Adventists offered an immediate public statement of nationalism and support for the Party. They implemented changes to remove the language of the Hebrew Scriptures from their liturgy and arranged to co-operate with the state in their extensive church welfare and medical care schemes. Most of the groups were able to welcome elements of National Socialism and to persuade the authorities that they did not present the immediate threat that had been feared.

The Nazis had intended to close all sects and undoubtedly could have done so, but there emerged a series of pragmatic compromises in which the sects either voiced support for the Party or gave practical aid where they could, or went quietly underground. Whilst their activities were carefully monitored, no immediate action was taken against them. Their ultimate fate, like that of the Free Churches, once the war had been won, was different. For the time being, they had purchased, one way or another, a right to an uneasy co-existence with the Nazi state.

From within the minority groups who managed, one way or another, to purchase a stay of execution, there emerged individuals or groups of individuals who faced arrest and even death for making a personal stance, particularly against Nazi racial policies. Members of the schismatic 'Seventh Day Adventist Reform Movement' refused, for example, all compromise and faced bitter persecution. Christian Scientists and Quakers, amongst others, found themselves in prisons or camps for their 'anti-Nazi activities' and particularly for having given assistance to Jewish people. Three young Mormons were involved in active resistance to Nazi policies. They were arrested for their activities and one of them was beheaded. Such individuals were undoubtedly influenced by their religious beliefs, but it was as individuals that they took action whilst the religious institutions to which they belonged were largely silent or even compliant with the public face of National Socialism.

The Case of the Jehovah's Witnesses

The Jehovah's Witness story stands out as radically different in this context of confusion, political naïveté and compromise. This group made the decision from a very early date to ignore the ban on

Bochum, Germany. Five of the Kusserow children play outdoors at a family picnic in 1932. The children wear garlands of flowers on their heads.

For Further Reading

The video and work book 'Stand Firm' tells the story of the Jehovah's Witnesses in the Third Reich. It is a Jehovah's Witness publication but involves a large number of independent scholars and is an objective and scholarly account.

'Jehovah's Witnesses', a booklet on the Witness story produced by the Holocaust Memorial Museum, Washington DC.

C.E.King 'The Jehovah's Witnesses' in 'A Mosaic of Victims' edited by Michael Berenbaum, New York: University Press, 1990.

B.Bailey 'A Quaker Couple in Nazi Germany'. York, England: William Sessions Limited, 1994.

their missionary work and meetings and to continue to preach and meet. In their literature they publicly identified the evils of the regime, including what was happening to the Jews. The consequences were severe as members met the full force of police and Gestapo brutality. Initially imprisoned in civil prisons, by 1935 they were amongst the first Germans to be thrown into the labour camps. By 1945 there were Witnesses in all the major concentration camps across the Europe of the Third Reich. Here they were subject to special tortures and humiliations, whilst maintaining their faith and refusing even the smallest compromises, even when such could buy their freedom from the camp.

Jehovah's Witnesses believe that they are living in the 'last days' and are witnesses to Jehovah here on earth. Whilst tax paying, law abiding and following a highly moral code of behaviour, they consider themselves citizens not of any 'earthly' state but of God's kingdom and soldiers in his holy army. Thus they would not enlist in Hitler's army or offer the Hitler salute as a sign of Nazi citizenship. They continued to 'witness' in their door-to-door missionary work and to meet and share bible readings and teachings.

Such a response to National Socialism hit at the very heart of what that movement professed. National Socialism claimed the hearts and minds all its citizens and it demanded a loyalty beyond political compliance. The Witness resistance and their continued and obstinate refusal to bow the knee, whatever the personal cost, was something the system could neither understand nor tolerate. Thus it threw at this tiny movement, with a mere 20,000 members out of a population of over 60 million, the full brute force of the regime. Brutality was no answer in the face of the Witnesses' faith and their work continued, in and out of the camps, even as Witness children were taken away to be brought up in Nazi homes and families were split by imprisonment and death.

All Christians in Nazi Germany had choices not open to Jewish citizens. It is very dangerous to make judgments, in retrospect, about the choices made by the religious minority groups and about the information and understanding available to them at that time. The Witness story demonstrates, however, that it was possible for even a very small and politically powerless group of people to make a firm stand against what they quickly identified as evil. Witnesses were strengthened and informed in their behaviour by their beliefs and their membership of the movement, but it is important to acknowledge that each Witness faced their own challenge as an individual and made their own choices. We may or may not share their beliefs, but the fact that the vast majority were willing to face imprisonment and death rather than, as they saw it, deny their God, did make a difference. It continues to make a difference to our analysis of the difficult questions facing Christians during the Third Reich.

Helen Gotthold with her children Gerd and Gisela. Gotthold was a Jehovah's Witness and held anti-Nazi views. She was convicted, condemned to death and beheaded in the Ploetzensee concentration camp, December 8 1944. Gerd and Gisela survived the war.

Christine King (UK) is Vice-Chancellor of Staffordshire University in England, where she is also Professor of History. Her research and publications concentrate on the history of religious minority movements in the Third Reich.

A MOSAIC OF VICTIMS:
WHAT ABOUT NON-JEWISH VICTIMS
OF THE NAZIS?

Michael Berenbaum

Gypsy child.

'Not all victims of the Nazis were Jews, but all Jews were victims'

Elie Wiesel

Throughout Nazi rule, Jews were the major Nazi target, but not the only one, as a variety of groups of individuals suffered at the hands of the Nazis and their collaborators. Political dissidents, communists, socialists and liberals alike, as well as trade unionists, were all persecuted because of their politics. Dissenting clergy were arrested when they spoke out against the regime. All too few began their opposition early in response to the rise of Nazism. Others spoke out when specific events demanded their response as religious people, such as *Kristallnacht*, the November 1938 pogrom during which synagogues were burned, Jewish businesses looted, and 30,000 Jewish men were arrested, or the Nazi Euthanasia Program when 70,000 handicapped Germans were murdered. The mentally retarded, physically handicapped, and emotionally disturbed Germans were not viewed as suitable raw material for breeding the 'master race', so they too suffered at the hands of the Nazis and their collaborators. Henry Friedlander suggests that the roots of genocide can be seen in this so-called 'euthanasia' program. Other victims of the Nazis included Jehovah's Witnesses, who would not swear allegiance to the state nor serve in the army of the Third Reich. They were targeted, as were pacifists. Gypsies (or the *Roma* and *Sinti*), considered traditional outsiders, were distrusted and despised. Regarded by the Nazis as a menace, they were deported and incarcerated in concentration camps. Still later, many were murdered by the Nazis. Male homosexuals were arrested and their institutions destroyed because of their sexual practices. Lesbians, however, were often exempt.

As a rule, the Germans treated citizens of western nations with greater respect than those to their east. They harbored a particular animus toward Slavic nations and focused a campaign of decimation against the Poles. Polish political leadership was ravaged. They were arrested, tortured, incarcerated and murdered. Since Polish nationalism was linked with Roman Catholicism, many priests were persecuted and murdered. Some of the more gifted of Polish children, especially those who resembled the Aryan ideal of blond hair and blue eyes, were forcibly taken to Germany in a program of so-called Aryanization. Heinrich Himmler advocated a policy that would restrict education for Polish children and that would teach the Poles to be subservient to the so-called master race. Eighty-three thousand non-Jewish Poles were killed in Auschwitz.

Thus, 'some groups were victimized for what they did, others for what they refused to do; still others, for what they were.' In the Nazi mindset, the world was divided into a series of lesser races by color, ethnicity, culture or national identity. Blacks and Slavs were special targets of Nazi animosity. Once targeted for persecution or destruction, the victims of Nazism were pushed to the margins of society. They were forced, to use a term first suggested by American sociologist Helen Fein, outside 'the universe of obligation' where their fate was of little interest to Nazified German society and of no moral importance. Hence, even those who did not enthusiastically support Nazi racial ideology could approach the fate of its victims with indifference. Jews were regarded as mortal enemies of the state, a cancer on society; their elimination was essential to the well-being of the state and to the health of the German nation.

Gypsies

Unlike the Jews, Gypsies were subjected to official discrimination long before 1933, yet no comprehensive Gypsy law was ever promulgated. Until 1942 pure Gypsies were not targeted. Only those who intermarried with Germans were considered a threat to the 'purity of the race'. Local initiatives against the Gypsies preceded policy decisions from Berlin. Thus, in 1935 the city of Frankfurt established a fenced and guarded Gypsy camp. By 1936, the city had banned immigration of new Gypsies and had authorized 'biological heredity examinations.'

In 1936 the Reich Interior Ministry issued guidelines 'For Fighting the Gypsy Plague', which required the photographing and fingerprinting of the Gypsies. This information proved lethal when persecution and incarceration later gave way to murder. In 1937, 'preventative custody' in Nazi parlance, concentration camp imprisonment was authorized for Gypsies.

A leading professor proposed a biological solution: 'In the long term the German people will only be freed from this public nuisance when . . . [the Gypsies'] fertility is completely eliminated.' As the 'Final Solution' to the Jewish Problem unfolded after 1941, Gypsies shared much of the same fate as Jews. Some were sent to ghettos, some were killed by mobile

> 'Only by understanding the fate of the others who suffered, where it paralleled the Jewish experience and more importantly where it differed, can the distinctive character of the Jewish fate as a matter of historical fact be demonstrated.'
>
> Michael Berenbaum, ed., *Mosaic of Victims*, p. xv.

> Some groups were victimized for what they did, others for what they refused to do; still others, for who they were.

Male Gypsy prisoners in Dachau concentration camp.

killing units in newly invaded territory held by the Soviet Union, others were sent to concentration camps where they were gassed in family units. In Auschwitz, Dr. Josef Mengele experimented on Gypsy children as he had on Jewish children.

Jehovah's Witnesses

Jehovah's Witnesses were isolated and harassed from 1933 onward. Suspicion and harassment turned into bitter persecution as the Witnesses refused to surrender. They refused to enlist in the army, undertake air raid drills, stop meeting or proselytizing. 'Heil Hitler' never passed their lips. A mere 20,000 among 65 million Germans, the Witnesses entered the spiritual battle against the Nazis as soldiers of Jehovah in the war between good and evil. They taught that Jehovah's forces will defeat Satan. The Nazis could not tolerate such 'false gods'. Persecution began immediately in 1933 and continued until 1945. After 1937, Witnesses were sent to concentration camps. Outside the camps, Witnesses lost children, jobs, pensions, and all civil rights.

Throughout their struggle, Witnesses continued to meet, to preach and to distribute literature. Five thousand Jehovah's Witnesses were sent to concentration camps where they alone were 'voluntary prisoners,' because the moment they recanted their views, they could be freed. Some lost their lives in the camps, but none renounced their faith. As they understood why it was they were suffering, they maintained their spiritual dignity to a degree unusual among prisoners.

Homosexuals

Even though homosexuality had been outlawed in Germany for centuries, it was tolerated in Weimar Germany. Works advocating homosexuality were published, gay bars were to be found in each of Germany's major cities. Within weeks of taking office Hitler banned homosexual groups. On May 6, 1933, four days before the book burnings, Professor Magnus Hirschfeld's pro-homosexual Institute for Sexual Research was vandalized, its library and photo collections destroyed. By the summer of 1933, Stormtroopers were raiding gay bars. Homosexuals were soon sent to concentration camps marked with yellow bands with the letter A. Pink triangles would come later.

Political infighting and sexual politics were joined in June 1934 when Hitler purged his SA and initiated the murder of his faithful lieutenant Ernst Röhm, a known homosexual, and 300 of Röhm's

For Further Reading

Michael Berenbaum, ed. *A Mosaic of Victims: Non-Jews Persecuted and Murdered by the Nazis.* New York: New York University Press, 1990.

Michael Berenbaum, ed. *Witness to the Holocaust: An Illustrated Documentary History of the Holocaust in the Words of Its Victims, Perpetrators and Bystanders.* New York: HarperCollins Publishers, 1997.

Michael Burleigh. *Death and Deliverance: Euthanasia in Germany 1900-1945.* Cambridge, UK: Cambridge University Press, 1994.

Richard Plant. *The Pink Triangle: The Nazi War Against Homosexuals.* New York: Henry Hold and Company, 1986.

Donald Kenrick, Grattan Puxon. *Gypsies under the Swastika,* Hatfield: University of Hertfordshire Press, 1995.

Donald Kenrick, Gratton Puxon. *The Destiny of Europe's Gypsies,* London: Heinemann Educational Books, 1972.

Jehovah's Witness Erich Frost sits a piano in 1931. Frost worked for the underground until his arrest in 1936. While imprisoned he wrote two hymns which were smuggled out and distributed among Jehovah's Witnesses at large. These hymns are still sung today.

subordinates. Nazi disdain for homosexuals made these early murders palatable to the populace. Shortly thereafter, Himmler created a special criminal police office to fight homosexuality. By December 1934, homosexual intent was sufficient to warrant criminal prosecution.

The Murder of the Handicapped

Mass murder of the handicapped began slowly. At first authorization was informal and secret. Narrow in scope, it was limited only to the most serious cases. Within months, the creation of the T-4 program involved virtually the entire German psychiatric community. Operating at the Berlin Chancellery, Tiergarten 4, a statistical survey of all psychiatric institutions, hospitals, and homes for chronic patients was ordered.

Three medical experts reviewed the forms without examining individual patients or reading detailed records. Theirs was the power to decide life or death. Patients ordered to be killed were transported to six killing centers: Hartheim, Sonnenstein, Grafeneck, Bernburg, Hadamar, and Brandenburg. The SS donned white coats for the transports to imitate a medical situation.

The first killings were by starvation. Starvation is passive, simple and natural. Injections were then used. Children were simply put to sleep, never again to awake. Sedatives became overdoses. Gassing soon became the preferred method of killing. False showers were constructed, and Ph.D. chemists were employed. The process was administered by doctors; 15-20 people were killed at a time. After the killing, black smoke would billow up the chimneys as the bodies were burned.

A few doctors protested. Carl Bonhöffer, a leading psychiatrist, helped his son Dietrich contact church groups, urging them not to turn patients over to the SS. A few physicians refused to fill out the forms. Only one psychiatrist, Professor Gottfried Ewald of Göttingen, openly opposed the killing. Count von Galen, the Bishop of Münster, eventually openly challenged the regime. 'We must oppose the taking of innocent human life even if it were to cost us our lives,' he argued.

Identity photos of a Polish female prisoner in Auschwitz.

On August 24, 1941, almost two years after it began, the operation was seemingly discontinued although evidence suggests it was merely driven underground.

The killing did not end, as mass murder was just beginning. The physicians trained in the medical killing centers graduated to bigger tasks. Irmfried Eberl, MD, who began his career in the T-4 program, became the commandant of Treblinka. His colleagues went on to Belzec, Sobibor, Treblinka and Auschwitz, where killing took on massive dimensions.

For Reflection

Why is it important to examine Nazi ideological persecution in its broadest definition?

What does the reaction of the Christian Church to the persecution of 'Aryan' victims say of its attitude to the Jews?

What might the stand of the Jehovah's Witness community say of mainstream Christian practice of the time?

Some were victims of the Nazis "because of what they were in terms of genetic (or, to a lesser extent, cultural) origins." Others were victims "because of what they did." (Here one should distinguish between those who engaged in "ordinary" crimes and violations of generally accepted moral values - the homosexual victims, for example, from others whose crimes were political - listening to foreign broadcasts, for example.). Still others were victims of the Nazis "because of what they refused to do. Included here are men who refused military service altogether and members of the armed forces who refused to comply with orders they considered immoral."

Adapted from Gordon C. Zahn, 'Pacifists during the Third Reich' in Berenbaum, ed., *A Mosaic of Victims*.

Michael Berenbaum (USA), is the author of many books, including *The World Must Know: The History of the Holocaust as Told in the United States Holocaust Memorial Museum*. He was Director of the Research Institute at the US Holocaust Memorial Museum in Washington, DC.

The murder of the handicapped was a prefiguration of the Holocaust. Killing centers for the handicapped were the antecedent of death camps. They were often staffed by the same physicians who received their specialized training 'and lost their moral inhibitions' in this early exercise in mass murder.

Psychiatrists did save some patients for a time, but only if others were sent to their deaths. *Judenrat* leaders were later to face similar choices. The transport of the handicapped was the forerunner of deportations. Gas chambers were first developed at these killing centers. So too, body disposal by burning. In the death camps, thousands could be killed at one time and their bodies burned within hours.

Religious leaders protested the murder of the handicapped and the killing appeared to stop, but when Jews were being murdered almost all Church leaders were silent. The handicapped were Germans and from a religious perspective they were inside the universe of common obligation. When the murder of the Jews began in 1941, the Jews 'even those who had converted to Christianity and hence were Jewish by Nazi racial definitions, but Christian by religious definitions' had long ago been forced outside of society and been relentlessly portrayed as a mortal danger to the Germans. Thus, only a rare few Christians could see in the Jews, fellow human beings, children of God.

'The historical record during the Third Reich demonstrates all too clearly that not all victims of the Nazis were Jews. Millions of other people were swept into the Nazi net of death. If one calculates all the civilian casualties – not including those killed as part of the systematic mass murder, nor those who died as accidental victims of battles, air raids, and military operations, but only those categorized as subhumans and killed as a result of conscious persecution – the result is staggering. The Nazi reign of terror brought suffering and death to Jews, Gypsies, Jehovah's Witnesses, the mentally and physically disabled, homosexuals, Communists, Slavs, Poles, Russians, Ukrainians, political opponents and others. In short, anyone who opposed or did not fit into the Nazi worldview was vulnerable.'

Carol Rittner, 'Foreword: The Triumph of Memory' in Berenbaum, ed., *Mosaic of Victims*, p. xii.

THE REACTION OF THE CHURCHES IN NAZI-OCCUPIED EUROPE

THE CATHOLIC CHURCH IN POLAND AND THE HOLOCAUST, 1939-1945

Dariusz Libionka

'My father was hiding in the coal-shed of Father Krasowski's vicarage, across the street from Gestapo H.Q. The priest had been as good as his word. Asked for help, he gave it. . . . With the few remaining diamonds my father had managed to save, the priest had obtained false passports and papers for the three of us.'

Kitty Hart, Return to Auschwitz, p.44

The issue of the attitude taken by the Catholic Church in Poland when confronted with the destruction of the Jews in that country is a complex one, and must be understood within a broad context. Many factors played a role in influencing the behavior of the Church leaders in occupied Poland. Although one must not underestimate the importance of pre-war attitudes toward Jews and Judaism, it is equally important not to disregard the complicated situation in which the Church found itself under German occupation. The present article relates exclusively to the Catholic Church. It will not discuss the activities of organizations devoted to assisting Jews, such as the *Zegota*, nor will it relate to the influence of religion nor the Catholic faith on the conduct of the Polish population as a whole towards the Jews.

The Attitude of the Church to the Jews in the Inter-War Period

During the inter-war period, and in the 1930s in particular, many political streams in Poland saw the Jews – who were a large ethnic minority of over three million residing in Poland – as a 'problem'. The political right-wing was convinced that the Jewish minority posed an economic and a cultural threat, and a threat to Polish national identity. The Jews, according to right-wing ideology, had given birth to Bolshevism and were the reason for its successes. This approach was warmly adopted by many members of the Catholic Church, who supplemented and enriched right-wing anti-Jewish rhetoric with traditional elements taken from Church doctrine. The Church's desire was to shape a model of Polish nationalism that would be in accordance with the demands of Catholic moral doctrine. The pastoral letter composed by August Hlond, head of the Catholic Church in Poland, in February 1936 bore the title 'On the Principles of Catholic Morality'. This epistle serves as a clear example of the tensions between Polish nationalism and Church morality, which the Polish clergy attempted to combine. The obligation to respect the Jew as an individual, along with a prohibition against the adoption of tactics in political struggle that would conflict with Christian ethics coexist in the epistle with an extensive list of accusations against the Jews. According to Hlond, the Jews do battle against the

'During the interwar period and in the 1930s in particular, many political streams in Poland saw the Jews as a 'problem'.'

Church and serve as the vanguard of atheism and Communism. Furthermore, they corrupt morality, disseminate pornography, and deal in treachery and usury.

The Attitude of the Bishops to the Jews during the German Occupation

German policy toward the Church after the occupation of Poland was inconsistent. In the territories annexed to the German Reich, a process of dismantling and destroying the Church's infrastructure was adopted at once by the German authorities. Church leaders were arrested, Polish clergymen were sent to the General Government *(Generalgouvernement)*, and churches, monasteries and convents were closed. In the Chelmno diocese alone, a few hundred clergymen were arrested and murdered in 1939. In the General Government, the policy was different. There, although the Church and its leaders were persecuted, it was not dismantled and destroyed, and its fate there, although very harsh, cannot be compared with what took place in the territories annexed to Germany.

Bishops in the General Government and in the territories taken from the Soviet Union in 1941 were witness to the murder of the Jews. Their stances regarding the Jews' plight can be gleaned from their appeals to the German authorities in the General Government, from their correspondence with the Vatican, and from autobiographical materials.

Archbishop Hlond left Poland in September 1939, and in his place the Archbishop of Lvov, Adam Sapieha, was recognized as head of the Catholic Church in the occupied country. Sapieha was held in high esteem by the Polish public due to his open opposition to German terror and his intervention with the German authorities for the alleviation of that terror. Polish research tends to unanimously emphasize his intervention on behalf of the Jews, and points to the assistance provided to Jews by the clergy of the Cracow diocese, of which Sapieha was informed. In fact, however, this oft-cited assistance mostly took the form of intervention on behalf of Catholics who were of Jewish origin. Not one of the three Councils held by the Polish Bishops during the German occupation mentioned the mass murder of the Jews. This is true even of the Council that took place on June 1, 1943, less than two weeks after the liquidation of the Warsaw Ghetto, even though it is possible that this event had a direct impact on the exact timing chosen for the convention. On the other hand, Archbishop Sapieha personally provided the priests who helped Jews with baptism certificates intended for Jews who were in hiding in Cracow.

The sources mention a number of Bishops who were actively involved in providing aid to Jews. The Bishop of Pinsk, Karol Niemira, who worked in cooperation with an underground organization that maintained ties with the ghetto, was particularly noteworthy in this regard. In a meeting that took place on December 17, 1943, German officials reminded Cardinal Sapieha that a number of Jewish families had even found refuge in the Archbishop's home in Lvov. Polish apologetic literature cites the names

During the morning hours . . . war broke out between Germany and Poland . . . Poland alone will suffer the hardships of the war . . . We are witnessing the dawn of a new era in the history of the world. As for the Jews, their danger is seven times greater. Wherever Hitler's foot treads there is no hope for the Jewish people. Hitler, may his name be blotted out, threatened in his one of speeches that if war comes, the Jews of Europe will be exterminated . . .The hour is fateful. If new world arises, the sacrifices and troubles and hardships will be worthwhile. Let us hope that Nazism will be destroyed completely, that it will fall and never rise again.

From the diary of Chaim Kaplan, September 1, 1939.

of over ten Bishops who were active on behalf of the Jewish population. Given the paucity of reliable written sources, however, it is difficult to verify these assertions.

In contrast with Bishops' letters from other occupied countries, the Polish Bishops' correspondence with Rome makes scarcely any mention of the annihilation of the Jews. Even in the letters of Cardinal Sapieha himself, who worked ceaselessly to defend the Polish nation and the Polish Church, and who included in his letters detailed descriptions of the Germans' inhuman behavior, one finds no reference to the tragic fate suffered by the Jews of Poland.

The lack of determined public condemnations of genocide from a Christian moral point of view can be explained on the basis of the profound difference between the situation in occupied Poland as opposed to that which pertained to Western Europe. In Poland, any expression of opposition to the Germans' anti-Jewish policy presented a life-threatening danger. This, however, cannot serve as an explanation for the fact that no effort was made to inform the Pope of the crimes committed against the Jews in the Polish dioceses – information that the Bishops surely possessed. Nor can this be explained as resulting from fear of German reprisals against the Polish Church. The Bishops' silence seems rather to indicate that German persecution of the Church – and the Polish Church in particular – combined with the Bishops' attitudes toward the 'Jewish problem', made them unable either to comprehend the extent of the Jewish tragedy or to attribute much importance to it.

The Attitude of the Clergy and the Monastic Orders to the Jews

The attitude taken by the Catholic clergy and nuns to the Jews during the period of annihilation is representative of the attitude taken by the Polish population as a whole. There were instances of heroism and courage alongside cases of extreme opportunism. The difficulty in assessing the period is that Polish scholars have tended to focus primarily on those Church leaders who assisted Jews or who were sympathetic to their suffering. For this reason, one is forced to try to complete the picture on the basis of indirect or secondary sources. The possibilities for action which the priests had were largely conditional upon objective factors – the location of their diocese, their involvement with the Polish underground, and their contacts with the Jewish population.

The clergymen who helped Jews did so in a variety of ways and at different times. In almost all cases, their activity was the result of personal initiatives taken by the lower clergy. Up until mid-1942 – i.e. until the beginning of the peak period of the 'final solution' – the help provided usually took the form of care for baptized Jews, issuance of baptismal certificates that allowed the recipients to obtain documents necessary for survival, and a variety of philanthropic activities. At times, clergymen turned to their congregations from the pulpit and asked them to help Jews and to be sympathetic to them.

'As early as October there were a considerable number of antisemitic elements who collaborated with the Germans in waging war on the Jews. . . . The antisemitic feelings were intensified after the return of thousands of Poles from the territories that were first occupied by the Soviets and later by the Germans, with their stories of atrocities committed by the K.G.B. (itself described as Jewish, of course); atrocities like Katyn, in spite of the many Jewish names on the lists of the victims.'

Emmanuel Ringelblum. *Polish-Jewish Relations during the Second World War.* p.39

From mid-1942 onward, the priests' activity centered on hiding Jewish children in convents and monasteries and on providing assistance to refugees from the ghettos that had been liquidated. Many Church people joined in the activities of the *Zegota*, which was established in late 1942, in cooperation with Catholic groups.

Testimonies and documents often reveal negative attitudes toward Jews held by Church leaders. A report on the Catholic Church that was transmitted to the Polish Government-in-Exile in London in the summer of 1941 was written in the style of pre-war Catholic journalism and included the thesis that the Germans, in spite of the evil they had perpetrated, had been proven to possess a realistic attitude in 'liberating Polish society from the Jewish plague'.

The question arises as to what priests were involved in aid activity for the Jews. The antisemitic views held by many Church leaders did not prevent them from providing assistance in individual cases. It is unknown how many priests altered their views on the 'Jewish problem' in the wake of the genocide they witnessed or, on the other hand, how many of them clung to their views, even while feeling compassion for the persecuted victims.

Concluding Remarks

What was the extent of assistance, and to what degree was it in fact helpful? Polish literature on this question tends to accept as axiomatic the view that there were 769 people involved in aid activities throughout the period of 1939-1945. Among them were 17 bishops, 60 monks, and 265 nuns. However, due to the questionable reliability of some of the writings that serve as the basis for these calculations, these numbers are themselves highly questionable. Furthermore, I have been unable to find anywhere any interpretation of these numbers. The question has not been raised as to the numerical relation between those involved in activities of this nature and those who remained indifferent or uninvolved. No attempt has been made to characterize or to describe the most active clergymen, who appear to have numbered no more than a few dozen.

These numbers should not come as a surprise. This type of activity, after all, was extremely dangerous, and required determination, will-power, and a strong character. From late 1941 on, Poles who provided assistance to Jews faced a death penalty. Many priests, even had they wanted to help, could in fact do nothing. At the same time, however, the inactivity of certain priests stemmed directly from their pre-war views on the 'Jewish problem'.

Finally, the question must be asked as to whether the annihilation of the Jews, to which the Polish clergy was a witness, had any direct influence on changing the Church's attitude to the 'Jewish question'. Here too one must be wary of statements that pertain to the majority of the population in

'The Polish clergy has reacted almost with indifference to the tragedy of the slaughter of the whole Jewish people.'

Emmanuel Ringelblum,
Polish-Jewish Relations During the Second World War, p.206

For Reflection

To what extent do you think historical prejudice is linked to the outcome of our moral decisions in the present?

Do you think that Christians thought they were doing enough for their Polish-Jewish neighbors?

Is it ever justified to blame the victims of persecution for their own victimization?

For Further Reading

W. Bartoszewski. *The Blood Shed Unites Us. Pages from the History of Help to the Jews in Occupied Poland.* Warsaw: Interpress,1970.

W. Bartoszewski and Z. Lewin. *The Samaritans. Heroes of the Holocaust.* New York: Twayne, 1970.

E. Kurek. *Your Life is Worth Mine. How Polish Nuns Saved Hundreds of Jewish Children in German-Occupied Poland, 1939-1945.* New York: Hippocrene Books, 1997.

Emmanuel Ringelblum. *Polish-Jewish Relations During the Second World War.* Illinois: Northwestern University Press, 1992.

Rafael F. Scharf. *Poland, What Have I To Do with Thee....* Krakow: Taiwpn Universitas, 1996.

Dariusz Libionka is a scholar at the Historical Institute of the National Academy of Sciences in Warsaw.

question. In the immediate wake of the war, censorship made it impossible to hold any discussion of the annihilation of the Jews that was not subordinated to a political context. The new regime in Poland, which was Communist-inclined, increased the Catholic clergy's sense of threat. For this reason, one is hard-pressed to find many words in the journalism of the period that pertain to the destruction of the Jews. This does not mean, however, that the matter was ignored in official declarations. In his first sermon following his return to Poland, August Hlond, now once again head of the Church in Poland, described his vision for the future of the Polish nation: 'We have the possibility of working together with the Savior Jesus Christ, and in this way, of playing an important role in the re-organization of the world, or on the other hand, we might attempt to build without Jesus and thus risk the tragic fate that befell Jerusalem, which failed to recognize the advent of redemption.' Echoes of the traditional view, according to which Jewish suffering as punishment for their rejection of Jesus' appearance as savior, can be heard clearly in this statement.

In a statement made by Cardinal Hlond after the pogrom in Kielce of 1946, in which the surviving Jews who had returned to Kielce were killed by the Polish population, he blamed the Jews for the deterioration in Polish-Jewish relations. The Jews, he claimed, were again holding important positions and they wanted to impose a regime alien to the Polish nation. In the same speech he stressed the suffering of the Church and of the Polish nation, and the help provided by the Catholic clergy to the Jews during the period of German occupation. These became central motifs in the education provided by the bishops to their congregations, and they had great historical importance in terms of the next generation's historical consciousness. Like the bishops, the authors of journalistic articles and editorials in the Polish press during the first post-war years had no doubt that the Church's help to the Jews had been extensive and of great importance.

Influenced by the horrors of destruction and of concentration and death camps, many priests surely forsook the extreme positions they had held prior to the war. But the anti-Jewish views of the Polish Catholic clergy proved to be deep-rooted and vigorous, and they found renewed sustenance in the new political reality of the late 1940s.

THE RESPONSE OF THE POLISH CHURCH TO THE HOLOCAUST

John T. Pawlikowski

Any examination of the Polish Catholic Church's role during the Holocaust must be placed within the situation prevailing in Poland after the Nazi invasion in September 1939. Poland was a totally occupied country. One part of the country was formally incorporated into the Reich. The remainder was ruled by a military government headed by General Hans Frank (the so-called 'General Government' area).

In Poland anyone caught aiding Jews was subjected to immediate death, a penalty that could also be extended to their families. In Warsaw, where the largest community of Jews lived, the Jewish community was eventually sequestered in a tightly controlled ghetto which Christians would have great difficulty entering. Poles themselves, it needs to be remembered, were victims of the Nazi plan for so-called 'human purification.'

The Nazi invasion of Poland went far beyond military victory. Because the Poles were regarded as 'subhumans' they were to be reduced to virtual slave status with the total destruction of cultural, political and religious symbols that would provide them with any form of human identity. Some Nazi leaders such as Himmler, Hitler and Frank entertained on occasion the idea of the eventual total annihilation of the Poles in a manner similar to the Jews. But whether the Nazis, if given the chance, would have pursued such a plan remains an open question. But the fact that they contemplated it, and that they built the Auschwitz concentration camp as an integral part of their effort to subdue the Polish nation, shows that Poles were not merely victims of military conquest but of a genocidal attack.

The Nazis realized they would have to break the back of the Catholic Church in Poland if their plan of national subjugation was to succeed. When the Nazis partitioned Poland after the invasion, they seriously undercut the Church's own territorial structures by dividing up historic diocese. Thus weakened, Polish Catholicism, especially in the annexed areas, lost most of its hierarchy and clergy. Only in Poland did the Nazis systematically arrest and imprison bishops. By the end of the war many cities had suffered major losses in the ranks of the clergy: Chelmno, 47.8 percent; Lodz, 36.8 percent; Poznan, 31.1 percent. Overall 1,811 Polish diocesan priests perished under the Nazis out of a total of 10,017 in 1939. Many church buildings were also destroyed. In Poznan, for example, only two out of the thirty pre-war churches remained at the end of the war.

The city was bombed September 1, 1939, and was threatened by Hitler's encircling armies only a few days later . . . After the siege, which lasted several weeks, Warsaw – one of the last parts of the country still offering resistance – had to surrender. This marked the beginning of the tragic years of the occupation, which would, as everyone knew, be fraught with great hardships for the Poles. The large number of Jews in occupied Poland posed a problem.' 'The attempt to save them cannot be explained without knowing the conditions under which the Polish people were living.

W. Bartoszewski, *The Warsaw Ghetto: A Christian's Testimony*, p. 4.

'Polish nationalism was synonymous with Catholicism. The Church had always provided the foundation of Polish nationalism, especially during periods of oppression. If the Nazi policy of exterminating the Polish nation were to have any chance of success, the Germans realized they had to destroy the organization and leadership of the Church.'

Richard C. Lukas. *Forgotten Holocaust: The Poles Under German Occupation 1939-1944,* p. 13.

For Reflection

To what extent is it important to evaluate the actions of the Church in the context of the conditions of the time?

What do the activities of organizations such as Zegota demonstrate?

If overcoming antisemitism was difficult for the few Poles that did give humanitarian help to the Jews, what does this say about the impact of prejudice on our ability to react in other situations?

It is within this context of total control of the country by the Nazi forces and the systematic attack on the churches that the Polish Catholic response to the Holocaust must be evaluated. Seen in these difficult circumstances the Polish Catholic response was ambiguous. The secret courier for the Polish underground, Jan Nowak, in a public interview at the United States Holocaust Memorial Museum during the Museum's week of commemoration of Polish victimization and rescue efforts on the occasion of the sixtieth anniversary of the German invasion of Poland, said that in his experience there was less antisemitism in Poland during the Nazi occupation because people hated the Germans so much. This disdain prevented any organized collaboration with the Nazis of the kind that surfaced in places such as France, Slovakia, Hungary and the Ukraine. There were indeed blackmailers in Poland who betrayed Jews to the Gestapo, sometimes for a small payment, according to Nowak, and there were people who saved Jews. Both were in the minority as he remembers it. 'Everybody in Poland was mainly concerned with how to survive – how to get food, how to avoid arrest – and this made people indifferent.' (*Update,* United States Holocaust Memorial Museum, November-December 1999, p.7) Despite the struggle for survival that was Poland's daily fare under the Nazis, the point made by Michael Steinlauf in his challenging book *Bondage to the Dead: Poland and the Memory of the Holocaust* (Syracuse University Press, 1997) needs to be emphasized as well. While both Poles and Jews suffered severely under the Nazis, non-Jewish Poles were able to maintain some semblance of a normal life while Jews were not. Thus Polish Christians did have some possibility of saving Jews.

Two groups in particular showed remarkable courage in their efforts to save Jews. The first was the *Zegota* movement (a code name for The Council for Aid to the Jews) which was the only organization during the Nazi era founded specifically for the rescue of Jews. While Zegota was not directly connected with the Polish Catholic Church and included a number of socialists who were generally hostile to organized religion, it did involve very prominent Catholic lay leaders such as Wladyslaw Bartoszewski who eventually himself became Poland's foreign minister after the collapse of the Communist government. Bartoszewski himself has said that *Zegota's* effort was modest. It placed a particular emphasis on saving Jewish children. Reliable estimates are that *Zegota* was able to place some 2,500 children and youngsters in homes, convents, and orphanages in the Warsaw area alone. Perhaps another 2,500 children were sheltered by individuals and independent groups. Bartoszewski insists that no large-scale effort could be mounted because the Nazis would have quickly discovered it and because hiding Jews became so dangerous that often they could not stay more than one week at a time in a given location. Some members of *Zegota* endured physical punishment at the hands of the Nazis for their efforts.

The other exemplary group was Polish nuns. Italy and Poland are the two countries where

Catholic orders of women stood out in a coordinated effort twards the rescue of Jews. In Poland children were a special target of rescue for the nuns. Eva Kurek has described the contribution of Polish nuns in several of her books including *Your Life is Worth Mine*. Yet it needs to be noted that some of the nuns involved in the rescue efforts had a pronounced 'conversionist' mentality. While this does not diminish the nobility of their deeds at the time, and while one must recognize this as part of the prevailing mentality in the Church at the time, it is necessary to point out the clear theological limitations present in the mindset of some of the Catholic rescuers in a more direct way than scholars such as Kurek have done. This even applies to *Zegota* where a few of its leaders supported financially the Zionist effort to move Polish Jews to Palestine. While this is much more benign, it does reveal a mentality that Poland would be better off without Jews. While the Nazi method of *Judenrein* was reprehensible to these leaders, they had some sense of identification with the goal of ridding Poland of its large Jewish community.

On the negative side there existed widespread antisemitism at both the popular and episcopal levels in Polish Catholicism. There is no question that this antisemitism muted any consideration of involvement in the rescue of the Jews for many Polish Catholics. The classical Christian antisemitism was frequently combined with a strong sense of religious nationalism. To be a Pole is to be a Catholic. Non-Catholics, particularly Jews, were ruining Polish Catholic society with their liberal political and cultural views (including capitalism) on the one hand and by joining with the hated socialists and communists on the other. In either perspective Jews were public enemy number one, even for the leading Polish bishops. When some Polish church leaders such as Cardinal Hlond (who was also criticized by Polish Catholics for leaving the country during the war), Cardinal Kakowski, Archbishop Sapieha or Archbishop Teodorowicz did speak out against antisemitic attacks by the Nazis or others, they generally coupled their remarks with strong attacks on Jews as Communists and as agents of immorality in Polish society. While there certainly was some Jewish involvement in communist and socialist groups in Poland as there was Jewish commitment to liberal cultural and political views, realities that need further examination by Jewish historians, the episcopal statements were highly exaggerated. On the level of popular Catholicism preachers and publications such as *Maly Dziennik* which Ronald Modras has studied in his important volume 'The Catholic Church and Antisemitism: Poland, 1933-1939' took much the same line as the bishops, viewing Jews as a destructive, even at times demonic, element in Polish life. It took a strong humanitarian outlook for those who did engage in rescue efforts to overcome this pervasive antisemitism in Polish Catholicism. In recent years there have been several attempts to confront this antisemitic tradition. The Polish Episcopal Conference raised it in their January 1995 statement on the Holocaust, though they tend to restrict its significance.

For Further Reading

Irene Tomaszewski and Tecia Werbowski. *Zegota: The Rescue of Jews in Wartime Poland*.

Vladka Meed. *On Both Sides of the Wall*. Washington, DC: United States Holocaust Memorial Museum, 1993.

The Jews of Poland. Brookline, MA: Facing History and Ourselves National Foundation, 1994.

Antony Polonsky, ed. *My Brother's Keeper: Recent Polish Debates on the Holocaust*. Routledge, 1990

Secretariat for Ecumenical and Interreligious Affairs, The National Conference of Catholic Bishops. *Catholics Remember the Holocaust*. Published by the United States Catholic Conference.

Ronald Modras. *The Catholic Church and Antisemitism: Poland, 1933-1939*. Harwood Academic Press, 1994.

John T. Pawlikowski O.S.M.

(USA), Professor of Social Ethics at the Catholic Theological Union in Chicago, has been a member of the United States Holocaust Memorial Council since 1980. He currently chairs the Council's Committee on Church Relations. The author of many publications on the Holocaust and Christian-Jewish relations, including *The Challenge of the Holocaust for Christian Theology*, Pawlikowski is also a member of the National Conference of Catholic Bishops' advisory committee on Catholic-Jewish relations.

And Professor Jan Blonski began an intensive and heated debate in January 1978 in the Catholic newspaper *Tygodnik Powszechny* when he suggested that, despite the severity of the Nazi occupation, Catholics might have done more to rescue their fellow citizens. This debate continues today and consensus is not likely to occur any time soon.

From the August 1942 leaflet, Protest, issued by the 'Front for the Revival of Poland', a Catholic underground group in Poland; authored by Zofia Kossak-Szczucka, a prominent Catholic writer.

The total number of Jews killed has already surpassed one million and the number grows with each passing day . . . The world beholds this crime - more terrifying than any in the past - and utters not a word. The massacre of millions of innocent people is being carried out amidst universal, ominous silence. The henchmen say nothing, they do not brag about their deeds. Neither England nor America speaks out. Even the influential international Jewry, so sensitive in the past to every wrong against its own, holds its tongue. The Poles are silent, too. Polish political friends of the Jews confine themselves to newspape notices, whereas Polish opponents of Jews show lack of interest in the matter which does not concern them. The Jews die amidst Pilates washing their hands.

This silence can be tolerated no longer. No matter what its motives are, it is abominable. Those who remain silent in the face of murder become murderer's accomplices. Those who do not denounce it - condone it.

We, Catholic-Poles, raise our voices. Our feelings toward Jews have not changed We continue to deem them political, economic and ideological enemies of Poland. Moreover, we are aware that they hate us more than they hate Germans, that they blame us for their misfortune. Why, on what grounds-this remains the mystery of the Jewish soul, yet it remains an incontrovertible fact. This fact, however, does not release us from the duty of damnation of murder.

We do not want to be Pilates. We are incapable of actively resisting German murders, we cannot help in anything, we cannot save anyone, but we do protest from the depth of our hearts, filled with compassion, indignation and dread. This protest is demanded of us by God, who does not allow us to kill. It is demanded by our Christian conscience. Every creature calling itself human merits neighborly love. The blood of the innocent cries to heaven for revenge. Those who do not join us in this protest are not Catholics.

THE CATHOLIC HIERARCHY IN FRANCE DURING THE WAR AND THE PERSECUTION OF THE JEWS

Renée Bedarida

The behavior of the French Catholic Church and its faithful, in response to the antisemitic persecution, has never been absent from the debates about the past. During the past quarter of the century, however, the subject has become more prominent with the reawakening of the Jewish consciousness and the many studies carried out that have placed the problem at the very core of Vichy historiography. Hence the question: Is the Church guilty for its silence and passivity in the face of the antisemitic policy conducted by the Pétain government and the extermination policy pursued by Nazi Germany starting in 1942?

The answer to this is far from simple. The data are complex and ambivalent, all the more so because we must guard ourselves against anachronism. Following the French defeat in the war, France was divided into two zones. The north was governed by the German occupation forces, while the south was unoccupied and a French government was established on July 10, 1940, headed by Marshal Pétain and seated in Vichy. The Vichy government replaced the principles of the French Revolution (Freedom Equality and Fraternity) with a return to nationalistic values.

It is a historical fact that in 1940 the problem of the Jews living in France was not a priority issue for the majority of the French people, for French Catholics, or for the religious hierarchy, which was concerned chiefly with maintaining its institutions, protecting its believers, and adapting itself to a new regime that seemed to be sympathetic to the Church and its interests.

Although violent persecution of the Jews did not begin immediately, official antisemitism began to rage as soon as October 1940 with the promulgation of anti-Jewish legislation; French Jews were deprived of their rights and foreign Jews of their liberty. But these actions were taken and applied in an atmosphere of almost total indifference. People were much more concerned with the terrible trauma of the defeat, with the sundering of France into two zones, with the absence of more than a million and half young Frenchmen still held prisoner in Germany. The French were not yet aware of the danger of Nazi ideology and could not imagine the deadly consequence of the first antisemitic

Drancy camp near Paris. One of the camps in France in which the Jews were held before their deportation to the east.

'I must make heard the indignant protest of the Christian conscience, and I proclaim that all men, Aryan or non-Aryan, are brothers, because they are created by the same God; that all, whatever their race or religion, are entitled to respect from individuals and the State. The current antisemitic measures are in contempt of human dignity, a violation of the most sacred rights of the individual and the family. . .'
Bishop Pierre-Marie Théas, France

'What I did for the Jewish people . . . was but an infinitesimal contribution to what ought to have been done in order to prevent this horrible slaughter, unprecedented and satanic, of more than six million Jews, which will undoubtedly remain the foulest stain in all of human history, a shame affecting all who participated or who allowed it to happen.'

Father Marie-Benoit, France

Father Marie-Benoit, a Capuchin priest, used his monastery in Marseilles, France, as a rescue center. He aided French Jews by manufacturing false passports, identity cards, certificates of baptism, as well as smuggling Jews into Spain and Switzerland.
On a visit to Rome on July 16, 1943, Benoit presented a plan for the rescue of French Jews to the Pope. The plan, which involved obtaining more humane treatment for Jews in French concentration camps and transferring some 50,000 Jews to North Africa, was approved by the Pope. However, the project failed when German troops invaded the Italian Zone of France..

laws. Accordingly, silence prevailed among the Catholic hierarchy when the first law against the Jews was issued on October 3, 1940.

In offering full support to the 'National Revolution' regime installed by Marshal Pétain, and for fear of endangering the Vichy program of restoration of the country, the Catholic hierarchy refrained from protesting against the unjust decree punishing the French Jews and kept silent. They maintained the same silence when foreign Jews (October 4, 1940) were shamefully confined in 'special camps' of evil character.

In June 1941, Vichy promulgated the second Jewish Law, which worsened the Jews' condition. The episcopate on both sides of the line of demarcation persisted in its silence, even when, in the spring of 1942, the occupation authorities required Jews living in the southern zone to wear the yellow star. From then on, antisemitic measures followed one upon another at an accelerated pace.

On July 15 and 16, 1942, the great *Vel d'Hiv* roundup took place in Paris: 13,300 men, women, and children were arrested by the Paris police and huddled together in camps. The Church raised no public protest in the face of this shameful event. The assembly of cardinals, and archbishops of the Northern Zone, met on July 22. In spite of their real disapproval, they maintained their public silence, leaving the faithful unaware of the danger of falling in with Nazi neopaganism, and they chose to send a protest letter to Marshal Pétain personally.

Deprived of information and instructions from their hierarchy, most Catholics – like many other French people – were unaware of the dangers run by their Jewish compatriots following the armistice. We must recognize that antisemitic and xenophobic propaganda – widely spread by the press in the late thirties and rendered more intense and listened to in the climate of political and economic crisis prevailing in France – had penetrated entire sectors of society. Besides, many Catholics carried with them the traditional Christian background of anti-Judaism, more or less conscious, but deeply rooted in the mind, on which the antisemitic slogans of the official press could build.

However, following the roundups of foreign Jews carried out in the Free Zone in the summer of 1942, there was a crucial change in the attitude of Catholics and their spiritual leaders. Several bishops had proclamations read out in the churches and distributed quietly in the parishes, despite all the efforts by the Vichy police to intercept them. The result was that thousands of priests, monks, nuns, and lay persons performed acts of charity toward the persecuted Jews, acts that were at the same time a show of defiance toward the Pétain government.

There were a total of six of these indignant messages, which reflected the reawakening of the Christian conscience, written by three archbishops and three bishops. From August 23, 1942 until September 20, Msgr Saliège, Archbishop of Toulouse, followed by Msgr Théas, Bishop of Montauban,

Msgr Delay, Bishop of Marseilles, Cardinal Gerlier, Archbishop of Lyon, Msgr Vanstenberghe of Bayonne and Msgr Moussaron, Archbishop of Albi wrote messages to be read out in their churches.

Of course the number of Episcopal protests may seem to be negligible – six, at a time when there were around a hundred bishops in France. But their impact was considerable, because the denunciation of the brutality of the roundups was tantamount to an attack on the entire system of brutal persecutions and deportations. As a result of the movement in public opinion set off by these protests, from then on a rift gaped wide between the Church and the Vichy government, a breach that grew wider several months later, in the wake of the imposition of compulsory labor service.

To tell the truth, a minority of Catholics had not waited for the Episcopal proclamations of the summer of 1942 to hear the voice of conscience; they had already rejected the poison of Nazi ideology and provided assistance and shelter to persecuted Jews, to the extent possible. One must quote the organization named *Amitié chrétienne*, run by the Jesuit Pierre Chaillet, the famous Abbé Glasberg and Catholic and Protestant lay persons, created as soon as 1941. In fact, all over France, thousands of the clergy and faithful performed many similar acts of charity and discreet operations. If a majority of the Jews in France, aliens and citizens alike, survived the genocide it was to a very great extent thanks to the help they received from Catholics and Protestants – sometimes as individuals, more often through their institutions (convents, boarding schools, presbyteries, associations, families) – where the potential victims were hidden and protected.

> To tell the truth, a minority of Catholics had not waited for the Episcopal proclamations of the summer of 1942 to hear the voice of conscience; they had already rejected the poison of Nazi ideology and provided assistance and shelter to persecuted Jews, to the extent possible.

We must not deduce from the Catholic authorities' change of heart toward the persecuted Jews that they had reached the point of rising against the Vichy regime and condemning Pétain himself for supporting the roundups. There were many Catholics who were willing to hide, shelter, and rescue Jews, especially children, at the risk of their freedom or lives, but who had no doubts about the merits of the National Revolution. In *When Memory Comes*, Saul Friedlander relates that the religious institution that saved him, in full cognizance of the danger, venerated Marshal Pétain, whose portrait adorned the classrooms, dormitories, and dining room, alongside that of Jesus.

In the summer of 1943, intervention by the hierarchy once again saved a number of recently

'We are all the children of Abraham, the 'sons of the Bible",' declared his Eminence Cardinal Vedier . . . 'Why need those who today practice the faith of Israel be outcasts in their own country?'
From the appeal of the President of the Jewish Consistory in France to Marshal Pétain, July 1941.

For Reflection
What triggered Church protest in France? At what point did Church leaders decide to speak up? What was the high point of Church protest and was there a line the bishops would not cross in denouncing the deportations of the Jews of France?

75,000 of the 300,000 Jews of France perished during the Holocaust. Is there a connection between these figures and the fact that the change in public opinion permitted many Jews to find refuge among the French?

For Further Reading

Michael R. Marrus & Robert O. Paxton. *Vichy France and the Jews,* Stanford, California: Stanford U.P., 1981.

W.D. Halls. *Polictics, Society and Christianity in Vichy France.* Oxford: Providence, 1995.

Susan Zuccotti. *The Holocaust, The French, and the Jews.* New York: Basic Books, 1993.

Richard M. Weisberg. *Vichy Law and the Holocaust in France.* New York: New York University Press, 1998.

Robert O. Paxton. *Vichy France: Old Guard and New Order, 1940-1944.* New York: Columbia University Press, 1990.

Renée Bedarida (France) has done extensive research on the French Church during World War II and has published many books in French on the subject.

naturalized Jews. The Germans, furious at not having been able to lay hold of the number of deportable Jews they had sought in the roundups of 1942-1943, demanded that Petain's regime revoke the citizenship of naturalized Jews. Msgr Chappoulie, the official spokesman of the Church, sent a letter to the government in which he solemnly warned that any new deportations would provoke strong feelings and protests in Catholic circles and force the bishops to speak up once again. As a result, Pétain rescinded the order.

This last example forces us to ask a question that cannot be evaded: in those troubled times, when so many of the faithful were deeply confused, should not the hierarchy have clearly restated the principles of justice and respect for human beings in order to light up the conscience of the faithful? Should it not have intervened whenever and wherever human rights as well as Christian rights were being trampled underfoot? The fact remains that after the war, the bishops declined to examine their consciences and simply considered that they had done their duty. By their lights, they had fulfilled their mission by protecting the institutions of the Church, especially the youth movements, and reached the conclusion that they had done well, without claiming so and without showing it.

The years have passed, but the memory of the attitude of the French Church between 1940 and 1944 continues to trouble the French people and notably the Christians among them. This is why, on September 30, 1997, standing at a symbolic site – the Drancy camp – the episcopate issued a public statement of repentance, before God, before human beings, especially the Jews. After having recalled that throughout the occupation years the spiritual authorities were kept prisoners of an attitude of conformity, prudence, and silence, the authors of the Declaration – the bishops of the dioceses where the major internment camps for Jews had been located – recognized the failure of their Church and its responsibility toward the Jewish people. They concluded: 'We confess this fault. We implore God to forgive us and ask the Jewish people to hear this cry of repentance.'

'On July 16-17, 1942, the Vèlodrome d'Hiver, an indoor sports arena in Paris, was turned into an internment center for Jewish families that had been rounded up. These were victims destined for Drancy, a northeast suburb of Paris, which served as an antechamber to Auschwitz. The ultimate objective was to seize the 28,000 Jews in the greater Paris area, a task to be carried out by nine thousand French police. Only half the objective was achieved on this roundup - 12,884 Jews, a disappointment from the German point of view. The victims, it appears, remained stunned and incredulous to the very end. But, according to one source, there were more than a hundred suicides during the roundup and in subsequent days.'

John Cornwell, *Hitler's Pope: The Secret History of Pius XII,* pp. 285-286.

LÉON BÉRARD

Léon Bérard was one of Vichy France's ambassadors to the Holy See. In the autumn of 1941, Marshal Pétain, head of the Vichy government in France, wrote to Bérard. Pétain was concerned about possible negative reactions of the Vatican to the anti-Jewish legislation enacted by the Vichy government. He wanted Bérard to find out in Rome what the Vatican's reaction might be. In response to Pétain's request, M. Bérard prepared a long report about the Vatican's views concerning the persecution of the Jews. This report became a frame of reference for Vichy officials, particularly for Pétain and his Prime Minister, Pierre Laval.

> 'In his report M. Bérard points out that he had heard of no misgivings on the part of Vatican officials to acts of persecution and harassment against Jews on the part of Vichy France. He maintained that the Vatican was not interested in the anti-Jewish laws.'

In his report M. Bérard points out that he had heard of no misgivings on the part of Vatican officials to acts of persecution and harassment against Jews on the part of Vichy France. He maintained that the Vatican was not interested in the anti-Jewish laws. According to church teaching, argued Bérard in his letter, there was a fundamental conflict between racism and Church doctrine. Nevertheless, religion was not the only distinguishing characteristic of Jews; there were also some ethnic, not racial, factors that set them apart. There was, therefore, every reason 'to limit their activity in society and . . . restrict their influence . . . It is legitimate to deny them access to public offices . . .'

The report maintained that the only objections to the French anti-Jewish legislation regarded the inclusion of converted Jews and the attempt to limit mixed marriages. In addition, the laws should be applied with regard for 'law and justice'.

Bérard stated that his report was based on consultations with Vatican officials. His letter became a key factor in Pétain and Laval's conduct towards the Jews. It stood in contrast to the different opinion voiced by Msgr. Valerio Valeri, Papal Nuncio in France. Valeri tried to help Jews, particularly baptized Jews. He argued openly with Pétain about the contents of Bérard's letter.

Looking at this story now it is quite clear that Bérard did consult with some senior officials in the Vatican when he prepared his letter. It was meant to ease Pétain's worry about repercussions by the Vatican to his anti-Jewish policy. It served this purpose well.

'Msgr. Valerio Valeri, Papal Nuncio in France, was 'an opponent of the Statut des juifs . . .' When Valeri suggested that the Marshal [Pétain] must have misunderstood the intentions of the Holy See, Pétain replied good-humoredly that it was the Nuncio who was out of line. Pétain offered to show Valeri the text of the letter. Valeri took him up on the offer. Writing to the papal secretary of state, Cardinal Maglione, Valeri protested that the antisemitic laws contained 'grave indiscretions [inconvenienti]' from the religious viewpoint. He wondered openly who had given Bérard his information. Maglione thought the matter worth pursuing and looked into it. Bérard's sources, it turned out, were highly placed within the secretariat of state and included monsignors Tardini and Montini (the future Pope Paul I).'

Michael R. Marrus and Robert O. Paxton, *Vichy France and the Jews.* p. 202.

FRENCH PROTESTANT CHURCHES AND THE PERSECUTION OF THE JEWS IN FRANCE

Michael R. Marrus

Generally speaking, French Protestantism was more sensitive to the predicament of the Jewish minority in France than the Catholic majority. Numbering about 600,000 on the eve of the war, Protestants were divided into several confessional groups, gathered under the umbrella of the *Fédération Protestante de France*. Themselves a minority, Protestants had a long history of being outside the religious mainstream and carried a historical memory of fierce persecution during the Sixteenth and Seventeenth Centuries. Further, they often had Jewish or German-sounding names, and of course were normally unable to produce baptismal certificates, useful in proving that the bearer was not Jewish. Ever since the advent of the Vichy regime, as pressure mounted against Jews and Freemasons, Protestants harbored fears of 'a new clericalism,' of which they too might become victims. In the summer of 1941 Pastor Marc Boegner, president of the *Fédération Protestante*, heard widespread rumors that Protestants were next on Vichy's list of enemies.

Along with a handful of other Protestants, Marc Boegner was among the first to protest Vichy's anti-Jewish legislation. Of Alsatian background, and profoundly patriotic, Boegner was widely respected at Vichy as a figure of international standing. His words could not be ignored. Under instructions from the *Eglise réformée de France*, of which he was also the head, he expressed his objectives in two letters, sent in March 1941, one to the head of government Admiral François Darlan (himself of Protestant origins) and the other to Isaïe Schwartz, then Chief Rabbi of France. The latter was made public, appearing in the antisemitic newspaper *Au Pilori* in Paris, and widely distributed in the unoccupied zone.

Boegner couched his appeal in polite terms, and in deference to official doctrine on the 'Jewish Problem', he made an unsubstantiated reference to the 'hasty and unjustified naturalizations' of the 1930s. (Such references were common at the time, reflecting a sincerely held but erroneous belief about the magnitude of Jewish immigration into France in the decade before the war, and also, perhaps, expressed a desire to make the most credible appeal to the Vichy Government.) But the thrust of his statement was a dignified and open challenge to the injustices of the anti-Jewish

'The people of Le Chambon-sur-Lignon not only resisted the Nazis, they resisted the policies of their own country, Vichy France. While there is no single explanation for their actions – perhaps we should leave that to future social scientists – the most important fact for us to know is that they were brought up to understand all the idioms of the language of love. When their hearts spoke to them, they first listened, then they acted.'

Pierre Sauvage in Rittner and Myers, eds., *The Courage to Care*, p. 99.

legislation. He told the Chief Rabbi: 'Our Church, which has known suffering and persecution in the past, has an ardent sympathy for your communities which have seen their freedom of worship compromised in certain places and the members of which have been so abruptly struck by misfortune. We have undertaken and we will continue to pursue our efforts to bring about the necessary changes in the [anti-Jewish] law.'

Like many at the time, Boegner assumed incorrectly that Vichy had acted under Nazi pressure. Consequently, he may have been optimistic for a change in policy, if only Vichy would show more independence.

If such were the Protestant leader's hopes, they were dashed in the months which followed. In May, Darlan told Boegner that his sole concern was protecting the Jews who had been in France for several generations, *'des Français Israélites'*, as they were generally known, to distinguish them from the unassimilated *'Juifs'*. 'As for the others,' Boegner reported Darlan's views, 'he only wants to see them leave.' Interventions became more numerous after the June 1941 anti-Jewish law and the beginning of the aryanization of Jewish property in the unoccupied zone. Boegner wrote to the Vichy head of state, Marshal Philippe Pétain, at the end of August, and apparently mobilized Cardinal Gerlier to make some representation on behalf of Catholic opinion. Simultaneously, a dramatic and forceful appeal came from an associate of Boegner, René Gillouin, the son of a Protestant pastor and an authentic traditionalist who was in close and frequent contact with Pétain.

In these and other expressions of protest from the Protestant camp, beyond the points we have mentioned, was a sense of common biblical heritage which Protestants shared with Jews – a link to the Old Testament and to Jesus himself. In his letter to the Chief Rabbi of March 1941 Boegner affirmed this tie, echoing sentiments in the Protestant underground press. This also emerged during an important meeting of sixteen Protestant leaders at Pomeyrol, near Tarascon in the Bouches-du-Rhône, in September 1941. The Pomeyrol group had profound religious objections to antisemitism:

'Founded on the Bible, the Church recognizes in Israel the people that God elected to give a savior to the world, and that is to be, amidst the nations, a permanent witness to the mystery of its fidelity. That is why, while recognizing that the state finds itself faced with a problem which it has to solve, it raises a solemn protest against any law placing Jews outside the human community.'

Such themes were not universally accepted by Protestants, of course. Like the Catholic Church, Protestants were divided. Notably, the conservative and Calvinist Independent Reformed Evangelical Church was far more respectful of Vichy and more favorable to the anti-Jewish laws than the Protestant mainstream. There was even a group of royalist and nationalist Protestants, led by Pastor Noël Noguet, who objected to the Pomeyrol statement on the grounds that Israel would benefit from the punishment inflicted upon it. But generally speaking such dissent was extremely limited and Boegner

'In March 1942, Pastor Boegner had written to the Chief Rabbi of France about the laws specifying that 'access and exercise of public functions . . . are prohibited to Jews' and that 'foreign immigrants of the Jewish race may be interned in special camps'. His letter offers a clue to the attitude of the French Protestants and their willingness to broach burning issues: 'Our church, which has suffered persecution in the past, feels an ardent sympathy for your communities where in certain places the freedom of worship is already compromised and where the faithful have been so abruptly thrown into affliction.' Boegner's letter did not receive unanimous approval; sadly there were Christians who found theological justification for antisemitism, some going so far as to affirm that the punishment of the Jews was part of God's plan.'

André Jacques, *Madeleine Barot*, p.33.

spoke for most Protestant groups. Uneasiness about the anti-Jewish legislation was both deep and genuine among various Protestant communities.

Persecution of Jews in France reached a new intensity in mid-1942. First came the imposition of the Yellow Star in the occupied zone – decreed at the end of May by German forces for all Jews over the age of six. Following quickly upon this decree came a series of Nazi ordinances excluding Jews from public life north of the demarcation line. Within days, the deportation trains carrying them to Auschwitz began to roll. In the year 1942 over 42,000 Jews were deported; several thousand of them came from unoccupied France, rounded up in the massive manhunts conducted by French police and various French auxiliary forces.

French propaganda poster with the photo of Marshal Pétain
'You are not sold, betrayed or abandoned. Have confidence. Come with me!'

Apart from the interventions of Boegner and some Protestant associations, Church opposition to the persecution of the Jews in France before the beginning of the deportations had been rather limited or muted. Direct and specifically Christian attacks on antisemitism fell to individuals or to small groups. However, for the first time in the course of the occupation, the deportation caused a substantial number of churchmen to denounce the persecution of the Jews. Along with important Catholic voices of protest, the Protestants added a public message – an eloquent statement by Pastor Boegner, circulated to almost all Protestant pulpits on September 22, 1942 to be read a few days later. *'The Eglise réformée de France,'* it said, 'cannot remain silent in the face of the suffering of thousands of human beings who have found asylum on our soil . . . Divine law cannot accept that families willed by God can be broken, children be separated from their mothers, the right of exile and compassion be unrecognized, respect for the human person be violated, and helpless individuals be surrendered to a tragic fate [*livrés à un destin tragique*] . . . The Gospel obliges us to consider all men without exception as brothers for whom the Savior died on the cross. How can the Church ever forget that it was from that people from whom the Jews are descended that came in the flesh the Savior of the world?'

Throughout the Vichy period, some churchmen were active in France at all levels, providing practical aid for the Jews escaping persecution. Hundreds of Jewish children were hidden, thanks to the work of Protestant and Catholic religious institutions. Rescue activity began even before the turning point in the summer of 1942, but vastly expanded thereafter, when Jews were literally being hunted down and were often in desperate need of false papers, aid and shelter. Such work was usually clandestine, often dangerous, and conducted frequently in relatively isolated areas.

Protestants who had been members of pre-war youth movements were prominent among those

For Reflection

Just how important, how determinant of the active empathy that developed between French Protestants and the Jews was the sense of being a member of a minority?

What qualifies as resistance? Do conventional male values limit our perspective on resistance during the Holocaust?

What sort of leadership is needed to encourage the dynamics of collective resistance, as in Le Chambon during World War II and the Holocaust?

who provided assistance to the Jews. Vital relief and later resistance efforts were organized by CIMADE *(Commission Inter-Movements auprès des Evacués)*, a relief organization originally established to assist internees in 1939, led by Madeleine Barot and Pastor François Delpech. In heavily Protestant areas, such as the isolated communes of the Haute Loire, the Hautes Alpes or the Tarn, Jews found shelter and sometimes assistance in leaving the country. Le Chambon-sur-Lignon (in the Haute Loire) is perhaps the most famous of these Protestant villages, virtually an entire commune that mobilized for rescue. Frequently cut off by snowdrifts during the winter, this almost homogeneously Protestant enclave helped thousands of refugees who passed through it. Jews there received the solid support of the local population, as well as the Cévenole school, headed by two nonviolent Protestant pastors, André Pacal Trocmé and Edouard Theis.

Looking back, one is impressed by the diversity of response among French Protestants and other churchmen, whose reactions to the persecution of Jews extended from the support given to Vichy's anti-Jewish laws by Protestant enthusiasts in 1940, to the wholehearted plunge into rescue activity by Protestant youth groups who provided Jews with false identity papers or smuggled them across the Spanish frontier. There was no single 'Protestant' reaction, just as there was no single reaction from French society. That there was significant Protestant aid extended to Jews, that there was a sense of human brotherhood, and that there was a kinship between some Protestants and Jews is obvious from the many instances of practical help and occasional heroism to which many survivors of the Holocaust in France can testify.

> '. . . the armed resistance produced heroes like General de Gaulle himself, and the passionately beloved coordinator of the French Resistance, Jean Moulin.
> There are no such nationally known names in the story of Le Chambon. When France was liberated, there were no triumphal marches for André Trocmé and his villagers through the streets of Paris or Marseilles. And this was as it should have been: they had not contributed directly to saving the life of the French nation. They were not so much French patriots as they were conscientious human beings.'
>
> Philip P. Hallie, *Lest Innocent Blood Be Shed*, p. 10.

For Further Reading

Emile C. Fabre. *God's Underground: CIMADE 1939-1945*. St. Louis, MO: The Bethany Press, 1970.

Stephen Hawes and Ralph White, eds. *Resistance in Europe: 1933-1945*. Baltimore: Penguin Books, 1976.

André Jacques, *Madeleine Barot*. Geneva: WCC Publications, 1991.

Michael R. Marrus. *The Holocaust in History*. New York: New American Library, 1987.

Michael R. Marrus and Robert O. Paxton. *Vichy France and the Jews*. New York: Basic Books, 1981.

Michael R. Marrus (Canada), Dean of Graduate Studies at the University of Toronto, is a Fellow of the Royal Society of Canada and a Fellow of the Royal Historical Society. He is the author of many essays and books, including *The Holocaust in History; The Unwanted: European Refugees in the Twentieth Century* and, with Robert O. Paxton, *Vichy France and the Jews*.

JULES-GÉRARD SALIÈGE

Jules-Gérard Saliège was the Archbishop of Toulouse. During the war he was already old and frail, but still a man of great popularity and authority. He stood out against Vichy from the start. In fact, he first voiced concern about Nazism in 1937, when Pope Pius XI published his pastoral letter, *With Burning Concern*, which dealt with anti-Christian aspects of Nazism. Saliège expressed his own concerns in line with the Pope's letter in his sermons and writings.

Archbishop Jules-Gérard Saliège

After France was defeated in 1940 he publicly denounced racism. In 1941 he was a leading voice against the anti-Jewish laws proclaimed by the French collaborationist Vichy Government. In this, Saliège stood in stark contrast to the attitude represented by Léon Bérard's letter, condoning anti-Jewish measures. In 1942, when the deportation of French Jews started, Saliège published a pastoral letter of his own, denouncing the deportations:

'That children, that women, fathers and mothers should be treated like animals, that family members should be separated and sent off to an unknown destination, it has been reserved for our own time to see such a sad spectacle. Why does the right of sanctuary no longer exist in our churches? Why are we defeated? . . . The Jews are real men and women. Foreigners are real men and women. They cannot be abused without limit. . . . They are part of the human race. They are our brothers like so many others. A Christian cannot forget it.'

Susan Zuccotti reports in her book, *The Holocaust, the French and the Jews* that when officials heard about Saliège's letter, they tried frantically to head it off. Saliège refused to withdraw it, so officials prohibited its public reading. 'Most priests, ignoring orders from local mayors, obeyed their archbishop. In parishes where the letter was not mentioned on August 23, it was read on August 30.' Four other French bishops in the unoccupied zone of France followed Saliège's example and issued pastorals.

'The Jews are real men and women. Foreigners are real men and women. They cannot be abused without limit . . . They are part of the human race. They are our brothers like so many others. A Christian cannot forget it.'

Archbishop Jules-Gérard Saliège

After the publication of his pastoral letter Saliège became one of the leaders of the efforts to stop the deportation of the Jews. His opposition to the deportations and to the persecution of the Jews brought about a change in French public opinion. As a result of this change, more Jews could now find hiding places with the French population. Vichy officials asked the Papal Nuncio to send Archbishop Saliège on a retreat with the hope that his influence on French Catholics and on French public opinion would diminish.

Jews being deported from France.

THE DUTCH PROTESTANTS, THE THIRD REICH AND THE PERSECUTION OF THE JEWS

Ger van Roon

The question of the significance of historic events may only be examined satisfactorily if the events are not isolated but viewed in their historic context, as a link in a chain. In this regard, during the years of Nazi occupation there were two opposing concepts: (a) one should regard the measures taken by the German occupiers, their step-by-step methods, as an isolated case; (b) one should regard the occupation in the light of what had happened in Germany in the years 1933-1940 and of National-Socialist ideology. Yet to obtain a clearer overall picture of the attitudes of the Dutch Protestants towards the German occupation and its policies, it is likewise necessary to delineate various phases.

Although one can observe initial reactions of opposition and resistance, the period from May 1940 to the end of the first six months of 1941 was largely dominated by 'neo-neutralism'. For many, the war seemed to have ended after the capitulation. There was much speculation about the rights and duties of the occupying power. This was expressed in a rather abstract and legalistic fashion. The Franco-German War was mentioned in this context and the provisions of the Land War Regulations prior to the First World War were cited, as if they could offer guarantees for an occupied country in a period of 'total' war. People were lulled to sleep again by friendly comments of the *Frankfurter Zeitung*.

> *'We have no illusions. We are fully aware that we cannot expect that your excellency will listen to the voice of the Church . . . but what we cannot humanly expect, we may hope for in our Christian faith. God Almighty has the power to change Your Excellency's heart . . .'*
>
> Joint appeal by the Dutch Churches to the German Commissioner, May 1943, regarding the plans to sterilize Jews living in mixed marriages.

> *'I felt it was my duty. That's the way I was brought up. When someone is in need, you help them. . . . It was a Christian act done in Christian love. We felt it was our duty because they were God's people.'*
>
> Henrietta Wiechertjes-Hartemink, Netherlands

The fact that the Dutch Government was in London and the war had not actually ended was scarcely ever mentioned openly during this phase. In consonance with the prevailing tendency of this period, clergymen omitted the intercession for the Queen and had to be expressly reminded of it. Some older politicians and Church leaders who had a vivid memory of the First World War, had already taken steps even before the start of the *Westfeldzug* to avoid, to every possible extent, conflicts with the future occupier. To this end, economic ties with Germany were strengthened in the hope of thus reducing political opposition. But organizational measures were also taken. Preparations were made in the Protestant Church sector for the establishment of a small inter-church executive body, the *Convent van Kerken*, to which the conservative churches of the 'Reformed' trend were admitted and represented by individuals personally invited. Because radical enunciations by the Dutch ecumenical authorities were feared, it was held that they had to be 'overruled' through the establishment of the new inter-church executive body. The 'Convent's' method was somewhat obliquely described by Slotemaker as acting 'in uniformity with the authorities and, if possible, centrally.' Whereas the German occupiers were understood to be the 'authorities', Slotemaker's emphasis on the 'central' function followed a directive issued by a high official church body in The Hague, the Board of Secretary-Generals. The fact that during the course of 1941 the attitude of the 'Convent' gradually began to change was a consequence of the fact that two members who held a minority viewpoint began to be more active and that the measures taken by the Germans made it increasingly difficult to continue pursuance of the 'neo-neutralist' line. Further, as a result of protests within the various churches, other delegates were eventually sent to the 'Convent', which in turn helped bring about a change in the 'Convent's' policy.

Jews awaiting deportation from Amsterdam

The Dutch Reformed Church was the first Protestant Church that in the 'May Days' addressed a message of resistance to its members. Although the true situation and actual problems were handled rather curiously, a Protestant Church began once again to speak and bear witness. And it occurred more than just this once.

A predominantly Reformed resistance group in the first phase was the so-called *Lunterse Kring*, some forty clergymen and members of various Protestant Churches who in August 1940 first convened in Lunteren. The purpose of the meeting was threefold: information on the *Kirchenkampf* (Church Struggle) in Germany and how it affected the general situation; discussions on current affairs; and the setting up of an underground organization to provide better information to members of the Churches and in this way reach as many people as possible. The *Lunterse Kring* demonstrated a clear continuity with experiences and activities from the late thirties. For example, the *Amersfoortse Sellingen* was strongly impressed by the *Kirchenkampf* in Germany from Dutch contact with Germans in the Confessing Church. The German experience indicated to them what might happen to their Church under National Socialism. The *Lunterse Kring* was an early example of national action from the lower ranks of Dutch Protestant circles, directed against synodal authorities reacting too slowly to the new situation.

The years 1941-1942 may be regarded as a second phase in the Dutch Churches' reaction toward the German occupation. Initially the Germans respected the Churches and only took action against a number of so-called 'political' individuals. The German offer to grant exceptional status to Christian Jews, too readily accepted by the Churches, typifies this initial period of the occupation. Clearly, the occupiers wanted to win over the Dutch population to National Socialism. Soon, however the process of Nazification would commence, a process which would also affect the Churches profoundly. Increasingly the Churches would be required to collect funds for the *Winterhilfe*, the Church press would be subjected to Nazi influence, persons of Jewish origin would be expelled from Protestant schools, religious radio programs would be censored, church proclamations and church services would be supervised by the Nazis. The Churches' influence was steadily reduced to the area of 'personal spiritual care'. This induced an increase in the number of conflicts between the Churches and the occupation authorities, and the Churches were thus faced with the dilemma: to concede or refuse.

National cooperation was sought with the Roman Catholic Church to acquire a stronger position through joint action. On February 17, 1942 a three-man delegation of Dutch Protestants and Catholics protested to *Reichskommissar* Seyss-Inquart against the violation of three fundamental principles: justice, humanity and freedom of conscience. The protest was followed by a pulpit proclamation in April 1942 in most churches, in which National Socialism as a principle and as a system was openly rejected.

During a third phase in the reaction pattern, from early 1943 to mid-1944, resistance to the occupation intensified. As a consequence, in May 1943 the authorities called up all Dutch servicemen and placed them in camps in Germany. Simultaneously, thousands of students were transported to Germany. The Dutch retaliated with a nationwide strike. A few months previously, in February 1943, the Churches had protested once more to the *Reichskommissar*, this time against the terrifying consequences of the National-Socialist system including the persecution of Jews, *Arbeitsdienst* (work service), execution of captives and mass arrests.

During the fourth and last phase (September 1944 to May 1945), with defeat imminent, the occupation authorities resorted to deeds of desperation. In a final protest to Seyss-Inquart in November 1944, the Churches reminded him of God's justice and warned that the crimes of the occupying regime had caused so much hatred that an enormous gap had been created between the occupied and suppressed people and the occupiers.

For Reflection

During the Nazi occupation in the Netherlands, there were many courageous rescue attempts and extreme expressions of solidarity as well as indifference, numerous cases of denunciation and collaboration. What is the significance of such a duality in Dutch society?

What made people decide to join one side or the other?

A relatively small part of Dutch Jewry was saved: around 105,000 out of 130,000 Jews in the Netherlands in 1940 were deported to the death camps. In this reality, what is the significance of choosing the Jewish saying 'Whoever saves a single life, saves an entire universe' to be inscribed on the medal awarded by Yad Vashem to those who rescued Jews?

For Further Reading

G. Jan Colijn and Marcia S Littell. *The Netherlands and Nazi genocide,* New York: The Edwin Mellen Press, 1992.

Louis de Jong. *The Netherlands and Nazi Germany.,* Cambridge, MA: Harvard Press, 1990.

Louis de Jong. *The Destruction of Dutch Jewry.* Amsterdam: 1965.

Jacques Presser. *Ashes in the Wind: The Destruction of Dutch Jewry,* London: 1968.

Corrie ten Boom. *The Hiding Place,* New York: Bantam, 1971.

Ger van Roon is professor of Modern History at the Free University, Amsterdam, where he also coordinates The Research Group Long Term Fluctuations. He is a fellow of the Royal Historical Society, London.

'Thou shalt pursue light even in the darkness, for light remains light.'

From 'The Dutch Ten Commandments to Foil the Nazis', which were distributed throughout the Netherlands

After the beginning of the occupation of the Netherlands, the German authorities, under orders from Berlin, promptly sought to isolate the Jews. The dispatch with which the measures were carried out surprised most people. Protests against these measures came earlier from Protestants than from Catholics and rather from pastors, priests and laity than from bishops and Church leaders. The *Lunteren* Group was distressed by the measures against the Jews and the lack of protests on the part of the Churches. They warned against the antisemitic propaganda of the occupiers and their Dutch allies. When new civil servants had to declare their Aryan or non-Aryan descent, one of the higher civil servants, De Graaf, protested. He resigned, but before leaving, in a meeting with colleagues from his department, he warned of the consequences of complying with this measure. In a leaflet of the *Lunteren* Group his words became known to the entire country. His behavior, however, was an exception.

One month after the workers' strike in February 1941, seven Protestant Churches made an official protest. They declared that they could not comply with the anti-Jewish measures, and decried the injustices of antisemitic actions and terror. When the deportations of Dutch Jewry started, all Dutch Churches demanded, in a telegram of July 11, 1942 the rescission of this measure. A pastoral letter followed on July 26. Seyss-Inquart tried to neutralize the objections, and promised that Christian Jews would not be deported. The Church leaders, who returned herewith to a strategy of self-defense, accepted this. Here we are at the limits of Church protest in the Netherlands.

Throughout these years, however, pastors, priests and laity went further than their leaders. Thousands of Jews were hidden in different parts of the country. This spontaneous aid by pastors, priests and laity stands in sharp contrast to the diplomatic and tactical behavior of most of the Church leaders. The reactions of the Churches in the Netherlands against the persecution of more than 100,000 Jews reveals the weak sides of a Christianity divided among many denominations. Though the protests of the Churches in the Netherlands were an early and ecumenical example of Church action against anti-Jewish measures, these protest exceeded only for a short time the general line of self-defense and were, to say the least, most insufficient.

Excerpted from Kulka, Otto Dov & Mendes-Flohr, Paul R., eds. *Judaism and Christianity Under the Impact of National Socialism.* The Historical Society of Israel and the Zalman Shazar Center for Jewish History, Jerusalem 1987. With Permission.

DENMARK AND THE HOLOCAUST

Carol Rittner

The story of the Danish Jews is *sui generis*, and the behavior of the Danish people unique among all the countries of Europe – occupied, allied with the Axis, or neutral. Denmark was a country where the Holocaust failed. Why? According to sociologist Helen Fein in *Accounting for Genocide*, two factors accounted for the higher or lower degree of victimization of Jews during the Holocaust: 1) the pre-World War II level of antisemitism in each of the occupied countries, and 2) the pattern of relationships between Jewish and non-Jewish communities in those countries.

Jews in Denmark

Jews had lived in Denmark since the 17th Century. When they first arrived in 1622, Jews were allowed to live only in certain towns, but by 1814 they were granted full Danish citizenship. When Denmark abolished its absolute monarchy in 1849 and adopted its free Constitution, Jews received full political equality, with access to the university, to commercial opportunity, and to social status. They were accepted and respected as full partners in the new democracy, but even with such an enlightened attitude, and with a tradition of religious tolerance, Denmark wasn't completely free of antisemitism.

The Invasion and Occupation of Denmark

When Nazi Germany invaded Denmark on April 9, 1940, the Royal Danish Army put up scant resistance. The Royal Navy surrendered without firing a shot. In the beginning, whatever negative attitudes the Danes had about the Germans were expressed through passive resistance, or giving them the 'cold shoulder,' rather than by open defiance, armed resistance, or sabotage. The Danes were given a degree of autonomy unheard of in any other German occupied country in Europe.

Throughout the occupation, the Danish Government insisted there was no 'Jewish problem' in Denmark. They were like all the other citizens of Denmark and would be treated no differently. In practice, this meant that Jews were not forced to wear the yellow Star of David, were not segregated or isolated and were not barred from restaurants, public places, schools, cinemas, or theaters. Their property was not confiscated, and they were never dismissed from their jobs. Their movement was

'Why did the Danes side with and shelter Jews, at great risk to themselves, when most of Europe did not? We met with some of them, heroes and heroines now in their seventies and eighties, and asked them why they behaved so nobly. And every time, the reaction was the same . . . Wouldn't you have helped your neighbors if they had been in trouble?'

Robert McAfee Brown, '*They Could Do No Other*' in *The Courage to Care: Rescuers of Jews During the Holocaust*, p. 143.

not restricted, by day or night. Jewish communal activities remained undisturbed despite the presence of German troops. Still, democratic Denmark had been defeated and occupied by a foreign country. Danes began to ask themselves whether or not as a conquered people they could maintain a democratic way of life. Can confidence, identity, and unity be restored when national pride is shaken to its core?

The Public Significance of Ideas

It was not the first time Danes had been confronted by such challenges. In 1864, after being defeated by the Prussians, Denmark was swept by a profound malaise. It was Nikolai F. S. Grundtvig (1782-1873), a remarkably talented and versatile poet, educator, historian, theologian and Christian humanist, who reinvigorated the Danish spirit of democracy and humanity. Grundtvig was a man of deep biblical faith, with a high level of tolerance and respect for other cultures and religious traditions of the world. His spirit was ecumenical. In all that he did and wrote, he emphasized the biblical doctrine of creation: 'First a human being, then a Christian: this alone is life's order.' People, he said, 'are bound to one another with ties more profound than any of the barriers of human history, including the history of religion, may have constructed. Through the Danish folk high schools, which he founded for young people, his ecumenical spirit caught on among 'ordinary' people in Denmark. In the Twentieth Century, during the German occupation when the Danes again needed help in restoring their national, Grundtvig's ideas proved their enduring significance.

Hal Koch (1904-1963), a theologian and professor of church history at the University of Copenhagen, recognized that fascism and Nazism were dangers to democracy. After the April 1940 invasion and occupation, Koch decided to give a series of lectures, open to the general public. He knew well that Denmark was privileged compared to other conquered countries. He had even supported the 'policy of negotiation,' but he was becoming more aware of the 'high price' Denmark paid for its relative autonomy under German occupation: 'We have said many a Yes and many a No which have not come from our hearts, and have taken on a fateful hypocrisy.'

Like Grundtvig before him, Koch found in the language of biblical morality the principles of civic virtue. These principles prompted certain questions: Am I my brother's/sister's keeper? Who is my neighbor? What are the boundaries of obligation? What is the connection between the actions of individuals and the common good? What is the relationship between how we Danes act and our self-understanding as citizens?

Examining the biblical tradition so familiar to Danes, Koch highlighted its public significance. He

For Reflection

Who is part of your universe of obligation today?

Why is public and religious leadership important in a time of national crisis?

After the war, journalists re-enact the escape of the Jews from Denmark to Sweden.

helped people to find, embedded in their biblical roots, universally accepted ideas. He illuminated and emphasized the self-understanding Danes held about themselves and about democratic values and ideals in their society.

From Apathy to Action

Between April 1940 and August 1943, Danish attitudes toward their German occupiers underwent significant transformation. German demands kept escalating until the Danes were no longer willing to compromise, to engage in the 'policy of negotiation,' to rely only on passive resistance and the 'cold shoulder' technique. By the Fall of 1942, the Danish resistance movement began to gain support. In the summer of 1943, sabotage activities, reprisals, strikes and street unrest across Denmark mounted to a high pitch. In addition, Danes were unhappy with the Germans because they were experiencing food shortages.

On August 28, 1943, SS *Obergruppenfuhrer* Dr. Werner Best informed the Danish Government that it was declaring a 'state of emergency.' Public gatherings of more than five persons were prohibited, as were strikes and financial support for strikers. An 8.30 p.m. curfew was imposed. Firearms and explosives were confiscated, press censorship was imposed, and Danish special tribunals for dealing with infringements of these prohibitions and regulations were to be established. Sabotage was to be punished by death.

At the end of September 1943, news of an impending German *Aktion* reached the Jews through Danish political leaders who were forewarned by Georg F. Duckwitz, the German legation's attaché for shipping affairs in Copenhagen. On the eve of *Rosh Hashanah*, Wednesday, September 29, 1943, Rabbi Marcus Melchior told his congregation that the Germans planned a mass roundup of Jews the next day, when the Nazis knew families would be gathered in their homes for the holiday. 'The situation,' Rabbi Melchior said, 'is very serious. We must take action immediately.'

As word spread, non-Jewish Danes 'spontaneously' began to do what they could to help. Friends and even strangers hid Jews in their homes and in hospitals, churches and convents in Copenhagen and up and down the east coast of Denmark. Every imaginable group protested German efforts to round up the Jews. Political parties issued statements; underground newspapers published articles. Virtually the entire country responded to German threats to harm the Jews, including the official State Church of Denmark, the Lutheran Church.

Ninety per cent of the Danish population belong to the Lutheran

Rabbi Marcus Melchior was responsible for conveying the impending threat of deportation to the Jews of Denmark at Jewish New Year, 1943

For Further Reading

Helen Fein. *Accounting for Genocide: National Responses and Jewish Victimization During the Holocaust.* Chicago: The University of Chicago Press, 1979.

Leo Goldberger, ed. *The Rescue of the Danish Jews: Moral Courage Under Stress.* New York: New York University Press, 1987.

Eric Silver. *The Book of the Just: The Unsung Heroes Who Rescued Jews from Hitler.* New York: Grove Press, 1992.

Johan M. Snoek. *The Grey Book.* New York: Humanities Press, 1970.

Leni Yahil. *The Rescue of Danish Jewry: Test of a Democracy.* Philadelphia: Jewish Publication Society, 1969.

Harold Flender. *Rescue in Denmark,* London: W.H.Allen, 1963

On board a vessel bound for Sweden.

Church. Between 1940 to 1943, the Danish Lutheran Church took decisive measures to combat anti-semitism and to include Jews within the bounds of the 'universe of concern'. When the crisis – the impending round-up of the Jews – came in September-October 1943, the Church was ready. The Bishop of Copenhagen, Dr. Hans Fuglsang-Damgaard (1890-1979) prepared a written statement which he signed on behalf of all the Danish Lutheran bishops. It was sent to the German occupation officials and was dispatched, via theological students, on Saturday, October 2, 1943 to all the churches in his diocese. On Sunday, October 3, the protest was read aloud in Lutheran churches throughout Denmark. The Danish Lutheran Church helped to rally the people and provided immeasurable amounts of assistance – from hiding people and Torah scrolls to gathering money, food, and other resources.

Almost the entire rescue operation was successful – nearly 8,000 Jews in Denmark were saved – but there were some failures. On the night of October 6, 1943, for example, some 80 Jews hiding in the attic of the Gilleleje Church, located in a fishing village north of Copenhagen, were betrayed, arrested and deported. While the tragedy at the Gilleleje Church was an exception to the 'spontaneous' help given to the Jews by the Danes, it is instructive to remember that even in Denmark, where the Holocaust failed, some people forgot that Jews were within the 'boundaries of obligation' we owe one another as fellow human beings.

Unlike so many in Nazi-occupied Europe, most Danes saw themselves as human beings linked to others through a shared humanity, not as individuals inhabiting a world divided into 'us' and 'them'. The Danes helped for a variety of reasons – because they were paid to do a job; because they hated the Germans; because they wanted to outwit the Germans; because they were determined to prevent the Nazis' genocidal policies from being implemented in Denmark. Whatever the reason, the civic and religious institutions played decisive roles in preparing the Danish population to respond. While we must not discount the role of the Danish Lutheran Church in this effort to help the Jews in Denmark during the Holocaust, the Danes probably responded, as Thomas Merton once wrote, not so much because they 'were Christians, as [because] they were human. How many others were even that?'

'Why did a course of action which worked so simply and so well in Denmark not occur to all so-called Christian nations of the West just as simply and just as spontaneously?'

Thomas Merton

Carol Rittner R.S.M. (USA), Distinguished Professor of Holocaust Studies at The Richard Stockton College of New Jersey, is the author or editor of numerous essays and books, including *Different Voices: Women During the Holocaust* and *Anne Frank in the World: Essays and Reflections.* Dr. Rittner is the co-editor of *The Holocaust and the Christian World.*

BULGARIA AND THE HOLOCAUST

Edward McGlynn Gaffney Jr.

In *The Book of Destruction* Professor Geoffrey Hartman wrote: 'The Holocaust threatens a secular as well as a religious gospel, faith in reason and progress, as well as Christianity . . . It challenges the credibility of redemptive thinking.' Redemptive thinking becomes believable in the face of the extraordinary witness of those who resisted the Final Solution, whether out of explicitly religious motivation or out of general humanitarian concerns.

Those who acted to save the lives of Jews during the *Shoah* were too few, but the rescuers surely deserve to be remembered as much as the perpetrators, lest moral victory be ceded to the Nazis. The loss of the life of each person who perished in the Holocaust is incalculable. For that very reason, the life of each person saved from the death camps is immeasurably good. As the *Talmud Sanhedrin* puts it, 'One who destroys a single life, it is as though he has destroyed the world; and one who saves a single life, it is as though he has saved the world.' In the case of Bulgaria, nearly 50,000 Jews – all Jews living within the pre-World War II borders of Bulgaria – were saved from being deported to the Nazi killing centers.

As in Germany, the plan to eliminate the Jews proceeded through stages in Bulgaria. In 1938, Bulgaria's powerful monarch, King Boris III, entered into a series of agreements with the Third Reich relating to trade, loans and armaments. More ominously, he secured the adoption of a Bulgarian racial purity law patterned on the infamous Nuremberg Laws of 1935. Known as the 'Law for the Protection of the Nation,' this pernicious legislation had the immediate effect of persecuting Jews, who were dismissed from their jobs, exiled from their homes, stripped of all civil liberties and in many instances forced into slave labor camps.

The debate on this legislation in the Parliament was not extensive, but those who objected deserve to be remembered. The Lawyers' Association objected to the proposed law on constitutional grounds. Leading intellectuals and writers signed petitions objecting on the ground that it betrayed the principles of Bulgarian national harmony. Monsignor Van Theelen sent to Queen Johanna a petition from the Jews of Ruse urging the blocking of the legislation. The principal Christian community in that country, the Holy Synod of the Bulgarian Orthodox Church, raised its voice against the legislation. All the bishops of the Church signed a joint letter condemning the discriminatory treatment of the Jewish minority as unjust and violent.

'I appeal to the state authorities not to enslave the freedom-loving, democratic and friendly Bulgarian spirit . . . to foreign indoctrination, influences, and orders . . .
I beg those who steer the ship of state to remove any policy of estrangement, division, and persecution.'

Metropolitan Stefan of Sofia

For Further Reading

Michael Bar-Zohar. *Beyond Hitler's Grasp: The Heroic Rescue of Bulgaria's Jews.* Holbrook, MA: Adams Media Corp, 1998.

Frederick B. Chary. *The Bulgarian Jews and the Final Solution.* Pittsburgh: University of Pittsburgh Press, 1970.

David Wyman, ed.. 'Bulgaria', in: *The World Reacts to the Holocaust.* Baltimore: Johns Hopkins Press, 1996.

Alexander Matkowski. The Destruction of Macedonian Jewry in 1943, *Yad Vashem Studies*, 3 1959.

Vicki Tamir. *Bulgaria and Her Jews: The History of a Dubious Symbiosis.* New York: Yeshiva University Press, 1979.

Vasileva, Nadejda Slavi. 'On the Catastrophe of the Thracian Jews: Recollection.' *Yad Vashem Studies*, 3 1959.

The opposition was unavailing. King Boris waited until after the Feast of the Epiphany and signed the anti-Jewish legislation into law on January 23, 1941. Perhaps the worst feature of the new law was its creation of a bureaucracy given plenary regulatory power over the Jews without any accountability even to the Parliament that conferred these sweeping powers upon the regulators. These bureaucrats, the Commissariat for Jewish Affairs, infiltrated Jewish life and prepared detailed lists of the names and addresses of Jews for the purpose of deporting them to Poland.

Bulgaria formally allied itself with the Axis powers in December 1941. On January 20, 1942, the Wannsee Conference set in motion the apparatus of the 'Final Solution'. A year later Adolf Eichmann sent his personal representative, Theodor Danneker, to Sofia to negotiate Bulgarian participation in the plan to annihilate all of Europe's Jews. Within a month he secured an agreement with the Bulgarian government to transport 20,000 Jews, all Jews from the two new territories Germany had placed under Bulgarian supervision – Macedonia and Thrace – as well as about 8,000 Jews within Bulgaria.

In March 1943, Bulgarian soldiers rounded up 11,343 Jews of Macedonia and Thrace, and deported them to Treblinka in Bulgarian boxcars, where all of them perished. When the secret plan to kill the Jews was exposed, Bulgarians rose up in protest. The former Attorney General, Dimitur Peshev, led a protest in Parliament, for which he was stripped of his position as Deputy Speaker. Again, lawyers, doctors, writers, and Communist activists were prominent in their opposition to the deportation order.

The response from Orthodox leaders was prompt and powerful. On his way to an Orthodox monastery on the evening of March 9, Metropolitan Stefan of Sofia saw a train full of Jews 'packed like sardines' into cattle cars in a manner that he said 'exceeded the notions of horror and the terms of inhumanity.' When he reached the monastery, he immediately sent a telegram to Boris, demanding that the King relieve their 'unbearable conditions' and demanding 'that they not be sent to Poland, that has a sinister ring even in the ears of babies.' On the day that Metropolitan Cyril of Plovdiv learned of the arrest of the Jews in his city, he also sent a telegram to King Boris stating that he was prepared to lie down on the railroad tracks in front of any train carrying Jews off to the death camps. The deportation order was postponed.

On April 2, the Synod of Bishops convened in an extraordinary session to address the government's policies towards the Jews. The Synod roundly condemned the policy of deportation, and took practical steps to implement its teaching, including the issuing of baptismal certificates to Jews desiring them as a safeguard against the deportation plan. The government tried to stop the church from holding mass 'baptisms'. Metropolitan Stefan refused to back down: 'I shall not obey such an order, and I shall order the Sofia churches to hold [the baptismal] services as usual.' When the Prime Minister, Bogdan Filov, branded Stefan as a 'troublemaker,' the Metropolitan accepted the term as the equivalent of King Ahab's scornful title for the prophet Elijah (1 Kings 18:17). The Bishop chose to read the insult as a compliment, a sign that he was doing the right thing.

The plans to kill the Jews were not cancelled in March; only postponed. The next raid on the Jews of Sofia began at dawn on May 24, a major national holiday in Bulgaria celebrating Saints Cyril and Methodius as the patrons of literature and learning. Metropolitan Stefan was on his way to preside at the public civic celebration when leaders of the Jewish community intercepted him and told him what was happening. As soon as he heard the news, he telephoned the Royal Palace to protest the deportation order, which he described as an 'absolutely unjustified persecution.' He told the head of the Royal Chancellery: 'The cries of injured Bulgarian citizens of Jewish origin rise up in protest against this injustice.' And he demanded that the King 'show wisdom and statesmanlike foresight in the defense of the rights of men to freedom and dignity.'

Stefan then walked to the public celebration. The King was absent, but in the presence of all the ministers of the government Stefan declared: 'This year our celebration is flawed by the persecution undertaken against the Jews. . . I appeal to the state authorities not to enslave the freedom-loving, democratic and friendly Bulgarian spirit. . . to foreign indoctrination, influences, and orders. . . In this holiday of our great teachers [Cyril and Methodius] I beg those who steer the ship of state, to remove any policy of estrangement, division, and persecution.'

Prime Minister Filov warned Stefan to stop interfering with the 'State necessity' of the government's treatment of the Jews. Stefan then wrote a long letter to the King, demanding that he cancel the deportation order immediately: 'By this act, Your Majesty, you would remove the suspicion that Bulgaria is a prisoner of Hitler's anti-Jewish policy.' Filov threatened to arrest the Metropolitan for 'anti-State activity.' Unimpressed with the threat, Stefan fired off another protest to the King. All the bishops of the Holy Synod confirmed the rightness of Stefan's actions in a joint statement read at all Orthodox churches throughout the country on the following Sunday.

These actions of courageous church leaders, joined with the vigorous protest of intellectuals and of leaders of the legal and medical professions, led the King ultimately to cancel the deportation order. Nearly 50,000 Bulgarian Jews were saved from Treblinka. Their descendants – most of them Israelis – now number nearly half a million souls.

For Reflection

May human life be sacrificed in a compromise made in the name of nationalism or ethnicity?

Is a person less worthy of protection if he or she is not of the same faith as me?

What responsibility do we have to help other human beings when they are in danger?

Edward McGlynn Gaffney is Professor of Law at Valparaiso University School of Law, where he teaches Constitutional Law and a seminar on religious freedom. He is the Book Review Editor of the *Journal of Law and Religion*, and a frequent contributor to *Commonwealth* magazine. For decades he has been involved in inter-religious dialogue between Christians and Jews. He is currently engaged in a project to produce a documentary film on the rescue of the Bulgarian Jews.

THE CHURCHES AND THE DEPORTATION AND PERSECUTION OF JEWS IN SLOVAKIA

Livia Rothkirchen

The Slovak People's Party, founded before World War I by the Catholic priest Father Andre Hlinka, became a significant political vehicle in the Slovak struggle for national identity. It was actually during the period of the Czechoslovak Republic (1918-1938) that that the Catholic clergy began to play an important role on the parliamentary and social scene. Dr. (Msgr.) Josef Tiso, a priest, became the leader of the Hlinka party in 1938 and then the first Prime Minister and President of newly independent Slovakia. The Slovak State, proclaimed in March 1939 'in the name of God and from the will of the Slovak nation', adopted a National Socialist program and, in fact, became a satellite of Nazi Germany. The paradox of the National Socialist state, which boasted being Christian as well, seemed contradictory and as such was viewed critically by the Holy See. Although the revival of Church life and the growing prestige of Catholicism were appreciated by the Vatican, the involvement of the hierarchy in state affairs 'when a war is raging' was opposed by Pope Pius XII himself and criticized by certain cardinals.

From the first months of Slovak independence, anti-Jewish legislation imposed a number of restrictions on Jews witrh the intention of ousting them from economic life. The Jewish Codex, promulgated on September 9, 1941, containing 270 articles, was drafted largely upon the German model. Both the Catholic and Protestant churches reacted in letters of protest against the Jewish Codex; however, their sole concern was baptized Jews. The Vatican Secretary of State, Cardinal Luigi Maglione, expressed the grievance of the Holy See in a note of November 14, 1941, re-emphasizing the fact that a pronouncedly Catholic state was about to initiate legislation based on the principle of race which contradicted the principles of the Catholic religion.

While the *Wehrmacht* made its victorious advance on the Eastern Front, assisted by Slovak troops, Tiso and his Prime Minister, Voytech Tuka, visited Hitler's headquarters in October 1941. During this meeting Tuka brought up the deportation of the Jews from Slovakia. Consequently, in February 1942 the Slovak government and the German Ambassador in Bratislava concluded the agreement for the first transports of young Jewish men and women aged 16 to 35. The Slovak

'Beginning in April 1942, people who had succeeded in escaping from the camps in Poland began to turn up in Slovakia bringing detailed information about what was taking place in Poland. Thus, it became clear beyond a doubt that deportation meant extermination, even though some of the deportees were still being held in labor camps in the Lublin area.'

Leni Yahil. *The Holocaust: The Fate of European Jewry.*

The hotel in Munich where Chamberlain signed the Munich agreement with the Nazi hierarchy. The signing of this agreement lead to the break up of the Czechoslovak Republic, and the founding of the Independent Slovakia.

government agreed to pay 500 *Reichsmarks* for every deported Jew. At the beginning of March, five assembly points were set up where deportees were being concentrated before their deportation. The first transport of 999 young women left from Poprad to Auschwitz on March 26, 1942. Thereafter, transports regularly left for Auschwitz and Lublin. From the beginning of April 1942, entire families were dispatched. About 60,000 Jews were deported until October 1942, when the deportations came to a standstill.

Slovak military personnel had witnessed massacres carried out by the *Einsatzgruppen* units in the Soviet territories. Wild rumors circulated about the fate of the stateless Jews who had been deported from the former Slovak areas annexed to Hungary and who had been massacred in Kamentetz Podolsk by the SS. While the public learned of the atrocities from hearsay and from occasional references of soldiers on leave, the higher echelons were briefed officially and in detail. The chaplain of the Slovak army informed Msgr. Giuseppe Burzio, the Apostolic delegate in Bratislava, as early as the late summer of 1941 about the mass killings. President Tiso was also briefed by one of his generals.

When rumors of the imminent deportations reached Msgr. Burzio, he informed the Vatican and protested to Prime Minister Tuka. He then reported to Rome that Tuka saw 'nothing inhumane or contrary to Christian principles' in the expulsion. The Jewish leadership launched appeals in the name of the Jewish communities and the Rabbis of Slovakia. The appeals were circulated amidst various religious and political leaders and a copy was sent to the Papal Nuncio in Budapest, Msgr. Angelo Rotta, who in turn forwarded it to the Vatican. The plea of the Rabbis, addressed to President Tiso, implored him to consider 'that in existing circumstances the deportations meant physical extermination'. The Jewish community and its leaders who had hopes of getting assistance from the Church were gravely disappointed by its indifference. Although both churches of Slovakia, the Protestant and the Catholic, sent letters of protest against the deportation, they were concerned only with obtaining privileges for baptized Jews.

While the majority of the Catholic hierarchy supported the Government's anti-Jewish policy, some

'Because of what I learned about Christianity in the Nazi era, I have sought, throughout my service to the church, to use the moral prerogatives of the ministry to remove barriers and to build bridges between religious traditions in the hope that the hatreds and ignorance of the past would not take root in the present.'

Douglas K. Huneke. *The Stones Will Cry Out: Pastoral Reflections on the Shoah.*

'We must believe in human beings, in spite of human beings.'

Elie Wiesel in *Hope Against Hope: Johann Baptist Metz and Elie Wiesel Speak Out on the Holocaust*, p. 63.

Chamberlain signs the Munich agreement. September 30, 1938.

For Further Reading

Raul Hilberg. *The Destruction of European Jews* (revised and definitive edition). 3 vols. London: Holmes & Meier, 1985.

Vojtech Mastny. *Czechs Under Nazi Rule: The Failure of National Resistance 1939-1942.* New York: 1971.

Yad Vashem Studies. Jerusalem: *Martyrs' and Heroes'* Remembrance Authority, 1957.

Yeshayahu Jelinek. *The Paris Republic: Hlinka's Slovak People's Party, 1939-1945,* New York: 1976

leading Slovak Church representatives nevertheless spoke out in strong terms. On April 20, 1942, the Vicar of Bratislava, Augustin Pozdech, addressed a moving appeal which reached the Vatican through the good offices of Msgr. Rotta, the Papal Nuncio in Budapest: 'I am distressed to the depth of my heart that human beings whose only fault is that they were born Jews should be robbed of all their possessions and should be banished, stripped of the last vestiges of their personal freedom, to a foreign country, and, moreover, as slaves . . . It is impossible that the world should passively watch small infants, mortally sick old people, young girls torn away from their families and young people deported like animals, transported in cattle wagons towards an unknown place of destination, towards an uncertain future.' Another appeal by Msgr. Jozef Carsky, Bishop of Presov, urged his colleagues to take decisive steps: 'If we remain passive while the daughters of the Jewish people are forcibly torn from their families, what shall we do when our own maidens will be taken away?' The Greek Catholic Bishop of Presov, Msgr. Pavol (Petro) Gojdic, beseeched the Vatican in his letter of May 1942 to induce Tiso, in the interests of the Church, to resign, and have a secular statesman take over his function and thus avert worse evil.

The majority of the Slovak population reacted to the persecution of the Jews with complete indifference. The Catholic priests in Slovakia had an immense influence on the mainly Catholic population whose religious beliefs were deeply rooted and connected with their everyday life. In addition to antisemitic traditions, the Church's unconcern was to a certain extent the outcome of Hlinka Party propaganda to the effect that if 'Judo-Bolshevism' conquered Germany, the Church and religion would be destroyed. Furthermore, the fact that the head of the State was a Catholic priest, acknowledged by the Holy See, gave *a priori* sanction to the Government and weakened any resistance of ecclesiastical authorities. President Tiso, preaching at a holiday mass, on August 15, at Holic, declared that it was a Christian deed to expel the Jews, since it was to the benefit of the Slovak nation to free itself of 'its pests'. On this occasion he also cited Hlinka's dictum that 'a Jew remains a Jew even if he is baptized by a hundred bishops'.

A few months after the deportations came to a standstill, Minister Mach, in a speech given in February 1943, alluded to the renewal of transports. The Jewish organizations launched a protest campaign. Their appeal was brought to the knowledge of the Papal Nuncio in Istanbul, Msgr. Angelo Roncalli (later Pope John XXIII). His energetic intervention with the Vatican, together with the steps taken by the Apostolic Delegate at Bratislava, bore fruit. The Holy See intervened in vigorous terms. Msgr. Burzio, at a meeting on April 7, 1943, remonstrated with Tuka on the fate of the Slovak Jews exterminated in Poland and Ukraine, warning him of the 'verdict of history and consequences of the post-war world'. Tuka replied that he was a practicing Catholic, that he had a clear conscience and the consent of his confessor. In addition to this demarche, the Vatican expressed its condemnation of the renewal of the deportations in a note of May 5, 1943.

A pastoral letter condemning totalitarianism and antisemitism was issued on March 8, 1943 by the Catholic episcopate. It was read in Latin from the pulpits, but many priests modified the original text. In reality, some official Slovak circles were inclined to keep the Jews concentrated within the State rather than to expel them from the country. One has, of course, to remember that the most vociferous protests against the deportation of Jews coincided with the period that followed the German debacle at Stalingrad and the political climate created in the country by the turn of the tide of the war. Heavy losses in fighting on the Eastern Front and the great number of Slovak soldiers defecting to the Soviets affected many Slovak families. With the approach of the Red Army towards the frontiers of the country, the Slovak underground movement called on the people to revolt. The suppression of the uprising sealed the fate of the remaining Jews. German troops together with Hlinka Guards organised roundups for Jews. Between October 1944 and March 1945, about 13,500 Jews were deported. The first five transports were directed to Auschwitz and the rest were dispatched to other concentration camps in Germany.

Msgr. Burzio visited President Tiso on October 6, 1944, and begged him to spare at least the lives of the Bratislava converts concentrated for deportation. Upon the instructions of the Pope, the Apostolic Delegate delivered a grave warning to Tiso, saying: 'the injustice wrought by his government is harmful to the prestige of his country and enemies will exploit it to discredit clergy and the Church the world over.' Tiso remained adamant, and Burzio reported to the Vatican: 'I couldn't see a shred of compassion or understanding for the persecuted'.

In the final analysis, Tiso had been reprimanded, curbed and warned by the Holy See. The fact that Slovakia was Catholic state, headed by a clergyman, made the Vatican more sensitive to its actions. Nevertheless, Dr. Tiso was not excommunicated. 'Vatican diplomacy . . . was content to limit itself to the narrow confines of strictly Catholic interests, and an opportunity for a great moral and humanitarian gesture was lost,' wrote Father John Morley in his book, *Vatican Diplomacy and the Jews during the Holocaust 1939-1945.*

For Reflection

Why did the Orthodox leaders in Bulgaria protect Jews while the churches of Slovakia sanctioned the killing?

What does it mean to 'simply remain human'?

'Vatican diplomacy . . . was content to limit itself to the narrow confines of strictly Catholic interests, and an opportunity for a great moral and humanitarian guesture was lost.'

John Morely, *Vatican Diplomacy and the Jews during the Holocaust, 1939 - 1945.*

Livia Rothkirchen (Israel) was the Editor of *Yad Vashem Studies*. She is the author of *The Destruction of Slovak Jewry*, and other studies on the Jews of Czechoslovakia and Hungary during the Holocaust.

THE CHRISTIAN CHURCHES AND THE PERSECUTION OF JEWS IN THE OCCUPIED TERRITORIES OF THE USSR

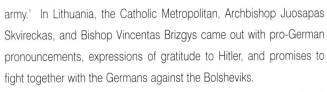

Yitzhak Arad

There were a number of Christian Churches active in the territories of the USSR occupied by Nazi Germany during World War II, despite the anti-religious campaign and policy of the Soviet Government. The Churches and the majority of the clergy in the occupied territories of the Soviet Union gladly received the invading Germans. The German troops who entered Lvov, the capital of western Ukraine, were welcomed by the head of the Uniate Church (an Eastern Rite Church which recognized the Vatican and the Pope), Metropolitan Szeptyckyj. He issued a proclamation expressing the gratitude of the Ukrainian people to the German army for liberating them and calling for collaboration with them. The heads of the Autocephalous Church (a Ukrainian nationalist church that had declared its independence from the Russian Orthodox Church in 1919), Polykarp and Ilarion called for 'the mobilization of the energy of the Ukrainian people to extend real help to the German army.' In Lithuania, the Catholic Metropolitan, Archbishop Juosapas Skvireckas, and Bishop Vincentas Brizgys came out with pro-German pronouncements, expressions of gratitude to Hitler, and promises to fight together with the Germans against the Bolsheviks.

The Russian Orthodox Church in the occupied territories found itself in a peculiar position. On the eve of the Nazi invasion, Metropolitan Seraphim of Berlin, the head of a pro-German Eastern Orthodox Church that consisted mainly of anti-Soviet Russian émigrés, appealed to 'all faithful sons of Russia, to join in the crusade under the great leader of the German people who has raised the sword against the foes of the Lord.' On the other hand, on the first day of the invasion,

Aktion reprisal; eleven men hanging in public.

the head of the Russian Orthodox Church in Moscow, Patriarch Sergius, issued a proclamation 'to the whole Church' damning the 'Fascist bandits' who had invaded Russia and blessing 'with heavenly grace the people for their heroic battle.' This call from the Moscow Patriarch formally obliged the

Russian Orthodox Church in the occupied territories, which recognized him, to resist the Nazi invasion.

During the first months of the German occupation there was a definite revival of religious life which had been suppressed during the Soviet times. Many churches were reopened, and the number of people who attended services increased. Most of them were peasants and women, but even in the cities there was an upsurge of religion.

There was no mention of the Jews in the pro-Nazi proclamations issued by the heads of the Autocephalous and Uniate Churches in the Ukraine and by the heads of the Church in Lithuania and other places in the occupied territories. Moreover, in the large number of documents relating to all the Churches in the occupied territories of the Soviet Union and their activities, there is almost no direct or indirect reference to Jews and the atrocities perpetrated against them. In fact, the first days after the German occupation, while the Churches extended warm greetings to the German army as the liberators from Bolshevik rule in the Ukraine and in the Baltic States, were the beginning of the nightmare for the Jews. Even before the *Einsatzgruppen*, the special units of the SS, began the mass killing of the Jews with the help of local auxiliaries, pogroms were carried out by the native population, killing thousands of Jews in Lvov, Kovno and many other localities in the Ukraine, Lithuania and Latvia. The heads of the Churches in those areas were silent when their followers carried out these atrocities. Furthermore, their pro-German proclamations and their blessings for the liberation from Bolshevism could be and were understood by the faithful adherents as an encouragement to kill the Jews. Large parts of the local population identified the Jews with the unpopular Bolshevik rule. Therefore, a combination of basic antisemitism and hatred of Bolshevism instigated these pogroms. It is to be stressed that this was not the intention of either Szeptyckyj in Lvov, who was known as a friend of Jews, or of Brizgys in Kovno, who had friendly connections with Jews. Nevertheless, this was the outcome. Undoubtedly, their pro-German proclamations contributed to the extent of the pogroms in which tens of thousands of Jews were massacred.

In Kovno on July 9, 1941, two days after thousands of Jews were rounded up by the Lithuanian police and shot, the Jews of the city were ordered by the Germans into a ghetto. The Germans claimed this was a response to a demand that had been made by the Lithuanians. A Jewish delegation, headed by Rabbi S. Snaig, went to meet Bishop Brizgys, the acting head of the Church of Lithuania, to implore him to intervene with the German commander. Brizgys replied: 'With all my regrets, I cannot do it. [For] this may endanger the position of the Catholic Church in Lithuania. Such a responsibility I cannot take upon myself.'

Unlike in other countries of Europe, in the Soviet territories the extermination of the Jews by the Nazis was a known fact and was witnessed by the local population. The expulsions and extermination actions were carried out by the German authorities with the active participation of tens

'The attitude of the Church regarding the Jewish question is, in general, clear. In addition, Bishop Brizgys has forbidden all clergymen to help Jews in any form whatsoever. He rejected several Jewish delegations who approached him personally and asked for his intervention with the German authorities.'

From the Operational Situation Report No. 54 of the German *Einsatzgruppen*, 1941.

'The Christian Church constantly reminds its believers of their duties as Christians, and first and foremost, the obedience to the Lord's laws. However there are times when we have to insist and emphasize these commandments . . . we believe such a time has come.'

Metropolitan Andrei Szeptyckyj, 1941.

of thousands of Lithuanians, Latvians, Estonians, and Ukrainians, who were organised in special police battalions, and the local police forces, which consisted of local population who had enlisted in the German service. Most of these people were presumably faithful members of the Christian Churches. Hence, condemnation by the Church of the massacres of the Jews would undoubtedly have worked to lessen the extent of the active participation of its members in the killing operations. Furthermore, the Church could have influenced the majority of the population, who were for the most part indifferent bystanders, to extend help to the Jews. It should be stressed that by remaining passive the population actually helped the Germans, because at that time the rescue of Jews demanded active help.

There is no information or documentation that indicates any relation between the Russian Orthodox Church in the German occupied territories and the Jewish tragedy. As far as we know this Church ignored the fate of the Jews and did not come out in their defence. To be sure, the Russian Orthodox Church was in an unfavourable position under Nazi rule. Its leader, Metropolitan Voskresenskii Sergeii, was killed by the Nazis in April 1944. Yet, his Church's silence on the Jewish tragedy leaves a big question mark as to its spiritual and moral behavior.

> 'Dear merciful people, I beg you and warn you, do not give a piece of bread to a Jew . . . No trace of a Jew is to remain. We should erase them from the face of the earth. When the last Jew disappears from the face of the earth, we shall win the war.'
> From the Sunday sermon of a priest in Kowel, May 1942.

The Catholic Church in Lithuania was also in an influential position, which could have been used to help the Jews in view of the large-scale participation of Lithuanian police battalions in the anti-Jewish actions, even outside Lithuania. A further indication of the Church's involvement was that Lithuanian chaplains served in some of these 'units of death'. The Lutheran Church in Latvia and Estonia assumed a similar attitude. In these Baltic countries the ruling Churches remained silent. Toward the end of 1943 and the beginning of 1944 however, there was some change. Disappointed with the Germans, some small groups of Catholics in Kovno, Lithuania began hiding a limited number of Jewish children. L. Garfunkel, a Jewish leader in the Kovno ghetto, wrote that Bishop Brizgys preached in his church against the atrocities being perpetrated against the Jews.

The Ukrainian Autocephalous Church was, according to existing testimonies, the most anti-Jewish Church in the occupied Soviet territories. Sermons were delivered in its churches calling on parishioners to kill the Jews. In the city of Kowel in Wolyn, on June 2, 1942, the Ukrainian police unit entered the church with its commander and received the blessing of the Chief Priest, Iwan Guba, before beginning an extermination action, in which thousands of Jews were shot on the outskirts of the city.

For Further Reading

Raul Hilberg. *The Destruction of the European Jews,* New York & London: Holmes and Meier,1985.

Andreas Hillgruber. 'War in the East and the Extermination of the Jews.' *Yad Vashem Studies vol. 18* (1987): pp. 103 - 132.

Dov Levin. *Fighting Back: Lithuanian Jewry's Armed Resistance to the Nazis, 1941-1945.* New York: Holmes and Meier, 1985.

Arkady Vaksberg. *Stalin Against the Jews.* Alfred A. Knopf, 1995.

There is no documentation relating to the attitude of the Ukrainian Autonomous Church or its leaders with regard to the Jews and their extermination. In Lvov, the head of the Uniate Church, Metropolitan A. Szeptyckyj, published a pastoral letter in November 1942, entitled *Thou shalt not kill*. It mentioned the basic Christian duties of love, the sanctity of human life and refraining from killing. Szeptyckyj did not mention Jews.

There were many cases in which individual priests gave assistance to Jews, provided them with hiding places, forged identity cards for them, and also influenced some of their congregants to help them. Certain priests baptized Jews and Jewish children. Some of them did so for humanitarian reasons, others for missionary purposes. Some of these priests were executed by the Nazis for their aid to Jews, or were sent to prison and concentration camps. Such individual cases were to be found in all the Churches. The small Baptist Church in the Ukraine was active in saving Jews; so was the Church of Old Believers in Latvia.

In the occupied territories of the Soviet Union, the attitude of the Churches toward Nazi Germany and the Jews was affected more by their people's nationalistic inclination and aims than by a general Church policy. The Churches in the Baltic states and in the Ukraine were part of the nationalistic upheaval there. They cannot be whitewashed of the guilt of their people in the large-scale collaboration and participation in killing the Jews, even beyond their national boundaries (in the death camps, the Warsaw ghetto, etc).

The Nazi policy with regard to the depoliticization and atomization of the Churches restricted the scope of possible Church intervention there – in some cases even terror was used against them, but this does not diminish their spiritual responsibility.

The silence of the Churches, except in the case of the pastoral letter of Szeptyckyj, and their blindness to the Jewish tragedy and the annihilation of the Jewish people, which was carried out openly, leaves a stain on Church activity in the occupied territories of the Soviet Union, and a question mark with regard to their moral and spiritual fortitude.

Meeting between Stalin, Truman, and Churchill.

For Reflection

Was the scope of possible church intervention restricted because of the many existing denominations and the atomization of the Churches?

As in Poland, the mass murder of the Jews was a publicly known fact. To what extent did the Germans know they had the support of the local population for their policy and that there was no need to hide it?

Could church leaders who opposed the murder have prevented their faithful from actively participating in the mass murder of the Jews?

Yitzhak Arad (Israel), former Chairman of the Directorate of Yad Vashem, the Holocaust Heroes' and Martyrs' Remembrance Authority, is currently working on a comprehensive history of the Holocaust in the Nazi occupied territories of the Soviet Union. Dr. Arad has written many articles and books in English and in Hebrew.

Round up of Jews by the Einsatzgruppen; victims sitting at the edge of their grave.

ANDREI SZEPTYCKYJ

Szeptyckyj came from an aristocratic Polish family. He adopted the Greek Catholic faith in 1888 and joined the Basilian Order. In 1899, at the age of 34, he was appointed as Bishop of Stanislawow, and one year later became the metropolitan of the Uniate church. Szeptyckyj was active in the struggle for national rights for the Ukrainian minority within the Polish state. The Ukrainian national movement, which had many sympathizers within the Uniate clergy and lay adherents, was strongly influenced by fascist and Nazi ideology. Szeptyckyj adopted a pro-German orientation and in 1941 welcomed the invading German army as liberators. Hoping the Germans would give the Ukrainians independence, he pledged his support for Hitler and urged Ukrainians to cooperate with Germany. He supported the formation of the Ukrainian army division within the SS and had his deputy officiate at a solemn mass in Lvov Cathedral to celebrate the establishment of the division.

In December 1939, Szeptyckyj wrote a letter to Rome where he complained about the many Jews who fled from German occupied Poland into the Soviet territories. He maintained that they had made a bad impression and were attempting to dominate the economic life of the region, accusing them of avarice and unethical business dealings.

Andrei Szeptyckyj

In spite of the anti-Jewish attitude manifested in this writing and his pro-Nazi views, Szeptyckyj was opposed to the German policy of extermination of the Jews. The Metropolitan strongly supported Ukrainians enlisting in German auxiliary forces, but was troubled by their participation in the massacres. It was probably his failure to keep them from participating in the murder of the Jews that prompted the Metropolitan in 1942 to write to the head of the SS, Heinrich Himmler, asking him to exclude the Ukrainian police from these operations. Moreover, in the following months, during the deportations and mass murder of the Lvov Jews, he enabled several dozens of Jews to take refuge in monasteries under his control and harbored Jews in his own residence for varying periods of time. Szeptyckyj's brother, who helped hide the Jews told one of them, David Kahana, 'It is a very hard task. Not every person has reached this level of dedication and will endanger his life for a Jew. Not all were educated in this way . . .'

JOZEF TISO

Jozef Tiso was born to a Slovak lower middle class family. He was trained as a priest and received a doctorate in theology in 1910. He served as a Member of Parliament and Minister of the Czechoslovak Government in the 1920s. He belonged to the clerical wing of the Slovak People's Party, advocating an authoritarian Catholic government. In 1938, Tiso became the leader of the party and following the creation of an autonomous Slovak entity in the same year, became its Prime Minister and was later nominated President. Tiso declared Slovakia's independence and brought the country into the Nazi camp, remaining loyal to the German Reich until the very end.

Msgr. Jozef Tiso delivering a speech.

Tiso's government surrendered the Slovak Jews and did not oppose their deportation. He kept up an anti-Jewish policy despite several protests from the Vatican. The Apostolic Delegate in Bratislava protested personally to Tiso, appealing to his 'feelings as a priest of the Catholic faith'. The fact that the Slovak state had a clergyman at its head and that there were priests in the political leadership certainly helped to sanction the anti-Jewish measures in the eyes of wide circles of the Slovak population. Tiso showed some concern for baptized Jews. He issued some eleven hundred exemptions from deportation, mainly to baptized and wealthy Jews. On the other hand he is quoted as having given a speech in August 1942, after 55,000 Slovak Jews had been deported, in which he said 'it is a Christian action to expel the Jews, because it is for the good of the people, which is thus getting rid of its pests.' It is probably his being a priest that lent the anti-Jewish policy a certain legitimacy and weakened possible opposition of the Catholic clergy and of believers.

In 1945 Tiso, who was on the Allies' list of war criminals, fled to Austria. He was captured and extradited to Czechoslovakia where he was tried, sentenced to death and executed.

Following the November 1989 'Velvet Revolution', the regained freedom brought along some negative trends in Slovak historic memory. Extreme Slovak nationalist elements appeared on the scene again. The first plaque in memory of Jozef Tiso was unveiled on the wall of the Roman Catholic Teachers' Institute on July 8, 1991, at Banovce nad Bebravou. Ever since, there have been attempts in the press and in various publications to rehabilitate Jozef Tiso as a martyr.

'The mass deportation of the Jews from Slovakia served as a trial run for the planned deportation method, and its organizational and political success was so important to Eichmann that he personally visited Slovakia several times and made contact with Slovak leaders. Among other matters, he assured the Slovaks that the Jews being deported to Poland were being treated there in humane fashion.'

Leni Yahil, *The Holocaust: The Fate of European Jewry*. p. 354.

ORDINARY MEN, EXTRAORDINARY EVIL: DIFFICULT QUESTIONS ON THE PERPETRATORS

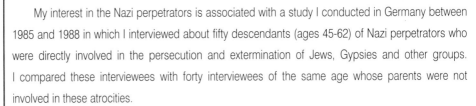

Dan Bar-On

My interest in the Nazi perpetrators is associated with a study I conducted in Germany between 1985 and 1988 in which I interviewed about fifty descendants (ages 45-62) of Nazi perpetrators who were directly involved in the persecution and extermination of Jews, Gypsies and other groups. I compared these interviewees with forty interviewees of the same age whose parents were not involved in these atrocities.

Among the descendants of perpetrators in my sample were people whose fathers' had killed Jews in their community during the *Reichskristallnacht* (an organized pogrom of the Nazis in Germany during the night of November 9-10, 1938 when synagogues were burned and thousands of Jews were arrested and sent off to concentration camps). I also interviewed descendants of physicians who participated in the so-called 'Euthanasia Program' in which the Nazis executed crippled and mentally handicapped Germans who, according to Nazi ideology, contaminated 'Aryan blood'.

These atrocities were preliminary to the massive extermination of Jews, Gypsies and other groups of *Untermenshen* (subhumans, according to Nazi racial ideology) that began with executions carried out by the *einsatzgruppen* (special Nazi killing squads which executed civilian populations during the invasion of the Soviet Union in June 1941). This was later extended into 'industrialized killing" through gassing with the use of gas-vans in Chelmno and by gas chambers at the death camps of Belzec, Majdanek, Treblinka, Auschwitz and Sobibor. In addition, many victims of the Nazis died of hunger, disease, overwork and other forms of torture in ghettos, where they were concentrated under inhuman conditions, and in work camps all over Nazi-occupied Europe. Most of my interviewees' parents were involved in this later phase of the Holocaust as low echelon executioners, as perpetrators of what has been defined as the 'middle range', or as top decision-makers who gave the orders for the killing.

What do we know about Nazi perpetrators? We know most of them were not mentally impaired, that they were not identified as sadists at home or in their social environment. We also know there were no simple demographic markers to identify the population of the Nazi perpetrators.

Einsatzgruppen

'Human history is filled with terrible examples of brutality, cowardice, complicity, and indifference to suffering. There have always been bystanders: people in various walks of life who might have changed the course of history, had they chosen to become more actively involved.'

Victoria Barnett, *Bystanders: Conscience and Complicity During the Holocaust*, p. xiv.

Among the perpetrators, we find educated and well-to-do people, as well as simple and church-affiliated people (although it is true that during the Nazi era there was public pressure to renounce religious affiliation). We find people who were loving parents as well as people who were not involved in the Nazi party or its antisemitic ideology. In the death camps, in addition to members of the SS, we find there were simple people from Ukraine, Latvia, Lithuania and Croatia who collaborated willingly with the Nazis in the extermination process. In Lithuania, we know that the local population began to turn against their Jewish neighbors even before the Nazi forces arrived. And we know that toward the end of the war, during bombing raids by the Allies, there were cases in which victims succeeded in escaping from trains headed for the death camps and fleeing into the woods (near the German town of Celle, for example, which is close to Bergen-Belsen). There, the civilian population, encouraged by Nazi authorities, hunted Jews in the woods like animals, killing most of them. Another thing we know is that one should not assume that during the Holocaust, evil behavior can only be attributed to specially designated German SS units, because we know the *Wehrmacht* (the regular German army) was also involved in brutalities on the Eastern front. What we know is that most were, as Christophen Browning called them, 'ordinary men'.

One of my interviewees, a priest, told me about an incident that happened toward the end of the war, when bombing by the Allies caused a fire-storm in his town which reached a shelter where 400 Russian forced laborers were locked up. No one in the community went to open the shelter when the fire started. As a result, all the Russians workers were burned to death. When my interviewee wanted to discuss this event with his congregation in 1985, forty years after the war, members of his congregation warned him that they would leave the congregation if he raised the topic.

At this point, it is appropriate to ask: What motivated so many people to actively take part in massive killing during the Holocaust? Was it fear, indifference or actual hatred. Was it perhaps a combination of all three? It is not easy to answer this question. While people like Daniel Jonah Goldhagen, in his book, *Hitler's Willing Executioners,* tend to emphasize hatred towards Jews, other researchers like Christopher Browning (in his book, *Ordinary Men*) tend to emphasize indifference towards Jews. The Nazis knew how to manipulate hatred and create dehumanization of their victims, turning them into scapegoats of their own inner contradictions and self-hatred.

But could this have worked without some deep fear of the consequences of refusal to go along with the authority? A number of perpetrators used the argument, in retrospect, that they had

For Reflection

How could people be loving parents and spouses while at the same time they viciously killed other children and women?

What makes the difference between people who chose to become rescuers during the Holocaust and those who chose to become perpetrators or bystanders?

What does it mean to 'work through' the burden of man-made atrocities? How can such atrocities be forgiven?

'Shakespeare's Hamlet said: 'To be or not to be, that is the question.' But that is no problem. We all want to be. The real problem, biblically speaking, is how to be and how not to be; that is our challenge, and it is what makes the difference between the human and the animal.'

Abraham Joshua Heschel, 'Choose Life' in *Moral Grandeur and Spiritual Audacity*, p. 252.

For further reading

Dan Bar-On. *Legacy of Silence: Encounters with Children of the Third Reich*. Cambridge MA: Harvard University Press, 1989.

Dan Bar-On. *The Indescribable and the Undiscussable: Reconstructing Human Discourse after Trauma*, Budapest: Central European Press, 1998.

Christopher Browning.. *Ordinary Men*. New York: Harper Collins, 1990.

Susannah Heschel, ed. *Moral Grandeur and Spiritual Audacity*. New York: Farrar Straus Giroux, 1996.

Elie Wiesel and Philippe de Saint-Cheron. *Evil and Exile*. Notre Dame, IN: University of Notre Dame Press, 1990

participated in the killings against their will, 'otherwise they or their families would be in danger.' But we do not have supportive evidence for this argument. Goldhagen, who investigated one hundred cases of Nazis who refused to participate in the shooting or the gassing of Jews and other victims, found that nothing happened to most of them and that they were just transferred to other tasks in the regime.

How could the perpetrators of these atrocities maintain a moral self-image during the Nazi era? In his book, *The Nazi Doctors*, Robert Jay Lifton claims they were able to do it mainly through the psychological mechanism of 'doubling': that is, they succeeded in building a kind of inner wall between what they did at the killing-site and how they continued to live their personal lives. There were a few people who collapsed during mass-executions, like Rudolf's father, a deeply religious person who broke down after witnessing the execution of his Jewish workers near Para Via Novo in Belarus (see further, Chapter 9, *Legacy of Silence*), but they were exceptions. Others consumed large quantities of alcohol in order to keep going. There were others who described the process of becoming involved in atrocities as a step-by-step procedure: there comes a point when one crosses a threshold and then anything is possible.

We also know the Nazis were sensitive to public resistance to their extermination process. They stopped the 'Euthanasia Program' when church leaders protested, and they also tried to hide the 'Final Solution' of the Jews, by using cover-language – euphemisms – to hide their real intentions and activities. In 1943, for example, when the non-Jewish wives of Jewish men who had been arrested by the authorities staged a spontaneous protest in front of Gestapo headquarters in Berlin, their husbands were released the next day and never arrested again.

Nazi leadership also paid attention to the psychological inhibitions of the executioners. In his speech at the Poznan meeting of SS Major Generals on October 4, 1943, Heinrich Himmler said, 'I want to talk to you quite frankly on a very grave matter . . . I mean the evacuation of the Jews, the extermination of the Jewish race.' In this speech, Himmler referred directly to what he considered the 'psychological hardships' of having to exterminate the Jews, but he says, 'To have stuck it out and at the same time – apart from exceptions caused by human weakness – to have remained decent fellows, that is what has made us hard . . . We shall never be rough and heartless when it is not necessary, that is clear. We Germans are the only people in the world who have a decent attitude toward animals . . .' (see further, Michael Berenbaum, ed., *Witness to the Holocaust*, p. 178).

How did Nazi perpetrators manage to function after the war, when the Nazi regime with its mental and physical support were gone? Did they return to their religious congregations and try to confess to the atrocities they had perpetrated? I tried to find out by interviewing priests and clergymen. Out of eighty contacts, only two could tell about a confession of a perpetrator after the war. In one case, a former soldier confessed that after being ordered to do so, he stabbed a six-years-old girl who ran to him out of the ruins of the Warsaw Ghetto after the Jewish uprising. He confessed that ever since the 'brown eyes of this girl never gave him peace.' Perhaps it was not by coincidence that he chose as his confessor a priest who was himself the son of a famous perpetrator (see further, Chapter 8, *Legacy of Silence*).

I highlighted two aspects of this confession: first, that there was a 'double wall' between the perpetrators and their social surrounding which helped former perpetrators to maintain a 'conspiracy of silence' in post-war Germany around the atrocities they had committed; secondly, that the perpetrators developed a paradoxical morality after the war, by which I mean that most of them did not become post-war criminals. Rather, they gave attention to the moral upbringing of their own children. In regard to their own atrocities, however, they maintained only the memory of a single vignette in which they felt guilt and shame. With the help of this single memory, they established a sense of their own humanness, but they also forgot all the other atrocities in which they had been involved.

How were descendants of the Nazi perpetrators able to live with this part of their family biography? Many never married or had children. Some are unable to find out for sure what atrocities or crimes their parents committed during the Holocaust, and they are burdened by this uncertainty. Quite a few of my interviewees have searched for meaningful ways of trying to correct the crimes their parents committed during the Holocaust by becoming religious or by choosing an occupation through which they could help unprivileged children or adults. A few of my interviewees also organized themselves into a self-help group that met regularly for four years in order to try to work through this painful part of their identity. In 1992 they began meeting regularly with a group of descendants of Jewish Holocaust survivors from Israel and USA. This group continues to meet annually.

From this short presentation of the Nazi perpetrators, we can learn several things that I think are relevant to the topic of this book, *The Holocaust and the Christian World*:

1. Except for a small number of the architects of the extermination process and a few sadists who enjoyed taking part in it, most of the perpetrators were ordinary men and women who could not be identified, *a priori*, as having the personalities of killers;

2. We have to assume that the potential for such atrocious behavior exists in most of us, as does the potential for becoming either rescuers or indifferent bystanders. Sometimes it is difficult to predict which of these potentials may become dominant at a given moment. The evil part may more easily become dominant when a whole society loses its basic respect and dignity for the 'others' who live among us.

3. Once the atrocities were activated, they have long-lasting effects, among both the survivors and their descendants and the perpetrators and their descendants.

'This, this was the thing I had wanted to understand ever since the war. Nothing else. How a human being can remain indifferent. The executioners I understood; also the victims, though with more difficulty. For the others, all the others, those who were neither for nor against, those who sprawled in passive patience, those who told themselves, 'The storm will blow over and everything will be normal again,' those who thought themselves above the battle, those who were permanently and merely spectators – all those were closed to me, incomprehensible.'

Elie Wiesel, *The Town Beyond the Wall*, p. 159.

Dan Bar-On (Israel) is Professor of Psychology at Ben Gurion University of the Negev, Beer Sheva and co-director of PRIME (Peace Research Institute in the Middle East).
Professor Bar-On has written many books and articles, most recently, *The Indescribable and the Undiscussable: Reconstructing Human Discourse after Trauma*.

'IN THE INTEREST OF MAINTAINING MILITARY DISCIPLINE...' THE MASSACRE OF CHILDREN IN BYELAYA TSERKOV, MILITARY CHAPLAINS AND THE WEHRMACHT

Ernst Klee, Willi Dressen, and Volker Riess

Byelaya Tserkov (Bialacerkiew) is a Ukrainian village, 70 km from Kiev. In August 1941 the *Feldkommandant* of Byelaya Tserkov requested the intervention of *Sonderkommando* (SK) 4a to kill its Jewish inhabitants. The extermination orders were received by a unit (*Teilkommando*) of SK 4a which was under the command of *SS-Obersturmführer* August Häfner. The unit consisted of regular members of SK 4a and a platoon from 3rd Company, SS Special Operations Battalion (*Waffen-SS*) under the command of *SS-Oberscharführer* Jäger. Between 8 and 19 August the Waffen-SS platoon – with the help of the Ukranian militia – executed several hundred Jewish men and women by firing squad. Scene of the crime: a rifle-range near the barracks . . .

The children of those murdered were initially locked up in a building on the edge of the village. On the evening of 19 August some of the children were transported in three full lorry-loads to the rifle-range and killed there. Some ninety children were kept back in wretched conditions. The following day, 20 August, the Catholic military chaplain, Ernst Tewes, and his Protestant colleague, Gerhard Wilczek, were having lunch together in the mess. Both were soldiers of officer rank. A distraught non-commissioned officer came and pleaded with Tewes (who was ordained a bishop after the war) to take 'remedial action'.

The military chaplains visited the children and informed the divisional chaplain of 295th Infantry Division (ID), who was in the area for a few days. Then the Catholic divisional chaplain, Dr. Reuss (who was ordained bishop in Mainz after the war) and his Protestant colleague Kornmann (presumed dead), together with Tewes and Wilczek, visited the awful scene. In the afternoon divisional chaplains Dr. Reuss and Kornmann reported to the *Generalstabsoffizier* of the division, Lieutenant-Colonel Helmuth Groscurth (killed in action) on their visit.

In order to carry out special security - police duties [the murder of Jews] which are outside the army's domain, it will be necessary to employ special SD detachments in the zone of operations.

Order by Chief of Staff of Wehrmacht, March 28, 1941 in : Yitzhak Arad, et al, eds *The Einsatzgruppen Reports.*

What follows – the actions of the Wehrmacht up to the officially condoned murder of the children on 22 August – can be found in the passages printed below.

Report by the military chaplain, Dr. Reuss, to Lieutenant-Colonel Groscurth, 1st Generalstabsoffizier, 295th Infantry Division

Catholic Divisional Chaplain

Division command post

to 295th Infantry Division

20 August 1941

I submit the following report to 295th Infantry Division:

Today in the afternoon towards 14.30 hours Military Chaplains Tewes and Wilczek, Military Hospital Division 4/607, came to the Protestant divisional chaplain and myself and reported the following:

They told us that German soldiers had drawn their attention to the fact that Jewish children aged between a few months and five or six years, whose parents are said to have been executed, are locked up in a house in intolerable conditions under guard by Ukrainian militiamen. These children can be heard whimpering continuously. They said that they went there themselves and had confirmed this fact but had not seen any members of the *Wehrmacht* or any other authority responsible for keeping order here or carrying out guard duty. They reported that there were only a few German soldiers there as spectators, and that these men had expressed their indignation at this state of affairs. They asked us to report to our headquarters.

Their description of these incidents made it reasonable to suspect that this was an arbitrary action on the part of the Ukrainian militia. In order to be able to report the matter accurately, I myself, accompanied by the two military chaplains and the Protestant Divisional Chaplain, *Wehrmachtsoberpfarrer* Kornmann, paid a visit to the house, where we discovered the following:

In the courtyard in front of the house the crying and whimpering of children could be heard very loudly. Outside there were a Ukrainian militiaman keeping guard with a rifle, a number of German soldiers and several young Ukrainian girls. We immediately entered the house unobstructed and in two rooms found some ninety (I counted them) children aged from a few months to five, six or seven years old. There was no kind of supervision by the *Wehrmacht* or other German authorities.

A large number of German soldiers, including a sanitation officer, were inspecting the conditions in which the children were being kept when we arrived. Just then a military policeman, who was under the command of the *Ortskommandantur* or the *Feldkommandantur*, also arrived. He stated that he had

Einsatzgruppen guard a column of Jews.

'Humanity, in the vocabulary of the SS, meant lightening [their] thankless task, both physically and morally: physically by protecting the killers from nasty accidents at work . . . morally by saving them from corrupt or weakening thoughts, such as equating their high calling with murder or seeing Jews as fellow human beings.'

Lord Dacre of Glanton in *Those were the Days*, p xiv.

The Last Jew of Vinnitsa

Wilhelm Kube, Gauleiter of White Russia . . . believed . . . that German Jews . . . were a cut above East European Jews and should not be indiscriminately exterminated with them. What a torrent of denunciation this heresy would bring on him from the former theology student and commander of Einsatzkommando 2, now head of the SS in White Russia . . . Dr Eduard Strauch! The Gauleiter should be sacked at once, demanded Strauch . . .

Lord Dacre of Glanton in *Those were the Days*, pp xiii-xiv.

come only in order to investigate a case of looting which was said to have been carried out by guards from the Ukrainian militia.

The two rooms where the children had been accommodated – there was a third empty room adjoining these two – were in a filthy state. The children lay or sat on the floor which was covered in their faeces. There were flies on the legs and abdomens of most of the children, some of whom were only half dressed. Some of the bigger children (two, three, four years old) were scratching the mortar from the wall and eating it. Two men, who looked like Jews, were trying to clean the rooms. The stench was terrible. The small children, especially those that were only a few months old, were crying and whimpering continuously. The visiting soldiers were shaken, as we were, by these unbelievable conditions and expressed their outrage over them. In another room, accessible through a window in one of the children's rooms, there were a number of women and older children, apparently Jews. I did not enter this room. Locked in a further room there were some other women, among them one woman with a small child on her arm. According to the guard on duty – a Ukrainian boy aged about sixteen or seventeen, who was armed with a stick – it had not yet been established whether these women were Jews or not.

When we got back into the courtyard an argument was in progress between the above-mentioned military policeman and the Ukrainian sentry who was guarding the house. This guard was being accused of the looting and also of destroying several passes which had been issued by the German military authorities to other Ukrainians (who were in fact women). The pieces still lay scattered on the ground. The military policeman disarmed the Ukrainian guard, had him led away and then went away himself. Some German soldiers who were in the courtyard told me that they had their quarters in a house right next door and that since the afternoon of the previous day they had heard the children crying uninterruptedly. Sometime during the evening of the previous day three lorry-loads of children had already been taken away. An official from the SD had been present. The lorry-driver had told them that these were children of Jews and Jewesses who had already been shot and the children were now going to be taken to be executed. The execution was to be carried out by Ukrainian militia. The children still in the house were also to be shot. The soldiers expressed extreme indignation over the conditions in which the children were being kept; in addition, one of them said that he himself had children at home. As there were no Germans there in a supervisory role I asked the soldiers to make sure that nobody else, particularly members of the local population, entered the house, in order to avoid the conditions there being talked about further.

Meanwhile a senior medical officer from the Wehrmacht whom I did not know had visited the children's rooms and declared to me that water should be brought in urgently. In such conditions the risk of an epidemic could not be excluded.

I consider it necessary to report this matter to my HQ for two reasons: first, there is no German watch or supervision at this house and second, German soldiers are able to enter it any time. This has indeed already happened and has provoked a reaction of indignation and criticism.

Dr. Reuss

Military Chaplain

Report by Wehrmachtoberpfarrer Kornmann

Wehrmachtoberpfarrer Kornmann O.U.

Protestant Divisional Chaplain

21 August 1941

to 295th Infantry Division

I submit the following report to 295th Infantry Division:

Yesterday (20 August) towards 1500 hours two military chaplains from a military hospital unit in this area came to see me and the Division's Catholic Military Chaplain and reported to us that near by, some 500 m away, about 80 to 90 children from babies to school-age were being held in the upper storey of a house. The children could be heard from a long way off shouting and crying and as they had already been there 24 hours, the soldiers quartered in the neighbouring houses were being sorely disturbed at night. The two military chaplains had been made aware of the presence of the children by the soldiers themselves. Together with the two chaplains and my Catholic colleague, I went to the house in question and saw the children lying and sitting about in two small rooms. They were partly lying in their own filth, there was not a single drop of drinking water and the children were suffering greatly due to the heat. A man from the Ukrainian militia was standing guard downstairs. We learned from him that these were Jew children whose parents had been executed. There was one group of German soldiers standing at the watchpost and another standing at the corner of the house. Some of them were talking agitatedly about what they had heard and seen.

As I considered it highly undesirable that such things should take place in full view of the public eye I hereby submit this report. The two military chaplains were from Military Hospital Unit 4/607 and were named Wilczek (Protestant) and Tewes (Catholic).

Kornmann F.d.R

Wehrmachtoberpfarrer

signed: signature

Lieutenant and O.1 (1. Ordonanzoffizier)

For Relection

Did they fulfil their duty appropriately?

If such chaplains had knowledge of mass shootings, what should they have done?

Is there a difference between moral, spiritual, human and military responsibility?

Finkovski actually displays extraordinary energy and distinguishes himself in his whole personality from other Greek Orthodox priests. . . .The desire to become bishop might, of course, be a strong motivation, in any case, Finkovski is presently the man who influences the population more than German propaganda.

Operational Situation Report USSR No. 90 Einsatzgruppen B., Smokask, Einsatzgruppen Reports, 144

For Further Reading

Erst Klee. Willi Dressen, Volker Reiss. *Those were the Days: The Holocaust through the Eyes of the Perpetrators and Bystanders.* (Trans. Deborah Burnstone.) London: Hamish Hamilton, 1991.

Yitzhak Arad. Shmuel Krakowski, Shmuel Spector (eds). *The Einsatzgruppen Reports.* New York: Holocaust Library, 1989.

Christopher R. Browning. *Ordinary Men: Reserve Police Battalion 101 and the Final Solution in Poland.* New York: Harper Collins, 1993.

Where on earth would we have found enough bread for ninety children? Even in the unlikely event that we had succeeded in doing so and we had managed to bring over some water, we would have only slowed down the whole action. Our priority was to try to effect an order that could help the children. It was not that we wanted to protect our own lives. It was also not the case that if someone had refused to carry out an order he would have been immediately put against the wall. What was needed then were stronger steps. We could have coped with the difficulties. By difficulties I mean that we assumed that we would have been reprimanded for our actions. What they would have done with us, I do not know, nevertheless I don't suppose it would have been something particularly awful. We had nothing to do with the SD; we belonged to the army.

Former military chaplain Gerhard Wilczek

Report by military chaplains Tewes and Wilczek

Protestant and Catholic O.U.
Military Chaplains
22 August 1941
to Military Hospital 4/607

We hereby submit the following report to 295th Infantry Division as instructed:

On 20 August 1941 at 13.00 hours we heard from German soldiers that quite a large number of children had been locked up in intolerable conditions in a house near our quarters. A Ukrainian was

Members of the *Ortskommandantur*

said to be guarding these children. As we suspected this to be some arbitrary action on the part of the Ukrainians we went over there straight away. We found about ninety children packed together into two small rooms in a filthy state. Their whimpering could be heard in the vicinity of the house. Some of the children, mainly infants, were completely exhausted and almost lifeless. There was no German guard or supervision present, only a Ukrainian guard armed with a rifle. German soldiers had free access to the house and were expressing outrage over these frightful conditions. As these events were taking place under the aegis of the German *Wehrmacht* and would therefore damage its reputation, we immediately went and reported to the *Ortskommandantur.* The *Ortskommandant* went with us to the house, inspected the conditions and then took us to report to the *Feldkommandantur*. At the *Feldkommandantur* none of the competent gentlemen was available for us to talk to and we were advised to call later. As the matter seemed to us to be one of utmost urgency and we assumed that the divisional commander of 295th Infantry Division stationed in the area was the most senior-ranking officer, we went to see the two divisional chaplains of 295th Infantry Division and informed them of what was happening so that they could report to their HQ.

Tewes, Military Chaplain

Wilczek, Military Chaplain

F.d.R.

(signed) Spoerhase

Lieutenant and O.1

SS-Obersturmführer August Häfner on the killing of the children

. . . Then Blobel ordered me to have the children executed. I asked him, 'By whom should the shooting be carried out?' He answered, 'By the Waffen-SS.' I raised an objection and said, 'They are all young men. How are we going to answer to them if we make them shoot small children?' To this he said, 'Then use your men.' I then said, 'How can they do that? They have small children as well." This tug-of-war lasted about ten minutes. . . . I suggested that the Ukrainian militia of the *Feldkommandant* should shoot the children. There were no objections from either side to this suggestion. . . . The children were taken down from the tractor. They were lined up along the top of the grave and shot so that they fell into it. . . . They fell into the grave. The wailing was indescribable. I shall never forget the scene throughout my life. I find it very hard to bear. . . . The execution must have taken place in the afternoon at about 3.30 or 4.00. . . . Many children were hit four or five times before they died.

SS-Obersturmführer August Häffner

Excerpted from: *Those were the Days: The Holocaust through the Eyes of the Perpetrators and Bystanders.* trans. Deborah Burnstone. London: Hamish Hamilton Ltd., 1991, pp. 138, 141-43, 144, 150, 151-52. Used with permission.

THE VATICAN, THE POPE AND THE PERSECUTION OF THE JEWS

UNDERSTANDING THE VATICAN DURING THE NAZI PERIOD

Michael R. Marrus

It is not always fully appreciated that the Vatican was neutral during the Second World War, having committed itself from the very outset to a policy of conciliation that marked church diplomacy in the inter-war period. To the Vatican, neutrality meant remaining apart from the two power blocs and, most important, maintaining an environment in which the church could operate as freely and openly as possible. Particularly since the presentation of Rolf Hochhuth's angry play, *Der Stellvertreter* (The Deputy) in 1962, this posture has been subjected to withering criticism. The Vatican has responded with the publication of a voluminous collection of documents on the role of the Holy See during the war, generating one of the most extensive historical discussions of the many ethical questions associated with the history of the Holocaust.

Historians generally see the policy of Pius XII as consistent with a longstanding tradition of Vatican diplomacy. During political storms of the depression years, this tradition was interpreted by Eugenio Pacelli, Cardinal Secretary of State under Pius XI and later to become the wartime Pope. Pacelli exemplified a profound commitment to the spiritual and pastoral mission of the Holy See; he saw his role as avoiding association with power blocs and forging diplomatic links with conservative or even fascist regimes. As fascism extended its influence in Europe during the 1930s, the Vatican remained aloof, occasionally challenging fascist ideology when it touched on important matters of Catholic doctrine or the legal position of the Church, but unwilling to interfere with what it considered to be purely secular concerns. Beyond this, the Vatican found most aspects of right-wing regimes congenial, appreciating their patronage of the Church, their challenge to Marxism, and their frequent championing of a conservative social vision.

The Vatican quarreled with both Hitler and Mussolini on race, but hardly out of concern for the welfare of Jews. Throughout this period the Church seldom opposed anti-Jewish persecution and rarely denounced governments for discriminatory practices; when it did so, it usually admonished governments to act with 'justice and charity', disapproving only of violent excesses or the most extravagant forms of oppression. Much more important for church policy was the clash between the pseudo-biological bases of racism and the fundamental principles of Catholicism and church authority. The tendency of fascist movements, especially Nazism, to use race as a foundation of their

'For the professing Christian, of all the questions that arise out of the study of the Third Reich and the Holocaust the most terrible are these: What were the churches doing? How could such a monstrous crime be committed in the heart of Christendom by baptized Roman Catholics, Protestants, and Eastern Orthodox who were never rebuked, let alone excommunicated? Where were the Christians?'

Franklin H. Littell. 'Foreword' in Aimé Bonifas, *Prisoner 20-801: A French National in the Nazi Labor Camps,* p. vii.

regimes directly challenged the Church's claims in the fields of baptism, marriage, and, more broadly, the definition of who was and who was not a Catholic. The Holy See sometimes muted its opposition, usually preferring conciliation and diplomacy even on fundamental questions such as these. Nevertheless, conflict could break through the surface. One notable occasion was March 1937, when the Papal Encyclical *Mit Brennender Sorge* (With Burning Concern) condemned the false and heretical teachings of Nazism. The Holy See openly protested Mussolini's turn toward racism the following year. Yet at the same time the Vatican strove to avoid an open breach – as it was to continue to do throughout the war. As always, the goal was political neutrality and the safeguarding of the institutional interests of the Church in a perilous political world.

Church policy toward Jews during the war can be seen in this historical perspective. For the first few years persecution seems to have caused few ripples at the Vatican and awakened no more interest or sympathy than in the 1930s. Church diplomats continued to speak in favor of 'justice and charity', but were largely unconcerned about the persecution of Jews by Nazi or collaborationist governments. A striking illustration comes from the Autumn of 1941, when the French Ambassador to the Holy See, Léon Bérard, sent an extensive report to Vichy on the Vatican's views. According to this diplomat the Holy See was not interested in the French antisemitic laws and worried only that they might undermine Church jurisdiction or involve occasional breaches of 'justice and charity'. So far as the French were concerned, the Vatican essentially gave them a green light to legislate as they chose against Jews.

When mass killings began, the Vatican was extremely well informed through its own diplomatic channels and through a variety of other contacts. Church officials may have been the first to pass on to the Holy See sinister reports about the significance of deportation convoys in 1942, and they continued to receive the most detailed information about mass murder in the east. Despite numerous appeals, however, the Pope refused to issue explicit denunciations of the murder of Jews or call upon the Nazis directly to stop the killing. Pius determinedly maintained his posture of neutrality and declined to associate himself with Allied declarations against Nazi war crimes. The most the Pope would do was to encourage humanitarian aid by subordinates within the Church, issue vague appeals against the oppression of unnamed racial and religious groups, and try to ease the lot of Catholics of Jewish origin, caught up in the Nazis' net of persecution. And with distinguished exceptions, the corps of Vatican diplomats did no better.

As Léon Papéleux makes clear, the Vatican's posture shifted during the course of the war, as did that of other neutrals: the Holy See gradually became more forthcoming in its démarches on behalf of Jews and more overt in its assistance to the persecuted. But the Pope remained reluctant to speak out almost until the very end. In the autumn of 1943, with Rome under German occupation, the Nazis

'Why, it has been asked repeatedly, did the Pope not utter a solemn denunciation of this crime against the Jews and against humanity? . . . Why, it has been demanded, did he not give a clear moral and spiritual lead to Catholic priests throughout Europe? In June 1941, when the Vichy French government introduced 'Jewish laws' closely modeled upon the Nuremberg Laws, the Pope responded to appeals from French bishops by stating that such laws were not in conflict with Catholic teaching. Later efforts by the British, Americans and Poles to persuade the Vatican to publish a specific condemnation of Nazi extermination of the Jews fell on deaf ears. The Pope, came the reply, could only issue a general condemnation of wartime atrocities.

A strong and openly voiced papal line might have silenced those Catholic bishops throughout Europe who actively and fervently collaborated with their Nazi masters. . .'

Ronnie S. Landau, *The Nazi Holocaust*, pp. 216-217.

> 'Our distress is not so much the result of concern for the outward peace and security of the Holy See . . . It is much more the unnamed hardships in the war zones and of the troops led into battle, calamities which reach our ears daily and which cannot be satisfactorily countered by peaceful means . . . the moral devastation of war, especially for matrimony, family and youth . . . and steadily growing hatred between nations . . . Efforts which verge on the inhuman are necessary in order to keep the Holy See above the strife of the warring parties . . . It is to such an extent that it is often painfully difficult to determine whether reserve and cautious silence are required, or whether open speech and resolute action are called fo. This torments us more bitterly than the dangers threatening peace and security in our own home.'
>
> Excerpt from a letter of Pope Pius XII to German Archbishop Joseph Frings of Cologne, dates March 3, 1944.

began round ups of Jews virtually on the doorstep of the Papal Palace. On a knife's edge, the Pope seems to have balanced carefully, fearing at any moment that the SS might descend on the Vatican itself. In his signals to Berlin, the German Ambassador to the Holy See, Ernst von Weizsäcker, portrayed a pro-German Pope, alluding to his reluctance to protest the assault on the Jews. Was Weizsäcker delicately trying to subvert the intentions of the SS by suggesting the high price the Reich might have to pay for the persecutions? Was he trying to protect the Pope from direct Nazi moves against him? Or was he accurately reporting the perspectives of the Holy See? Interpretations of this episode vary widely – from those who see Pius playing a delicate, complicated game with Nazi occupiers, expressing himself cryptically, to those who read the incident as a further indication of Church reluctance to take any risks on behalf of Jews.

Our understanding of Church policy now extends considerably beyond Hochhuth's accusations and related charges of pro-German and antisemitic pressures at the Vatican. It is true that Pacelli had served many years as Papal Nuncio in Germany and feared mightily during the war that the defeat of the Nazis would lead to the triumph of Bolshevism in Europe. But Vatican documents do not indicate a guarded pro-Nazism or a supreme priority of opposition to the Soviet Union. Nor do they reveal a particular indifference to the fate of Jews, let alone hostility toward them. Rather, the Vatican's communications, along with other evidence, suggest a resolute commitment to its traditional policy of reserve and conciliation. The goal was to limit the global conflict where possible and above all to protect the influence and standing of the Church as an independent voice. Continually apprehensive of schisms within the Church, Pius strove to maintain the allegiance of Catholics in Germany, in Poland, and elsewhere. Fearful too of threats from the outside, the Pope dared not confront the Nazis or the Italian Fascists directly. Notably, the Papacy maintained its reserve not only against Jewish appeals but in the face of others as well. The Holy See turned a deaf ear to anguished calls from Polish bishops to denounce the Nazis' atrocities in Poland; issued no explicit call to stop the so-called

For Reflection

What, if anything, is the difference between neutrality and indifference?

How can individuals and/or institutions that call themselves 'Christian' ever remain neutral in the face of atrocity?

Once Church authority loses credibility, can it ever recover? How?

euthanasia campaign in the Reich; deeply offended many by receiving the Croatian dictator Ante Pavelic, whose men butchered an estimated 700,000 Orthodox Serbs; and refused to denounce Italian aggression against Greece. Beyond this, there is a widespread sense that, however misguided politically, Pius himself felt increasingly isolated, threatened, and verging on despair. With an exaggerated faith in the efficacy of his mediative diplomacy, Pius clung to the wreckage of his pre-war policy – 'a kind of anxiously preserved virginity in the midst of torn souls and bodies,' as one sympathetic observer puts it.

Individual churchmen of course reacted otherwise, and there is a long list of Catholic clergy who saw their Christian duty as requiring intervention on behalf of persecuted Jews. Often the deportation convoys galvanized priests to action. In some cases, as with the intervention of the apostolic delegate Giuseppe Burzio in Catholic Slovakia, such appeals may well have made a difference. In Bucharest, Nuncio Andreia Cassulo pleaded with the Rumanian Government for humane treatment for the Jews and actually visited Jewish deportees in Transnistira. In Budapest Nuncio Angelo Rotta intervened repeatedly with Admiral Horthy on behalf of Hungarian Jews and may have helped secure papal intervention in the summer of 1944. Angelo Roncalli, the apostolic delegate in Turkey and the future Pope John XXIII, was among the most sensitive to the Jewish tragedy and most vigorous in rescue efforts despite his reflection, at the time, of traditional Catholic attitudes toward Jews. Elsewhere, on the other hand, church leaders replicated the posture of the Vatican itself – or even deferred with greater or lesser sympathy to those directing the machinery of destruction. Outstanding in this respect was the timid and pro-Fascist Cesare Orsenigo, the Nuncio in Berlin, who appeared wedded to the views of the German government. The Pope did not dictate policy on such matters to his subordinates and allowed them to go their own way. His timidity in this respect may be one of the most important charges against him.

In retrospect, some historians have come to appreciate the tactical caution of the Holy See. Günther Lewy, for example, suggests that a 'flaming protest' by the Pope against the perpetrators of genocide would almost certainly have failed to move the German public and would likely have made matters worse – especially for the half-Jews as well as for practising Catholics in Germany. Others claim that much of the present condemnation of Vatican policy springs from mistaken assumptions about Church doctrine. It may be quite correct to say, as does Father John Morley, that the Vatican 'betrayed the ideals it set for itself'. But sincere churchmen at the time could certainly judge those ideals otherwise. As Leonidas Hill reminds us, 'the theology of the Church lays far less emphasis on saving lives than on saving souls through the consolations of religion'. Seeing the institutional church as a supreme value in its own right, those in charge of its fortunes tended unhesitatingly to put these ahead of the victims of Nazism.

For Further Reading

Harry James Cargas. *Holocaust Scholars Write to the Vatican.* Westport Connecticut: Greenwood Press, 1998.

J. Cornwell. Hitler's Pope: *The Secret History of Pius XII.* Viking, 1999.

S.I. Minerbi. 'Pius XII', in: I. Gutman, (ed) *Encyclopedia of the Holocaust* (Macmillan, 1990), Volume 3, pp.1135-1139.

John S. Conway. *The Nazi Persecution of the Churches 1933-45.* N.Y.: Basic Books, 1968.

Michael R. Marrus (Canada), Dean of Graduate Studies at the University of Toronto, is a Fellow of the Royal Society of Canada and a Fellow of the Royal Historical Society. He is the author of many essays and books, including *The Holocaust in History; The Unwanted: European Refugees in the Twentieth Century* and, with Robert O. Paxton, *Vichy France and the Jews.*

WHO WAS PIUS XII?

Eugene J. Fisher

Pius XII was a man. He was neither a demon nor an angel, though he reigned as Pope (1939-1958) during arguably the most demonic and certainly most destructively evil period in human history. Opinions on him range from adulatory, as was expressed virtually universally on his death, to condemnatory, as in the recent screed by John Cornwell, *Hitler's Pope*, which blames him not only for the political success of Hitler in Germany (and thus for World War II) but for starting World War I as well! As usual, truth for historians lies somewhere in the complex ambiguities in between these extremes. This is as it should be.

Pope Pius XII.

> Pius XII . . . he was neither a demon nor an angel, though he reigned as Pope (1939 – 1958) during arguably the most demonic and certainly most destructively evil period in human history.

Please allow me to give you just a sampling of this very mature Jewish-Christian exchange, which I believe may become a model for future discussions of what I have previously called a 'radioactive' issue (having taken the term from the very wise Rabbi A. James Rudin's early analysis of the Auschwitz Convent controversy, to give credit where it is due). One problem, as it was discussed, is often that available evidence can be read quite honestly by scholars in more than one way. For example, some have argued that the fact that the Pope made no public statements on the one-night Nazi roundup of Jews in Rome in 1943, illustrates his 'indifference'. These scholars will bring out the report sent back to Berlin by the German ambassador to the Vatican as evidence, since it states that the Pope 'does not wish' to go public on the matter. Others, myself among them, argue the opposite. The German ambassador, Weizsäcker, was a Catholic, and like others was fearful that the Nazis would invade and ransack the Vatican. Yet he had to communicate Pius' ultimatum: Stop the roundup of the Jews of Rome or the Pope will go public. So this is how he did it, gently and encouragingly to his superiors in Berlin. The proof, I would argue, is that the Nazi roundup of Roman Jews stopped and never started again. Most of those picked up that first night were lost. But the majority of the Jews of Rome were saved, hidden largely in the convents and monasteries of Rome, and fed by a Vatican van that went around distributing food. Obviously, this was with the direct knowledge and approval of Pius XII. It could not have happened otherwise.

So there was no public protest. But there was direct and in this case effective action to save the Jews of Rome. Is Pius to be declared a demon for thus saving thousands of lives? Is he to be declared a prophet for not publicly protesting the fact that the Jews rounded up that first evening were sent to their deaths? That is a hard, moral choice with no easy answers. One sees it also in the fact that the Pope made no specific public protests over the systematic murder by the Nazis of the civil and religious leadership of Catholic Poland.

How is one to weigh Pius XII's policy of neutrality in World War II, a policy carefully crafted by his predecessors over centuries going back to lessons learned the hard way during the Protestant Reformation, the French Revolution, and the emergence of the modern nation-state in the 19th and early 20th Centuries? Was it a policy reflecting indifference to the moral evils of Nazism? A basically decent response to what was happening in Europe up to the eve of World War II, that was simply overwhelmed by massively catastrophic evils that had virtually no precedent in European history?

There is a great deal of evidence to show that behind the officially neutral stance, Pius and his nuncios throughout Europe were very actively engaged in a wide variety of efforts to stop the deportations of Jews where they could and to save and hide them where they could not. In Italy, 80% of the Jews were saved, and thousands more in other places (such as Southern Croatia) by the Italian Army, often with the direct urging of the Pope or his representatives. Archbishop Angelo Rotta in Budapest (see page 164), for example, worked closely with Raoul Wallenberg of Sweden to save Jews. Indeed, it was Rotta who first organized the four 'neutral' embassies to try to protect the Jews. Wallenberg was sent to Budapest to join Rotta's activities. This dangerous activity, such as forging false papers for Jews, of course was reported back to the Vatican's Secretary of State, who responded, 'Bravo, Monsignor!' Numerous interventions for the Jews were made with the Government of Hungary, initially with some success.

But, as Father Pierre Blet points out in *Pius XII and the Second World War*, most of the Vatican's efforts were in the end unsuccessful. Blet concludes that it is 'remarkable . . . that despite the fact that so many repeated interventions ended with only tenuous results in comparison with efforts expended, the Vatican in the midst of the uncertainties and the darkness within which it had to take action, continued in its life-saving work to the end.' Looking at much, if not all of the same evidence, however, Father John Morley in *Vatican Diplomacy and the Jews during the Holocaust 1939-43*

> *How is one to weigh Pius XII's policy in World War II, a policy carefully crafted by his predecessors over centuries going back to lessons learned the hard way during the Protestant Reformation, the French Revolution, and the emergence of the modern nation-state in the 19th and early 20th Centuries?*

For Further Reading

Pierre Blet. *Pius XII and the Second World War.* New York: Paulist Press, 1999.

John Morley. *Vatican Diplomacy and the Jews during the Holocaust 1939-43.* KTAV, 1980.

John S. Conway, 'Records and Documents of the Holy See Relating to the Second World War', in: M. Marrus, (ed.) *The Nazi Holocaust* and *Bystanders to the Holocaust,* Volume 3, pp. 1227-1245.

For Reflection

Would you agree that 'historical truth lies somewhere in the ambiguities between extremes'?

In the face of extreme evil, to what extent do you think neutrality is possible?

Do you think it is possible or desirable for religious leaders to predict and intervene in the process and outcome of political events?

Eugene J. Fisher (USA) is Director of Catholic-Jewish Relations for the Secretariat for Ecumenical and Interreligious Affairs of the National Conference of Catholic Bishops, Washington, DC. He is also Consultor to the Vatican Commission for Religious Relations with the Jews. Dr. Fisher is the author or editor of sixteen books and over 200 articles in major religious journals.

concluded more starkly that the Pope's emphasis on 'reserve and prudence' acted in the end to restrain his diplomats from 'other options', such as 'ecclesiastic sanctions on the guilty parties or nations' that might have been utilized if the Pope had spoken out more forcefully. In any event, the simplistic word 'silence' that has been used by some with reference to Pius XII is not helpful to an understanding of the complexities involved.

Two recent initiatives may shed, not so much 'new' light, as the light of dispassionate reason on the symbolically charged questions surrounding the pious Italian Catholic convicted in the world press today as ultimately responsible for virtually all the evils of the first half of the Twentieth Century; that is to say, everybody's all too convenient scapegoat. The first is an academic conference in April 2000, organized by the editors of this collection. Good scholars are involved. One can only have the expectation that the results, while not resolving all the issues, will at least clarify them and bring the discussion to a better understanding of the complexity of the questions that must be honestly faced.

The second initiative is a longer-term process co-sponsored by the Vatican and the International Jewish Committee for Inter-religious Consultations (IJCIC). Again, very good scholars are involved; this time just six; three Catholics appointed by the Holy See and three Jews appointed by IJCIC. As the 'Catholic Coordinator', I can say at this point that the joint project is well begun. The joint statement, issued at their first meeting in New York on December 7, 1999, is available on the web site of the US Catholic conference (www.nccbuscc.org) and the Jewish/Christian dialogue web site created by Fritz Voll of Calgary (www.jcrelations.com). These list the scholars as well.

It will be most interesting to see how the joint historical commission of Catholic and Jewish scholars frames from first-hand evidence these awesomely difficult historical questions and *post facto* judgments.

PIUS XII AND THE HOLOCAUST

Jonathan Gorsky

The Role of the Vatican during the Holocaust years remains highly controversial. The argument is focused upon the alleged failure of Pope Pius XII to speak out on behalf of the victims of the Holocaust and explicitly condemn Nazism.

Supporters of the Pope point to thousands of Jews rescued by Catholic institutions in Rome and across Europe, as well as the endeavors of nuncios (papal ambassadors) on behalf of Jews in different countries occupied by Nazi Germany. They note that in the post-war years distinguished Jewish figures expressed gratitude to the Vatican for their endeavors and a forest was planted in Israel in memory of the Pope on his death in 1958. They argue that controversy was only stirred up when Rolf Hochhuth's play, *The Representative*, appeared in 1963 and accused the Pope of complicity with Nazism, motivated by fear of the bolshevik threat sweeping across Europe.

Papal Critics

Papal critics point to the failure of Pius XII publicly to condemn either Nazism or the Holocaust. There was no explicit Papal reference to Jewish suffering throughout the war years, nor was there clear condemnation of Nazism in the Pope's addresses. Information received by the Vatican from 1942 onwards was not disseminated, nor was direction given to Bishops and the Catholic faithful with regard to the treatment of Jews. Church efforts on behalf of Jews in the occupied countries depended on local initiative and the particular inclinations of the nuncios, who might or might not be sympathetic. It was only late in 1944 that the Vatican responded adequately in helping to forestall the deportation of the Jews of Hungary, and throughout the war the Vatican appeared indifferent to the horrors perpetrated by a Catholic government in Croatia.

Each case requires careful analysis, for neither set of arguments is as clear-cut as its protagonists maintain.

The Vatican endeavored to find places of refuge for Jews after *Kristallnacht* in November 1938, and the Pope instructed local bishops to help all who were in need at the beginning of the war.

The rescue of thousands of Jews during the Holocaust, and the opening of Catholic institutions as places of shelter, could not have occurred in the face of Papal disapproval. This is especially true with regard to institutions within the confines of Rome and the Vatican. The fact of the rescue is not

> *Supporters of the Pope point to thousands of Jews rescued by Catholic institutions in Rome and across Europe . . . Papal critics point to the failure of Pius XII publicly to condemn either Nazism or the Holocaust . . . Each case requires careful analysis, for neither set of arguments is as clear-cut as its protagonists maintain.*

"For a long time during those frightful years I waited for a great voice to speak up in Rome. I, an unbeliever? Precisely. For I knew that the spirit would be lost if it did not utter a cry of condemnation when faced with force. It seems that that voice did speak up. But I assure you that millions of men like me did not hear it and that at that time believers and unbelievers alike shared a solitude that continued to spread as the days went by and the executioners multiplied.

"It has been explained to me since that the condemnation was indeed voiced. But that it was in the style of the encyclicals, which is not at all clear. The condemnation was voiced and it was not understood! Who could fail to feel where the true condemnation lies in this case and to see that this example by itself gives part of the reply, perhaps the whole reply, that you ask of me. What the world expects of Christians is that Christians should speak out, loud and clear, and that they should voice their condemnation in such a way that never a doubt, never the slightest doubt, could rise in the heart of the simplest man. That they should get away from abstraction and confront the blood-stained face history has taken on today."

Albert Camus. Statement made at the Dominican Monastery of Latour-Maubourg, 1948.

disputed. Although critics have maintained that some of the figures adduced by Papal supporters are considerably exaggerated, no one has denied the significant scale of Catholic rescue activity, and gratitude was indeed expressed by leading Jews after the war.

Crucial Testimony

However compilations of Jewish post-war responses in Vatican documents have tended to ignore the crucial testimonies of Gerhardt Riegner and Rudolf Vrba. Riegner manned the office of the World Jewish Congress in Geneva throughout the war years and endeavored to convey information about the Holocaust to the Allies. He was more closely involved with the Vatican than the Jewish figures whom Pius XII's supporters tend to cite. Rudolf Vrba escaped from Auschwitz in April 1944 and, like Riegner, made desperate efforts to solicit help in the free world. He too had important contact with the Vatican. Riegner maintains that the Vatican was unhelpful until 1944, and Vrba, who had a six-hour meeting in that year with a Papal diplomat, claims that none of his material was ever circulated or publicized.

The argument adduced by Pius XII's supporters that the Papal policy commanded general assent until the Hochhuth play in 1963 also requires qualification. The Pope was aware of criticism during the war, and it was not confined to Jewish spokespersons, who tended to be quite reserved. At the highest level, the French Cardinal Tisserant wanted a forthright condemnation of Nazism, and Jacques Maritain was a notable post-war critic of Papal policy. Other dissenters included the leader of the Polish Government in Exile and the United States Representative in the Vatican. It is important to note that criticism was not only voiced by Jews, but by others who were looking for a forthright religious stand on Nazism and German behavior in occupied Europe. It has also been claimed that the Pope himself agonized over his wartime policy and believed that he was confronted by moral dilemmas that were apparently insoluble.

The key criticism of Pius XII revolves around his 'silence', that is, his failure to speak out explicitly about the Holocaust. Critics, particularly at popular level, tend to assume that the issues were straightforward and require no analysis. In consequence they have not attended to the Pope's own stated position.

Guarded Statements

It is important to note that the Vatican strongly condemned Nazi ideology in the late '20s and throughout the '30s. Cardinal Pacelli, as Pius XII then was, was particularly outspoken. But even his supporters do not dispute that Papal pronouncements during the war were extremely guarded.

At its strongest, the case for this policy is that explicit attacks on the Nazi regime would have had serious consequences for Catholics throughout occupied Europe, and might have made the situation even worse for Jews and anyone the Church sought to defend. The examples usually cited are the reprisals taken against Catholics of Jewish origin in Holland in 1942, after an outspoken condemnation by Holland's Catholic bishops of the deportation of Dutch Jewry. Catholic institutions were able to shelter victims of Nazism, only provided their neutrality was respected by German forces.

This is a substantial argument, albeit one that has in turn been open to controversy. The Dutch example, when the bishops clearly decided where their duty lay, is not the only instance of religious protest in occupied Europe and there are equally well-known cases when no reprisals were taken, notably Cardinal von Galen's indictment of the Nazi euthanasia policy in 1941.

Pius XII's position appears to have been formulated soon after the Nazi occupation of Poland. In 1937, Cardinal Pacelli, as Pius XII then was, helped draft *Mit Brennender Sorge*, his predecessor's powerful critique of Nazism; and his own first encyclical, issued soon after the invasion of Poland in 1939, included a strong statement about Polish suffering, although it did not explicitly condemn German aggression. But he was informed by some leading Polish Catholics that similar statements made over Vatican radio were leading to vicious Nazi reprisals and the Papal responses to the invasion of the Low Countries in 1940 were noticeably muted.

Sister Pasqualina

In 1998, Sister Pasqualina, who supervised the Pope's household during the war years, claimed that the Pope had intended to write about Jewish suffering in 1942, but stopped short when he heard about the savage response to the Dutch bishops' endeavors in Holland. There is also evidence that the Pope instructed church leaders to act positively at local level, if they felt that some good could be achieved, but he appears to have believed that the consequences of a Papal statement were dangerously unpredictable, as such a statement would be heard in every part of occupied Europe, regardless of particular circumstances.

> Throughout the war, the Pope was determined to maintain Vatican neutrality, and in the early years he hoped to be able to negotiate peace between Germany and the Allies. The Pope was following a well-established Vatican policy in times of war, but clearly Nazism represented an unprecedented political evil, and in the circumstances of World War II, such neutrality raised complex moral issues,

Throughout the war, the Pope was determined to maintain Vatican neutrality, and in the early years he hoped to be able to negotiate peace between Germany and the Allies. The Pope was following a well-established Vatican policy in times of war, but clearly Nazism represented an unprecedented political evil, and in the circumstances of World War II, such neutrality raised complex moral issues, exacerbated by a lack of interest in Vatican mediation on the part of the belligerents. Furthermore, the

For Reflection

Do you evaluate the sense of moral concern any given participant in history feels by what they do?

Does the apparent inaction of the Vatican concern its indifference towards the plight of the Jews?

Why did the Vatican not follow th example of other Church leaders who did make statements on behalf of the Jews?

For Further Reading

N. Perry, and F. M. Schweitzer. *Jewish-Christian Encounters Over the Centuries.* NY: Peter Lang, 1994.

Saul Friedlander. *Pius XII and the Third Reich.* New York: Alfred A. Kanpf, 1966.

C. Falconi. *The Silence of Pius XII.* Boston: Little, Brown & Co., 1970.

policy of neutrality inhibited the Vatican's capacity to act on behalf of the victims, and might have been responsible for the obstacles encountered by Gerhardt Riegner.

Some commentators have emphasized the Papal Concordat with Hitler's Germany signed in 1933 and negotiated by Cardinal Pacelli as Papal Nuncio. Combined with the Pope's profound hostility to Bolshevism, this seems to provide damaging insight into Vatican policy, but the argument has considerable weaknesses. By the period of the Holocaust, Vatican relations with Germany were very tense, and little remained of the Concordat. Nazi intentions for the Catholic Church were made very clear in the Warthegau, a Polish territory assimilated to the Reich, where the Church was subject to draconian legislation, as well as in Germany itself. Also, the Vatican did not recognize German territorial expansion, and offered no support for Operation *Barbarossa*, when Germany invaded Soviet Russia in 1941. American Catholics who had qualms about working in armament factories supplying weapons to Russia were privately reassured by the Vatican. The Roman Catholic Church indeed opposed Bolshevism, but as the Russian people had been attacked, they were entitled to defend themselves.

Vatican Archives

Controversy in recent years has also focused on the unwillingness of the Vatican to open its wartime archives to public scrutiny. The Vatican has in fact published twelve volumes of important archive documents but only one has been translated into English – the others appear in the original languages with introductory essays in French. The material is copious and has been mined by a number of historians, notably Professors John Conway and Owen Chadwick, who drastically revised Hochhuth's damning verdict on Pius XII's involvement in the 1943 deportation of 1,000 Jews from Rome, but there is also material that has been used by Pius' critics. The archive documentation was edited 'in-house', by Catholic scholars selected by the Vatican, and inevitably this has been a source of disquiet. Also the editors have been faulted for their failure to include the 1942 Riegner Memorandum, which provided the Vatican with crucial information about the Holocaust, but the material that has appeared is substantial and important.

It is important to note that we are not dependent on Vatican archival material alone for our understanding of Papal policy during the war. Vatican radio transcripts and *Osservatore Romano*, the Vatican newspaper, are available, as are the public speeches given by the Pope. Memoirs, diaries and diplomatic archives published by the belligerents provide vital sources of information. Carlo Falconi's examination of the papers of Croatian emissaries to the Vatican yielded material of great importance, as did his study of similar papers from Poland. (Falconi's highly critical analysis of the Croatian material has as yet elicited no satisfactory response from Vatican supporters.)

The role of the Vatican in the Second World War leaves many moral dilemmas unresolved. During the war the Vatican remained neutral, and did not endorse the Allied campaign. Historic Vatican policy in times of war is to remain equally available to all sides as a peacemaker. This role would be compromised by partisan support. But when an evil of the magnitude of Nazism arises, is neutrality really an option for religious leadership?

There were major Roman Catholic communities on both sides of the conflict and from the perspective of Roman Catholic belief the preservation of the Church is of paramount importance, for it is the decisive instrument of human salvation. But Croatia in particular exposes the dilemma that supporting Church interests might run counter to clear moral obligation in time of horrific suffering. The Catholic regime in Croatia was perceived as being of great significance for the Church, but its murderous behavior was unacceptable to religious morality. Failure to condemn this behavior obviously sent messages to the Croatian regime.

The Ultimate Dilemma

Two clear positions do emerge from the debate about Pius XII. For his supporters, the Pope avoided making public statements because there was a strong possibility that they would expose innocent people to drastic Nazi reprisals. They emphasize that Catholic institutions rescued thousands of Jews. Papal opponents focus on the particular evil that Nazism represented and maintain that in such circumstances religious leadership must be clear, forthright and outspoken. Nazi aggression and brutality should have been explicitly condemned; Roman Catholics might have been inspired to do more for Jews and other victims of persecution, who would at least have had the comfort of knowing that the world was not indifferent to their fate. The argument exposes the dilemmas facing religious leaders who confront political tyranny: these dilemmas have much contemporary relevance in both religious and political spheres and clearly warrant further exploration.

Jonathan Gorsky (UK) is Education Advisor to The Council for Christians and Jews, UK. He teaches and writes about the Holocaust and Christian-Jewish Relations, and is editor of *Common Ground*, the journal of the Council of Christians and Jews.

THE VATICAN
AND THE HOLOCAUST

John T. Pawlikowski

At a major international Jewish-Christian Conference in Vienna in 1988 Bernard Lewis strongly cautioned against excessive generalization with regard to the role of the church during the Nazi era. He urged instead a painstaking country by country analysis in Europe, taking into account the church's particular social and political position in each nation. Only such an approach can lead to a fair assessment of the Catholic response. One of the best examples of such an approach is found in the volume *Judaism and Christianity under the Impact of National Socialism: 1919-1945* edited by Otto Dov Kulka and Paul R. Mendes-Flohr.

There is little question that Vatican policy on the rescue of Jews was very reserved. This does not mean that no actions were taken, directly or indirectly. On the contrary, recent archival research, by Pierre Blet S.J. and others, has uncovered more activity than was once imagined. But just about all of it was behind the scenes, sometimes undertaken by papal nuncios rather than by officials in the Vatican itself. And it is clear that the rescue of Jews was never a high priority for the Vatican. Nonetheless, while theological anti-Judaism was commonplace in church circles during this period, there is little evidence to suggest any significant sympathy for the Nazi extermination of Jews within the Vatican hierarchy, including Popes Pius XI and Pius XII. What blocked greater Vatican commitment to Jewish rescue was the much higher priority accorded other Catholic concerns during this difficult time.

One impeding obstacle to a more concerted effort was Pius XII's perception of himself and that of the Vatican as a peacemaker in Europe. Professor John Conway has argued that Pius XII inherited this viewpoint from his mentor Pope Benedict XV. While Conway may somewhat overemphasize the significance of this 'peacemaker' perspective, there is no doubt that it played an important role in generating a policy of supposed 'neutrality' on the part of the Vatican in the hope that it could broker a peace between the Third Reich and the Allied governments. There is also some evidence, far from conclusive however, that important persons in the Vatican were convinced of an ultimate Nazi victory during the early stages of the war. It is only in the later stages of the war when the tide began to turn

'. . . a year ago in the columns of Tygodnik Powszechny . . . Ewa Berberyusz [wrote]: 'Possibly even if more of us had turned out to be Christian, it would have made no difference to the extermination, but maybe it would not have been such a lonely death'. Jerzy Turowicz said: 'If we had not had such antisemitism in Poland before the war, perhaps we would still not have been able to save more Jewish lives, but our attitude to the extermination taking place before our very eyes would have been different.' This is in my opinion the crux of the matter.'

Victor Erlich in *My Brother's Keeper? Recent Polish Debates on the Holocaust*, ed. Antony Polonsky, p. 199.

towards the Allies and the devastation wrought by Nazi policies was becoming increasingly apparent to everyone that the Vatican began to move away from this policy of neutrality.

An even more critical factor in shaping Vatican policy during the war was the Vatican's goal of preserving the status of the Catholic church at all costs. Church preservation was a goal it shared with many Protestant churches, especially in Germany, during the Third Reich, as the contributors to the work edited by Robert P. Ericksen and Susannah Heschel, *German Churches and the Holocaust: Betrayal,* clearly demonstrate. Pius XII's efforts to secure the Concordat with Hitler is one example of this. He became convinced that, while the Nazis might well violate some provision of the Concordat, the agreement would on balance stabilize the Catholic church's position in Germany and restore it to a status it had not enjoyed since the time of Otto von Bismarck. The Vatican was also committed to the preservation of the old classical social order in Europe. Despite their grave reservations about aspects of Nazi policy, particularly its racial dimensions, those who fundamentally molded Vatican policy concluded that the Third Reich represented an important bulwark against the advancing forces of liberalism and Bolshevism. While the Vatican itself did not directly engage in strong criticism of Jews for supporting these two 'enemy' ideologies, it raised no strong objections when Cardinals and bishops in such countries as Poland and Germany did so. The signal was given that it was permissible policy to fault the Jews on this score. It was only in his Christmas radio addresses of the early forties that Pius XII gave some hint of moving away from the support of the old classical social order in Europe in light of the war.

Leading historians such as Fr. John Morley and Michael Marrus have confirmed this overriding priority of church preservation on the part of the Vatican. In his important study *Vatican Diplomacy and the Jews,* KTAV, 1980, Morley argued that the Vatican could have done far more to save Jews and other Nazi victims through the judicious use of papal nuncios. Papal nuncios were in fact effective in this regard in such places as Budapest (Angelo Rotta) and Istanbul (Angelo Roncalli, the future Pope John XXIII). Morley sees the problem as centered not in crass Papal indifference to Jews but in the tone of Vatican diplomacy which Pius XII set during this era. Prudence and reserve were its prevailing characteristics. It studiously tried to avoid offending any nation, the Third Reich included. This approach had a straitjacket effect on Vatican diplomacy and in no way differentiated it from the posture of the civil states. In fact, on occasion representatives of the Allied camp such as the Polish Government-in-Exile in London spoke more candidly and specifically about the Jewish question than the Vatican. Michael Marrus of the University of Toronto also locates the muted response of the Vatican to Nazism fundamentally in the diplomatic style Eugenio Pacelli had helped to shape during the political storms of the Depression era as Pius XI's Secretary of State. He acknowledges Vatican

The former Great Synagogue, one of the Warsaw Jewish community's beautiful buildings, lies in ruins like much of the Ghetto around it.

'Marking the fiftieth anniversary of the liberation of Auschwitz, Pope John Paul II said that many people of different nationalities had died in Nazi death camps, but 'in particular the children of the Jewish people, for whom the Nazi regime had planned a systematic extermination, suffered the experience of the Holocaust. . . . Let us pray and work so that this does not happen. Never again antisemitism. Never again the arrogance of nationalism. Never again genocide.'

Nechama Tec, 'The Vatican, the Catholic Religion, the Jews' *in Holocaust Scholars Write to the Vatican,* ed. Harry James Cargas. p. 34.

For Further Reading

Helen Fein. *Accounting for Genocide: National Responses and Jewish Victimization during the Holocaust.* Chicago: University of Chicago Press, 1984.

Otto Dov Kulka and Paul R. Mendes-Flohr eds., *Judaism and Christianity under the Impact of National Socialism.* Jerusalem: The Historical Society of Israel, 1982.

Henri de Lubac. *Christian Resistance to Antisemitism: Memories from 1940-1944.* San Fransisco: Ignatius Press, 1990.

Michael R. Marrus. *The Holocaust in History.* New York: New American Library, 1987.

Marvin Perry and Frederick M. Schweitzer (eds.), *Jewish-Christian Encounters over the Centuries: Symbiosis, Prejudice, Holocaust, Dialogue.*

arguments both with Hitler and Mussolini on racial questions, but insists that the opposition had more to do with the Christian theology of baptism than it did with deep concern about the plight of the Jews. Even after the publication of *Mit Brennender Sorge*, the Papal Encyclical against Nazism issued in 1937 by Pius XI, the Vatican strove to prevent an open breach with the Third Reich. The primary goal remained, in Marrus' words, 'a political neutrality and the safeguarding of the institutional interests of the Church in a perilous political world.' ('The Vatican and the Holocaust', *Congress Monthly,* January 1988, p.7.) The first few years of the war saw little Vatican protest against growing Nazi hostility towards the Jewish community, no more in fact than in the 1930s. Catholic representatives spoke generally about justice, but remained largely unconcerned about the antisemitic campaigns being developed by the Third Reich and collaborationist governments. When the murder of Jews began in earnest, says Marrus, the Vatican refused to issue more than the most general of condemnations despite its excellent information on the seriousness of the Jewish condition.

Marrus joins many other historians in arguing that the root cause of the limited Vatican response was diplomatic style. Vatican documents, he insists, do not show any guarded pro-Nazism or a supreme priority of opposition to the Soviet Union. In fact, Pius XII was known to have sheltered several hundred Jewish orphans at the Papal summer residence. Clearly neither simple hostility, nor deep-seated antisemitism, nor callous indifference explain the Vatican's posture during this time. What extant documents establish beyond all doubt is the dominance of a policy of 'reserve and conciliation' under Pius XII which not only shaped his approach but served on the whole as a model for the Church's diplomatic corps as well. For Marrus, the controlling reality under Pius XII was preservation of the Church. All else took second place. The same perspective is shared by another Holocaust historian, Nora Levin, though she attributes somewhat more direct influence to the bolshevik factor as a principal threat to Catholic survival than does Marrus. This priority of Church survival led Pius XII and the Vatican, in Levin's words, to view the Jews as 'unfortunate expendables'. (*The Holocaust*, Schocken, 1973, p. 693.) In the terms of Helen Fein, they fell outside the 'universe of moral obligation'.

There were certainly examples of Vatican intervention on behalf of Jews. They were not a total 'non-priority'. Often these interventions came as a result of intensified pressure from Jewish organizations or Allied governments rather than being initiated by the Vatican. The best examples are in Hungary where Admiral Horthy received a strongly worded 'open telegram' and the Vatican seemingly supported the intensive efforts of the Papal Nuncio Angelo Rotta to issue letters of protection for Jews (some 13,000 according to Rotta's report to the Vatican) and in Slovakia where President Tiso (a Catholic priest) relaxed pressure against the Jews after a Papal appeal. There was also some effort made in Romania though Gerhardt Riegner tends to attribute this intervention more to local Catholic leaders than the Vatican itself. In France the Vatican's reaction to the Jewish condition in the unoccupied regions, while critical of Vichy policy, was much weaker in tone than the statements of several French bishops such as Bishop Saliège and Bishop Théas who strongly condemned the Vichy government's anti-Jewish legislation and its willingness to deport Jews into the hands of the Nazis.

Notice also must be taken of rescue activities undertaken by Catholic nuns in Italy and Poland in particular and by members of Catholic resistance groups in France and Italy (the Assisi Underground). These groups felt, and in some cases were assured, that they had the support of Pius XII for their activities. How much 'credit' the Vatican can be given for such regional interventions is a matter of dispute among historians. Consensus is surely lacking whether more public and sustained efforts by the popes of the Holocaust era and their Vatican staff would have made much difference in the end in terms of Jewish survival. Many people think it would have. Some prominent historians such as Günther Lewy, himself a critic of Vatican policy during the Third Reich, think not. The more fundamental issue today is to assess whether the 'reserve' diplomacy served the Church well during the Nazi period and whether, even if it had not made much difference in the actual number of Jewish survivors, church leadership had a moral obligation to speak out in protest to preserve its moral integrity as the late Catholic historian Edward Gargan and others have always insisted. These questions need to be pursued in earnest by contemporary Christians.

Building of the Warsaw Ghetto wall

For Reflection

How can Christians and Jews 'work together,' as Pope John Paul II put it, 'to prevent the repetition of such heinous evil'?

To what extent is it possible to avoid offending evil without condoning it?

John T. Pawlikowski O.S.M.
(USA), Professor of Social Ethics at the Catholic Theological Union in Chicago, has been a member of the United States Holocaust Memorial Council since 1980. He currently chairs the Council's Committee on Church Relations. The author of many publications on the Holocaust and Christian-Jewish relations, including *The Challenge of the Holocaust for Christian Theology*, Pawlikowski is also a member of the National Conference of Catholic Bishops' advisory committee on Catholic-Jewish relations.

THE CASE OF PIUS XII: CHRISTIANS AND JEWS IN CONFRONTATION

Albert H. Friedlander

Emerging out of the miasma of the 'Holocaust Kingdom', all of us were damaged within the core of our being. When we try to confront this today, we come to realize human imperfections, which are embedded within that history; but we also see traces of human greatness. My wife's aunt, for example, was smuggled from convent to convent during the darkest years, and lived on for over 50 years to express her gratitude to her saviors. I was a child in Berlin, with memories of Christians who tried to protect me in school and who hid me during the days of the national pogrom of November 1938. In all the years that followed, particularly after I became a rabbi, I felt close to the Christian community – whether walking alongside Martin Luther King from Selma to Montgomery, or in Great Britain working with the CCJ in the company of the late Cardinal Hume and the Archbishop of Canterbury. In Germany, I have given papers at the *Katholischentag* (every two years, between the meetings of the Protestant *Kirchentag*); I have been asked to address my friends on theological concerns which we share.

The 'case' of Pius XII brought my dialogue/confrontation to a new level of thinking. Last year, at conferences I attended in Prague, Vienna, and Trier, this issue both united and divided me with my Catholic colleagues. Both the sanctification of Edith Stein, and the proposals regarding the beatification process of Pope Pius XII gave us problems, which remained unresolved. I had been asked by the London Catholic periodical *The Tablet* to express a Jewish view on this burning issue. The request worried me greatly. Still, my text appeared in *The Tablet*, London, January 2, 1999.

Should a rabbi enter the internal discussions of the Church, particularly in regard to Church doctrine? Should not the Catholic Church engage in its soul-searchings without interference from the outside? And I was clearly not an objective judge in an area where I and my family had suffered in the Holocaust. Yes, I was mindful of the goodness I had encountered from Christians at that time. Still, I carried a great deal of emotional baggage into this issue. Could I really act as the categor, the biblical accuser who is normally played by Satan (see the Book of *Job*)? Each individual – or Church – must probe into its own conscience to make its decision.

> 'We tend to be very selective in our memories and this is particularly true of religious traditions . . . we like to defend ourselves by our good memories, by the lives of saints . . . but there are also tragic memories . . . it is important for Christians to remember, liturgically if possible, the Holocaust.'

In an elegant, philosophic mode, Hegel referred to our conscience as this deepest, inner loneliness within itself. On that level, the Church and the individual Catholic must turn inwardly, without advice from the outside. Nevertheless, the Church lives in this world; its thoughts and actions of yesterday and of today affect its neighbors. And yesterday was the time of the Holocaust.

Have all of us really confronted that world in terms of the inheritance it has left us? My Christian colleagues start with the assertion that we are all sinners. I have my doubts: if we all sin – nobody sins! I know a rabbi cannot tell Christians what to believe; but should he not criticize actions by neighbors, which hurt his own community? Memories should not be flawed. I do recall Jews who collaborated with the Nazis because they were powerless victims, placed alongside those who became involved with the Nazis without being forced to do so; I find myself making judgments but know that we must look at individual cases and not issue blanket condemnations. We must also examine the history. The Church was under pressure from the Nazis, and at times took the easy road which was seldom the right road. Must we not look at it? It could hide from its conscience inside doctrines, which became rationalizations. At times, its theology was wrong; and this pains me. Religion must be prepared to suffer; it cannot always be diplomatic. And today, even an act of contrition and remembering the Holocaust in that fashion can be wrong enough for a rabbi to express his disappointment in a faith and its leaders whom he respects highly.

> *Religion must be prepared to suffer; it cannot always be diplomatic.*

And so I look at recent theological decisions of the Church. In a sermon given in the St. Vitus Cathedral in Prague, I acknowledged the Pope's desire to place the Holocaust into the prayers and memories of the Church through Edith Stein. That is another issue. But what about Pius XII?

It becomes clear to me that we cannot just examine the Holocaust as historians. We must place this anguish into our liturgy so that our faith can confront it. This also carried dangers with it. Elie Wiesel and I wrote a prayer book to be used by Christians and Jews on Holocaust Memorial Day. In his introduction to it, Cardinal Hume wrote: 'We tend to be very selective in our memories and this is particularly true of religious traditions . . . we like to defend ourselves by our good memories, by the lives of saints . . . but they are also tragic memories . . . it is important for Christians to remember, liturgically, if possible, the Holocaust'. (Wiesel and Friedlander *The Six Days of Destruction* pp. 9-10.)

The case of that Pope is an internal matter – or is it? Cardinal Hume's words, 'We like to defend ourselves by our good memories. . . by the lives of saints', have a direct impact here. It is clear that the Vatican's role during the Holocaust is the issue here, and that the Jewish community is addressed. Are there not doubts here even within the Catholic community? How, otherwise, could it permit a direct

For Reflection

Do you think that the Christian religion is self critical?

Do you think that religious traditions and people of faith should be self critical?

Do you think that Christians are sufficiently sensitive toward and informed about the traditions and perspectives of other faiths?

For Further Reading

'The Tragedy of Pius XII' in *The Tablet*, London: 2 January 1999.

'Pius XII as he really was' in *The Tablet*, London: 13 February 1999.

John Cornwell. *Hitler's Pope: The Secret History of Pius XII*. New York: Viking, 1999.

George Bull. *Inside the Vatican*. New York: 1982.

Jonathan Steinberg. *All or Nothing: The Axis and the Holocaust 1941-43*. London: 1990.

antisemitic attack by the vice-postulator Fr. Kurt-Peter Gumpel in Rome in defense of the beatification procedure for Pope Pius XII?

In an article in *The Tablet* which followed my text, Father Gumpel states that: 'The materials in my possession confirm that no one of whatever station or organization did as much to help the Jews as did Pius XII and, at his explicit instruction, the Roman Catholic Church' ('Pope Pius XII as he really was', *The Tablet*, 13 February 1999).

He takes the Jewish awareness of the Pope's 'timidity' to be a direct attack upon the Vatican, and demands that one should now examine the Jewish attacks upon Christianity through the centuries. Is this a way for the Church to defend itself? Do his wildly inaccurate claims for Pius XII as a defender and savior of the Jews during the Holocaust advance the beatification process? And what are the facts of this case? The recent book by John Cornwell, *Hitler's Pope: The Secret History of Pius XII*, cannot be ignored by serious scholars.

It is easier to dismiss Fr. Gumpel – even if he *can* point to the tragic history of his own family – as an old-fashioned bigot whose claim to be 'a friend of the Jews' falters when he looks at his neighbors. The Jewish community sees Fr. Gumpel as bigoted, which he is – but what is happening within the Church? Again, the voices from outside should lead to an inner examination. Has the Church taken any action of censure against Fr. Gumpel for his intemperate remarks? And does the pain expressed by the Jewish community have any impact upon the deliberations leading to sainthood for Pius XII? A rabbi cannot put himself into the position of being the advocate for the devil; the procedure within this process must express its own doubts within its own system. Yet it would be disastrous for all of us, Jews and Christians, if this debate were to result in a closing of ranks and of the mind in Rome. The fact remains that the dark history of the time of the Holocaust is part of any assessment of individuals during that testing period.

Who is a saint in the time of evil? The rabbis take the Genesis text: 'And Noah was a righteous man in his time' and examine it closely. Did it mean that 'in his time' suggests that the standards were much lower? Anyone who was not totally evil could be called righteous. Or does it mean that in such an evil time anyone fighting it had to be particularly good? The end decision was in Noah's favor, even though his actions after leaving the ark cause much concern. In the time of the Nazis, we find a similar situation: does silence or indirect action constitute the moral resistance required when one does not put one's life at risk? Many

> 'The question is *not* whether the Pope was evil, but: was he a saint? I must ask the Church to re-assess its conscience. Does not 'sainthood' indicate a superhuman effort? And: if the Church wants to be a teaching testimony to everyone, should it not take extra care, even if it leaves the establishment of those days less than perfect?'

individuals had to make that choice. As I indicated, there were moral failures among the victims as well. But I am concerned with the apathetic onlookers. Standing on the outside, I would and should not act as judge. The question is *not* whether he was evil, but: was he a saint? I must ask the Church to re-assess its conscience. Does not 'sainthood' indicate a superhuman effort? And: if the Church wants to be a teaching testimony to everyone, should it not take extra care, even if it leaves the establishment of those days less than perfect? After the loneliness of the inner search, we have to confront one another face to face; and we have to share the common pain alongside the moments of light which reach out from our past.

'After the loneliness of the inner search, we have to confront one another face to face; and we have to share the common pain alongside the moments of light which reach out from our past.'

Albert H. Friedlander (UK), a rabbi, is Dean of Leo Baeck College, London and Vice-President of the Council of Christians and Jews. He is an established author and commentator on the Holocaust and its implications for Jews and Christians.

DOCUMENT:
HUMANI GENERIS UNITAS

Humani Generis Unitas (The Unity of the Human Race): Excerpts from an Encyclical Never Published

In June 1938, after his attempts at diplomacy with Nazi Germany and Fascist Italy had failed, Pope Pius XI ordered an American Jesuit priest, Father John LaFarge, to draft an encyclical letter for him denouncing racism and antisemitism. The result was Humani Generis Unitas, but, for a variety of reasons, not least among them that Pius XI died in early 1939, the encyclical was never published. In 1997, the full text in English was published by Georges Passelecq and Bernard Suchecky in their book, The Hidden Encyclical of Pius XI (New York: Harcourt Brace & Co., 1997), pp. 176-275. What follows is an excerpt from the English text of Humani Generis Unitas. The numbers at the beginning of each paragraph refer to the numbered paragraphs in the text itself.

2. . . . at a time when so many contradictory theories are leading to increased disorder in human life in society, the church has a duty to speak to the world. . . .

3. In doing so, the Church is not encroaching on foreign terrain; she does not seek to engage in "politics," pursues no personal interest; she is carrying out the pastoral mission of teaching with which she is entrusted by her divine Founder. This teaching mission concerns not only the immediate or mediate content of Christian revelation, but also everything required to enlighten and direct consciences in everyday life. . . .

111. When we arrive at the issue of race, we find a striking example of the harm caused by the false, sentimental, and almost mystical way of speaking that has been applied to the ideas of nation, people, and state. . . .

116. . . . racism denies, practically if not theoretically, that there are objective goals and values common to humanity as a whole.

117. Let us examine racism's moral teaching, whose essential thesis we have recently been obliged to condemn. "The strength of the race and the purity of its blood must be preserved: any means that serves this end is, for that reason alone, good and legitimate." That is the rule of racist morality. We ask: Doesn't such a principle deny the essence of an objective moral order valid for all men and all times? Doesn't it abandon that order to the arbitrary will and instinct of particular races?. . .

119. . . . the existence of a natural moral law, which all men carry in their hearts, and which is

written by the Creator, is taught by Holy Scripture. Hence the racist rule of morality is once again in conflict with Catholic teaching in matters of faith and morals. It constitutes in addition a permanent threat to the security of public and private life, and to every kind of peace and order in the world. The world has become aware of the crisis it is suffering. . . .

120.   But racism is not satisfied with denying the value of a universal moral order as a blessing that unites humankind . . . we have already drawn attention to the false racist thesis that asserts that "Religion is subordinated to the law of race and must be adapted to that law." . . .

122.   . . . our Catholic faith teaches us as a fundamental truth that there is one God for all men and races, "the Father of our Lord Jesus Christ" (Ephesisans 1:3). The Christian religion, the only true religion, is thereby fundamentally adapted to all and ordained for all races. Anyone who denies this truth contradicts an essential manifestation of the Church's life, which is, moreover, expressed in the universal mission with which she was entrusted by her Founder . . .

123.   Simple respect for reality, as manifested in its consistency, in the light of divine revelation, many sciences, and experience, does not allow the Catholic to remain silent when confronted by racism. For as a Catholic, respect for what is must always be his essential trait. Therefore it must be repeated that racism cannot stand up to the test of the third negative criterion already established [earlier in the document]. According to this criterion, any group that claims an extensive totality, that is, which judges the content of all other purposes and values from the standpoint of its own purpose and fundamental scale of values, destroys the basic structure on which humanity depends in order to achieve true unity in authentic plurality. Thereby it reveals its inner falsity and its poverty. Now that is precisely what racism does, either in theory or in its practice. It makes the fact of racial grouping so central to its system, assigns it such an exclusive significance and efficacy, that in comparison all other social bonds and groupings no longer have a distinct, relatively independent individuality or foundation in law. . . .

131.   Those who have placed race illegitimately on a pedestal have rendered mankind a disservice. For they have done nothing to advance the unity to which humanity tends and aspires. One naturally wonders if this end is faithfully pursued by many of the principal advocates of so-called racial purity or if their aim is not rather to forge a clever slogan to move the masses to very different ends. This suspicion grows when one envisages how many subdivisions of a single race are judged and treated differently by the same men at the same time. It is further increased when it becomes clear that the struggle for racial purity ends by being uniquely the struggle against the Jews. Save for its systematic cruelty, this struggle is no different in true motives and methods from persecutions everywhere carried out against the Jews since antiquity. These persecutions have been censured by the Holy See on more than one occasion, but especially when they have worn the mantle of Christianity. . . .

THE CHALLENGE
OF THE EXCEPTION

A GLIMMER OF LIGHT

Nechama Tec

Jan Karski

'Courage is never alone, for it has fear as its ever-present companion. An act deserves to be called courageous if, and only if, it is performed in spite of fear. The greater the fear, the more courageous the action that defies it. Thus, it is only when fear and anxiety rule supreme that courage can truly assert itself.'

Shlomo Breznitz in *The Courage to Care: Rescuers of Jews During the Holocaust*, p. 149.

In the past, and now, I heard Jan Karski say, 'Jews were abandoned by all world governments but not by all individuals'. (Jan Karski, Personal Communication, 1999.) A Polish Catholic, a "Righteous Among the Nations", a World War II hero, an emissary for the Polish underground and the Polish Government-in-Exile, a professor of political science, Karski's observation grew out of his personal experiences. Mixed in with Karski's wartime political and humanitarian preoccupations was a strong opposition to the Nazi policies of the biological annihilation of the Jewish people. He tried to stop it by alerting the leaders of the free world to the systematic murder of the Jews.

In preparation for one of his illegal transatlantic journeys, Karski met with Jewish leaders in Poland and agreed to deliver their messages to the Allies and to others whom they saw as influential in the free world. In addition, with the help of the Jewish underground leaders, Karski smuggled himself twice into the Warsaw Ghetto, to gain first-hand knowledge of the Jewish plight. Then, for a report of another phase of Jewish destruction, dressed as a guard, Karski entered Izbica, which served as a looting, murdering and holding camp for Jews destined for the death camp, Belzec. Not only was Karski risking his life through these visits, but he endangered his psychological well-being as well. Confronted by the camp's degrading conditions, he suffered a nervous breakdown, which only magnified the threats to his life. (T. Thomas Wood and Stanislaw M. Jankowski, Karski, *How One Man Tried to Stop the Holocaust*, pp.124-130.)

Later, in the free world, Karski met with influential leaders including President Roosevelt and the British foreign minister, Anthony Eden. Karski's reports about the Jewish plight and the messages from the Jewish leaders that inevitably pleaded for help fell on deaf ears. For the Allies, as for other governments, the German systematic murder of the Jews was definitely not a priority. These personal contacts with high-ranking governmental officials must have convinced Karski that the Jews were abandoned by all world governments.

Karski's intellect and humanitarian spirit taught him some other lessons. He believes that even though in wartime Europe the murderers of Jews by far outnumbered those who wanted to save them, it is counter-productive to concentrate only on the murderers of Jews and ignore the minority that was determined to save them. This assertion Karski explains is based on two reasons. First, because it is historically untrue. Thousands of Christians tried to save Jews and were ready to die for them. Some did. Second, because this kind of an emphasis perpetuates the idea that 'everybody hates the Jews'. Not everyone hates the Jews. Christian rescuers felt that the Jews were valuable enough to risk their lives for them. In short, it is both historically incorrect and psychologically unhealthy to concentrate on the idea that no one wanted to save Jews (Jan Karski, *Personal Communication*, 1999).

It is generally agreed that in addition to the more than 16,000 Christians, recognized by Yad Vashem as Righteous Among the Nations, many more thousands of Christians tried to rescue Jews but for many reasons remain unknown. While the exact number of those who risked their lives to save Jews, for obvious and not so obvious reasons, will probably never be known, knowledge about the exact numbers is less important than insights about this kind of behavior. Such insight carries a promise of positive lessons.

Under the German occupation the appearance of Christians who selflessly risked their lives to save Jews signaled an opposition to the Nazi policies of Jewish destruction. Aid to Jews was illegal and endangered the lives of the rescuers and their families. And yet, each country under the German occupation had some individuals who endangered their lives for Jews. Significantly, too, of the Jews who survived in the illegal Christian world, practically all had benefited from some kind of aid. Moreover, my research is based on evidence from 309 Jews who survived the war by hiding or passing in the forbidden Christian world and who mention 565 Christian rescuers who tell that over 80 per cent of their protectors offered aid without any expectation of concrete rewards. (I, myself, benefited from the help of Christian rescuers who were motivated by profit. See: Nechama Tec, *Dry Tears, The Story of a Lost Childhood*. New York: Oxford University Press, 1982.) To be sure, there were some who saved Jews for money but they made up less than 20 percent. As a group, Christian rescuers who tried to save Jews without motivation for personal gains fit into the definition of altruistic rescuers. (For a comparison of altruistic and other kinds of rescuers, see: Nechama Tec, *When Light Pierced the Darkness, Christian Rescue of Jews in Nazi-Occupied Poland*. pp. 70-109.)

Concentrating on altruistic rescuers, what characteristics did they share? Who among the non-Jews was likely to try to overcome the many barriers and rescue Jews? Who was most likely to stand up for the persecuted Jews, traditionally viewed as 'Christ-killers' and blamed for every conceivable ill?

If we were a part of a group of people that included altruistic rescuers, we could not distinguish these rescuers from the rest of the group. Traditional ways for placing people into certain categories are of no help. When I compared large numbers of non-Jewish rescuers in terms of social class, education, political involvement, degree of antisemitism, extent of religious commitment, and friendship with Jews, they were very heterogeneous. Some of them came from higher, some from lower classes. Some were well-educated, while others were illiterate. Comparisons in terms of

'Once or twice in my life God has called me, and I have been there and responded to the call . . . Across the horrors [of the Holocaust] I thank Providence for making it possible for me to obey the commandment in Deuteronomy to love one's neighbor, a precious heritage of the election of Israel'

Olga St. Blancat-Baumgartner, France

religious and political affiliations also show much diversity. From these comparisons I had to conclude that conventional ways of categorizing people do not predict rescue.

A few examples of the Righteous Among the Nations illustrate their diversity. Returning to Jan Karski, a Righteous Gentile and an honorary citizen of Israel, he came from a socially privileged background. As a young university graduate he entered the Polish Foreign Service and was an aspiring young diplomat. His mother instilled in him tolerance for people who differed from him; this included Jews. The idea of social justice was a part of his upbringing and it meant standing up for the less fortunate. Catholicism played an important part in Karski's life. But religious practice did not interfere with the high value placed on independence.

'A brave act, by definition implies risk-taking. The issue to consider is, for whose sake is the risk taken? Is it for the sake of the individual himself or herself, a close relative, a dear friend, or is it a commitment to one's group or society? The more distant and intangible the cause, the greater the courage implied by the action. At the farthest extreme of motivation we find those who do not act for themselves or for their close kin but, like Emile Zola, for the sake of an abstract idea.
I maintain that there is even something more courageous than that. It is when one human being risks everything in order to help save another human being who has been hunted down, degraded, and abandoned by all.'

Shlomo Breznitz in *The Courage to Care: Rescuers of Jews During the Holocaust*, p. 151.

'Some people have asked me whether I was ever afraid. Oh, God, yes! I was scared to death. And very near death also.
At one point I was in the hands of the Gestapo, my husband was in jail, and the Nazis were doing a lot of house searching.
We were hiding 36 people, 32 Jews and four others who were also being sought by the Gestapo . . .
It was not always easy and often we were frightened but we were able to help a little bit, and we did it because we believed it was the right thing to do.'

Johje Vos, honored by Yad Vashem, along with her husband, Aart, as a Righteous Gentile, in *The Courage to Care: Rescuers of Jews During the Holocaust*, p.27.

In contrast, Stanislawa Dawidziuk (Szymkiewicz), a young factory worker in Warsaw, came from a poor working-class family. She had only a few years of schooling and completed her elementary school education after the war. Under the German occupation Stanislawa shared a one-room apartment with her husband, a waiter, and a teenage brother, an orphan. In 1943, at the husband's request she agreed to add to her cramped quarters a woman whose looks betrayed her Jewish background. The woman, Irena, was brought by Ryszard Kaminski, a Polish policeman, who begged

Stanislawa's husband to keep her just for one night. Next day Kaminski could not find a new home for Irena. Irena's single-day stay soon stretched into weeks. Stanislawa's husband refused to continue risking his life for their guest. He became adamant and demanded that his wife dismiss Irena. Stanislawa objected. She knew that Irena's appearance in the street would lead to her death. Eventually, in protest, Stanislawa's husband stormed out of the apartment, never to return.

In his absence Stanislawa gave birth to a boy. She arranged a special place behind a movable closet for Irena. Kaminski continued to visit, supplying them with modest provisions of food. Despite serious threats and several close calls, Stanislawa Dawidziuk insisted that Irena stay on. When, after the Warsaw uprising, in 1944, the Germans were evacuating the Polish population, it was rumored that mothers of small children could stay on. Because Stanislawa worried about Irena's 'Jewish looks', she bandaged her face, pretending that it protected her from a toothache. Stanislawa insisted that Irena should claim the baby as her own. She felt that by staying in the apartment with the baby Irena would be safer. In the end, all were given permission to stay on.

Stanislawa did not quite fit into her antisemitic environment. She was not concerned with what others thought about her. She was surprised that I was interested in her story. Saving Irena was just something she felt she ought to have done. She insisted that she could not have acted in any other way.

After the war Irena emigrated to Israel, where she died in 1975. Stanislawa Dawidziuk remained in Poland, and in 1981 she was recognized by Yad Vashem as Righteous Among the Nations.

Coming from a different background, Marion van Binsbergen (later Pritchard) somehow resembles Stanislawa Dawidziuk. Marion was 20 years old when the Germans occupied her native Holland. She was the daughter of a prominent judge and an English mother, both of whom instilled in her tolerant values, a keen sense of justice, and a fierce independence.

Appalled by what she saw around her, from 1942 till 1945, van Binsbergen devoted all her energies to anti-Nazi activities; that involved the saving of Jews, most of whom were young children. She would locate hiding places, help them move, and provide them with food, clothing and ration cards. She also lent moral support to the Jewish fugitives as well as the families who hosted them. One extraordinary way in which she saved Jewish lives was by registering newborn Jewish babies as her own. She managed to register several of these children within a span of five months.

Then van Binsbergen (Pritchard) was asked by a Dutch resistance leader to find a hiding place for a Jewish friend with three young children. When she could not find one, she moved with the fugitives into a small house in the country. There she was soon confronted by a Nazi collaborator, who was about to discover the hidden Jews. To prevent this from happening, van Binsbergen shot the intruder though she had never fired a gun before. She continued to take care of this family for two

For Further Reading

Philip Friedman. *Their Brothers' Keepers*. New York: Holocaust Library, 1978 (1957).

Mordecai Paldiel. *The Path of the Righteous, Gentile Rescuers of Jews During the Holocaust*. Hoboken, NJ: KTAV Publishing House Inc., 1993.

André Stein. *Quiet Heroes: True Stories of the Rescue of Jews by Christians in Nazi-occupied Holland*. Toronto: Lester & Orphen Dennys, 1988.

Nechama Tec. *When Light Pierced the Darkness, Christian Rescue of Jews in Nazi-Occupied Poland*. New York: Oxford University Press, 1986.

Thomas T. Wood and Stanislaw M. Jankowski. *Karski, How One Man Tried to Stop the Holocaust*. New York: John Wiley & Sons, Inc., 1994.

years, until the end of the war. Marion talks in a matter-of-fact way about her rescue of Jews.

Marion van Binsbergen Pritchard has received the Yad Vashem Medal of the Righteous Among the Nations and has become an honorary citizen of the State of Israel. (Based on Nechama Tec, 'Righteous Among the Nations' in *The Encyclopedia of the Holocaust*, to be published by Yale University Press.)

As I mentioned earlier, comparisons of large numbers of rescuers in terms of conventional ways of categorizing people, such as class, education, religion, politics and more, show great difference. When, however, these individuals are examined at close range, a cluster of shared characteristics and conditions emerge. One of these characteristics, sometimes referred to as individuality, separateness, or marginality, suggests that the rescuers did not quite fit into their social environments. Not all of them were aware of this tendency, but whether they were conscious of it or not, the individuality of these rescuers appeared under different guises and was related to other shared attributes and conditions.

Being on the periphery of a community means being less affected by the community's expectations and controls. Therefore with individuality comes freedom from social constraints, and a higher level of independence, offering an opportunity to act in accordance with personal values and moral precepts even when these are in opposition to societal demands.

The rescuers I studied seemed to have had no trouble talking about their self-reliance and their need to follow personal inclinations and values. Nearly all defined themselves as independent. They were motivated by moral values that do not depend on the support and approval of others but on their own self-approval. They are usually at peace with themselves and with their own ideas of what is right or wrong. One of their central values involved a long-standing commitment to protect the needy. This commitment was often expressed in a wide range of charitable acts extending over a long period of time. Risking their lives for Jews during World War II fits into a system of values and behaviors that had to do with helping the weak and the dependent.

This analogy, however, has its limitations. Most disinterested actions on behalf of others might have involved extreme inconvenience, but only rarely would such acts suggest that the givers had to make the ultimate sacrifice of their own lives. For these righteous rescuers, the war provided a convergence between historical events demanding complete selflessness and their predisposition to help. People tend to take their repetitive actions for granted. What they take for granted they accept, and what they accept they rarely analyze or question. Therefore the constant pressure of, or familiarity with, ideas and actions does not necessarily translate into knowledge or understanding. On the contrary, easy acceptance of customary patterns often impedes understanding.

For Reflection

What does the Holocaust suggest about our nature as ethical beings?

Imagine that you were faced with the decision of whether or not to rescue a Jewish person during the Holocaust. What do you think you would have done? Are you happy with the first answer that comes to your mind?

What insights can we derive from the history of the Holocaust for our responsibilities today?

Starving children in the Warsaw ghetto.

A related tendency is to view the actions that one habitually repeats as ordinary, regardless of how exceptional they may appear to others. And so the rescuers' history of helping the needy may have been in part responsible for their modest appraisal of their life-threatening actions. Rescuers seem to have seen in their protection of Jews a natural reaction to human suffering. Many insisted that saving lives was not remarkable and was unworthy of special notice.

Given such matter-of-fact perceptions of rescue, it is not surprising that aid to Jews often began spontaneously and without planning. The unpremeditated start underscores the rescuers' need to stand up for the poor and helpless. This need to assist those in distress overshadowed all considerations of their personal safety and that of their families. Most protectors, when asked why they had saved Jews, emphasized that they had responded to the persecution and the suffering of other human beings, and said that the fact that the sufferers were Jews was entirely incidental to their impulse to act. A minority of rescuers claimed to have helped out of a sense of Christian duty or in protest against the German occupation.

This ability to disregard all attributes of the needy except their helplessness and dependency points to universalistic perceptions. The compelling moral force behind the rescuing of Jews, as well as the universal insistence that what mattered were the victims' dependence and unjust persecution, combined to make such actions universalistic.

To recapitulate, Christians who selflessly risked their lives shared, closely related, six characteristics and conditions: individuality or separateness from their social environment; independence or self-reliance; a commitment to helping the needy; a modest self-appraisal of their extraordinary actions; unplanned initial engagement in Jewish rescue; and universalistic perceptions of Jews as human beings in dire need of assistance. The close interdependence of these six characteristics and conditions offers a preliminary explanation of altruistic rescue of Jews by Righteous Christians. (Much of this discussion is taken from Chapter 10, 'A New Theory of Rescue and Rescuers' in my book *When Light Pierced the Darkness*, pp. 150-183.)

Nazi policies of Jewish biological destruction led to extreme cruelty, devastation and evil, and much less frequently to expressions of extreme goodness epitomized by the Christian rescuers of Jews. The selfless sacrifices of these Christian rescuers may serve as a model for others to imitate now and in the future.

> *Nazi policies of Jewish biological destruction led to extreme cruelty, devastation and evil, and much less to expressions of extreme goodness epitomized by the Christian rescuers of Jews. The selfless sacrifices of these Christian rescuers may serve as a model for others to imitate now and in the future.*

Nechama Tec (USA), Professor of Sociology at the University of Connecticut, Stamford, CT, is the author of six books and numerous articles. Since 1977, she has been conducting research about compassion, altruism, resistance and the rescue of Jews during World War II. Dr. Tec is currently writing a book about the destruction of European Jewry and gender, which will be published by Yale University Press.

THE MEMORY OF GOODNESS

Eva Fleischner

For Reflection

What motivates people to help others?

What impedes people from helping others?

What kind of education do we need to encourage to enable people to develop an altruistic personality?

A number of years ago, I interviewed some French Catholics about what they had done during the Holocaust to help Jews. One woman I spoke to was an 87-year-old nun who lived in a house for retired sisters near Paris. She was still formidable, despite her short stature and age. Fifty years ago she had been director of a large boarding school in Paris, where she must have been immensely impressive. Her position at the time made it relatively easy for her to take in and hide Jewish children until she could arrange to send them across the border into the unoccupied zone. Often she took them to the train herself. On one occasion she needed 15,000 francs to pay a woman who had agreed to take a Jewish baby across the demarcation line. Where did she get that kind of money? I asked her. She shrugged and said, 'I don't remember, but it always came when I needed it.'

She told me about a confrontation she once had with a French policeman sent to take the Jewish children away. When she refused to hand them over, the man, embarrassed, said to her: 'What am I to do? I have my orders.'

'If you are afraid for your skin,' she told him, 'give me a week to hide the children. Then come back and arrest me! What you are doing is a disgrace. How could you do such a thing? Can you really imagine that I would give you the children?' The man went away. In the week that followed, she spirited the children away in all directions: 'Luckily I had the addresses of many convents,' she said. The policeman never came back.

What explains her actions? As far as I can tell, not her background. Like many aristocratic families in France, her family tended to be antisemitic – although the war changed that and they began to help her. Nor did she speak in theological terms. Rather, I felt in her an instinctive response to a crisis, to a situation of terrible injustice. Her position enabled her to help, and help she did.

Another person with whom I spoke was a priest, Father Albert Gau. During the war he opened a restaurant (ostensibly run by a woman he knew), which served as a front for Jews and other refugees from the Germans. I asked him whether he had had the support of his bishop. With some hesitation he said, 'Yes, up to a point.' Then, he told me of the time his bishop had warned him to stop this 'dangerous business'. That day Father Gau's doorbell rang. Before him stood an extremely pregnant Jewish woman. He welcomed her, then he telephoned his bishop: 'Bishop I have a pregnant Jewish woman here. You told me to stop, so I shall send her over to your place. You have plenty of room!'

The worried bishop told Father Gau to keep the woman, and so he did. He saved the woman and her child and continued to do his rescue work.

Father Gau also spoke of his network of helpers, including a Carmelite convent outside his town. The Superior of that convent helped save a Jew sent to her by dressing him in a Carmelite habit when the Germans searched the place because he had been seen entering it.

What made Father Gau act as he did? People were not always able to answer such questions themselves when I put it to them, but two things seem clear in regard to Father Gau: he is a profoundly compassionate man – he kept referring to all that the Jews had suffered – and he is a man of great independence of spirit. As a young man, when he had decided to become a priest, he chose not to go to the local seminary because it was too provincial and narrow, but instead to the seminary of St. Sulpice in Paris, where he was exposed to a great breadth of ideas and to great teachers.

We should not think of people who helped Jews during the Holocaust as heroes or saints, not only because they themselves refuse this label, but because it would let us off the hook too easily. If we put them on a pedestal, we deprive ourselves of the possibility of identifying with them. These women and men can become models for us – not to be admired and venerated, but flesh-and-blood creatures who embody the potential for goodness that exists in us all, the capacity we all have for what Jewish tradition calls 'hesed', and Christian tradition 'grace'.

Some rescuers – a minority in my experience – already had a real love for Jews and Judaism before the war. Rolande Birgy is one of them. She spent much of the war in the French Alps, the Haute Savoie, because it is close to the Swiss border. She always made sure, in finding families who would hide Jewish children, that the children's faith would be respected. On the day of the week when French children were away from school in order to attend catechism classes, Rolande saw to it that the Jewish children were taught their own scriptures by a priest.

Eventually she was arrested by the French police. An official came to her cell to interrogate her, asking her why she helped 'those Jews who killed Christ.' Her answer was clear: 'My dear sir, let me tell you something. Anyone who has had any catechism at all knows that it was not the Jews who killed Christ, but our sins.' We have here an example of both 'the teaching of contempt' and the overcoming of it.

On August 23, 1942, when the deportation of French Jews was under way, the Archbishop of Toulouse (later Cardinal), Msgr. Jules-Gérard Saliège, ordered a pastoral letter read aloud in the churches of his diocese. In it, he vehemently condemned the inhuman treatment of Jews. The letter caused a sensation throughout France because it was the first occasion when a bishop of the Roman Catholic Church had spoken publicly on behalf of the Jews.

'. . . instead of excusing the bystanders, awareness of the selfless protection of Jews only underlines the bystanders' failure to help. Had some of those who claim that nothing could have been done engaged in rescue, fewer Jews would have perished.'

Nechama Tec, 'Foreword' in Cries in the Night: Women Who Challenged the Holocaust, p. xiii.

For Further Reading

Eva Fogelman. Conscience & Courage: Rescuers of Jews During the Holocaust. New York: Doubleday, 1994.

Mordecai Paldiel. Sheltering the Jews: Stories of Holocaust Rescuers. Minneapolis: Fortress Press, 1996.

Michael Phayer and Eva Fleischner. Cries in the Night: Women Who Challenged the Holocaust. Kansas City: Sheed and Ward, 1997.

Carol Rittner and Sondra Myers, eds. The Courage to Care: Rescuers of Jews During the Holocaust. New York: New York University Press, 1986.

Michael Smith. Foley: The Spy Who Saved 10,000 Jews. London: Hodder & Stoughton, 1999.

> *'Whoever saves one life, it is as if they had saved the whole world.'*

'In France, I think the fact that some of the 'elite' of the churches – people like the Cardinal of Toulouse, the Archbishop of Lyons, and the head of the Protestant Church – spoke up, also helped. It meant that there were whole organizations that walked with them. But then there were also other isolated individuals who were just humanists, just right-eous people, who were not afraid to help.'

Gaby Cohen in *The Courage to Care: Rescuers of Jews During the Holocaust*, p. 73.

Eva Fleischner (USA), Professor Emerita, Montclair State University, New Jersey, is a teacher, lecturer, and author of several books and articles, most recently, *Cries in the Night: Women Who Challenged the Holocaust*. She is a member of the US Bishops' Office of Catholic-Jewish Relations and of the International Commission formed to study the Vatican archives relating to the Holocaust.

Inspired by Saliège's example, the bishop of Montauban, Msgr. Pierre-Marie Théas, also wrote a pastoral letter to his diocese. Marie-Rose Gineste, a young social worker and member of the resistance, told him that if it were mailed to parish priests, it would be stopped by the censors. Consequently, she volunteered to deliver it herself by bicycle throughout the diocese, even though this meant cycling more than 100 km. a day. The following Sunday morning Bishop Théas' pastoral letter was read aloud in all the Catholic churches of his diocese.

The Catholics of Toulouse and Montauban had the support and blessing of their bishops. Others were not so fortunate. Out of eighty French bishops, only four spoke out. Should we describe these few as insignificant because they were not typical? Indeed, they were not typical. All the more reason not to dismiss them, but instead to celebrate and honor them. They are proof that human beings can overcome evil, can choose decency and compassion over apathy and hatred.

People acted for many different motives: patriotism, personal contact with Jews, obedience to authority, a sense of justice, resistance to the hated Germans, the influence of a teacher, the demands of Christian faith, and so on. One motive, however, was common to all: compassion, humanitarian concern. Again and again I was told, 'They were victims, they needed help, they had nowhere to go.' Everyone knew that the Jews were the most exposed of all the Nazis' victims. As such, they had to be helped. This was usually said in a matter-of-fact manner, often without any reference to the person's Christian faith, even by priests and other religious persons.

While I am unable to draw a single profile of these rescuers, they all do have one thing in common: none of them think of themselves as heroic, as having done anything out of the ordinary.

I was told again and again, 'I don't really have anything to tell you, I didn't do anything.' Or, 'We did so little, given all there was to do.'

Before I started my work I knew that I would not find very many just ones, although I found more than I expected. I also knew that, no matter how many I might find, their number would still be very small compared to the millions who stood by and did nothing or who actively collaborated. Knowing this, I found comfort in Jewish tradition, which does not measure goodness in numbers: 'Whoever saves one life, it is as if they had saved the whole world.' May we be inspired by their example to do likewise.

RESCUERS:
THEIR MOTIVES AND MORALS

David P. Gushee

When the Nazis embarked on their evil effort to destroy the European Jews, the 300 million non-Jews of Europe were forced to decide what stance they would take toward their Jewish neighbors. Essentially, these Europeans – the great majority of them professing Christians – had three options: to help the Nazis, to help the Jews, or to do nothing either way.

The situation was, of course, more complex than any summary can adequately convey. The Nazis did not post some kind of notice indicating that they were planning to annihilate the Jewish people. Information about the exact fate of the Jews was not readily available, though anyone who was looking could see that the Jews were in deep trouble. Further, non-Jews had varying opportunities to help Jews, and varying resources with which to help; some were on the run from the Nazis themselves, and in any case the situation in each European country had its own particular dynamics.

Still, it is fair to say that for many tens of millions of Europeans, there was at some point during the war a choice to be made. A Jewish mother and child were at their door, begging for help, for food, for a place to stay: what to do? Rescuers, or 'righteous gentiles of the Holocaust' were those who said 'Yes' when the request for help was made. Over 16,000 such rescuers have been identified officially by Yad Vashem, and no one knows how many more there may have been. They are the lone bright spot in the pervasive darkness of the Holocaust.

Several researchers, myself included, have sought to identify the motives and convictions of those who rescued Jews during the Holocaust. This is an important question for a number of reasons. Without succumbing to any kind of naïve hope of capturing and bottling the secret of moral goodness, it is true that if we study those who rise to the peaks of human goodness and moral courage, we can learn much that is valuable about how to live this life ourselves. Christians, in particular, should be interested in the rescuers because, on the European scene during the Holocaust, they are the only non-Jews whose behavior can be considered genuinely in keeping with the moral teachings of the Christian faith.

The way we know about why rescuers acted as they did is primarily through interviews with them that have been conducted since the war. It is also possible to gain insights about the motives of

'My family was Dutch and Christian. Even when we were quite young, my parents always encouraged us, my sisters and me, to read the Bible and to believe that love was the aim of our lives. My mother and father taught us that Moses got the instruction from God that tells us 'to love our neighbors as ourselves'. And we also know from the Bible that Jesus Christ, who was Himself a Jew, had said that the greatest commandment was 'to love God and to love your neighbor as yourself'. Both at home and at school, our education was directed toward love, compassion, and service to others.'

John Weidner, honored by Yad Vashem as a Righteous, in *The Courage to Care: Rescuers of Jews During the Holocaust*, p. 58.

rescuers through articles and books written by the rescuers or by those they rescued. By now we have enough information to draw some tentative conclusions, though we must always keep in mind that the number of rescuers about whom such information is available is still relatively small.

It is helpful to draw a distinction in the motivations of rescuers between those who acted for explicitly religious reasons and those who did not. Some have mistakenly assumed that every rescuer was a Christian, and that every Christian acted as he or she did due to religious motivations. Neither assumption is correct. Some rescuers were atheists and agnostics; especially in south-eastern Europe some were Muslims. There were convinced Communists who rescued Jews.

Among what might be called the general or non-religious reasons for rescue, the most important motivation appears to have been a personal relationship with a Jewish person who needed help. Jews turned to the non-Jews around them who, they hoped, could be trusted to help; these were usually, though not always, friends, co-workers or colleagues in various organizations. Rescuers sometimes were embedded in families or friendship networks or religious groups in which rescue was expected. Here is 'peer pressure' put to its most positive use. Some rescuers were motivated by patriotic or political ideologies. For example, the Jews of Denmark were aided by their non-Jewish neighbors in part as an act of national resistance to Nazi oppression. Many rescuers acted out of a sense of justice or a strong emotional reaction to the suffering of fellow human beings.

Of that 'minority within the minority' who rescued Jews for explicitly Christian reasons, it is possible to identify several different types of motivation. Some Christians, in a remarkable reversal of historic Christian antisemitism, rescued Jews due to a sense of special religious kinship with them. This might be called Christian philosemitism, and it was most often found among those Christians in the Calvinist or Reformed theological tradition, and sometimes among deeply devout Christians of other theological perspectives.

There were some Christians who rescued Jews due to a sense of obedience to biblical teachings about compassion, love, and justice. They read biblical passages such as the story of the Good Samaritan, or the command to love God and neighbor wholeheartedly, and became convinced that these texts applied directly to the grave situation at hand. To disregard these teachings would be to disobey God, and this they were unwilling to do despite the risks that rescue created.

Christian leaders sometimes – though not often enough – helped Christians understand what was at stake by articulating the moral evil of Nazism and its murderous policies. Resistance at this level was led by theologians and church leaders (Catholic, Orthodox and Protestant, in different contexts) who preached and taught that Nazism was a heresy and/or that the mass murder of the Jews was a horrible evil. Their words, and sometimes their deeds, inspired grass roots Christians to participate in rescue activities.

For Further Reading

David P. Gushee. *The Righteous Gentiles of the Holocaust: A Christian Interpretation.* Minneapolis: Fortress Press, 1994.

Philip Hallie. *Tales of Good and Evil, Help and Harm.* New York: HarperCollins Publishers, 1997.

John J. Michalczyk, ed. *Resisters, Rescuers and Refugees: Historical and Ethical Issues.* Kansas City: Sheed & Ward, 1997.

Samuel P. and Pearl M. Oliner. *The Altruistic Personality: Rescuers of Jews in Nazi Europe.* New York: Free Press, 1988.

Gay Block and Malka Drucker. *Rescuers, Portraits of Moral Courage in the Holocaust,* New York: Holmes & Meier Publishers, Inc, 1992

Most explicitly Christian rescuers were deeply devout men and women whose actions are incomprehensible apart from their sense of a vital relationship with God. Here we face a really quite troubling paradox: while baptized Christians were murdering Jews or collaborating with murderers, and while God seemed all too silent, Christians could be found scattered all over Europe, who experienced the presence and direction of God, and rescued Jews on the basis of this religious sensibility.

That is perhaps as good a place as any to conclude a discussion of rescuers and their motivations. It should have been possible for any humane individual, and certainly for any thoughtful Christian, to understand that the murder of innocent men, women, and children was evil and had to be resisted. The moral treasury of Western civilization had many resources that could have grounded such resistance intellectually and spiritually. A small percentage of Europeans found reasons to resist and courageously did so. A great majority sat on the sidelines and did nothing, while scores of thousands organized and carried out the murder of six million Jews and millions of others. We look to the rescuers for hope and insight, while still grieving the actions and inactions of their neighbors.

Japanese Diplomat, Sempo Sugihara, rescued Jews in Kaunas

Swedish Diplomat, Raoul Wallenberg. Rescued Jews in Budapest

For Reflection

Do you think that rescue was morally required of every non-Jew in Europe during the Holocaust? Why or why not?

Why did so many Europeans, including Christians, react indifferently to the plight of their hunted Jewish neighbors?

If you were making the best religious case for rescue that you could, what resources of your faith tradition would you draw upon?

'I do not have a scientific answer for why those who helped did it. I have asked myself that question over and over. For those of us who were young Jewish people at the time, it is not difficult to give an answer as to why we took the risks. We young Jews felt that it was our duty to help the helpless, to help those who were even in more danger than we were. But, for the Catholic and Protestant families who took risks to help our children, it is not so easy for me to answer why. I believe they were just good people, and I can say that there were hundreds of them, maybe even thousands.'

Gaby Cohen, The Courage to Care: Rescuers of Jews During the Holocaust, pp. 72-73.

David P. Gushee (USA) is Graves Professor of Moral Philosophy at Union University, a Southern Baptist school located in Jackson, Tennessee (USA). He is the author of a Christian study of rescuers called *The Righteous Gentiles of the Holocaust* (Fortress, 1994), and has lectured extensively on rescuers both in the United States and in Europe.

METROPOLITAN CHRYSOSTOMOS

When the Second World War broke out, there were 275 Jews on the Greek island of Zakinthos in the Ionian Sea. Until 1943 the island was under Italian occupation and the Jews remained unharmed. However, after Mussolini's fall the Germans occupied the Italian territories and on September 9, 1943 a German force landed on the island.

The German commander ordered all Jews to be assembled so that they could be deported to the mainland and from there to the camps in Poland. To prepare for the deportation, the German officer summoned the Greek mayor, Karreri, and ordered him to prepare a list of all the Jews on the island.

Metropolitan
Chysostomos.

The mayor went to the local Metropolitan, Chrysostomos, for assistance. The Metropolitan volunteered to negotiate with the Germans himself and told Karreri to burn the list of Jewish names. He then approached the German commander and implored him not to deport the Jews. The Jews were Greek citizens, he said; they had done nothing bad to their neighbors and did not deserve to be punished by deportation. When the German would not listen to the Metropolitan's reasoning and insisted on receiving the list of all local Jews, Chrysostomos took a piece of paper, wrote his own name on it and handed it over: 'There is the list of Jews you requested'.

After the failure of their attempt to have the deportation stopped, the mayor and Metropolitan warned all the Jews to leave their homes and go into hiding in the mountains. Chrysostomos promised that the Greek islanders would provide the Jews with food and shelter. Two thirds of the Jews left their homes and stayed in hiding until liberation.

In August-September 1944 three small German boats came to deport the Jews; however the small force of Germans was unable to search for them and round them up. The Jews of the island of Zakinthos were the only Jewish community in Greece that was left unharmed, and that was saved from extermination.

Chrysostomos was awarded the title of 'Righteous Among the Nations' by Yad Vashem for his courageous rescue operation. He was following in the footsteps of Archbishop Demaskinos of Greece who on March 23, 1943, after the first deportation trains left Salonika for Auschwitz, published an outspoken condemnation of the deportations of Greek Jews. Demaskinos was known to have said: 'I have taken up my cross. I spoke to the Lord and made up my mind to save as many Jewish souls as possible.'

LE CHAMBON-SUR-LIGNON

Le Chambon is a village in southern France with a population of about 3,300, that served as a focal point for the sheltering of thousands of Jews during most of the Nazi occupation. In the winter of 1940-1941 a Jewish woman from Germany approached Pastor Andre Trocmé's wife and asked her for help. Magda. Trocmé asked for the advice of the village's head, but was astonished when he told her to send the woman away and not risk the safety of the village. The Trocmés decided to help the woman anyway. Pastor Trocmé called on the people of the village to help Jews, claiming that their persecution was contrary to God's will and the Christian faith. The small town's overwhelmingly Protestant population responded to the Pastor's call to extend aid to fleeing Jews. Despite the danger to anyone harboring Jews, refugees were housed in public institutions and children's homes or with local townspeople and farmers. With the help of others some were then taken on dangerous treks to the Swiss border. The entire community banded together to rescue Jews, seeing this as their Christian obligation.

Survivors celebrate their liberation in the main square of Le Chambon sur Lignon, June 1944.

Andre Trocmé and his wife, Magda, initiated and presided over this vast rescue operation, at times jeopardizing themselves and their family. The Vichy authorities knew what was taking place, since it was impossible to hide such wide-scale rescue activities over time. They demanded that the Pastor cease his activities. His response was clear-cut: 'These people came here for help and for shelter. I am their shepherd. A shepherd does not forsake his flock. . . I do not know what a Jew is. I know only human beings.' The Pastor was eventually arrested along with a number of his friends, but he was released after a few weeks, without having been persuaded to sign a commitment to follow government orders in the future. His cousin, Daniel Trocmé, who directed the Children's home at Le Chambon, was betrayed, arrested and sent to Majdanek concentration camp where he perished in 1944. The villagers continued to shelter Jews even when Pastor Trocmé was forced to go into hiding.

It is estimated that between three and five thousand Jews found shelter in Le Chambon and its environments at one time between 1941 and 1944. 'We were doing what had to be done and we were lucky to be there at the time. . . It was the most natural thing in the world to help these people,' said a resident, when asked about his motivations in helping the Jews.

Rescued Jewish children in Le Chambon. The man located in the center of the photo was the nephew of the Chief Rabbi of Lyon. (USHMM)

MSGR. ANGELO ROTTA

Msgr. Angelo Rotta was the Papal Nuncio in Budapest, Hungary. During the deportations of the Slovak Jews in 1942, he wrote a letter to Pope Pius XII, calling his attention to the fact the Slovak head of state, Msgr. Jozef Tiso, was a priest. He urged the Vatican to exercise its influence on him on behalf of the Jews. Attached to this letter was an appeal from the Jewish Community in Bratislava. In many respects Msgr. Rotta became the source of information for events in Slovakia, and later in Croatia.

In March 1944 when the Nazis occupied Hungary, the fate of the Jews there was sealed. This was the last large Jewish community – approximately 700,000 people – left in Europe. In the following months of April-July 1944, the Germans deported some 475,000 Hungarian Jews to Auschwitz, where most of them perished, being sent to the gas chambers immediately on their arrival.

These were the final months of the war, the German army was in the retreat on all fronts and the reality of the Final Solution was already widely known. Msgr. Rotta joined a group of diplomats – among them were Angel Sanz Briz and Giorgio Perlasca of the Spanish embassy, and Fredrich Born of the International Red Cross – who tried to help Jews in Budapest. Msgr. Rotta pressured the Vatican to call upon Hungarian Bishops, who so far had not opposed the deportations, to do their Christian duty and help. The Pope too sent a letter with a message to the Hungarian Regent asking him to reverse the Hungarian policy on the Jews. This effort bore fruit: the bishops published a public protest and the Pope appealed to the Hungarian head of state. The Papal protest along with other objections undoubtedly contributed to the Hungarian decision to stop the deportation. This is reflected in the Hungarian Regent's answer to the Papal letter: ' . . . I am doing all in my power to see that the demands of Christian and humane principles are respected. May I be permitted to ask that in the hour of grievous trial Your Holiness may continue to look with favor on the Hungarian people . . . '

In October 1944, the Hungarian Nazi party, Arrow Cross, seized power in Budapest, and its members resumed the killing of Jews, shooting them on the banks of the Danube river. Once again Msgr. Rotta joined in rescue efforts by diplomats stationed in Hungary. These diplomats issued documents to Jews, making them protected citizens of their countries. Msgr. Rotta issued 13,000 such documents and helped other diplomats to find safe houses for Jews where they were sheltered from shootings and from the death marches.

Msgr. Angelo Rotta has been honored by Yad Vashem as one of the Righteous Among Nations.

'Rescuers do not easily yield the answer to why they had the strength to act righteously in a time of savagery. It remains a mystery, perhaps a miracle. Many helped strangers, some saved friends and lovers. Some had humane upbringings, others did not. Some were educated, others were barely literate. They weren't all religious, they weren't all brave. What they did share, however, was compassion, empathy, an intolerance of injustice, and an ability to endure risk beyond what one wants to imagine.'

Malka Drucker, In the *Introduction to Rescuers: Portraits of Moral Courage in the Holocaust,* Gay Block and Malka Drucker. p. 5.

Msgr. Angelo Rotta, Papal Nuncio to Hungary during the Holocaust.

SISTER MARGIT SLACHTA

Sister Margit Slachta was very active in promoting political rights for women, and was the first woman elected to the Hungarian Parliament in 1920-21. During the war she headed the Benedictine Order in Hungary. From the very beginning, she was outspoken against attacks against Jews and was involved in many rescue activities during the years of the Holocaust.

In the summer of 1941 the Hungarian government deported some 20,000 Jews from its recently annexed territories to the Ukraine. Slachta protested to the Hungarian officials. 'We raise our voices in opposition to the fact that officially-sanctioned mass atrocities can take place in our country. We do this as members of the human race, as Christians and as Hungarians. . .' She even went to investigate the situation of the deported Jews. After that visit, having seen the plight of the Jews with her own eyes, she became even more committed to the cause of saving Jews.

In her efforts to help the Jews, Slachta tried to enlist the help of clergy in and outside Hungary against the deportation of Slovak Jews that had started in March 1942 and against the expropriation of Jewish property in Hungary. She even turned to the Pope and met with him in March 1943 to appeal to him on behalf of the Jews. During her audience with Pius XII she reported the situation of the Jews in detail and showed him documents she had brought with her.

Slachta instructed the convents of her order to open their doors to Jews and shelter them. One of the nuns was killed while trying to protect Jews. Her society in Budapest supplied and distributed food, clothing and medicine to the Jews of Budapest during the last months of the war.

When the Germans came to inspect a convalescent home for children that was attached to a convent Slachta confronted them personally. She refused to let them speak to the children and interrogate them about their family background. The Germans left the place and the children who were hidden were saved.

'Do not let yourself become preoccupied with evil in the negative sense, but strive to achieve good. Have zeal for the good rather than fear for evil, have zeal for good deeds, rather than having fear and trembling brought on by sin.'

Sister Margit Slachta was awarded the title of Righteous Among the Nations by Yad Vashem.

> *'Do not let yourself become preoccupied with evil in the negative sense, but strive to achieve good. Have zeal for the good rather than fear for evil, have zeal for good deeds, rather than having fear and trembling brought on by sin.'*

ANTONINA SIVAK

Antonina Sivak

Antonina Sivak lives today in Lachovice, a small town in Poland. During the war she worked as a maid in Lwow, serving the family of a German officer stationed there. One day, as she was cleaning a rug on the porch, she met another maid. It was Rivka Hollander, a Jewish woman who came to Lwow hoping to find work. She was alone in Lwow, as her husband was in the Russian army. The two maids became friends. Rivka asked Antonina to help her bring about the release of her sister from the labor camp in which she was held and to bring her to Lwow. She gave Antonina a diamond ring and told her she could sell it and use the money for the rescue. Antonina returned without Rivka's sister. She had been unable to release her from the camp. She returned the precious ring to Rivka, although she could have kept it for herself.

In 1942 all Jews in Lwow were ordered to move to a ghetto. Antonina, or Tonia in short, was worried about Rivka, and proposed that she should not go to the Ghetto, but hide in her room in the German officer's apartment.

Tonia hid Rivka with her for three years. During that period there were several moments of great danger for both of them. Rivka's hiding place was behind the large closet in Tonia's room. During the day she could come out and stretch, sometimes she would use the sewing machine in the room. When no one was at home she would help Tonia with the housework. One day she was sitting at the sewing machine, when the German landlady came into the room unexpectedly. Rivka continued sewing, pretending she was just a friend of Tonia's. On another occasion, one of Tonia's friends was arrested as a member of the Polish underground and Tonia was interrogated by the Nazis. It became very dangerous for Rivka to stay in the room, so she left and roamed the countryside for a while. When she found nowhere to go to, she returned to Tonia's. As it had become too dangerous to stay in the German officer's home, Tonia rented a room for Rivka. At the end of the war she waited with Rivka until they heard from her husband.

Antonia is one of the Righteous among the Nations honored by Yad Vashem in Jerusalem. When asked why she had saved Rivka, risking her life every day, even every minute, she said: 'I had been told Jews were satanic, but here I saw a young woman in great danger. She was not Satan, she was a human being in need. This was the most Christian deed one could do. I could not have acted differently.'

MOTHER MARIA SKOBTSOVA

Mother Maria Skobtsova (born 1891) emigrated from Russia after the Russian Revolution. She settled in Paris, where she devoted herself to the service of the needy, principally her fellow refugees. It was the death of her four-year-old daughter in 1926 which prompted her to accept what she called an 'all-embracing motherhood', and this was the reason that she took her vows as a nun of the Russian Orthodox Church (1932). Hers was to be an unremitting labor of love. In the service of the Russian down-and-outs of France she shared the rigors of their life and sacrificed her personal security as part of her commitment. Not that she was ever dour or solemn. One of the best-remembered of her attributes was her infectious good cheer.

The occupation of France by Hitler's armed forces created a new category of outcasts, the Jews. Mother Maria was immediately at hand with offers of support, together with her colleagues. Foremost among them was the chaplain at her house, Father Dimitri Klepinin (born 1900). It was he who began to issue false certificates of baptism to Jews who felt that they might benefit from their protection (1940-43). After the decree of June 7, 1942, which required that Jews should wear the Star of David, there was need for them to be protected in almost every aspect of their life. Many were sheltered at Mother Maria's premises, many were conveyed to comparative safety in the south of France. 'If we were true Christians we would all wear the Star,' she said, 'the age of confessors has arrived.' Her poem on the Star was widely distributed and encouraged many.

When mass arrests of Jews took place in Paris, Mother Maria gained access to the stadium where they were confined. She supported the prisoners as best she could. But she was anguished at the limitations of her role.

When Father Dimitri was arrested (1943), he was offered his freedom as long as he discontinued his assistance to the Jews. He showed his interrogator the crucified figure on his pectoral cross. 'And do you know this Jew?' he asked. Father Dimitri was to end his days in Dora concentration camp (1944).

Mother Maria was sent to Ravensbrück (1943), where she was to spend her last two years. Her fellow-prisoners remember her vitality and generosity in the most dismal situations. At the same time she accepted suffering for herself, and anticipated death as 'a blessing from on high'.

Her generosity extended to the very moment of her death. Mother Maria escaped selection for the gas chambers on Good Friday, 1945. But she saw panic in the midst of those selected. It was then that Mother Maria took the place of one of the condemned. In this way 'she went voluntarily to her martyrdom so as to help her companions to die.'

Two triangles, a star,

The shield of King David, our forefather.

This is election, not offence.

The great path and not an evil.

Once more in a term fulfilled,

Once more roars the trumpet of the end;

And the fate of a great people

Once more is by the prophet proclaimed.

Thou art persecuted again, O Israel,

But what can human malice mean to thee,

Who have heard the thunder from Sinai?

Mother Maria Skobtsova, center.

ZEGOTA

Zegota is the name of an underground organization in Nazi occupied Poland that was helping Jews. It was founded by Zofia Kossak-Szczucka, a Polish writer and devout Catholic. She was a member of a Catholic organization, FOP, and well known for her nationalist views. In the summer of 1942 she wrote an illegal leaflet 'Protest' in the name of her organization, in which she condemned the Nazi crimes against the Jews. The leaflet clearly reflects Kossak-Szczucka's anti-Jewish feelings, but at the same time it condemns the murder of the Jews and insists in no uncertain terms on the duty to help the persecuted Jews. 'The silence can no longer be tolerated . . .', she wrote, 'Therefore - we Catholics, Poles - raise our voice. Our feeling toward the Jews has not changed. We continue to deem them political, economic and ideological enemies of Poland. . . . This fact, however, does not release us from the duty of damnation of murder. . . . This protest is demanded of us by God, who does not allow us to kill. It is demanded by our Christian conscience.'

Alongside five Polish organizations, the board of Zegota included two Jewish organizations, thus proving in the midst of war and misery that human empathy and compassion should be common to all religions. Its major operation was supplying Aryan papers to Jews, enabling them to survive without the immediate danger of capture and deportation to death camps. Tens of thousands of such identity papers, including baptism and marriage certificates, were forged by Zegota activists and handed out to Jews. Hiding places with Polish families were located and equipped. Zegota had a special department for children. The organization found safe houses for them, and helped the sheltering families to take care of these children, paying for their expenses. This included providing medical care for the Jewish children in hiding by physicians who were members of the underground. Over 2,500 children were hidden by Zegota in Warsaw alone. Remembering that hiding and helping Jews was a major crime punishable by death, we can better understand what it took to operate such a network. Zofia Kossak-Szczucka herself was caught and sent to Auschwitz. The leaders of Zegota sent many messages to the Polish Government in exile in London, urging the Polish dignitaries to help the Jews and to proclaim punishment to those Poles who collaborated with the Nazis and helped them hunting down the Jews. Despite all the dangers, the organization was active from December 1942 until Poland was liberated.

Zofia Kossak-Szczucka, one of the founders of Zegota.

CORNELIA TEN BOOM

Cornelia ten Boom was born in Amsterdam in 1892 and moved to Haarlem at a very young age. During the war her family spearheaded a rescue operation in Holland that helped many Jews. Motivated by their Christian faith, they hid Jews in their own home and risked their lives while finding hiding places with other families, getting food supplies and food coupons for rationed foodstuffs for the many hidden Jews in their care. They had built a secret hiding room in their home, concealing the entrance behind a cabinet. There were four permanent residents in this place, but it also served as a temporary refuge for Jews who were waiting for more permanent shelter. When a new family was found that was willing to help Jews, Cornelia ten Boom would go there and see to it that a proper hiding place was built. She would also visit the Jews in hiding regularly to make sure they were safe. She provided medical care for the concealed Jews, and sometimes had to make arrangements for burial in Christian cemeteries for Jews who had died in hiding.

The whole family and many others were involved in the rescue operations, and eventually paid a very high price for their courageous deeds. The whole family was arrested, betrayed by a traitor. Cornelia's elderly father died in prison, and she and her sister were sent to Ravensbrück, the concentration camp for women in Germany. Even in the camp, Cornelia was a source of support and comfort for her fellow inmates, telling them stories from the Bible and helping them to keep their faith. After the war Cornelia said that she sensed God's presence in Ravensbrück more than she had ever known before. This helped her make sense of her suffering. She related that the Lord clearly said to her and her sister Betsie: 'It is for My People you must suffer.' Cornelia was eventually released from the camp, but her sister Betsie died there. Her brother died of an ailment that resulted from his imprisonment.

'If Jesus says to love our enemies, He gives us the love that He asks from us. I have always believed, and now I know from personal experience, that the light of Jesus is stronger than the deepest darkness. A child of God cannot sink deeply endlessly; the arms of the Eternal are always deeper.'

The ten Boom family before the war. Four members of the ten Boom family perished, having been arrested for helping Jews: Cornelia's father, Casper ten Boom (who is shown sitting center), her brother Willem, her sister Betsie and their nephew Kik.

RIGHTEOUS AMONG THE NATIONS

Country	Number Honored (as of December 1999)
Poland	5,264
Netherlands	4,174
France	1,786
Ukraine	1,216
Belgium	1,049
Hungary	475
Czech Republic + Slovakia	418
Lithuania	414
Russia + Belarus	402
Germany	327
Italy	240
Greece	211
Yugoslavia (all countries)	189
Austria	82
Latvia	65
Romania	55
Albania	53
Switzerland	23
Moldova	31
Denmark	14
Bulgaria	13
Great Britain	11
Norway	7
Sweden	7
Armenia	3
Spain	3
Estonia	2
Brazil	1
China	2
Japan	1
Luxembourg	1
Portugal	1
Turkey	1
USA	1
Total	16,542

AFTER THE HOLOCAUST: HOW HAVE CHRISTIANS RESPONDED?

AFTER THE *SHOAH*: CHRISTIAN STATEMENTS OF CONTRITION

Peggy Obrecht

In August 1947, after the horrors of the Nazi concentration camps had been fully exposed to the world, an international gathering of Christian and Jewish leaders came together in Seeligsberg, Switzerland, to examine contributory factors in the growth of antisemitism over the centuries. At the Seeligsberg conference the participants drew up a ten-point document outlining steps Christianity needed to take if it were to strip future Church teaching of negative images of Judaism and replace them with a new positive theological understanding. As important as the *Ten Points of Seeligsberg* and a resolution on antisemitism by the World Council of Churches fourteen years later both were, it was not until Vatican Council II (1962-1965) and the Roman Catholic Church's 1965 pioneering statement on the Church's relationship to Judaism and the Jewish people, *Nostra Aetate* (*In Our Time*), that a virtual revolution in Christian thinking occurred. Since that conciliar document, Christianity as a whole has witnessed within many of its other denominational bodies a reversal of almost 1900 years of what Jules Isaac (1877-1963) called 'the teaching of contempt'.

When the voices from most of the major denominations joined in the new conversation, it was often with an expression of contrition for the painful mutual history of these two great faiths – Judaism and Christianity – and with a recognition that the murder of millions of Jews during World War II and the Holocaust (*Shoah*) took place in the heart of Christendom. Although the declarations are markedly different in style and content, there are important similarities. For most, the assertion of God's continuing covenant relationship with His people Israel and the responsibility to teach about Judaism from Judaism's own texts are two central affirmations. As the late Protestant theologian Paul Van Buren remarked, the early Church Father Justin Martyr was correct: 'It is bad business to learn about Jews except from Jews.' Their texts are the tools needed to enable others to interpret the reality of Judaism and the Jewish people. To do otherwise is to perpetuate the canards that have marked traditional church teaching down through the centuries.

In Germany, the first synod of the Evangelical Church of Germany (E.K.D) to produce a statement acknowledging some culpability on the part of Christianity, and specifically on the part of the German Churches, for the fate of Jews during the Nazi era, was the provincial Synod of the Protestant Church in the Rhineland. In 1980 it approved a statement calling for a 'new relationship of the Church to the Jewish people,' adding its 'recognition of Christian co-responsibility and guilt for the Holocaust.' Having looked deep within the soul of the Church at its failure to live up to the moral imperatives of its own tradition, the Synod statement affirmed the permanent election of the Jewish people as the people of God, and the belief that righteousness and love are the admonitions of God for both faith traditions. For Christianity, this demonstrated a radical turn in its historical understanding of Judaism.

Four years later (1984) a statement of the Evangelical Synod of Baden, also decrying the Church's teaching about Jews as a rejected people, like the Rhineland statement before it, confessed that Christians in Germany bore a joint responsibility and guilt for the Holocaust.

In anticipation of the 50th Anniversary of Germany's surrender in May 1945, the German Roman Catholic bishops produced two statements acknowledging the failure and guilt of many of their own people. Recalling an earlier joint statement (1988) by the German and Austrian Bishops' Conference on the occasion of the 50th Anniversary of *Kristallnacht*, they confessed in the January 1995 statement that the 'Church which we proclaim as holy, and which we honor as a mystery, is also a sinful Church and in need of conversion.' They further charged that not a few of their members 'got involved in the ideology of National Socialism and remained unmoved in the crimes committed against Jewish-owned property and the life of Jews. Others paved the way for crimes or even became criminals themselves.' In April 1995, the Catholic bishops reiterated their declaration that the Church had failed to intervene effectively as Nazism was on the rise. In that same month, they joined the Council of Protestant Churches in a statement which promised that in the future both groups must 'devote our strength to the protection of human life.'

The German and Austrian bishops were not the only European Catholic leaders to voice contrition and to call for repentance for the complicity of some of their own in the crimes of the Third Reich. During Advent in 1994, a statement was issued from the Hungarian Roman Catholic Bishops and the Ecumenical Council of Hungarian Churches. Theirs was timed to coincide with the 50th Anniversary of the year Hungary experienced the full brunt of Nazi rule. Declaring the Holocaust to be a sin which 'burdens our history,' the statement went on to acknowledge that there were those who professed to be Christian but who, 'out of fear, cowardice and compromise did not raise their voices in protest against the mass humiliations, deportation and murder of their fellow Jewish citizens. Before God we ask pardon for their negligence and omission in the face of this catastrophe fifty years ago.'

In 1995, Roman Catholic bishops of Poland issued their Declaration of the Polish Episcopal

'We Catholics in the dialogue know something, only something, of the Jewish horror of the Holocaust. We have heard the Jewish charge of Christian silence and maybe we are still too silent. More and more Christian scholars are dealing with the theological implications of the Holocaust for Christian theology. Surely this represents a turn in history.'

Bishop Francis J. Mugavero DD, "Nostra Aetate Twenty Years On: A Symposium" in *Christian Jewish Relations*, vol. 18, #3, pp. 33-35.

Commission for Dialogue with Judaism. The bishops of the Netherlands, that same year, in their statement *Supported by One Root: Our Relationship to Judaism,* praised their fellow Polish and German bishops for recognizing 'co-responsibility for the persecution of the Jews in the past' adding that 'in all sincerity, we join them in this sentiment.'

Later in the decade, Italian, Swiss and French Catholic leaders prepared responses of their own. In September 1997, at a ceremony at Drancy, the transit camp outside Paris where many Jews had awaited deportation to Auschwitz during the Nazi era, the French bishops read from their *Declaration of Repentance.* The time had come, they wrote, for the Church 'to submit her own history to critical examination and to recognize . . . the sins committed by members of the Church and to beg forgiveness of God and humankind.' Decrying the inaction of Church leaders when France's Nazi collaborationist Vichy government first deprived Jews of their rights, they acknowledged their own silence 'in the flagrant violation of human rights . . . leaving the way open to a death-bearing chain of events.' Unhesitatingly, they affirmed that the Church, called at that moment to play the role of defender, did in fact have considerable power and influence, and 'in the face of the silence of other institutions, its voice could have echoed loudly by taking a definitive stand against the irreparable.'

In North America, as in Europe, the Protestant Churches also have issued statements of contrition. Following the precedent set by the Vatican in its Conciliar statements of 1965 (*Nostra Aetate*), 1975 (*Guidelines for Implementing* Nostra Aetate), and 1986 (*Notes on the Correct Ways to Present Jews and Judaism in Preaching and Catechesis in the Roman Catholic Church*), and after examining how Judaism had been presented in their own texts, these denominational bodies began the process of correcting the teaching of the past in their own traditions. The Disciples of Christ, for example, in a lengthy Statement on Relations between Christians and Jews (1993) called upon its Church to review thoroughly the long and painful mutual history of Judaism and Christianity. It suggested examining biblical texts, the laws against Jews enacted by synods of the Church, subsequent patterns of religious persecution through the ages and finally the *Shoah* itself. In an effort to help its members gain a greater understanding of the bonds which link the Jewish and Christian people, it recommended that resources from the Church's Commission on Theology be used in future study.

In 1987, the Presbyterian Church (USA) adopted a study paper entitled *A Theological Understanding of the Relationship Between Christians and Jews.* Like other denominational bodies, it affirmed the ongoing covenantal relationship of the Jews with God. The paper also called for repentance for the church's 'long and deep complicity in the proliferation of anti-Jewish attitudes and actions.' Not disseminated for broad use, it was nonetheless published with the Presbyterian General

'Pope John Paul II unambiguously claims that "the crime which has become known as the Shoah remains an indelible stain on the history of the century that is coming to a close. . . . [The Church] calls for sons and daughters to place themselves humbly before the Lord and examine themselves on the responsibility which they too have of the evils of our time."'

Thomas F. Stransky, CP, Preface in Pierre Blet, *Pius XII and the Second World War: According to the Archives of the Vatican*, p. xv.

Assembly proceedings in 1987. That same year, at the 16th General Synod of the United Church of Christ, the delegates overwhelmingly approved a resolution which was hailed as a breakthrough for their Church's relationship with the Jews. Again one finds the affirmation that, all earlier positions of the Christian Church to the contrary notwithstanding, 'God's covenant with the Jewish people has not been abrogated.' As had the Disciples of Christ, the UCC called for new educational resources for its seminaries and local churches. Additionally it directed its inter-agency bodies, local congregations and regional judicatories to engage in dialogue with the Jewish community in an ongoing effort to establish firm relationships of trust.

In 1994, a document entitled *The Declaration of the Evangelical Lutheran Church in America to the Jewish Community* was adopted by the E.L.C.A. at their Church Council. The one page declaration expressed pain and sadness at both 'certain elements in the legacy of the reformer Martin Luther, and the catastrophes, including the Holocaust of the Twentieth Century, suffered by Jews in places where the Lutheran Churches were strongly represented.' Recalling Luther's 'stand for truth' and his witness to 'God's saving Word,' it expressed, nonetheless, the compelling need to acknowledge his anti-Judaic diatribes and the 'violent recommendations' against the Jews within his later writings. Recognizing all antisemitism as an affront to the Gospel, the Church pledged to oppose in the future 'the deadly working of such bigotry, both within our own circles and the society around us.'

Within the Baptist denomination, it was the Alliance of Baptists, in their 1995 statement, which expressed most forcefully a need for contrition. Recalling that *Nostra Aetate* heralded a significant change in Jewish-Christian relations, first among Roman Catholics and soon thereafter among Protestant Christian bodies, they affirmed the influence of this invitation to dialogue begun by Vatican II. They called for a public confession of sins; first for the sin of interpreting sacred writings in ways deleterious to the Jewish people, then for the sins of complicity, silence, and indifference, and finally for 'inaction to the horrors of the Holocaust'. As others had before them, they called for the Church to affirm that the gifts of God to the Jewish people are irrevocable, and emphasized their members' need to be educated about Judaism.

At the United States Holocaust Memorial Museum in the fall of 1997, His All Holiness Ecumenical Patriarch Bartholomew of the Greek Orthodox Church, before a gathering of Christians and Jews, recalled the indifference of so many peoples during the *Shoah* as their neighbors were taken away. While praising those who risked their own lives to save others, he acknowledged that the 'bitter truth for so many Christians of that terrible time was that they could not connect the message of their faith to their actions in the world.' He went on to attest that 'silence in the face of injustice, silence in the darkness of Auschwitz's bitter night will never again be allowed.'

For Reflection

To what degree do you think the new teaching about Judaism is filtering down to the congregants?

What might explain the absence of some denominations in today's conversation?

Is it enough to voice contrition? What else must be done?

For Further Reading

Jack Bemporad and Michael Shevack. *Our Age: The Historic New Era of Christian-Jewish Understanding.* Hyde Park, NY: New City Press, 1996.

Marcus Braybrooke. *Time To Meet: Toward a deeper relationship between Jews and Christians.* Philadelphia: Trinity Press International, 1990

Michael Shermis and Arthur E. Zannoni, eds. *An Introduction to Jewish-Christian Relations.* New York: Paulist Press, 1991.

The United States Catholic Conference. *Catholics Remember the Holocaust.* Washington, D.C: 1998.

Clark M. Williamson. *A Guest in the House of Israel.* Westminster: John Knox Press, 1993

Peggy Obrecht (USA), has been the Director of Church Relations for the United States Holocaust Memorial Museum, Washington, DC since 1989. An Associate Member of the National Association of Catholic Chaplains, she also is the coordinator of Adult Education for Brown Memorial Presbyterian Church, Park Avenue, Baltimore, MD.

Although a resolution is not due out for a few years, it should be mentioned that one of the most far reaching and promising study papers ever to be drawn up within Protestantism is *Bearing Faithful Witness*, a 59-page document of the United Church of Canada. It will, no doubt, prove to be a significant and far-reaching theological and pastoral statement when it is published.

While Pope John XXIII (1958-1963) began the revolutionary process in Roman Catholic Christian Church thinking which changed forever the course of Christian-Jewish relations, it has been Pope John Paul II (1978-) who has made the relationship between Catholicism and Judaism a central concern of his pontificate. The wealth of biblical and liturgical scholarship during his time as Pope, the statements forthcoming from the Vatican, and the actions he has taken with regard to the Jewish communities within countries around the world have helped to bridge solidly what was once regarded as an unbridgeable chasm. The final document of the century to emanate from the Vatican, *We Remember, A Reflection on the Shoah*, has not been without its critics. But it is offered up as yet another text to help strengthen the bonds between the Catholic and Jewish faiths as the two continue on in conversation. It must be added that similar degrees of critical assessment have been applied to many of the Protestant statements by both Christian and Jewish leaders.

Unfortunately there are Churches which have not entered into the interfaith discussion at any level, preferring, for reasons of their own, to ignore or discount this troubled history. For them the choice has been to avoid giving serious consideration to the damaging effects anti-Jewish references in teaching have had, and will continue to have, not just on the Jewish people, but on their own congregants as well. Perhaps in time more will recognize what is at stake in following the lead set by denominations such as the Roman Catholic Church and the United Church of Christ. To those Church bodies which, in a spirit of cooperation and caring, have labored long and hard in confronting their past, gratitude and recognition must be given. By understanding what this history has meant and by attempting through education to bring about repentance, change and reconciliation, they have ensured that the next millennium holds the promise of untold opportunities for all, Christians and Jews alike, to grow in religious faith and understanding.

HOW HAVE THE CHURCHES RESPONDED TO THE HOLOCAUST?

Eugene J. Fisher

The initial work in confronting the *Shoah* came from individual Christian theologians, not institutional leaders. For years even before World War II, towering figures such as James Parkes, Jacques Maritain, and Paul Tillich had led the way to a *heshbon haNefesh*, 'reckoning of the soul', among reflective Christian thinkers. Most were Protestant. Most, too, were Protestants who signed the famous *Ten Points of Seeligsberg* under the auspices of the International Council of Christians and Jews in 1947. While it did not mention the *Shoah*, Seeligsberg did systematically and effectively attack the theological and alleged biblical underpinnings of what Jules Isaac, who researched negative Christian attitudes toward Jews and Judaism even while hiding from the Nazis during the war, aptly called the Christian 'teaching of contempt'.

It must be stated also at the outset that the first official Catholic response to the implications of the *Shoah* for Christian teaching came a relatively belated twenty years after the end of World War II and the liberation of Auschwitz. Already in 1948, however, the First Assembly of the World Council of Churches in Amsterdam had issued a statement on *The Christian Approach to the Jews* which began with a call 'to look with open and penitent eyes on man's disorder' with respect to 'the extermination of six million Jews.' 'To the Jews,' the statement affirms, 'our God has bound us in a special solidarity linking our destinies together in His design.'

While maintaining the Protestant tradition of 'missions to the Jews as a normal part of parish work', the document acknowledged candidly that 'The Churches in the past have helped foster an image of the Jews as the sole enemies of Christ, which has contributed to antisemitism in the secular world. . . Antisemitism is a sin against God and man.' This call to combat antisemitism was repeated by the Third Assembly of the WCC in New Delhi in 1961.

These considerations were developed with greater depth in the 1968 Report of the WCC's Faith and Order Commission, and 'recommended for further study'. That document delved, again with candor and now at some length, into the historical sins of Christians against Jews over the centuries.

'In the face of the risk of a resurgence and spread of anti-Semitic feelings, attitudes, and initiatives, of which certain disquieting signs are to be seen today, and of which we have experienced the most frightful results in the past, we must teach consciences to consider anti-Semitism, and all forms of racism, as sins against God and humanity. In order to ensure this education of consciences and effective cooperation in general, it is to be hoped that there can be set up joint committees [of Christians and Jews].'

Pope John Paul II
Papal Visit to Hungary, Address to
Jewish Leaders in Budapest
August 18, 1991

But it could not resolve the central theological question of whether the Jews, after Christ, have a role to play in God's design that is not exhausted in giving birth to Christ and which will result in their conversion to Christ. Some maintained the permanent election of Israel in its own right, while others felt that Israel's history was and is oriented toward its 'fullness' in Christ, as is all of creation. Placing the 'two views' side by side as equal options, of course, was in itself a remarkable advance from the entirely negative views of Judaism that had prevailed in all of Christianity since Patristic times. For while the great Reformers of the 16th Century had taken a critical (and as we Catholics would now, albeit again belatedly acknowledge most helpful) look at virtually all other aspects of Christian thought up to their time, the Church's negative stance toward Jews and Judaism was not taken up for close examination. So by the time of the rise of Nazism, all the churches of Europe had essentially the same theological stance on Jews and Judaism, a stance so negative, as Pope John Paul II said in 1997, that it 'lulled the consciences' of Europe's Christians so that they did not react as the world had a right to expect.

This brings us to the Catholic entry into the battle against antisemitism: the deceptively short section 4 (15 sentences in Latin) of the Second Vatican Council's declaration, *Nostra Aetate* ('In our Time' – or as some referred to it: 'It's About Time!'). Like Seeligsberg, the Council did not acknowledge the *Shoah* as its reference point. That did not happen until the 'implementing' guidelines were issued by the Holy See's Commission for Religious Relations with the Jews in 1974. Still, that was the background for the debate in the Council. Jules Isaac met with John XXIII in 1960 and the Pope gave a mandate to Cardinal Augustin Bea, a German and a scripture scholar, to include a schema on the Jews in the materials for the Ecumenical Council he envisioned. Bea did just that, and through enormous effort, supported especially by the bishops of the U.S., France, and Germany, pulled off what Bea and his successor, Cardinal Willebrands, considered to be the very first 'systematic' reflection on the relationship between the Church and the Jewish people on the level of a Council in Catholic history.

Briefly, the 2,221 bishops who signed the declaration stated on the one hand, that one cannot hold responsible for Jesus' death all Jews of his time, and certainly not those of succeeding generations, nor can the Jews be presented in Catholic teaching as 'rejected by God or accursed as if this followed from Sacred Scripture'. On the other hand, the Council pointed to the Jewishness of Jesus, his mother and his apostles, so that it is when the Church 'delves into' her own mystery she encounters the mystery of Israel and its 'irrevocable' covenant with God. Seeligsberg writ large! Subsequent documents of the Holy See's Commission, in 1974, 1985 and 1998 have adumbrated these brief but revolutionary teaching dicta of the Catholic Church. They were promulgated

For Further Reading

Catholics Remember the Holocaust, USCC publication #5-290.

Eugene J. Fisher and Leon Klenicki, eds. *In Our time: The Flowering of Jewish-Catholic Dialogue.* Stimulus Foundation: New Jersey, 1990.

David Novak. *Jewish-Christian Dialogue, A Jewish Justification.* Oxford: Oxford University Press, 1989.

Geoffrey Wigoder. *Jewish-Christian relations since the Second World War.* Manchester: Manchester University Press, 1988.

supportively with reference to statements of local Catholic episcopal conferences, notably France in 1973, the US in 1975 and 1988, and Poland in 1991.

In 1990, in Prague at the opening of a meeting of the International Catholic-Jewish Liaison Committee, Cardinal Edward I. Cassidy of the Holy See's Commission noted the need for, the Whole Church to make an act of 'repentance (*teshuvah*)' for its role in preparing the way for and in perpetrating, through so many of its members, the *Shoah*. Beginning in 1994 with the Catholic bishops of Hungary, the episcopal conferences of Europe, each in their own particularity, began to do so. The bishops of Germany, Poland, the US and the Netherlands all issued statements of repentance in 1995 on the occasion of the 50th anniversary of the liberation of Auschwitz. The French bishops in 1997 and the Italian bishops in 1998 added their own most remarkable confessions to this self-examination by the Catholic Church of the sins of its past.

In March 1998, with the statements of particular local churches as its backdrop, the Holy See's Commission promulgated *We Remember: A Reflection on the Shoah*. Like the Conciliar declaration itself and its two previous implementing documents, *We Remember* was received critically. But it contains an extremely strong mandate for continuing Catholic reflection on the *Shoah* and for Holocaust Education in every Catholic educational institution in the world. As such, it begins a process rather than, as its critics fear, closing the door to further progress in Catholic-Jewish relations. In this country, therefore, the U.S. bishops' conference published all of the above statements together in a single volume, *Catholics Remember the Holocaust*, with Cardinal Cassidy's own (by definition definitive) statement, in the light of the criticism, of what the Commission intended to say in its document.

Read as a whole and together with the numerous statements of Pope John Paul II on the subject, I believe that the Catholic Church, in the person of its hierarchy, is truly and efficaciously beginning to grapple with the evils that enmeshed it and its teachings in the past.

Stepping Stones to Further Jewish-Christian Relations. New York: Paulist Press, 1987. (vol.1) and 1985 (vol.2)

Eugene J. Fisher (USA) is Director of Catholic-Jewish Relations for the Secretariat for Ecumenical and Interreligious Affairs of the National Conference of Catholic Bishops, Washington, DC. He is also Consultor to the Vatican Commission for Religious Relations with the Jews. Dr. Fisher is the author or editor of sixteen books and over 200 articles in major religious journals.

PROTESTANT RESPONSES TO THE HOLOCAUST

Stephen R. Haynes

Those who study the relationship between Christianity and the Holocaust have very concisely described the connection: although Christian anti-Judaism did not by itself make the Holocaust possible, the murder of six million Jews by the Nazis and their accomplices could not have occurred without Christianity. This means, very simply, that the Holocaust is a Christian event, a watershed in the Church's history. If we move our focus from Christianity to Christians, the picture is more nuanced, but no less bleak.

Protestant Christians are implicated in the mass destruction of European Jewry in myriad ways. Thousands and perhaps millions of baptized Protestants participated in the 'Nazi Final Solution of the Jewish Question' as perpetrators. While it is tempting for Christians to deny that any 'genuine' Protestant could participate in mass murder – much less against members of God's chosen people! – the fact is that persons from virtually every Protestant tradition aided the genocide. Many Protestant Christians who did not perpetrate violence against Jews were nonetheless collaborators in Nazi antisemitism. This group included 'theologians under Hitler' such as Emanuel Hirsch, Paul Althaus, and Gerhard Kittel, as well as the roughly two-thirds of the German Evangelical Church that was affiliated with or supported the pro-Nazi German Christian Movement. More happily, Protestants also resisted the Holocaust in a variety of ways. From the beginning of the Nazi era, a minority of Protestants resisted Nazi policies that impinged on the Church's life and witness. This resistance was focused in organizations such as the Pastors' Emergency League and the Confessing Church, in theologians and churchmen like Karl Barth (1888-1968), Dietrich Bonhoeffer (1906-1945), Martin Niemöller (1892-1984), and Heinrich Gruber (1891-1975), and in confessional statements such as *The Bethel Confession* (August, 1933) and *The Barmen Declaration* (May, 1934). Furthermore, Germany's Jehovah's Witnesses staged a long, courageous, and consistent campaign of resistance against the Nazi state. Once Nazi aggression placed Jews in mortal danger, Protestants in many parts of Europe became rescuers.

Among the Protestant rescuers motivated by religious convictions were the Huguenot community of Le Chambon sur Lignon, France (led by Reformed Pastor Andre Trocmé), and the ten Boom family of Holland. The vast majority of Protestant Christians, however, were neither perpetrators

'After the Holocaust, a credible Christian theology must begin in and result in a practical, lived theology.'

Sidney G Hall, *Christian Anti-Semitism in Paul's Theology.*

The refusal of German Protestants in the 1930s to speak or act on behalf of Jews is particularly tragic, since at this time effective resistance to Nazi totalitarianism may still have been possible.

nor resistors. Rather, they were bystanders who did not contribute directly to the murder of Jews, but did nothing to thwart it. The refusal of German Protestants in the 1930s to speak or act on behalf of Jews is particularly tragic, since at this time effective resistance to Nazi totalitarianism may still have been possible. In remaining safe and silent under Nazi rule, the majority of Protestants became collaborators in the genocide that unfolded between 1941 and 1945. *The Stuttgart Declaration* (1945), the first official Protestant response to the Holocaust, spoke soberingly of the guilt incurred by these Christian bystanders: 'We accuse ourselves that we did not witness more courageously, pray more faithfully, believe more joyously, love more ardently.'

Protestant Responses to the Holocaust

The earliest and most common Protestant responses to the Holocaust were those of shock and avoidance. Nevertheless, the grievous record of Christianity during the Nazi era has left Protestant Christians much to ponder. A small group of Protestant thinkers who experienced the war or who came to maturity in the post-war world, for instance, Eberhard Bethge, Franklin H. Littell, A. Roy Eckardt, Alice L. Eckardt, Jurgen Moltmann, and Clark M. Williamson have aided the churches in coming to terms with the Holocaust's meaning for Christians. Along with concerned pastors and lay people, these scholars have led conferences and workshops, influenced official Church statements, and nurtured a concern in the Church for Jewish-Christian dialogue. Still, their task of encouraging Christians to acknowledge the Holocaust as a Christian event has not been fully accomplished. Even Protestants who know a good deal about World War II, Nazism and the Holocaust are likely to be unaware of Christianity's role in perpetuating hatred for Jews and thus making the Holocaust possible.

For the most part, responses to the Holocaust in Protestant Churches have been more spontaneous than systematic; and they have differed among evangelical and mainline groups. Evangelicals often celebrate the stories of Christian rescuers, particularly Corrie ten Boom, author of *The Hiding Place*. Some groups, such as Jehovah's Witnesses, advocate an approach to the Holocaust that foregrounds their record of resistance to the Nazis. Liberal Protestants, on the other hand, emphasize non-proselytizing dialogue with Jews and revision of Christian doctrine as appropriate responses to the Holocaust. Interestingly, members of both groups are attracted by the legacy of Dietrich Bonhoeffer, the Lutheran theologian whose martyrdom by the Nazis has made him something akin to a post-Holocaust Protestant saint.

Commemoration of the courage and faith shown by Protestants who resisted the Nazi onslaught against the Jews comprises an important response to the Holocaust. But attention to Protestant heroes of faith can also obscure the less attractive aspects of the Church's record with regard to Jews.

For Reflection

David Gushee has written, 'The Holocaust is an event in the history of the Christian faith and the Christian church.' What does this statement mean?

Has your denomination issued an official statement dealing with the Holocaust or Jewish-Christian relations? Do you agree with the statement?

Does your congregation take seriously its responsibility to offer a response to the Holocaust? How?

For Further Reading

Craig A. Evans, and Donald A. Hagner, eds., *Anti-Semitism and Early Christianity*. Fortress, 1993.

Philip Hallie. *Lest Innocent Blood be Shed: The Story of Le Chambon and How Goodness Happened There*. New York: HarperPerennial, 1994.

Stephen R. Haynes. *Reluctant Witnesses: Jews and the Christian Imagination*. Westminster/John Knox, 1995.

The Theology of the Churches and the Jewish People: Statements by the World Council of Churches and its Member Churches, Geneva: WCC Publications, 1988.

Renate Wind. *Dietrich Bonhoeffer: A Spoke in the Wheel*, Grand Rapids, MI: Eerdmans, 1991.

Stephen R. Haynes (USA) is Associate Professor of Religious Studies at Rhodes College, Memphis, Tennessee. He has written several books dealing with the Holocaust, including *Prospects for Post-Holocaust Theology* (Scholars Press, 1991), and *Holocaust Education and the Church-Related College* (Greenwood, 1997). He is an ordained minister in the Presbyterian Church (USA).

An Ongoing Response

There are several specific areas in which Protestant response to the Holocaust will, and should, continue. One is the issue of the relationship between Christianity and antisemitism. In addition to Christianity's historic connection to Jew hatred, Protestants must deal specifically with the anti-Jewish dimensions of Scripture and Church confessions, the chief authorities for belief and life in most Protestant Churches. Thus, the scholarly debate about whether Christian antisemitism has its roots in the New Testament is a crucial one, given the role Scripture plays in defining the Protestant faith.

Another area in which work is needed is a consistent and faithful witness with regard to Jewish life and interests, and in particular attitudes towards the State of Israel. On one hand, Protestants must condemn and oppose antisemitism in all its contemporary forms. On the other hand, they must endorse attitudes and policies that balance support for both Arab and Jewish human rights, the desire to maintain a Christian presence in the 'Holy Land', and the duty to protect and support the State of Israel. Some Protestants have responded to the Holocaust with a Christian Zionism that eschews this balance for a theologizing of the nation state. While this response to the Holocaust is welcomed by some Jews, it makes others uneasy, and is neither a sufficient nor necessarily appropriate response to Christian responsibility in the Holocaust.

A third area of ongoing work is the search for a Christian conception of the Jewish people that recognizes their theological importance, but does not mystify them as eternally 'other'. Understandably, the ferment in Protestant thinking following the Holocaust has reasserted a 'biblical' view of Jews as God's elect people whose fortunes and misfortunes provide unique testimony to divine activity in the world. Many Protestants regard this theological perspective as a religious duty in light of the Holocaust and what it teaches about the effects of the Christian 'teaching of contempt'. Nevertheless, in the post-Holocaust world what many Jews expect from Christians is not philosemitism, but recognition of their status as normal human beings.

Much remains to be learned and assimilated with regard to the role of Protestant people and institutions in the Holocaust. How will the work that remains be accomplished? Because of the non-hierarchical structure of Protestant Churches, real progress will not come until the Holocaust, Christian anti-Judaism, and Jewish-Christian relations become staples of the seminary curriculum. This will allow pastors and educators to take the lead in transforming how Protestants think and behave, and in communicating to a new generation of believers a gospel that is free of anti-Judaism. In the meantime, it is encouraging that more and more Protestant students are being exposed to the Holocaust and its religious dimensions in their post-secondary studies. It is worrying, however, that as the Holocaust recedes into the past, fewer Protestants will recognize that they too live in its shadow.

AFTER THE HOLOCAUST: HOW HAVE CHRISTIANS RESPONDED?

ACTIVITIES

IN SEARCH OF *TIKKUN*

Marcia Sachs Littell

The Day of Remembrance (*Yom HaShoah*) is observed each year in the United States on the 27th of Nissan in the Jewish calendar. This date falls on the fifth day following the eighth day of Passover. It was adopted from the date chosen in Israel to commemorate the Holocaust.

Fixing the Date

The United States Congress enacted Public Law 96-388 on October 7, 1980. This law provided for appropriate ways to commemorate the Days of Remembrance as an annual, national, civic commemoration of the Holocaust. In America, official proclamations are issued and ceremonies are conducted by the President of the United States, governors, mayors of towns, all major branches of the military, government and community groups, universities, colleges and schools both public and private, and in the synagogues and churches. The decision was made by Congress to use the date fixed on the Jewish calendar for this observance.

On April 12, 1951, the Knesset in Israel declared the 27th of Nissan as *Yom HaShoah* (Holocaust Remembrance Day). However, throughout the 1950s this calendar day was ignored due to the clash of values and differing interpretations of the meaning of the Holocaust in Israel at the time.

It was not until 1959 that the Knesset actually legislated a national public commemoration of the day. Two years later it passed a law which closed all public entertainment on that day. The Zionist philosophy was sparked by Ben Zion Dinur, a labor Zionist who believed the Holocaust was the final proof that the Jewish people needed to focus on re-establishing itself on its land – not dwell on days of commemoration. To David Ben Gurion, the Holocaust was a negative event which had happened to the Jews. His theory was to focus on building the state. To Ben Gurion, the *Sabra*, the new Jew, would be different. More than 150,000 survivors settled in Israel. They focused their energy on building new lives and families. Their reluctance to open old wounds was understandable. They simply did not have the energy to focus on the debate on which date to commemorate this painful event. The religious Jews, the Orthodox community, did not want any date on or near to Passover which would ruin the joyous celebration. In fact the ultra-Orthodox did not want any commemoration at all. The last source pushing for commemoration in Israel were the ex-ghetto fighters, partisans and members of the underground resistance to the Nazis. In *The Jewish Way*, Irving Greenberg refers to the controversy as 'The Shattered Paradigm: *Yom Hashoah*' (pages 314-372).

In recent years, European countries have also begun to institute official days of commemoration and remembrance. No doubt, constructing appropriate programs for Christian commemoration will pose the same initial dilemmas for pastors and community leaders in Europe as it did in the United States. In the United States a volume to aid the lack of existing liturgy on the Holocaust, a book of varied program examples, was compiled. It includes numerous Christian and interfaith programs which are provided as examples for those wishing to construct commemoration programs. (See *Liturgies on the Holocaust: An Interfaith Anthology,* edited by Marcia Sachs Littell and Sharon Weissman Gutman.)

The Purpose

Yom Ha Shoah provides Jews and Christians in the community an opportunity for *tikkun,* to come together and engage in healing. *Yom HaShoah* is the time for non-partisan, interfaith, inter-religious services to take place. This is the time for all citizens in the community – both Jewish and Christian – to unite in healing, reflection, commemoration, cooperation and bearing witness.

The most effective forms of commemoration have taken place when synagogues and churches come together in interfaith remembrance and cooperation. To give an illustration of what can be done: in 1997, two lay leaders in the Methodist Church of Toms River, New Jersey, Virginia and Jack Lamping, organized an interfaith group of lay leaders and clergy to prepare a Holocaust Commemoration Program. The first year the program took place in the Methodist Church. Community members from the local synagogues and the Roman Catholic Church gathered with their Protestant brothers and sisters in the Methodist Church. The second year the interfaith community gathered in the synagogue. The third year the community service was held in a Catholic Church. The leaders plan to continue to rotate the service each year to the various houses of worship in the community. This has provided a strong foundation on which to build ongoing interfaith dialogue in this small American town.

Preparation

Before any Christian congregation decides to have a Holocaust Memorial Service it is imperative for the planners to be clear in their minds about the goals and purpose of the program. Why are they doing it? What do they hope the final outcome will be? These questions must be asked before engaging in a program. Some preparatory education in advance of the observance is helpful in building a successful program. This is especially true in communities where there are few or no Jewish residents and interfaith interaction is non-existent.

Developing a Christian liturgy on the Holocaust is a delicate task. While the victims of the *Shoah* were Jews, the murderers, accomplices and silent bystanders were Christians. There were rescuers,

For Further Reading

Marcia Sachs Littell and Sharon W Gutman. *Liturgies on the Holocaust: An Interfaith Anthology.* Valley Forge: Trinity Press International, 1996.

Hilda Schiff. *Holocaust Poetry.* London: Harper Collins, 1995

Cecilie Klein. *Poems of the Holocaust.* Jerusalem: Gefen Publishing House

Itzhak Tatelbaum. *Through Our Eyes: Children Witness The Holocaust.* Chicago: I.B.T. Publishing, 1985

but they were few in number. Thus, it is important for the congregation to understand the mass of the event. Recent films on the Holocaust produced for public consumption, such as *Schindler's List,* are helpful in paving the way to understanding and can be used as part of adult education seminars. The aim of observing *Yom Ha Shoah* is not to place guilt, but to seek reconciliation and to renew faith in humanity and commitment to life.

Resources

There are certain classical texts, which have been used again and again over the years. These have become a common liturgy and their repeated use provides symbolic recognition of the tragedy of the Jews. These are the descriptions and prayers that dramatically tell the story and transmit the significance of the event. Among these resources, the poems of Nelly Sachs, the Diary of Anne Frank, the poems of the children of Theresienstadt, *I Never Saw Another Butterfl*y, and the writings of Elie Wiesel are frequently used in services. (*Liturgies*, page 44.)

Many Churches have used the Reformed Judaism Movement's post-Holocaust liturgy, a '*Yom Kippur* confession', in their *Yom Hashoah* Liturgy:

> *For the sin of silence*
> *For the sin of indifference,*
> *For the sin of secret complicity of the neutral,*
> *For the closing of borders,*
> *For the washing of hands,*
> *For all that was done,*
> *For all that was not done . . .*

Most important for Christians is that this event should not be a one time occurrence. The telling of the story of the Holocaust should provide the opportunity for insight and for learning the lessons. The most important experience in the teaching, memorializing, and never forgetting, is the use of prayers, songs and readings among people who remember. It is in these sacred hours of remembrance and meditation that the suffering of the past may be transformed and that we may find hope for a better future: in a healed and repaired world – through *tikkun*.

Marcia Sachs Littell (USA) is Director of the National Academy for Holocaust and Genocide Teacher Training, and the Master of Arts in Holocaust and Genocide Studies at The Richard Stockton College of New Jersey. She is the Executive Director of the Annual Scholars' Conference on the Holocaust and the Churches, and Senior Consultant to The Philadelphia Center on the Holocaust, Genocide and Human Rights. Her publications include *Liturgies on the Holocaust: An Interfaith Anthology* (co-editor), *Confronting The Holocaust,* Parts 1 & 2 (co-editor) and *Holocaust Education: A Resource Book For Teachers and Professional Leaders.*

CHALLENGES FOR THEOLOGICAL TRAINING

Isabel Wollaston

Having taught courses on religious responses to the Holocaust and on Christian-Jewish relations for a number of years now, it is my view that such courses must, above all, be self-critical. Considerable claims are made concerning the progress that has been made. However, are such claims justified? There is much talk about 'Jews' and 'Christians', but who is actually talking to whom about what in this context?

Often there is a preference for speaking of 'Jewish-Christian' rather than 'Christian-Jewish relations'. There are two reasons for this. First, to signal the sensitivity of Christian participants (in the past Christians have presumed to define Jews and Judaism from a Christian perspective, but today claim that this is no longer the case). Second, to indicate the primacy ascribed to Judaism and the Hebrew Bible (Christianity is, in some sense, seen as derivative and dependent on its Jewish roots for its own self-understanding). Yet, such linguistic humility is misleading. We are still often dealing with a Christian-driven agenda. As the Vatican Guidelines note, 'The problem of Jewish-Christian relations concerns the Church as such, since it is when she is 'pondering her own mystery' that she encounters the mystery of Israel.' For Christians, the agenda is a theological one, motivated by the need to understand what it is to be Christian in the light of both the Holocaust and encounter with Jews and Judaism.

By contrast, many Jews insist that they have no such theological incentive: 'Since Jews can understand their faith without reference to Christianity, there is no internal need to engage in theological discussion with Christians at all.' (David Berger in *Essential Papers on Jewish-Christian Relations in the United States,* p.330). Eliezer Berkovits goes further in simply stating 'all we want of Christians is that they keep their hands off us and our children.' Furthermore, he insists that 'What is usually referred to as the 'Judeo-Christian tradition' exists only in Christian or secularist fantasy. As far as Jews are concerned, Judaism is fully sufficient. There is nothing in Christianity for them. Whatever in Christian teaching is acceptable to them is borrowed from Judaism.' (Faith after the Holocaust, pp. 47, 44-5).

Given such statements, any course on Christian-Jewish relations needs to address the basic question of whether there is, in fact, anything theological for Christians and Jews to talk about. Or are

> *The Vatican Guidelines note, 'The problem of Jewish-Christian relations concerns the Church as such, since it is when she is 'pondering her own mystery' that she encounters the mystery of Israel.' For Christians, the agenda is a theological one.*

we dealing with something that is of concern only to Christians struggling with questions concerning the role their religious traditions played in paving the way for the Holocaust, and/or the lack of response to the Holocaust on the part of many Christians?

In this context, it is important to remember that we are not dealing with relations between Judaism and Christianity, but with a whole range of (often contradictory) Judaisms and Christianities. Any course should reflect an awareness of the multiple Jewish and Christian perspectives to be found both in the world today, and in the past. Yet, such diversity is rarely reflected in the way that Christian-Jewish relations is taught. Often the focus is limited to those individuals or institutions that believe dialogue and encounter is a valid, even necessary approach. Yet, we must also acknowledge that many Jews and Christians are either reluctant to engage in dialogue, or are consciously excluded from this process. It is all too easy to discuss Christian-Jewish relations as if dialogue is clearly a 'good thing' when, for many Jews and Christians, it is not at all self-evident that it is either possible or desirable. To illustrate this point one might ask how many evangelical Christians, committed to the centrality of mission and/or to the belief that 'no one comes to the Father except by me' engage in dialogue? Likewise, ultra-Orthodox Jews are rarely, if ever, involved. Numerous Jews see no need for – or are reluctant to engage in – theological discussion. Many Orthodox Jews are reluctant to go beyond discussing social or practical issues common to both Jews and Christians. The former and now late Chief Rabbi of Great Britain, Immanuel Jakobovits, gave voice to such reluctance when he insisted that 'What we do not seek, at least within the Orthodox Jewish community, are theological dialogues in the narrow sense of subjecting each faith to the critical scrutiny of the other. Nor do we aspire to joint religious services, or to interfaith activities of a specifically religious nature, as a desired expression of mutual trust and respect.' ('Jewish Understandings of Interfaith Encounter', *Christian-Jewish Relations*, pp.15-6). Ironically, one area where there is consensus between many Jews and Christians lies in the exclusion of Messianic Jews. The existence of Jews who are self-professed Christians is clearly an embarrassment to many who advocate dialogue. Indeed, often the necessary precondition of dialogue or encounter is the implicit or explicit renunciation of mission on the part of the Christian partner; a precondition that can cause difficulties for many evangelical Christians.

Teaching within a Department of Theology in a secular British university, it cannot be assumed that staff and students share a particular faith perspective, or indeed adhere to any faith at all. The course under discussion here, 'Christian-Jewish Relations since 1945', is a single module – that is, ten two-hour sessions – for approximately twenty-five second and third-year undergraduates. Those taking the course are mainly students within the Department of Theology, with a small number from other departments, such as Drama or Philosophy, taking the course as an ancillary subject. While most students taking the course have completed first-year courses in 'Christian Theology' and 'Introduction

For Reflection

Do Jews and Christians have different reasons for wishing to engage in dialogue or encounter each other? If so, is this likely to generate problems for Christian-Jewish dialogue?

Why is 1945 held to mark a turning point in Christian-Jewish relations? Is the Holocaust the sole reason for the changes that have occurred in Christian-Jewish relations in the past 50 years, or have other factors also had a bearing on attitudes?

Is there any need for Jews to develop a Jewish theology of Christianity?

What is meant when people refer to 'the Judeo-Christian tradition'? Do you agree with Eliezer Berkovits that there is in fact no such thing?

to Judaism', this is not always the case. The majority of students on the course are practising Christians, or from Christian backgrounds, although a small number may be Jewish. The format of the class is a 60-minute presentation followed by a combination of discussion, small-group work, and the viewing of a video or slides. Assessment is twofold in order to give students the opportunity to engage with both specific texts and broader theoretical discussions, and consists of an essay and an analysis of one of a number of specific key Church statements.

The aim of the course is to enable students to identify and analyse the dominant issues and approaches in Christian-Jewish relations since 1945. There are three primary emphases:

(a)   The evolution of Christian-Jewish relations since 1945, with particular emphasis on the changing attitudes of the Churches as embodied in official statements.

(b)   Identification and analysis of recurrent questions and controversies, such as the relationship between Christian anti-Judaism and Nazi antisemitism, and attitudes to the State of Israel.

(c)   Analysis of theological models employed to represent the relationship between Christianity and Judaism, e.g. supercessionism (which regards Christianity as the fulfilment or successor of Judaism), or the interpretation of Christianity as 'Judaism for Gentiles', or as a second covenant. As a model, is it more helpful to represent the relationship between Judaism and Christianity as that of a mother and daughter (Abraham Joshua Heschel), or elder and younger brothers (Rosemary Radford Ruether)? Alternatively, should rabbinic Judaism and Christianity be seen as distinctive strands simultaneously emerging from a variety of Second Temple Judaism(s)?

The course concludes with three lectures by guest speakers who have practical involvement in the field on 'The Future of Christian-Jewish Relations'. These sessions illustrate the variety of possible perspectives, encourage students to think about possible future developments, and provide an opportunity to engage directly with those actively involved in this area. Throughout the course, consideration is given to the question of whether 'official' dialogue and encounter have had any real impact upon the situation as it is 'on the ground'. As one possible example of such a contrast, the course explores current debates over the Christianization of the Holocaust, such as the Carmelite convent controversy, the canonization of Edith Stein, and the presence of Christian symbols at Auschwitz. Students are encouraged to consider the ways in which such controversies are represented on the internet and reported in the media. Does the frequency of such controversies illustrate the progress or the lack of progress made in Christian-Jewish relations since 1945?

Teachers in this area have a responsibility to their students to be clear. However, such clarity should not be achieved by misrepresenting what is actually happening. A course on Christian-Jewish relations since 1945 should refelect developments and, by all means, offer a critique of that situation, but never present this situation as more straightforward than it actually is.

For Further Reading

Secretariat for Ecumenical and Inter-religious Affairs, National Conference of Catholic Bishops, *Catholics Remember the Holocaust*, United States Catholic Conference 1998.

Allan Brockway et al. *The Theology of the Churches and the Jewish People*, WCC Publications 1988.

Dan Cohn-Sherbok (ed.), *The Future of Jewish-Catholic Dialogue*, Edwin Mellen Press. 1999.

Carol Rittner and John Roth (eds.), *Memory Offended: The Auschwitz Convent Controversy*. Praeger 1991.

Isabel Wollaston (UK) is Lecturer in Theology at the University of Birmingham. She currently serves on the Advisory Board of the Centre for Jewish-Christian Relations, Cambridge, and the Steering Committee of the 'Holocaust, Genocide and Religion Group' of the American Academy of Religion. She is editor of *Reviews in Religion and Theology* and author of *A War against Memory? The Future of Holocaust Remembrance*, SPCK, 1996.

HOLOCAUST EDUCATION IN AMERICAN CATHOLIC COLLEGES AND UNIVERSITIES

Michael Phayer   Carol Rittner

'No dialogue between Christians and Jews can overlook the painful and terrible experience of the Shoah.'

Pope John Paul II, 'Address to the International Liaison Committee between the Catholic Church and the IJCIC in Rome', December 6, 1990.

Catholics were directed by Vatican Council II (1962-1965) to learn about Judaism and about God's First Covenant with the Jewish people, a covenant we Christians believe has never been abrogated. In their document, *Nostra Aetate* ('In Our Time'), the Council Fathers reminded the Church about 'the bond that spiritually ties the people of the New Covenant to Abraham's stock.' The bishops wanted 'to foster and recommend that mutual understanding and respect which is the fruit, above all, of biblical and theological studies as well as of fraternal dialogues.' Catholics were encouraged to study the Jewish roots of Christianity, to revise their teaching and educational materials so as to challenge anything which might suggest anti-Judaism or that might foster antisemitism. They were also encouraged to enter into genuine dialogue with Jewish people.

Roman Catholic Christians took seriously the directives of Vatican II. They began to study and do research, to revise their liturgy, to restructure their educational materials about Jews and Judaism, and to enter into dialogue with Jews. Very quickly Catholics learned that if they were going to seriously dialogue with Jews, they would have to be willing to talk about the Holocaust – Nazi Germany's attempt to annihilate Jewish life and culture in Twentieth Century Europe.

In addition to offering workshops, seminars and courses on the Old Testament (Hebrew Scriptures), or about the Jewish roots of Christianity, about the modern State of Israel or about Jewish life and literature, American Catholic colleges and universities began teaching courses on the Holocaust. They also began to join with Jewish organizations, synagogues, and survivor groups to offer students and the community at large – Jewish and Christian – opportunities to participate in programs commemorating the Holocaust.

For Reflection

If God's covenant with the Chosen People is still valid, what should the correct disposition of Catholics toward Jews be?

Why has the Holocaust been a 'wake-up' call for western civilization?

Why is it difficult for many Catholics to grasp why religious leaders like New York's Cardinal John J. O'Connor or Milwaukee's Archbishop Rembrant Weakland make public apologies for the Holocaust?

Some Pioneers

Msgr. John Oesterreicher, one of a small group of international pioneers who rethought Catholic-Jewish relations after the Holocaust, was a professor at Seton Hall Catholic University in Orange, New Jersey. There he published his journal, *The Bridge*, which explored the Jewish roots of the Christian heritage. For years, John Oesterreicher engaged in his work of teaching, learning, and from his Roman Catholic perspective, researching Jews and Judaism. For years, he labored in the field of Jewish-Christian relations, as did a number of his colleagues at Seton Hall, including Sister Rose Thering and Father John Morley, best known for his pioneering volume, *Vatican Diplomacy and the Jews, 1939-1943* (KTAV). While Sister Rose has been particularly involved in dialogue with Jews and Christians about the modern State of Israel, she and Father Morley have both written about, lectured, and taught courses about the Holocaust. Most recently, Father Morley was appointed as one of several Catholic and Jewish scholars to examine the eleven volumes of Vatican documents related to World War II and Pope Pius XII.

In the Midwest, when Harry James Cargas began teaching his courses on the Holocaust, Webster College was a small well-known Catholic college sponsored by the Sisters of Loretto. There, he inspired students and colleagues, Christian and Jewish, with his thoughtful and provocative books and lectures on the failures of the institutional Church during the Holocaust. For years, Cargas taught, organized conferences, invited speakers to seminars – Elie Wiesel being among the more famous – and produced radio and television programs about the Holocaust. He interviewed survivors about their experiences during the *Shoah*, publishing those interviews in journals and books. As Vidal Sassoon wrote in the Foreword to Cargas' book, *Reflections of a Post-Auschwitz Christian,* 'Harry James Cargas [was] one of the new breed of brave Christians who [realized] that the monstrosity of the Holocaust was a Christian tragedy.' The work he began at Webster, and tirelessly carried out for nearly three decades, is carried forward by Dr. Linda Woolf, who continues to teach courses on the Holocaust and genocide to students at Webster University.

Roman Catholic seminaries and theological schools also include courses on the Holocaust in their curricula. Father John Pawlikowski at Catholic Theological Union in Chicago has taught Holocaust-related courses for many years, earning scholarly respect from Jews and Christians in the USA and beyond. He has been particularly involved in the dialogue between Polish Catholics and Polish Jewish survivors of the Holocaust in the United States and in Poland. Some Catholic universities, like the University of Notre Dame in South Bend, Indiana have established Chairs in Christian-Jewish Studies. At Notre Dame, Dr. Michael Signer, a Jewish scholar, holds the Chair. Under his leadership and with the support of the university, major seminars and conferences related to the Holocaust have been held, attracting students, educators, and scholars from all over North America.

More than ten years ago, Seton Hill College in Pennsylvania (not to be confused with Seton Hall University in New Jersey) inaugurated a program to train interested educators – and others – about the Holocaust. Every year, Seton Hill's National Catholic Center for Holocaust Education co-sponsors

For Further Reading

Joyce Freedman-Apsel and Helen Fein, eds. *Teaching about Genocide: A Guidebook for College and University Teachers: Critical Essays, Syllabi and Assignments.* Ottawa: Human Rights Internet, 1992.

Harry James Cargas. *Reflections of a Post-Auschwitz Christian.* Detroit: Wayne State University Press, 1989.

Edward Bristow, ed. *No Religion is an Island: The Nostra Aetate Dialogues.* New York: Fordham University Press, 1998.

Zev Garber and Richard Libowitz, eds. *Peace, In Deed: Essays in Honor of Harry James Cargas.* Atlanta, GA: Scholars Press, 1998.

Stephen R. Haynes. *Holocaust Education and the Church-Related College: Restoring Ruptured Traditions.* Westport, CT: Greenwood Press, 1997.

'As people of religion and also people of the campus we are confronted by the Holocaust in painful ways. The more we examine the Holocaust the more we see how the church leadership failed the people. And we see how the products of the modern university, the alumni of the great universities of the Weimar Republic, the graduates of an institution once referred to as universitas fidelium, served an evil cause and even conceived evil programs.'

Marcia Sachs Littell. *The Role of the University in Rethinking Issues of Social Justice* in Zev Garber and Richard Libowitz, eds. *Peace, In Dccd*, p. 202.

Michael Phayer (USA) is Professor of History at Marquette University in Milwaukee, Wisconsin. He is the author of several books, including *Protestant and Catholic Women in Nazi Germany* (1990).

Carol Rittner R.S.M. (USA) is Distinguished Professor of Holocaust Studies at The Richard Stockton College of New Jersey and the co-editor of *The Holocaust and the Christian World: Reflections on the Past, Challenges for the Future.*

a four-week intensive course on the Holocaust for educators that is taught in Jerusalem in cooperation with Yad Vashem, Israel's Holocaust Memorial. Well over a hundred university, college and high school teachers from across the United States have participated in this program.

What Accounts for the Interest?

From Boston College to Loyola Marymount University in Los Angeles, from Barry University in Miami to Georgetown University in Washington, DC, from College Misericordia in Northeastern Pennsylvania to Marquette University in Milwaukee, and from St. Elizabeth's College in New Jersey to Catholic Theological Union (CTU) in Chicago, courses on the Holocaust are proliferating, being taught to undergraduate and graduate students, to members of the clergy and to interested lay people, Catholic, Protestant and Jewish.

What accounts for this profusion of interest in the Holocaust over the last 20 years at Catholic colleges and universities? There are many reasons, among them the revolutionary change in Catholic thinking about Jews and Judaism stimulated by Vatican II. The strong leadership of Pope John Paul II also has contributed to the interest of Catholic colleges and universities in this historical horror. Pope John Paul II has spoken more often and more directly about Jews, Judaism, and the *Shoah* than any other Pope in recent history, even more than the much beloved Pope John XXIII. These are important factors to take into account when asking the question about the basis for the interest in teaching about the Holocaust in American Catholic colleges and universities.

Other factors also deserve to be mentioned, including the obvious one that the Holocaust was perpetrated by a thoroughly modern country with a majority Christian population in the heart of Christian western civilization in the shadows of the great cathedrals and learning centers of Christendom. Young people want to know what their religious leaders did or did not do during the Holocaust. They have more than an intellectual curiosity, though undoubtedly they are curious. When asked, many of them say they feel 'morally obligated' to find out all they can, otherwise, what possibility is there of changing the future? Interestingly enough, in his book, *Holocaust Education and the Church-Related College,* Stephen R. Haynes comments that the results of a survey he did in the mid-1990s in preparation for writing his book indicated that 'nearly half of the colleges claiming to teach the Holocaust out of moral obligation are Catholic-affiliated'.

Undoubtedly, there will come a time when interest in the Holocaust will wane, but for the present, Catholic colleges and universities all across America are teaching students about the 'Tragedy of the *Shoah* and the Duty of Remembrance' (see further, *'We Remember: A Refection on the Shoah'*). They are doing so in an effort to 'invite all men and women of good will' to do what Pope John Paul II has encouraged them to do: 'to reflect deeply on the significance of the *Shoah*' so as 'to become fully conscious of the salutary warning it entails: The spoiled seeds of anti-Judaism and antisemitism must never again be allowed to take root in any human heart.'

JOURNEY TO POLAND: REMEMBRANCE AND RECONCILIATION A PERSONAL REFLECTION

Margaret Shepherd

Education about the Shoah is a central concern of the Council of Christians and Jews, which seeks an in-depth understanding of its impact on Jews, Christians and the relationship between them. Although we do therefore undertake many activities around this major issue, it was only with much hesitation and apprehension that I decided to organise a visit to the camps in Poland. My intention was simply to give members of the CCJ an opportunity, at the end of this pain-filled century, to take what I anticipated would prove to be a painful yet necessary journey.

Some twenty-seven people responded, Jews and Christians, of very different ages, backgrounds, life experiences - and expectations. They also proved to be very caring and mutually supportive. That Jews and Christians were making such a journey together was both unusual and special, affecting all that we saw, heard, experienced together. In the space of five days in October 1999, we visited Majdanek; the labour camp at Plaszow and Schindler's factory; Auschwitz-Birkenau; the Warsaw Ghetto, and Treblinka.

Guard towers at Majdanek. Photo by Ronald Channing.

It was hard for us all, especially on the first day, facing Majdanek in the gathering gloom of dusk with flocks of crows flying overhead, just hours after landing in Poland. I reflected that the shock of finding ourselves there, so suddenly, was nothing to the trauma of those who had been unceremoniously forced there to perish in their thousands. We stood in front of the trenches where thousands had been shot in one day; we stood inside the gas chamber; we saw the crematorium. Silently, with disbelief, we stood in front of the huge mound of the ashes of the dead. And right beside Majdanek runs the main road into Lublin; as if this is normality. The buildings and the watchtowers encircling the camp seemed recently built; a mundane part of today's reality. "What is reality?", I asked myself. How could this place have become a reality, accepted by the Christians of Lublin on whose outskirts it was built? Where did I, a Christian, fit into all this? What was it saying to me?

Birkenau was beyond the limits of my mind - and it shattered my soul. It was vast, stretching as far as the eye could see. It was eerie; silent, and unrelieved by birdsong. I felt numbed, chilled to the core of my being. A place of contradictions: apparently peaceful, but offering no peace; surrounded by beautiful, whispering birch trees, but under them, I knew, had sat mothers and children awaiting their turn to enter the gas chambers. We prayed that day beside a tranquil lake which Robin O'Neil, our scholar-in-residence, called the most sacred place in Birkenau. Its beauty was cruelly deceptive, for it contained the ashes of those who had been murdered there.

How can one pray in these places? We did. The group very much wanted to. But with hesitation, and enormous sensitivity. Nothing had been specially prepared. The focus was naturally on Jewish suffering and at Plasow, Kaddish was said, the traditional Jewish prayer for mourners. Elsewhere we used psalms and poetry and lit candles. One or two of the Christians in the group said to me afterwards that they would have liked other victims, non-Jews, to have been remembered specifically, perhaps with appropriate Christian prayers. I am sure the Jewish members of the group would have accepted that, despite the normal difficulties about Jews and Christians praying together. On this occasion it would have been a matter of being together to pray, each in his or her own way, each respectful of the other. I know that the prayers we said together helped some. For me, an alternative and deeply appropriate response would have been silence.

I had been to Treblinka before, but this time was very conscious of the fact that one of the Jews in the group had escaped from Warsaw in 1939 on the Kindertransport, leaving behind his parents and his little sister. All had perished in Treblinka and this was the first time he had been there to honor their memory. It was a privilege to be with him and his wife on this very personal journey. It brought home forcefully to me the pain of each one of those who had suffered in every possible way during those dreadful years - and those who go on suffering today. It doesn't stop. It isn't finished. It cannot be consigned to history. I stood with him that day, silent again, not daring to touch his pain with my words.

Since our return I have reflected deeply on the many issues raised by such a visit to places, at the heart of Christian Europe, where unspeakable suffering, degradation and death took place. How do we Christians cope with such a burden of responsibility, acknowledge it and face the future? To paraphrase the Roman Catholic theologian, Johanne Baptist Metz; no Christian theology can be done today except against the backdrop of the Shoah. At its very heart the Shoah challenges our theological reflection as Christians. Public admission by Christian churches has been made in recent years of the age-old sin of antisemitism and its dire effects on the Jewish community. It was indeed the seedbed in which the evil Nazi ideology flourished with devastating effect. We have rightly been

> *'Since our return I have reflected deeply on the many issues raised by such a visit to places, at the heart of Christian Europe, where unspeakable suffering, degradation and death took place. How do we Christians cope with such a burden of responsibility, acknowledge it and face the future?'*

Arek Hersh lighting a Yahrzeit Candle,
Auschwitz Birkenau.

called to repentance by our churches. Significant and important though all this is, more fundamental are the questions placed at the door of the Christian faith itself. I do not believe we can go on as before, as if the Shoah had not taken place.

When we visited Auschwitz I was all too conscious of the centrality of the cross in Christianity. We saw the building which had been the Carmelite Convent at the centre of the disturbing confrontation over the Community's presence there. Only in recent months has the subsequent problem of Christians planting numerous crosses at the site been resolved. It raises two major issues: firstly, how can the Polish nation and the Jewish people come to a mutual recognition of each other's suffering? For each, Auschwitz remains primarily a symbol of their own group's suffering rather than that of others. With patient understanding a way forward could be found to seeing Auschwitz as both a Jewish and a Polish tragedy. Both were victims. Secondly, what is a fitting memorial to the dead? For Christians, a cross is important, but this has been for Jews a sign of persecution for two thousands years, which makes the presence of huge crosses, especially at Auschwitz, a great problem. The Jewish preference is that there should be no memorial at Auschwitz. Some kind of uneasy compromise has been reached, not without difficulty, and what has become known as "the Papal cross" remains standing in the grounds of the former Carmelite Convent, but the controversy surrounding the whole question has left a bitter taste. As we left Birkenau, I was startled by the sight of a large, tall cross above a building which faces it, formerly part of the SS barracks. I was distinctly uneasy at its position and proximity.

I believe that we Christians have to question our understanding of the life and, especially, the death of Jesus, whom we call "Christ". For countless generations Jews have been falsely accused of causing his death, causing persecution, giving way to the blood libel, pogroms, expulsion and, finally, paving the way to the Shoah itself. That erroneous teaching was, of course, refuted by the Roman Catholic Church in its now famous 1965 document, Nostra Aetate, but how should we look at the death of Jesus, the Jew?

In thinking this through in depth I find Jürgen Moltmann helpful in his book, The Way of Jesus Christ: Christology in Messianic Dimensions. Jesus died a Jewish death at the hands of the pagan Romans. His sufferings are intimately linked with the sufferings of his people, especially the prophets before him, and with all who have come after him; and therefore with the sufferings endured in the Shoah. His was the Jewish God, who identifies with the suffering of His people, the Jewish people, through the ages and to the present day and therefore with the suffering of the Shoah. Jesus is not separate from but most intimately a part of his people, especially in his death as a righteous, innocent one at the hands of gentiles. If he had lived in the Twentieth Century, it is likely that he would have perished in Auschwitz.

For Reflection

If you have visited – or can imagine yourself visiting – any of the concentration/death camps, what issues arose/would arise for you as a Christian?

What do you think repentance and reconciliation mean to our Churches, to you, in the context of the Shoah?

How do we pray after the Shoah?

One of the Christians in my group sent me a Christmas card, which he had designed himself. On the front he had chosen words from the poet, William Blake: 'He who kisses the joy as it flies/ Lives in eternity's sunrise.' Inside, he had placed the reproductions of two photographs facing each other: on the left, a photograph of blown-up gas chambers at Auschwitz-Birkenau, with the caption, Black hole of the universe; and on the right, a photograph of Coventry Cathedral, almost totally destroyed by enemy action and rebuilt after the war, a sign of forgiveness and reconciliation, with the caption, Phoenix from the ashes. What would your comments be?

What is your understanding of forgiveness, in the light of the Shoah?

For Further Reading

Jürgen Moltmann. *The Way of Jesus Christ: Christology in Messianic Dimensions.* (Trans. Margaret Kohl.) Augsburg Fortress Publications, 1994. (see pp. 151-212, especially pp.167-168).

Martin Gilbert. *Holocaust Journey: Travelling in Search of the Past.* London: Weidenfeld & Nicolson, 1997.

Martin Gilbert. *The Holocaust: The Jewish Tragedy.* London: Harper Collins, 1986.

Primo Levi. *If This Is A Man.* London: The Orion Press, 1969.

Klaus Scholder. *The Churches and the Third Reich.* (2 vols.) SCM Press, 1977.

Peter Chave. *The Holocaust: Its Relevance to Every Christian.* London: CCJ, 1991.

Sister Margaret Shepherd NDS

(UK) is a Member of the Sisters of Sion and Director of the Council of Christians and Jews, UK. She regularly teaches, lectures and writes on Christian-Jewish relations and the Holocaust. She is widely known as an educator, writer and broadcaster.

Cross outside block 11 in Auschwitz.

This is not, however, how the suffering and death of Jesus is preached about in our churches or expressed in our liturgies. If it were, then so much would follow from such a new approach to the core of the Christian faith. Our understanding of incarnation; of the life of Jesus, with its central message of living according to God's values; of the resurrection; and of our life as followers of this Jew called Jesus. All this would impact on our relationship to the Jewish community of today. We have hardly begun to consider the radical reshaping of our Christian theology and, following on from that, a very different expression of our Christian faith. We need new images of our God and His Christ for our day, living, as we do, in the shadow of the Shoah. We need a new language to heal this shattered relationship between Jews and Christians - both "peoples of God". We need a common language, born out of the ashes of the Shoah, with which to speak honestly with each other.

This was borne out even in what I had called our special CCJ visit to Poland. I had struggled over this in the advertising for it. I did not want to call it a "tour" or a "trip". I had settled on "A Journey to Poland - Remembrance and Reconciliation". The word "remembrance" was clearly acceptable and certainly appropriate. In the words of the Eighteenth-Century founder of the Hasidic movement, the Ba'al Shem Tov, "Forgetfulness leads to exile, while remembrance is the secret of redemption". But "reconciliation"? I had unwittingly walked into a minefield, as some of the Jews in the group expressed their anger at thinking that I wanted them to be reconciled with the perpetrators - and their descendants. This had not been my intention. I had simply seen such a visit as a natural part of our concern at CCJ to bring about the healing of the shattered relationship between Jews and Christians. As we remembered the pain of the past and tried to come to terms with it, I hoped we might find cause for hope for the future. The healing of memories in order to find a way forward is part of the building of trust, mutual respect and real friendship. Only in this way can our Jewish brothers and sisters come to believe that things have changed between us, and our fellow Christians understand how radical is this changed relationship, so that together we can move forward in hope.

We are indeed now fostering a new relationship with Judaism, and have put the essential building blocks in place. But we have barely begun this delicate task. As for any radical review of our own Christian theology in the light of this new relationship, that task still awaits us.

WHERE MEMORIES MEET

Stephen D. Smith

Birkenau in January was difficult to absorb. Just a large bleak empty space with snow blowing from left to right across the 'ramp', the watchtowers empty, the trains long since gone. So too, the people. The majority were gassed and burned. As I surveyed the scene of desolation, I realised that there was nothing to connect me to the lives of those who perished there, nor anything to give me a sense of what to do next. Actually, I did not know what kind of place it was. A museum perhaps? But how can you possibly call a place of mass murder a museum? Birkenau is not a museum, or if it is, it should not be. Is it an artefact? Certainly, it is a relic of the past, a kind of rotting or semi-restored version of reality. But people died there, their ashes and the remains of their mortal bodies are still scattered just below the surface of the soil. Wherever you walk, the ground is soaked in the memory of forgotten souls. So how do you describe it? Birkenau is the final resting place of a million souls and yet there is no name, not one headstone, not even a sense of dignity of death, anywhere to be seen. It is

View of the 'ramp' at Birkenau from the Gate Tower.

a cemetery, and yet it never can be, as cemeteries are places of memory and this symbolises the absence of such. So too, the little towns and villages of Poland, the Ukraine, Belarus, Czechia, Slovakia, Lithuania and the towns and cities of Germany, France and Holland and other European countries remain bereft of much or all of their Jewish past. Still today, there is little or no evidence of appropriate forms of memorial in recognition of that past. We say we remember; but do we not more readily forget?

Standing there on the 'ramp', I cast my mind back just several months to the visit James, my brother, and I had made to Yad Vashem. There in Israel, we had confronted ourselves, our past and the impact of the mass destruction of European Jewry upon our somewhat naïve and idealistic Christian identity. I had thought, until then, that Christianity would do the right thing, would lead the moral campaign for a world free of violence and hatred and would demonstrate that peaceful co-existence was worth fighting for. And then I discovered that was not necessarily so. I also discovered that the Jews of Europe had been murdered *en masse* at the hands of 'Christian' people

'It is not enough to ask whether or not our memorials remember the Holocaust, or even how they remember it. We should ask to what ends we have remembered. That is, how do we respond to the current moment in light of our remembered past?'

James Young, *The Texture of Memory*

Jews have by and large been left to carry the burden of the Shoah. Is this right, in view of the fact that the perpetrators, collaborators and bystanders were not Jewish?

Rusting cutlery: Birkenau.

and that few seemed to care about that. James and I decided that we should do something to confront our compatriots and co-religionists with the consequences of the *Shoah* for non-Jews.

At Birkenau, we realised that the sites of mass destruction, as important as they are to our sense of history, are not places of memorial, but an insult to the memory of the individuals, families and communities that were wasted there. Not that the current guardians mean it that way: on the contrary, but it is part of the nature of the site and what happens there. It seemed that there also needed to be places wherein their memory could be honored, their story told and the consequences and issues addressed. Moreover, such places could and indeed should come from outside of the Jewish context as well as those created by and with the Jewish community. Jews have, by and large, been left to carry the burden of the *Shoah*. Is this right, in view of the fact that the perpetrators, collaborators and bystanders were not Jewish? Surely those who fall victim should not be responsible for addressing the causes of their victimization.

We traveled to the U.S. and visited some twelve or more museums, education centres and archives. We traveled to Israel and spent many weeks on many occasions at Yad Vashem, but also at Beit Lohamei Haghetaot and other places. We traveled around Europe, to the camps, the ghettos, the streets and forests of this history. And then we began to think, to struggle. . . and eventually to build.

Four years later, Beth Shalom, the House of Peace, came into being. Beth Shalom is not a monument, but a memorial to the victims of the *Shoah* and a center of learning for future generations. Tucked away in the rural idyll of Sherwood Forest, it is the place one would least expect to find such a confrontation with a past far removed from the North Nottinghamshire countryside. But this is of course exactly the kind of environment where such a center should be. Its very disconnection from the actual events of the *Shoah* forces one to bridge the gap between everyday life in Britain and the reality of mass murder and its consequences for all societies everywhere.

The vast majority of visitors to the United States Holocaust Museum in Washington DC are not Jewish. So too, Yad Vashem has many more Christian than Jewish visitors. This is the way it should be, not only because of relative numbers, but because the *Shoah* should mean something to an increasing number of non-Jews if it is ever to mean anything to society as a whole. However, the phenomenon of non-Jews visiting such sites of learning is now being further extended, as a number of Christians are beginning to create such places too. In Fukuyama, Japan, a small congregation began a center for learning about the Holocaust, coincidentally also called Beth Shalom. In Lithuania the new 'Atminteis Namai' (House of Memory) is founded by non-Jewish individuals concerned to see their society confront its past. In addition, Christians involve themselves in running and supporting

Jewish or state museums. The Austrian based, *Gedenk dienst* (or 'memorial service' – an alternative to doing national service) sends young volunteers around the world to work at sites or in museums dedicated to teaching about the *Shoah*. In local museums and sites young non-Jewish volunteers work alongside Jewish colleagues such as in the Lithuania Jewish State Museum, Vilnius, or the Anne Frank House in Amsterdam. These environments provide opportunity for the visiting public to appreciate and confront the history itself, but also encourage a fertile co-operation across communities.

> '*It seems apparent that 'never again' is a deceptively simple assertion masking a range of assumptions and intentions. One such assumption concerns the need for active remembrance: it is necessary to make a conscious effort to know what happened, and then to communicate that knowledge to others.*'
>
> Isabel Wollaston, *A War Against Memory?* p.8

Whenever we confront the *Shoah*, it seems we should do so learning together. Jews and Christians, survivors and young people, teachers and pupils; each should enrich the experience of the other. In the face of the *Shoah*, one does not achieve this through the presumptuous delivery of opinion, but in the humility of human wisdom in the face of such total suffering. What can I say? What can I conclude? What can I convey of something I understand so little? I could tell you facts, but will that help you understand? I could analyse the data, but is an intellectual thesis about the murder of someone else's family fitting? Or maybe I could build a memorial, or write a poem. There is plenty I can say and do. But always before I do, I know I should listen. I should listen to you, who survived, you who are older and wiser, you who are younger and fresher, you who preach, you who teach, you who just want the world to be a better place. In the listening, I despair with you, share with you, hope with you, cry with you. In the listening, at times there is nothing to say and then we are silent. And in the silence there is memory. Their memory, the forgotten memory, the memory that was never born nor borne, because no one witnessed that which should be remembered and no one really cared. And so we must learn to remember and to confront the absence of their memory and in some way to make it ours. We must learn to convey the inconceivable in words that will touch hearts and one day change lives.

In this way the memory of the destroyed communities becomes a part of my own. When I talk of 'them', 'the Jews', 'their' suffering, 'their' burden, 'their' experience, I reinforce the divide and

For Further Reading

Saul Friedlander. *Probing the Limits of Representation*. Cambridge MA: Harvard University Press, 1992.

Geoffrey H Hartman. *Holocaust Remembrance, the Shapes of Memory*. Oxford: Blackwell, 1994.

Harold Kaplan. *Conscience and Memory, Meditations in a Museum of the Holocaust*. Chicago: The University of Chicago Press, 1994.

Jean-François Lyotard. *The Differend: Phrases in Dispute*. Manchester: Manchester University Press, 1983.

Stephen Smith. *Making Memory: Creating Britain's First Holocaust Centre*. Newark: Quill Press, 1999.

James E Young. *The Texture of Memory: Holocaust Memorials and Meaning*. New Haven: Yale University Press, 1993.

Isabel Wollaston. *A War Against Memory?* London: SPCK, 1996.

Beth Shalom Holocaust Memorial Centre, Laxton, UK

For Reflection

How does memory shape our sense of identity?

Do you think that visiting sites, memorials and centers effects what we understand about the Holocaust?

Is remembering the Holocaust important? Why?

Stephen D. Smith (UK) is co-founder and director of the Beth Shalom Holocaust Memorial Centre, UK. He is a member of the Intergovernmental Task Force for Holocaust Remembrance, Research and Education. His publications include *Making Memory: Creating Britains' First Holocaust Centre* and he is also editor of *The Witness Collection*. Among his forthcoming publications is *Forgotten Places: The Holocaust and the Remnants of Destruction.*

recommit all Jews everywhere to the status of the 'other'. Who are 'they', these anonymous 'Jews', of whom we talk? They are a part of us; not as Christians, but us as a part of a shared humanity. As I often repeat, the *Shoah* was not about the suffering of the Jews, but about the suffering of humanity as experienced by the Jews of Europe. Therefore, even though these people suffered precisely because they were Jews, we who are not should come alongside the terrible burden which that imposes, and share in it, as co-members of humanity; if only in trying to show that it *does* matter.

In some small way the Beth Shalom Holocaust Memorial Centre is there to do just that. It says to the Jewish community that somewhat belatedly some Christians are beginning to realise that the *Shoah* is their problem too and are prepared to do something practical about its meaning for Jews and Christians separately and together. But also to say to non-Jewish people generally, and to Christians in particular, that the *Shoah* really is our problem and to steel ourselves to respond to it openly, publicly, daily. In this way, whether at a place such as Beth Shalom or in a plethora of museums and sites around the world, people should do more than confront the history of the *Shoah*. Such places

should not become a destination point on the tourist trail, but places of learning, of listening, of talking and of silence, where memories can meet. There is nothing that can be done to turn back the clock or to reinstate the wasted lives. There is nothing that can be done to alleviate the despair that lingers in the hearts and minds of the survivors or the anger that boils in any decent individual's soul when confronting such inadmissible evil. However, there is a future and that future is to be shared. Maybe such places help us to confront the dark reality of that past, if only to strengthen our resolve to make that future more certain, and for the sake of our shared humanity, more safe to live in.

School children learning from a mobile travelling exhibition at the Centre

AFTER THE HOLOCAUST: HOW HAVE CHRISTIANS RESPONDED?

ISSUES

ON CHRISTIAN MISSION
TO THE JEWS

Hubert G. Locke

> 'As Christians we must always remind ourselves that our faith began as a Jewish sect. In this fact lies the impetus, for some Christians, and the peril, for others, of efforts to convert the Jewish people to Christian belief.'

As Christians we must always remind ourselves that our faith began as a Jewish sect. In this fact lies the impetus, for some Christians, and the peril, for others, of efforts to convert the Jewish people to Christian belief.

The impetus can be traced to the effort of Jesus' first followers to convince other Jews that Jesus was the long-awaited Jewish Messiah. This was the core message in the preaching of Peter and other leaders of the church in Jerusalem – a congregation that, initially, had considerable difficulty accepting the insistence of Paul that the Christian message was intended for non-Jews as well. As Paul's point of view gained ground, Christian preachers and teachers found themselves faced with an inherent contradiction. On one hand, Christians proclaimed that theirs was a universal message of redemption and salvation, intended to be heard by and valid for the entire world. However, they could not escape the fact that this universal message had come to the world in the life and teaching of a Jewish carpenter, who preached his first sermon in a Jewish synagogue and surrounded himself with Jewish followers. This tension – how to acknowledge Christianity's Jewish origins while proclaiming its universal intent and implications – has troubled Christianity for almost two millennia since then.

The initial Christian response to this tension was to denigrate the Jewish religion by depicting it as theologically and spiritually inferior to the new Christian faith. Over time, the attack on Judaism as a religion became an assault on its Jewish adherents. What began as an attempt to persuade Jews regarding the claims of Christianity degenerated into a message of condemnation, not only of Judaism but also of the Jewish people themselves who were denounced as 'stubborn' and 'hardhearted' for refusing to acknowledge what, for Christians, had become their supreme proclamation – that Jesus was the Savior of the World.

This condemnation of the Jewish people – essentially for being Jewish and not converting to Christianity – set the stage and laid the groundwork for what has proven to be centuries of Christian ambivalence toward Jews. It has seen Christians vacillate between a condescending indifference, at best, and an outright hostility in its worst moments, toward Judaism and the Jewish people. When the Christian world has chosen to be indifferent to Jews it has treated them as second-class citizens not entitled to the privileges of Christian society. Where hostility has held sway, it has led to antisemitism or hatred of the Jews that has become part of the tragic legacy of the Western world. It is the contribution of Christianity to antisemitism that, for many Christians, stands as a rebuke to any attempt at undertaking a mission to the Jews. Antisemitism reached its lowest level in Europe in the 1930s and 1940s. In Germany, the most powerful nation in Europe – even after its defeat in World War I – a political regime headed by Adolf Hitler seized power and began a campaign of discrimination and oppression against Germany's Jewish citizens. A tiny fraction of Germanys' populace, many German Jews were forced to leave their homeland and emigrate to other parts of Europe or to North America. In 1938, the German military machine launched an assault that, a year later, spread all across Europe. As the military conquered new territory, special squads scoured the towns and villages rounding up Jews and marching them to the surrounding fields or forests where they were forced to dig their own graves before they were shot.

As the German army rolled through Eastern and Western Europe, the number of Jews encountered increased dramatically. By 1941, a more systematic process of annihilation was begun. In the major cities, particularly of Eastern Europe, Jews were forced to give up their homes and businesses and move into ghettos. From the ghettos they were transported to one of six death camps that had been established in central and southern Poland; here, Jews were 'selected' either for forced labor if they were relatively young and healthy, or for medical experimentation. The rest were led into gas chambers.

While this ghastly process went on, the Christians of Europe were, for the most part, silent. Here and there, courageous Christian voices spoke out against the murder of the Jews; small bands of Christians hid Jews and helped them escape across the borders of the occupied territories or took in Jewish children and raised them as their own. But these were frightfully small exceptions to a general climate of indifference toward the fate of the Jews who, in the brief space of three years, saw over five million of their numbers perish at the hands of the Nazis.

Tragically, it was not only the Christians of Europe who did not raise their voices in protest. In Canada, the United States, and elsewhere, reports of the annihilation of the Jews were widely reported in the media, including Christian journals and magazines. But commentators either considered the reports to be wartime propaganda or news of God's judgment on a 'stiff-necked people'.

In the aftermath of Germany's defeat and the end of the Second World War, Christians all over the world have had to re-examine their consciences and to ask themselves why the Church, with its message of God's love for all of humanity, did so little to aid the Jews in their hour of greatest peril. It has forced the Church to re-examine its preaching about the 'perfidious Jews' and to recognize the extent to which the Christian motif of 'the Jews as Christ-killers' helped to create an atmosphere in which the slaughter of Europe's Jewish populace could take place without widespread outcry and opposition.

Most Christian churches today, therefore, consider their primary task concerning the Jewish people to be genuine efforts to purge Christian teaching and preaching of its anti-Jewish sentiments, not attempts at conversion. Church Sunday School literature, devotional readings, and many other denominational materials continue to carry a subtle and often not so subtle message that perpetuates the image of the Jewish people as those who rejected Christ and of Judaism as an inferior, if not false, belief.

> For many Christians, the appropriate stance of the Church in the presence of the Jewish people is that of penitence, not proselytization.

A mission to any people obliges those who would undertake it to carefully examine themselves and their past with respect to those to whom the mission is directed, lest it be seen as a massive effort in hypocrisy. In the case of the Jews, there remains – in the words of Jesus – a huge beam in the eye of Christians that is two millennia of anti-Jewish attitudes, sentiments and behavior. Christians would do well to work on removing this beam, before thinking about any mission to the Jews.

For many Christians, therefore, the appropriate stance of the Church in the presence of the Jewish people is that of penitence, not proselytization. For many others, it is theologically best left to what Paul, in his letter to the church at Rome, termed the 'unsearchable widsom and knowledge of God' to deal with his people Israel.

For Further Reading

Franklin H. Littell. *The Crucifixion of the Jews.* Macon GA: Mercer University Press, 1986.

'Interreligious Dialogue: Stretching the Boundaries', *Journal of Ecumenical Studies,* Vol. 24, No. 3, 1997.

Michael Marrus. *The Holocaust in History.* New York: Penguin Books, 1987.

Hubert G. Locke (USA) is Dean and Professor Emeritus of the Daniel J. Evans School of Public Affairs, University of Washington. A member of the Church Relations Committee of the U.S. Holocaust Memorial Museum in Washington, D.C., he is author of *Exile in the Fatherland: Martin Niemoeller's Letters from Moabit Prison* and *Learning from History: A Black Christian's Perspective on the Holocaust* [forthcoming].

CHRISTIAN PREACHING AFTER THE HOLOCAUST:
ONLY GOOD THINGS CAN FOLLOW

Harry James Cargas

Since the end of World War II, I have had the opportunity to hear well over two thousand homilies in Catholic Churches throughout America. Never have I heard one on Jewish-Christian relations. I have listened to men in the pulpit trying to explain why it is a sin for men to wear Bermuda shorts, why nuns who abandon traditional religious garb were actually playing into the hands of the Communists; even one that began, 'Whenever we think of Easter, we think of the Easter bunny.' And what was the lesson of the day on the Sunday I am speaking of ? 'You're no bunny 'til some bunny loves you.' The priest proved to be a good fellow, one of us, going for laughs. He was not about to burden us with troubling theological insights. Easter is for eggs and chocolates and bonnets and, oh yes, triumph over death.

Our era is the time after the Holocaust. Why has that awesome event registered so little with our ordained Christian preachers? Why can't we, whose religious obligation includes repenting our sins, acknowledge that probably every killer of Jews in the *Shoah* – every single murderer – was a baptized Christian? And it takes a lot of people to kill a lot of people. Thousands of people at least, who called themselves Christians, massacred countless numbers of Jews, Romanies, Jehovah's Witnesses, homosexuals, and others. Hundreds of millions stood by in the world and allowed it to happen. How could this have been so? Why is my Church silent, and therefore its churches silent, over the greatest sin in our history?

None of this is to imply collective guilt, of course. Those not yet born during the war, those who were, themselves, victims or who did resist the policies of Nazis and others are clearly not culpable. But we Christians who do not renounce what the Holocaust was all about, who are willfully ignorant of the background, the event, and its implications are in danger of being post-Holocaust accomplices. We are in danger of continuing the iniquitous convention of antisemitism and thus, at its roots, anti-Christianity: one cannot hate and be a Christian at the same time. Unfortunately, some hate and call themselves Christian, but that is an impossible pairing.

What then is necessary to be done? The scapegoating idea that Jews were responsible for the death of Jesus is both bad history and bad theology. Nevertheless, for centuries Christians were able

Our era is the time after the Holocaust. Why has that awesome event registered so little with our ordained Christian preachers? Why can't we, whose religious obligation includes repenting our sins, acknowledge that probably every killer of Jews in the Shoah *– every single murderer – was a baptized Christian? And it takes a lot of people to kill a lot of people.*

to blame Jews (collectively no less) for the crucifixion without much fear of contradiction. Today it is somewhat different. Vatican II and *Nostra Aetate* specifically condemned antisemitism. But it might not be too much to say that most Catholics and other Christians are only vaguely aware of the implications, and some even prefer to ignore these teachings.

The very first step that Christians must take to become reconciled with Jews after the Holocaust is to acknowledge the role that Christianity in general and Christians in particular had in the monstrous tragedy. And along with admitting what truly happened must go repentance. In both the Testament adapted from the Jews and the Christian Testament, the concept of repentance for sins is prominent. Repentance signifies a change of mind or heart and connotes regret for one's past transgressions. Usually this is accompanied by acts of penance meant to atone for the sins committed.

Such acknowledgment must become apparent in Christian thinking about the Holocaust and nowhere more than in Sunday instructions given in worship services. Thus it is imperative that Christian seminaries require that their students study the history and implications of anti-Judaism in general and the Holocaust in particular. Many ministers and priests are shockingly ignorant of the facts surrounding negative attitudes towards Jews held by Christians for centuries, as well as the dreadful specifics of the World War II massacre of so many millions of people who had their religious roots in the soil of Christendom. This situation needs radical modification if anti-Judaism is to be eliminated. If it is not insisted upon in the seminaries, how can future clergy be expected to comprehend its gravity?

Liturgical calendars should include an annual service dedicated to remembering the Holocaust. This will inspire members of the Christian community to think and pray about the victims, the criminals, the policies and unconcern of so many, and will also be a sign to Jews that Christians are beginning to care enough to take the *Shoah* seriously on the congregational as well as the academic level.

Important topics will have to be addressed. One is a reminder to congregations of the essential Jewishness of Christianity. As I have written elsewhere, 'This point will need elaboration only for the theologically retarded.' It might be instructive for preachers to consider what has happened to the Christian psyche over the centuries. Christians glory in an inheritance of love, sacrifice, good works, and even martyrdom. And yet under some Christians, Jews, and others too, have endured persecution, exile, ghettoization, imprisonment, torture, and murder. Are we currently passing on any part of our legacy – glorious or evil – to our children, our community, and our unborn generations?

What follows is logical: any recognition of the Jewish roots of Christianity should pave the way for a discussion of Jesus as a link (rather than a divisive figure) between Christians and Jews.

For preachers to go deeper, they need to examine the idea of inspiration in Christian Scripture. This is threatening territory to many. Christians should not fear such a question, however. The

> *Why is my Church silent, and therefore its churches silent, over the greatest sin in our history?*

> *Important topics will have to be addressed. One is a reminder to congregations of the essential Jewishness of Christianity. As I have written elsewhere, 'This point will need elaboration only for the theologically retarded.'*

person on whom their faith has been founded urged a search for truth, insisting that 'The truth shall make you free.' Gregory Baum wrote this as a priest: 'If the Church wants to clear itself of the anti-Jewish trends built into its teaching, a few marginal correctives will not do. It must examine the very centre of its proclamation and reinterpret the meaning of the gospel for our times.' Among the questions to be considered are these: Are we misinterpreting the passages in the Christian Bible that appear to be antisemitic? Have certain words in Scripture been added to the original texts, as some scholars would have it? Are the antisemitic passages really there and if so how are we to regard them today?

As a part of the close investigation of Scripture called for, pastors and others need to find new terminology for what many now call the Old Testament and the New Testament. These titles are insulting to Jews. They imply arrogance: Christians have appropriated (most of) the Jewish texts and adapted them to their own interpretation. They have updated the Jewish Book and given their own explication to the meaning of events. Perhaps the designation 'Apostolic Writings' as suggested by Father John Pawlikowski would serve for the Christian texts and 'Hebrew Scriptures' would make it clear that the earlier writings belong to a separate religious tradition, but are shared by Christians. That might prove a beginning.

Most of the Christian pulpits are not available to women at this time, another area where improvements in Jewish-Christian relations could easily be effected. Without women ministers, churches prohibit to themselves a feminine perspective on every theological topic imaginable. Let the sermon time be open to the laity, women and men, especially those competent to speak on the history and meaning of Christian relations (including antagonism) with the Jewish people.

Finally, attempts by Christians to convert Jews to their faith must not only be abandoned but also discouraged by preachers in churches. Behind every missionary attempt is the usually unstated belief that we have the total truth; you have almost none. This, again, is a position of arrogance. Let one major example illustrate the direction that needs to be taken here. In 1846, a new religious order was founded by Marie Alphonse and Marie Theodore Ratisbonne, brothers who converted to Catholicism from Judaism. One of their objectives was the conversion of Jews to Christianity. Today however, their followers insist that proselytising must be completely abandoned, and lead in trying to bring both groups together in understanding based on equality and respect.

These are some suggestions for steps Christians can take to begin to become reconciled with Jews. It will take a long time; centuries of persecution will not be healed in a decade. But we must begin, collectively and individually. What will Jews do in response? That is a question that Christians need not ask. No matter how Jews receive our belated overtures, our own conversions to a Christianity free of antisemitism, we Christians must make the effort to be virtuous, open, loving. If we do, only good things can follow.

For Further Reading

Howard Clark Kee and Irvin J Borowsky. *Removing Anti-Judaism from the Pulpit.* New York: Continuum, 1996.

Sidney G Hall III. *Christian Anti-Semitism and Paul's Theology.* Minneapolis: Fortress Press, 1993.

A Roy Eckardt. *Jews and Christians: The Contemporary Meeting.* Bloomington: Indiana University Press, 1986.

Marcus Braybrooke. *Time To Meet: Towards a deeper relationship between Jews and Christians.* London: SCM Press Ltd, 1990.

Harry James Cargas, Professor Emeritus at Webster University in St Louis, published thirty-two books, nine of them on the Holocaust, including Conversations with Elie Wiesel and Voices from the Holocaust. Dr. Cargas was Vice President of the Annual Scholars Conference on the Holocaust and served on a number of editorial boards. He passed away in August, 1998.

ENCOUNTERING THE NEW TESTAMENT

Gareth Lloyd Jones

Since 1945 many detailed accounts have been written of anti-Jewish polemic in Christian literature. With few exceptions they begin with the major theologians of the Second Century C.E. Spurred into action by the claim that there is a direct link between the Nazi Holocaust and the Church's negative attitude towards Judaism, scholars have subjected the views of the early Christian fathers to close scrutiny. Their research has demonstrated that antipathy towards Jews is never far from the surface in the writings of some of the most influential theologians. Consequently, this 'teaching of contempt', as the Early Church's presentation of Judaism has been aptly described, is regarded as containing the seeds of modern antisemitism.

The Taproot of Antisemitism

Although Christians are ready to scour patristic texts for the slightest trace of anti-Judaism, there is a reluctance to subject the New Testament to the same critique. While the works of the fathers may justly be regarded as the source of much of the persecution suffered by Jews at the hands of Gentiles, such a charge cannot be levelled at the Scriptures. Many biblical scholars are adamant that there is no connection between the prejudicial statements about Jews and Judaism found in the New Testament and the barbarism of Hitler. They refuse to believe that what has been termed the 'theological antisemitism' of the Christian era has any basis in the Bible and deny any possible link between biblical teaching and Nazi anti-Jewish policy.

They refuse to believe, for instance, that the hard sayings about the Pharisees attributed to Jesus in Matthew 23, the pointed remarks of Paul about the inferiority of Judaism, and the phrase 'His blood be upon us and upon our children', which, according to Matthew 27:26, was on the lips of the crowd of onlookers at Calvary, could in any way have augmented the sufferings of the Jews over the past two thousand years. They do not concede that one of the most belligerent references to Jews in all Christian Scripture, found in 1 Thessalonians 12:16 where the author states that they are the deserved recipients of God's wrath, may have been taken by countless generations of Christians as licence to

'The question of Christian moral credibility had its origin centuries before the Holocaust. It was created by the New Testament attitude to Judaism and the Jewish people, and it is perpetuated by that outlook.'

Roy Eckardt, *Jews and Christians.*

harass and even murder their Jewish neighbors. They dismiss the antisemitic potential in Jesus' scathing description of his Jewish audience in John 8:44 as the children of the devil, and in John the Divine's reference to the 'synagogue of Satan' in Revelation 2:9.

But this standpoint has not gone unchallenged. Jewish theologians in particular have been vocal in their disagreement. Eliezer Berkovitz, for example, claims that 'Christianity's New Testament has been the most dangerous antisemitic tract in history. Its hatred-charged diatribes against the Pharisees and the Jews have poisoned the hearts and minds of millions and millions of Christians for almost two millennia. Without it Hitler's *Mein Kampf* could never have been written.' (*Judaism* 27, 1978, p.325.) Strong words which are totally unacceptable to many Christians. But Berkovitz, an Orthodox Jew, is supported by the eminent Reform theologian Samuel Sandmel. In the last book that he wrote, *Anti-Semitism in the New Testament?* (1978), he concluded that 'it is simply not correct to exempt the New Testament from antisemitism and to allocate it to later periods of history. It must be said that innumerable Christians have purged themselves of antisemitism, but its expression is to be found in Christian Scripture for all to read' (p.144).

Jewish scholars are not the only ones to come to this conclusion; their view is shared by reputable Christian theologians. The most extensive investigation to date of the negation of Judaism in Scripture is that carried out by Norman A. Beck, a Lutheran scholar. The subtitle of his book *Mature Christianity* (2nd. ed. 1993) indicates his concern: 'The recognition and repudiation of the anti-Jewish polemic of the New Testament.' In her controversial study of the theological roots of antisemitism, *Faith and Fratricide* (1974), the Roman theologian Rosemary Ruether argues that parts of the New Testament were intended by their authors to turn Christians against Jews. She asks pointedly, "Is it possible to say, 'Jesus is the Messiah' without, implicitly or explicitly, saying at the same time 'and the Jews be damned'?" (p. 246). James Parkes, the Anglican clergyman who ranks as a doyen in the field of Christian-Jewish relations, stated categorically that after more than fifty years studying the topic he was convinced that it is dishonest to refuse to face the fact that the basic root of modern antisemitism lies squarely in the New Testament.

Opposing Views of Scripture

Any consideration of the biblical roots of antisemitism must, therefore, take account of two diametrically opposed views. Both are espoused by distinguished scholars who are acutely conscious of the persecution suffered by Jews and are determined to eradicate the possibility of another Holocaust. However, the lack of agreement between the two sides suggests that the issue will remain on the theological agenda for some time to come and will continue to be vigorously debated.

For Further Reading

John Pawlikowski. *Jesus and the Theology of Israel.* Wilmington: Glazier, 1989.

C.M. Williamson. *Has God Rejected His People?.* Nashville: Abingdon, 1982.

D. Pollefeyt. *Jews and Christians:Rivals or partners for the Kingdom of God?* Grand Rapids: Eerdmans, 1997.

H.Clark Kee and L.J.Borowsky eds., *Removing Anti-Judaism from the Pulpit.* New York: Continuum, 1996.

G.Lloyd Jones. *Hard Sayings: Difficult New Testament Texts for Jewish-Christian Dialogue.* London. Council of Christians and Jews, 1994.

Lillian C.Freudmann. *Antisemitism in the New Testament.* New York: University Press of America, 1994

'After the Holocaust, a credi-ble Christian theology must begin in and result in a prac-tical, lived theology.'

Sidney G Hall. *Christian Anti-Semitism and Paul's Theology.*

'The question of Christian moral credibility had its origin centuries before the Holocaust. It was created by the New Testament attitude to Judaism and the Jewish people, and it is perpetuated by that outlook.'

A. Roy Eckardt

These two views are based on differing concepts of the nature and purpose of Holy Scripture.

The first view, that which denies any connection between the New Testament and later pogroms, is governed by dogmatic considerations. Its protagonists engage in an ideological defence of Scripture. In their opinion, to claim that the Bible is 'sacred' is tantamount to saying that it is morally unassailable and immune to human fallibility. While the Early Chuch Fathers may be justly condemned for the anti-Judaism because their writings are not considered to be inspired, the same criticism cannot be levelled at the New Testament because in dealing with the Bible the enquirer stands on holy ground.

Proponents of the second view, those who see a connection between Auschwitz and the Gospels, are not as reluctant to submit the Scriptures to searching criticism. They recognize that although Scripture is sacred, it also has a human element. It is linked to historical circumstances. Because the New Testament reflects the ecclesiastical tensions of the nascent Church, the circumstances surrounding its origin should be considered by all who seek to interpret its message in the contemporary world. The implications inherent in the fact that the Word of God comes to us in the words of men and women must be faced, not least with regard to those texts that are hostile to Jews.

The debate between these two standpoints is essentially concerned with authority. The central question is: Have we the right to criticize our religious traditions? Are we justified in repudiating certain New Testament passages because they are damaging to Jews? Those who use such terms as 'inerrant' and 'infallible' in relation to the Bible will deny the existence of such a right. Our Christian forefathers, however, had no qualms about engaging in subjective interpretation of their own Scriptures. The Early Church pressed selected portions of the Hebrew Bible into service to prove the superiority of Christianity, while neglecting the rest. Appropriate passages were used as a quarry for messianic prophecies and used to prove that the Messiah had come in Jesus of Nazareth, whereas laws governing diet and circumcision, to take but two examples, were given a meaning other than the literal.

Such selectivity and reinterpretation was not confined to the Hebrew Bible; it was applied to the New Testament as well. The stipulations about non-retaliation, almsgiving, self-denial, celibacy, and the role of women in the Church have been either ignored in practice or spiritualized by most Christians. If some aspects of New Testament teaching can justifiably be repudiated, in the sense of their not being regarded as binding the contemporary Christians, cannot the same principle be applied to passages that have proved injurious to Jews for almost two millennia?

Neutralizing the Antisemitic Potential

It is obvious that a deep antipathy to certain groups of Jews exists in Christian Scripture. Whatever we believe about the intention of the original writers, the dangerous power and antisemitic potential of what they wrote must be recognized. The negative stereotypes, still current in Christian thinking, are to be found in the Bible. Because Christians saw the Jews as children of Satan who killed Christ, it was thought they were rejected by God and replaced by the Church. In an attempt to neutralize this potential, many biblical scholars are insisting that the New Testament writings be put in their correct historical and sociological context.

To take but one example, the importance of discovering the context of John's Gospel for understanding the author's negative portrayal of Jews has at least three significant ramifications. First, it mitigates the harshness when we appreciate that the early Christians were on the defensive and that vilifying others was a way of defining themselves. Second, it reminds us that John expresses time-bound prejudices against the Jews of his own age, not global anti-Judaism valid for all time. Third, the recognition that the Gospel contains the meditations of a devoted disciple on the Jesus tradition reminds us that John's views of Judaism are his own and not necessarily those of Jesus.

If preachers and teachers over the past two millennia had taken such considerations into account and had wrestled, as we now must, with the limitations imposed on the Bible by the circumstances under which it was written, the Christian perception of the Jew would have been far less negative.

In the middle ages Jews were made to wear distinguishing clothes such as these pointed hats to mark them out in Christian society.

'We have at once to face an enigma. How could Christianity, born Jewish . . . succumb to antisemitism?. . . Christian antisemitism is an historic fact . . . We find it everywhere in our path.'

Jules Isaac, *The Christian Roots of Antisemitism.*

Gareth Lloyd Jones (UK) is Professor of the School of Theology at the University of Wales, Bangor. An Anglican priest and Canon-Chancellor of Bangor Cathedral, he is the author of several books on Jewish-Christian relations and biblical study, including *Hard Sayings: Difficult New Testament Texts for Jewish-Christian Dialogue.*

READING NEW TESTAMENT TEXTS

Jane Clements

'In 1942, a Slovak rabbi asked the local Roman Catholic archbishop to intervene to stop the deportations to the concentration camps. Since the rabbi knew nothing of the gas chambers, he stressed the dangers of hunger and disease for women, the children and the elderly. The archbishop replied, 'It is not just a matter of deportation. You will not die there of hunger and disease. They will slaughter all of you, old and young alike, women and children at once. It is the punishment you deserve for the death of our Lord and Redeemer.'[1]

The response of the Archbishop is shocking but represented an approach held by clerics throughout Christendom for centuries. Now, two generations after the Holocaust, most Christians overwhelmingly reject such a terrible response – and yet both the scriptural texts and, to a large extent, the theology which helped to give rise to such thoughts remain problematic.

Those who wish to promote the view that Jews collectively, vigorously and willfully opposed the teaching and authority both of Jesus and his church have no shortage of New Testament texts to use as illustrations. Here are a few:

John 8:44-45: Jesus to a Jewish audience: 'You are of your father the devil, and your will is to do your father's desires. He was a murderer from the beginning, and has nothing to do with the truth, because there is no truth in him. When he lies, he speaks according to his own nature, for he is a liar and the father of lies. But, because I tell the truth, you do not believe me.'

Or Matthew 27: 24-25: 'So when Pilate saw that he was gaining nothing, but rather that a riot was beginning, he took water and washed his hands before the crowd, saying, 'I am innocent of this man's blood; see to it yourselves.' And all the people answered, 'His blood be on us and on our children.''

1 Thessalonians 2:14-16: 'For you, brethren, became imitators of the churches of God in Christ Jesus which are in Judea; for you suffered the same things from your own countrymen as they did from the Jews, who killed both the Lord Jesus and the prophets, and drove us out and displease God and oppose all men by hindering us from speaking to the Gentiles that they may be saved – so as always to fill up the measure of their sins. But God's wrath has come upon them at last!'

These words, however problematic, may not simply be erased from scripture. What is important is how they are to be read. There is no problem for those who regard the New Testament as a human construct, with varying degrees of divine inspiration or none. But for the believer seeking to be inspired and instructed by the Scriptures as they stand – especially if he or she believes in the supremacy of scripture above all other Christian teaching – the problems remain. Whatever one's conviction, all reading of scripture is primarily a subjective experience. The question to be asked by Christians is: How are we expected to read the text? In seeking to maintain the integrity of Christian belief as a whole, it is imperative that any post-Holocaust approach to the New Testament promotes a commitment to the value of each human soul and encourages positive and creative attitudes – especially towards the Jews.

In some cases, a careful reading of the entire passage in context immediately produces a more enlightened view. However, of particular importance in this whole field has been the place of Biblical criticism which seeks to understand the historical context of a particular passage or the specific intentions and situation of the writer. Despite the problems created by Biblical criticism in the past, Christians of all traditions now agree that some sort of understanding of the historical, social and theological background of a text serves to enhance its meaning. This includes, for example, the individual concerns of the gospel writers, the 'factions' from which they emerged and the implications of certain themes for their contemporaries. Much work has been done in recent years on the above texts, although the explanations offered are by no means acceptable to all. By way of example, regarding John's gospel, scholars point to a period of probable conflict between the Johannine community and the local synagogue leadership which undoubtedly would have affected the evangelist and encouraged his hostile stance in such matters. Similarly, scholarship on the theology of Luke, as found in both his gospel and his Acts of the Apostles, suggests a supercessionist view – that is, that Luke aimed to demonstrate that the Christian church stepped in to fill the role previously played by the people of Israel. Therefore, Luke must be seen as taking every opportunity to portray antagonism between the Jewish religious leadership and early Christians. In another example, work on the Matthean Pilate passage suggests that it does not reflect in any sense an historical account. It becomes clear that a number of different approaches are being taken – the Johannine example suggests an historical or sociological approach, whereas the Lucan example is more concerned with theology.

But even for those who see problems in accepting elements of Biblical criticism, different passages of scripture require different approaches. A parable is read differently from a psalm, while many of the miracle stories in the gospels are generally read with a christological interpretation – their value being in what they tell the reader about the nature and person of Jesus. Reading and interpreting the New Testament is largely an acquired skill – which therefore places a moral responsibility on the teacher.

For Reflection

Should history and faith be kept separate?

How does an understanding of the life and events of Jesus' time relate to the worship of the Christ of the Church?

To what extent has European experience and tradition offered its own interpretation of elements within the New Testament?

Does the way in which the Church has historically approached texts about women, slavery, poverty or pacifism have anything to teach us about texts relating to 'the Jews'?

For Further Reading

David Flusser. *Jewish Sources in Early Christianity*. Tel Aviv: MOD Books, 1989.

ed. Kee & Borowsky. *Removing Anti-Judaism from the Pulpit*. New York: Continuum, 1996 .

Gareth Lloyd Jones. *Hard Sayings: Difficult New Testament texts for Jewish-Christian Dialogue*. London: The Council of Christians & Jews, 1997.

Daniel Smith-Christopher. *Text and Experience*. Sheffield: Academic Press, 1995.

N.T. Wright. *Jesus and the Victory of God*. London: SPCK, 1996.

1. As taken from Gareth Lloyd Jones, *Hard Sayings: Difficult New Testament texts for Jewish - Christian dialogue.*

Jane Clements (UK) is Education Officer at the Council of Christians and Jews, London. She is involved in teaching in schools and university education, and works with Christian and Jewish communities, preparing materials and leading study tours in Europe and Israel.

The disciplines of practical and pastoral theology demand their own approach. The Rev Vera Sinton, lecturer in pastoral theology at Wycliffe Hall, Oxford, wrote recently in the Church of England Newspaper (December 10, 1999) that pastoral theology promotes a subjective view of scripture, where 'we will pick up some of the threads that seem to us to be important, ignoring others.' This is done in order to increase the reader's effectiveness in terms of leading a Christian life, in accordance with scriptural principles.

In recent years, the term 'cultural exegesis' has emerged. This refers to the additional insights one might bring to the reading of the Bible from the context of one's own culture. A classic example is the native American who remarked 'I now realize that the Israelites were also a tribal people.' (*Text & Experience*, Smith-Christopher.) Inevitably, in this process the accent has been on non-European approaches to the text. Bearing in mind that the tragic history of Christian-Jewish relations and, indeed, the Holocaust itself are a part of the European experience, it is interesting to see how Christians from cultures without literary and historical traditions about Jews view the same apparently difficult passages of the New Testament. In such cases, Jews are not seen as stereotyped members of a distinct, identifiable group, but as representative of a more universal humanity. This whole approach presents an opportunity to explore the text afresh, appreciating the values of the Jewish tradition, and without the historical anti-Judaism which pervades the European experience.

In summary, while the existence of problematic texts cannot and should not be ignored, reading the New Testament – whether from a scholarly or confessional standpoint – need not perpetuate the poisonous use of phrases taken as they stand.

FLASHPOINTS OF CATHOLIC-JEWISH RELATIONS

A. James Rudin

There have been more positive encounters between Roman Catholics and Jews since the conclusion of the Second Vatican Council in 1965 than there were in the first 2000 years of the Christian Church. The Council's Declaration, *Nostra Aetate* ('In Our Time'), that focused on Jews and Judaism, gave extraordinary impetus to building constructive relations between two of the world's oldest faith communities.

Yet serious flashpoints have always remained, carrying with them the potential to weaken or even expunge some of the historic gains that have been achieved since 1965. It is important to recount several of these because they directly impact upon the latest crisis in Catholic-Jewish relations: the role and activities of Pope Pius XII during the Second World War.

Catholic conversion efforts aimed at Jews were an issue of contention after 1965, but in the years following the Second Vatican Council, the Church eschewed the 'targeting' of Jews as candidates for conversion. Especially important was Pope John Paul II's 1986 address in the Grand Synagogue of Rome in which he respectfully described Jews as 'our elder brothers in faith.'

The lack of formal diplomatic relations between the Holy See and the State of Israel was another source of friction until 1993, when the Vatican and the Jewish state signed the 'Fundamental Agreement' that led to full mutual recognition.

In June 1987, just three months before his scheduled visit to the United States, John Paul II warmly received Austrian President Kurt Waldheim at the Vatican. Many Jewish and Catholic leaders expressed profound disappointment and the meeting became a *cause célèbre* because of the serious accusations that personally linked Waldheim to war crimes that took place while he was a German army officer stationed in the Balkans during the Second World War.

The intense negative reaction to the Waldheim meeting threatened to cancel a major meeting in Miami between the Pope and American Jewish leaders scheduled for September 1987. It required a 'summit conference' at Castel Gandolfo involving John Paul II, other Catholic officials and representatives of the American Jewish community to repair the damage.

Perhaps the most toxic flashpoint was the Auschwitz convent crisis of the 1980s and 1990s. The issue centered on the presence of a small number of Carmelite nuns who established a convent in one of the Auschwitz death camp's original buildings. Indeed, the nuns chose the very site where the Germans had stored the lethal Zyklon-B poison gas used to murder over a million Jews at Auschwitz and nearby Birkenau during the *Shoah*.

In 1995, after a long, painful and public clash of religious symbolism and historical memory, the nuns finally left the building and moved into a nearby structure that was newly constructed for use as a convent. However, the satisfactory resolution of the crisis came only after the Pope directly intervened and urged the Carmelites to move.

This brief overview of earlier flashpoints is important in seeking to understand the controversy swirling around the role and record of Eugenio Pacelli whose nineteen-year pontificate as Pius XII began in 1939 on the eve of the Second World War.

The most serious charge made against Pius XII by his critics, both Catholic and Jewish, is that the wartime Pope was inactive, indifferent, and ineffective in confronting Nazi Germany during the Holocaust when 6,000,000 Jews were murdered. Critics further charge that Pius XII's 'silence' in effect 'sealed the fate of the Jews' in Europe.

Criticism surfaced as early as the mid 1960s when *The Deputy,* a play by the German Protestant playwright Rolf Hochhuth, presented a thinly disguised account of the Pope's activities during the Second World War. *The Deputy* created such a furor that Pope Paul VI ordered that over 5,000 pages of official Vatican records of the wartime period be released to counter Hochhuth's claim that Pius XII failed to respond adequately to the murderous antisemitism of the Nazi regime.

The eventual release of the Vatican documents, which was concluded in 1981, did not silence Pius XII's critics. In fact, just the opposite happened. Because the 5,000 pages represented only a carefully chosen partial record, demands intensified in the 1980s and 1990s that all pertinent Vatican records be made available to appropriate scholars for study.

The demands were consistently rejected even when made by the late Cardinal Joseph Bernardin of Chicago in 1992. Vatican officials cited a long-standing policy that 75 years must pass before records can be released. Some Catholic leaders also asserted that the 5,000 released pages were sufficient in any analysis of Pius XII's record during the wartime period.

Clearly, the potent issue of the *Shoah*, the Vatican and the 'silent' Pope will not go away. Indeed, with each passing year it has intensified, and it seems few people are neutral about Eugenio Pacelli's actions. Many Catholic leaders throughout the world have vigorously defended him. Under John Paul II's leadership, the process leading to Pius XII's beautification and canonization has commenced, as it also has for John XXIII who succeeded Pacelli as Pope in 1958.

In March 1998, the Vatican released 'We Remember: A Reflection on the *Shoah*.' In the brief sixteen-page document there is a spirited defense of Pius XII *vis-à-vis* the Jewish people during the

For Further Reading

Derek J. Holmes. *The Papacy in the Modern World: 1914 - 1978.* Burns and Oates Publishers.

Frederick M. Schweitzer. *Jewish-Christian Encounters Over the Centuries: Symbiosis, Prejudice, Holocaust, Dialogue,* Vol. 136. Peter Lang Publishing, 1994.

O. Chadwick. *"Weizsäcker: The Vatican and the Jews of Rome,"* in Michael R. Marrus. *Bystanders to the Holocaust,* Volume 3. KG Saur, 1999: pp.1263-1283.

Holocaust. To buttress its case, the Vatican authors cited positive remarks made about Pius XII by four post-war Jewish leaders, including the late Golda Meir, a former Israeli Prime Minister.

But just as with the release of selected Vatican documents, the pro-Pius XII material contained in 'We Remember' only intensified the controversy. I strongly believe it was an error to include a specific defense of Pius XII in 'We Remember,' a document that was intended to be a spiritual reflection on the *Shoah*.

By citing only carefully selected sources to bolster Pius XII's reputation, the authors of 'We Remember' have, perhaps unwittingly, permanently opened the debate and moved all future discussions of Pius XII into the realm of historic analysis and documentation. Just as the Vatican can muster its version of 'truth,' so can the critics of Pius XII.

A striking example of this predictable phenomenon was the publication in 1999 of John Cornwell's highly critical *Hitler's Pope: The Secret History of Pius XII* (Viking) and Pierre Blet's *Pius XII and the Second World War: According to the Archives of the Vatican* (Paulist Press). The latter volume attempts to support the claim that the Pope undertook positive steps to combat Nazism and save Jewish lives.

Sadly, neither Cornwell nor Blet, both Catholics, had access to all the key records of Pius XII's pontificate. Both sharply contrasting books are based upon incomplete data, but one thing is certain; the campaign to obtain all the relevant documents regarding Pius XII will only escalate.

This is bound to happen in the post-Cold War period when previously closed records from the former Soviet Union, East Germany, and a host of other countries have recently become available. It is bound to happen because a collective *Heshbon haNefesh* (Hebrew for 'inventory of the soul') is currently underway that includes a critical analysis of the roles played during the Holocaust by Switzerland, other neutral nations and the Allied governments, as well as by business, educational and religious bodies.

No institution, least of all the Roman Catholic Church, will be exempt from that kind of careful scrutiny. Hopefully, the Vatican archives and other centers of primary source material will soon be made available to teams of competent Catholic and Jewish scholars who, together, will finally bring closure to the vexing question of Pius XII and his wartime activities.

Until and unless this takes place, this issue will fester and foment continual friction. Indeed, the controversy can undo many of the extraordinary gains that have been achieved in Catholic-Jewish relations since 1965. Hopefully, this will not happen.

When other Catholic-Jewish flashpoints surfaced in the past, constructive steps were taken by the Vatican that successfully addressed the particular problem, and the same kind of action is needed now. The well-known cliché rings true: 'The ball is in the Vatican's court,' and all the world awaits the Holy See's response.

A. James Rudin (USA), a Rabbi, is the National Interreligious Director of the American Jewish Committee, New York. He is author of many essays and books on Christian-Jewish Relations

THE CANONIZATION OF PIUS XII

John T. Pawlikowski

The response of Pope Pius XII to the challenge of the Holocaust has been the subject of much discussion since the appearance of Rolf Hochhuth's play *The Deputy*, often cast in highly polemical language. For some writers such as Peter Gumpel, S.J., who has been examining the cause of Pius XII for possible canonization, there is little question that the Pope responded with great courage and humanity to the plight of Jews and other victims of the Nazis. He was responsible for saving hundreds of thousands of Jewish lives and therefore deserves eventual sainthood. Those promoting the canonization of Pius XII often cite statements by Jewish leaders such as Dr. Joseph Nathan of the Italian Hebrew Commission, Dr. A. Leo Kubowitzki of the World Jewish Congress, and Israeli Prime Minister Golda Meir who praised the Pope publicly for his efforts on behalf of Jews.

The critics of Pius XII, both Christians and Jews, argue that his public silence regarding the Jews contributed directly to the staggering loss of Jewish lives under the Nazis. They seriously question the claim that he saved "hundreds of thousands' of Jewish lives. Instead, they portray Pius XII as a rather cold, even callous personality, whose principal concern was preserving the institutional well-being of the church and consolidating papal power. While some would admit that he made a few important efforts to save Jews, Jewish rescue never became an important priority for him during the Nazi era. John Cornwell's book *Hitler's Pope* is an extreme example of such a perspective. A number of Jewish and Christian scholars have tried in different ways to find a middle ground in evaluating Pius XII's papacy. While critiquing his leadership, even seriously at times, these scholars, who include John Morley, Michael Marrus, John Conway, Michael Phayer and others, argue that Pius XII made some constructive efforts to save Jews, especially in the later years of the war, which have been insufficiently acknowledged. On the other hand, they believe there were serious defects in his overall approach to Nazi extermination policies that warrant much greater investigation and which demand that any canonization process be put on hold by the Vatican. It is regrettable that the discussion about Pius XII has become so polarized, for such an atmosphere makes it difficult for dedicated scholars to pursue an open, well-researched evaluation of Pius XII. For that reason it would be wise, and ultimately enhance Catholic integrity, if scholars were allowed to complete their research on his papacy without the immediate prospect of canonization hanging over their heads.

Referring to the thorough investigation of the record of the Lyons (France) diocese during the Nazi era mandated by the Archbishop of that city under the direction of respected historians, the late Cardinal Joseph Bernardin said in a plenary address to the Vatican-Jewish International Dialogue in Baltimore (May 1992) that 'it is only through candor and willingness to acknowledge mistakes where documentary evidence clearly warrants it that Catholicism can join in the pursuit of justice with full moral integrity.' The late Cardinal's words should become the framework for an investigation of Pius XII's record during the Nazi era.

An objective evaluation of the scholarly research thus far yields a very mixed picture. On the one hand, we now know from the published archives of the period released by the Vatican as well as from other documentation that Pius XII does not deserve the label of 'silent' because most who hear that term interpret it to mean he did nothing at all for Jews and other victims. There may be more of an authentic argument for the term 'silent' in the restricted sense of his not going public with criticism of the Nazis with specific reference to the Jews and Poles, but the general use of the term obscures the results of recent scholarship regarding some of the positive efforts he did undertake, almost exclusively through diplomatic channels. And the memoirs of the late Cardinal Henri de Lubac, S.J., a leader in the French Catholic resistance during World War II, show that at least some Catholics understood Pius XII's general public criticism of the Nazis as applying primarily to the situation of the Jews.

The writings of Vatican archivists such as the late Robert Graham, S.J., and his present successor Pierre Blet, S.J., demonstrate that Pius XII and his diplomatic representatives made important interventions in Slovakia on three occasions between 1942 and 1944. In Germany in October 1943, the Vatican Secretary of State Cardinal Maglione forthrightly confronted the Reich ambassador over the capture of Jews for transfer to the extermination camps in Nazi-occupied Poland. In Hungary in 1944 the Papal Nuncio Angelo Rotta released an 'open' telegram to the Hungarian leader Admiral Horthy protesting the attack upon people 'because of their nationality or race'. For researchers such as Graham and Blet, Hungary represents perhaps Pius XII's finest hour in terms of Jewish rescue. A Jewish leader of the period, Dr. Gerhart Riegner of the World Jewish Congress, does acknowledge the Vatican initiatives in Hungary in his published memoirs in French, though he remains far less enthusiastic about the Pope's overall record.

What issues do we still need to address with respect to Pius XII's record? The following areas are among those that require continuing scrutiny by scholars if we are to have a relatively complete assessment of his moral stature as a religious and a world leader during one of the critical periods of the last century.

For Further Reading

Robert P. Ericksen and Susannah
Heschel, eds. *German Churches
and the Holocaust Betrayal.*
Augsburg Fortress Publisher, 1999.

Richard C. Lukas. *The Forgotten
Holocaust: The Poles Under German
Occupation, 1939-1944.* New York:
Hippocrene Books, 1990.

Pierre Blet, S.J. *Pius XII and the
Second World War: According to the
Archives of the Vatican.* Paulist
Press, 1999.

1.   We must pursue in greater detail the actions of Pius XII in the early years of the Third Reich. One of the basic flaws in the analysis provided by Graham and Blet is their failure to confront the question, what if the Pope had acted sooner, and more decisively, in the initial phase of the Final Solution? Most of the examples of interventions they cite came in the latter period of Nazi onslaught. One argument made is that the Pope and other ranking Vatican officials were not fully aware of the extent of the Nazi attack on the Jews until this time. But Gerhart Riegner has raised an important question to which Vatican officials have not adequately responded. There was a letter transmitted by Dr. Riegner to the Vatican regarding the severity of the Nazi treatment of Jews considerably earlier than the Vatican has generally acknowledged knowing about the Nazi extermination plan for the Jews. This document is acknowledged in the archival materials released by the Vatican. But the letter itself is missing. This letter is critical because it would indicate that Pius XII's response was slow in coming after the Vatican was informed about the true nature of the Nazi program.

2.   We need to look at Pius XII's record immediately after the end of the war. Catholic historian Michael Phayer has criticized Pius XII's posture during this period, basing his criticisms in part on the archives of Jacques Maritain, the eminent French Catholic philosopher, who resigned his post as French Ambassador to the Vatican in protest over Pius' immediate post-war stance on German Catholic guilt.

3.   The research on Pius XII's response to the Nazi invasion of Poland needs greater emphasis. As historians such as John Morley and Richard Kukas have shown, Pius XII was severely criticized by many Catholic Poles for not speaking out publicly against the invasion and its aftermath and naming the Poles specifically as Nazi victims. In short, the same criticisms that have been made regarding Pius' approach to Jewish victimization. This is an important aspect of Pius' papacy because the critique comes from Catholics, not from Jews, and undercuts the claim made by some defenders of Pius that no serious criticism of Pius XII existed prior to the appearance of *The Deputy*.

4.   The question of Pius XII's attitudes towards liberalism and bolshevism needs to be explored in greater depth. Was he so overcome by opposition to these ideologies, and their potential threat to the existence of the church, that he was willing to mute criticism of the Nazis in the vain hope that Nazism would provide a buffer against these 'enemies' of the church? The significance of the signing of the Concordat with Hitler and the way in which the Center Party in Germany was neutralized by Pius XII need further investigation in this regard.

5.   We need both an opening of the Vatican archives (as the late Cardinal Bernardin and Cardinal O'Connor have urged) for this period as well as a comprehensive examination of other relevant archives from national governments and individuals (such as Ambassador Maritain) with close

connections to the Pope. Since he left no diaries and little in the way of personal letters, we need to obtain a better hold on how key people of the time regarded him. In the light of these remaining gaps in research, the process of fully investigating Pius XII's record should not be short-circuited by rating him 'blessed' or 'saint'. Perhaps the initial process in this regard might continue, though with a firm commitment that no action would be taken by the Vatican until there is a fuller scholarly assessment of his overall record. There is also need to widen the usual parameters of such a scrutiny relative to canonization with the inclusion of a wide range of scholarly assessments of his papacy. He was no ordinary Christian, but the leader of Christianity's largest denomination during one of the church's most challenging periods. Any final judgment on his moral stature and his spirituality must be viewed in that context.

John T. Pawlikowski O.S.M.
(USA), Professor of Social Ethics at the Catholic Theological Union in Chicago, has been a member of the United States Holocaust Memorial Council since 1980. He currently chairs the Council's Committee on Church Relations. The author of many publications on the Holocaust and Christian-Jewish relations, including *The Challenge of the Holocaust for Christian Theology*, Pawlikowski is also a member of the National Conference of Catholic Bishops' advisory committee on Catholic-Jewish relations.

EDITH STEIN'S CANONIZATION: ACKNOWLEDGING OBJECTIONS FROM JEWS AND CATHOLICS

Eloise Rosenblatt

Edith Stein, a Carmelite nun who died at Auschwitz in 1942, was beatified by Pope John Paul II in Cologne in 1987 as a martyr of the Church. The Pope canonized Edith Stein as Saint Teresa Benedicta in Rome on October 11, 1998, acknowledging her both as a 'daughter of Israel,' and as a member of the Carmelite order.

Aspects of the Debate

In the years since 1987, the central issue in the debate continues to be, from the Jewish community, the sainting of a woman who was not martyred at Auschwitz because she was Catholic, but who was murdered in the Holocaust under the Nazis because she was a Jew. Rabbi Leon Klenicki, interfaith affairs director at the Anti-Defamation League in New York, asked, 'Why canonize her as a victim when she was taken because she was Jewish?' The Church, from the Jewish perspective, seemed to sweep aside her Jewishness, and then both shame and attempt to proselytize Jews with the example of Stein's conversion. For some Jews, Stein was a woman who betrayed her people by abandoning her faith and then offering herself as atonement to God so that her people would accept their Lord. For other readers, both Jewish and Christian, the matter of Stein's 'conversion' is full of ambiguity because she never described the process by which she embraced Roman Catholicism. The evidence points to the reality that she always stood in solidarity with her Jewishness. Intriguingly, as Patricia Hampl notes:

"Edith Stein chose the one Catholic contemplative order whose roots extend past Christianity back into the hermetic tradition of the Old Testament. Carmelites, though they take their rule from Teresa and much of their tradition of contemplative practice from John of the Cross, look back to Elijah as the first 'Carmelite.'"

Edith Stein.

'Of course, she would never have been killed had she not had Jewish parents.'

Msgr. John M. Oesterreicher, *The Record*, Louisville, KY, Dec. 20, 1990.

For Edith Stein's living relatives, the ambiguity of her religious allegiance is not the determining factor in their relationship to her, for, the Biberstein family suggest, she is to be honored as a 'distinguished scholar and as a loving aunt'. Stein's relationship to her family is memorialized by her autobiography, *Life in a Jewish Family.*

She started this volume in 1933 after losing her teaching job when the Nazis took power and forbade Jews to hold professional positions. She wrote most of it after she became a Carmelite, though she never completed the account. The book is a loving tribute to her immediate and extended family and circle of friends. It was conceived as a testimony to counteract racial hatred and caricatures of Jewish life in German society. Through a truthful memoir of her Jewish upbringing and its representation of a real Jewish family, she hoped to reverse racial and religious discrimination based on ignorance.

Catholics argue that Stein's canonization is justified. She may be a 'daughter of Israel,' but she also died as a woman who, after her conversion, served as Catholic educator in a Dominican college preparing women for teaching careers, as a lecturer on women's issues, a contemplative nun, philosopher, autobiographer, linguist and mystic. Her theology and spirituality at the time of her arrest were Catholic in expression. Though her philosophical writings on the structure of the human person do not address the issue of religious belief, much of her intellectual legacy and writings are Catholic in focus, for she translated Thomas Aquinas and John Henry Cardinal Newman. She wrote a biography of John of the Cross and found spiritual guidance in Teresa of Avila.

Some Catholics express resentment at attempts by Jews to intrude as 'outsiders' into internal affairs of the Church regarding Edith Stein. This is similar to the chagrin they feel at 'interference' by Jews and 'non-loyal' Christians alike with the proposal to canonize Pope Pius XII because of questions raised by historians about the Pope's public silence on racial persecution by the Nazis.

Jewish leaders protest the Church's 'politicization of holiness' in choosing to canonize Edith Stein, as if this would bring premature closure to questions about the role of Church leaders during the Holocaust and after World War II in protecting former Nazis. Such a canonization can too easily disguise Christian guilt for the Holocaust by a manifestation of honor for those who suffered its horrors. Canonizing Edith Stein can distract from a mandate that Catholic institutions radically re-examine Christian theology for its contribution to the Holocaust. Christians must undergo conversion both individually and collectively, and radically revise those theological constructs which perpetuate antisemitic reflexes in preaching and anti-Jewish effects in interpreting scripture. The teaching of respect must replace the teaching of contempt.

Further, a claim to justify Stein's canonization based on her 'Catholic' writings bypasses

'The beatification of Edith Stein outraged many Israelis and other Jews. Why, critics wanted to know, was the Church placing the crown of martyrdom on the head of a single apostate Jew when millions of other Jews – children, grandparents, mothers, and fathers – had perished at the hands of the Nazis? Once again, it was said, the first Polish pope was attempting to rob the Holocaust of its specific intent – the genocide of European Jewry – by focusing attention on those Christians who were also Nazi victims. Was this not, it was suggested, an attempt to use the saint-making process to deflect attention from the Church's own complicity through silence in the Nazis' war on the Jews? Of all the Christians killed by the Nazis, why had the Church chosen a convert who had asked God in the midst of the Holocaust, to accept her life in atonement for the 'unbelief of the Jews.''

Kenneth Woodward, *Making Saints,* pp. 127-128.

For Further Reading

Patricia Hampl. 'Edith Stein,' p. 207, in *Martyrs: Contemporary Writers on Modern Lives of Faith*, ed. by Susan San Francisco: Bergman Harper, 1996, pp. 197-215.

Edith Stein. *Life in a Jewish Family (1891-1916): An Autobiography.* Trans. Josephine Koeppel, O.C.D. Washington D.C.: ICS Publications, 1986.

John Cornwell argues that Eugenio Pacelli, later Pius XII, held antisemitic biases himself, and this accounts for his failure to publicly condemn the Nazis for their persecution of Jews in World War II. The historical data in Cornwell's controversial volume, *Hitler's Pope: The Secret History of Pius XII,* Viking Press, 1999, has been challenged by Fr. Peter Gumpel, reporter for the beatification cause of Pius XII and by Pierre Blet, S.J., author of *Pius XII and the Second World War in the Vatican Archives,* Congregation for Catholic Education, 1999. See 'Vatican Presents Fr. Blet's Book Defending Pius XII' in the *Wanderer,* October 21, 1999, p.6 and Alessandra Stanley, 'Book Revives Issue of Pius XII and Holocaust' in *New York Times,* Nov. 3, 1999.

acknowledgment that the foundation of her corpus as a philosopher was inspired by her education in a Jewish intellectual milieu. Religious inquiry was neither the focus nor the foundation for her examination of the structure of the human person in her dissertation *On Empathy* in 1917, or personal individuation in *Finite and Eternal Being*, written in 1936.

Biographical Sketch

Edith Stein was born into a Jewish family in Breslau in Silesia, Germany, now Wroclaw, Poland, on the holiest day of the Jewish calendar, Yom Kippur, October 12, 1891. She pursued doctoral studies in Germany at Gottingen (1913-16) under the phenomenologist Edmund Husserl, and followed him to the University of Freiburg where she received her doctorate in 1917, writing her dissertation *On the Problem of Empathy*. One element in her conversion was her chance reading of the autobiography of Teresa of Avila in 1921, to which her response was, 'This is the truth'. Six months later, in 1922, she was baptized a Roman Catholic at the age of thirty-one. For several years she trained women for a teaching career at a Dominican sisters' institute in Speyer. For two years, 1931-32, she lectured on philosophy and feminist issues in Germany, Austria and Switzerland. She also attempted to regain a place in the university by taking up work as research assistant at Munster, but no one would sponsor her habilitation, the second thesis required for a university appointment. She knew that the possibility of a university career had been terminated when Nazis proscribed Jews from teaching in 1933.

She entered the Carmelite order in Cologne on October 15, 1933. As the Nazi oppression of Jews increased, she feared reprisals against the community. She asked to be transferred to a Carmel in Palestine, but the British had closed immigration to Jews from abroad. Sr. Teresa Benedicta finally crossed the border into Holland and took up residence in the Carmelite community of Echt in January, 1939. Her blood-sister Rosa joined her in Echt in the summer of 1940. When Holland was occupied by the Nazis, the community sought refuge for Edith and her sister at the Carmel of Le Pacquier in Switzerland, but months dragged on without getting the necessary papers from Holland, Switzerland and Rome.

Edith first buried her autobiography in the garden to prevent its discovery by the Nazis, hoping to avoid risk to all the persons named in the book, as well as reprisal against the Carmelite sisters for harboring her. Fearing it might be damaged in the ground, she dug it up after three months and finally entrusted its hiding to one of the Carmelites. On July 26, 1942, the Dutch bishops issued a pastoral letter denouncing Nazi policies against the Jews. On August 2, 1942, Edith and Rosa were arrested by the Nazis. Edith said to her frightened sister, 'Come, let us go for our people'. They were transported to Westerbork and then to Auschwitz. A terse Red Cross certificate issued February 15, 1950, verifies that she died at the hands of the Nazis in Auschwitz on August 9, 1942. Her autobiography was retrieved from its hiding place after the war.

Conclusion

Hampl proposes that Catholics be more sensitive to Jewish experience in dealing with the questions about which community should lay claim to Edith Stein.

'For if the church relinquished its claim on her martyrdom, Edith Stein could become for Christians the focal point of an act of contrition still desperately needed by the Western world in response to the mid-century horrors committed against Jews and Jewish life in Christian Europe. . . As a Catholic saint, she is folded into the canon of church history. But where she is needed is exactly where she placed herself: in between. . . She should remain. . . a figure forever calling Christians toward contrition – the proper Christian response to the Holocaust.'

For Further Reading

Katharina von Kellenbach. 'Overcoming the Teaching of Contempt', in A. Brenner and C. Fontaine, eds., *Reading the Bible: Approaches, Methods and Strategies*. Sheffield: Sheffield Academic Press, 1997, pp. 190-202.

Eloise Rosenblatt R.S.M. (USA) is a Sister of Mercy from Burlingame, California. In her academic career she has been a college, university, and seminary professor, as well as an administrator. She is the author of *Paul the Accused: His Portrait in Acts of the Apostles*, (Liturgical Press), 1995, and many articles in theological journals. She is presently pursuing a degree in Law.

THE DILEMMA OF FORGIVENESS

Alice L. Eckardt

'Non-Jews and perhaps especially Christians should not give advice about the Holocaust experience to its heirs for the next two thousand years. And then we shall have nothing to say.'

Martin Marty in *The Sunflower,* 1997 ed., p.201; 1976 ed., p.173.

'When real evil is done . . . detachment is immoral. The proper attitude towards evil is anger.'

Reinhold Niebuhr, *Anger and Forgiveness, Discerning the Signs of the Times.* Charles Scribner's Sons, 1946.

The issue of forgiveness has divided Christians and Jews perhaps more than any other with regard to the Holocaust. For Christians usually believe that they have been given an absolute commandment to forgive under any and all circumstances (though this does not mean that most Christians actually do this). And it appears that most Christians are ready to expect Jews to do just that with regard to those who were involved in the Nazis' attempt to annihilate the Jewish people. Thus Jews all too often are told to forgive, to forget, or are accused of being uncharitable and vengeful if they insist on remembering. Can or should the murder of approximately six million individuals be set aside this easily? (Consider another question: should Christians forget the murder of one Jew approximately two thousand years ago?) Is this the usual way people react to other large-scale killings and their perpetrators?

If we give more thought to the matter of forgiveness we find that there are many questions and angles to consider. For example, does it matter how extensively an individual was injured? Is it sufficient recompense if the person who did the injuring simply asks for forgiveness? What if the one who caused the harm shows no repentance? Or, more significantly, what if the person attacked was killed by the other's action? And deliberately so? In that case can someone else provide forgiveness to the killer? And what if the matter involves a national community or a whole generation? Is it likely that an entire nation will repent of the actions carried out by its collective society or its government? Even if possible, would repentance be sufficient for the deaths inflicted and the lives of so many others torn to shreds? Can one generation forgive a previous generation for its actions that harmed and killed others? How much time should elapse before such a nation or generation may be trusted?

Will forgiving in these situations benefit anyone? Will forgiving the perpetrators provide better security for potential victims of bigotry or hate, or will it do the opposite? Where does the matter of justice and the rule of law enter the picture? After all, it is almost universally believed that justice is rooted in the Divine Being and is seen as basic to the Creation. Are justice and forgiveness in conflict? Justice may be the mercy provided for society.

Jesus' teachings as recorded in the four gospels are often cited by Christians as the basis for insisting on forgiving in every situation. Yet Jesus always spoke only of person-to-person wrongdoing and responses, how one person should respond to being sinned against by another. Jesus urged almost endless willingness to forgive the wrongs done to oneself as long as the other repents and asks for forgiveness. At the same time, Jesus insisted that one should be reconciled with any person to whom one had done harm before approaching the altar with a gift to God. In none of these situations did Jesus speak about how anyone should respond to an attack on someone else.

Yet not too many years after the Holocaust a Christian foundation insisted that the world should not only forgive even those whose attitudes provoke us but should also 'draw a line under the whole business [i.e., the Holocaust], just as if nothing of consequence had ever happened' (cited by Paul Lindhardt, in *The Sunflower*, 1st ed., p.165). Contrast that with Jesus' insistence that 'it would be better that a millstone be put around someone's neck and he were cast into the sea than he should harm one of these little ones' (Matthew 18:6).

> *'Antisemitism is easy to analyse, to dissect, to condemn. It is infinitely more difficult to fight it effectively.'*
>
> Jules Isaac

Repentance (*teshuvah*) clearly lies at the heart of the matter of forgiveness. But it is more than merely saying 'I'm sorry'; it must be genuine and deep-seated, and involve a real turning around in one's behaviour and intention. The turning around should also attempt to make some kind of reparation for the harm one has done, at least to those who have managed to survive. In 1985 in another situation thousands of South African Christians signed and issued The Kairos Document which insisted there can be 'no reconciliation, no forgiveness and no negotiations. . . without repentance.' Have the murderers – all of those, in Europe, who participated in one way or another in the Nazis' killing policy – shown repentance? Almost none have done so! So what is the basis for forgiving (still less forgetting)?

But how does this apply to those of the younger generations? They are not guilty of their parents' or grandparents' crimes. In that sense it is not appropriate to speak about forgiving them. But they can certainly regret what their predecessors did and do everything possible to ensure that such hatreds and policies do not again prevail. Above all it is essential that they not attempt to bury the past by forgetting, for such forgetting becomes complicity.

We hear much more about the need to forgive those who have committed wrongs of one sort or another than we do about the need to help and sustain those who have been injured. Some years ago this very situation arose in the Netherlands when a number of church groups and individual

'. . . *some measure of justice is absolutely necessary to even consider forgiveness or reconciliation.*'

Sven Alkalaj in *The Sunflower*.

For Further Reading

Alice L. Eckardt. 'Suffering, Theology and the Shoah,' *in The Holocaust Now*, Steven Jacobs, ed. East Rockaway, NY: Cummings & Hathaway, 1993.

Alice L. Eckardt and A. Roy Eckardt. *Long Night's Journey Into Day: A Revised Retrospective on the Holocaust*. Detroit: Wayne State University Press, 1988.

Reinhold Neibuhr. *Anger and Forgiveness: Discerning the Signs of the Times*. Charles Scribner's Sons, 1946.

Simon Wiesenthal. *The Sunflower*. N.Y.: Schocken, 1976; revised and expanded ed. 1997.

Clark Williamson. *Has God Rejected His People?* Nashville: Abingdon Press, 1982.

For Reflection

Do our traditional theologies about suffering and evil cope with the enormity of the Holocaust? What is God's role in all of this?
How do you understand the meaning of Jewish survival?

What have been the Church's teachings about Judaism and the Jewish people over the centuries? And how have they fed not only anti-Judaism but also antisemitism?

What has been the experience of the Jewish people living within and under Christian rule since the early 4th Century?

How did the European churches and their leadership act during the Nazi period, and especially during the years of the 'Final Solution'? How did North American churches react to the plight of Jews in Europe?

Alice L. Eckardt (USA) has taught courses on the Holocaust at Lehigh University, Bethlehem, PA, and has written and spoken extensively on this and on the broader subject of Jewish-Christian relations. An author of many works, she also co-authored with her husband A. Roy Eckardt, *Long Night's Journey Into Day: A Revised Retrospective on the Holocaust.* Detroit: Wayne State University Press, 1988.

Christians sought the release of several Nazis held in Dutch prisons for war crimes. They argued that since these men were now in their later years and could do no more harm they ought to be allowed to live their last years in their homes. What these do-gooders had not even given thought to was how such action might affect survivors of the death camps living in Holland. Yet the mere thought of such a release caused extreme trauma in many cases. When those who were not victimised forgive the victimisers, those made to suffer – a second time – are the original victims (and their families).

This question of who may forgive, what may be forgiven, when, etc, is raised in Simon Wiesenthal's *The Sunflower*. Simon was led, as a Jewish prisoner of the Nazis, to the bedside of a dying SS man at the soldier's request. The young German wanted to confess to a Jew about his participation in the brutal killing of several hundred unarmed Jews during an attack on a Ukrainian village, hoping to receive forgiveness. Should Simon forgive him? Or not? Did he have the right to do so? The responses to those questions by a number of invited contributors – Christians, Jews, and a few others – challenge our thinking.

We cannot speak about forgiveness without confronting the issue of remembrance. A Lutheran layman wrote some years ago, 'this attempt to wipe Judaism from the face of the earth is. . . the most historic event of our aeon. . . which cannot and may not ever become merely a bygone fact of the past. What has been done even to the least of Jesus' brothers, to his Jewish brothers, has been done to him. . . if the Christian Church has any right to call herself the Church of Jesus Christ, it must be also her own suffering' (Wolfgang Zucker, Lutheran Forum, Sept. 1975, p.10).

> 'Christians must be aware that after Auschwitz the Jewish people suspect Christians as well as Christian theology. Jews have two thousand years of documented history on the danger of trusting Christians.'
>
> Sidney G Hall

CHRISTIANS IN A WORLD OF GENOCIDE

Franklin H. Littell

Historians, both Jews and gentiles, are generally agreed that the Holocaust is the most traumatic event in the experience of the Jewish people since the destruction of the Second Temple. No consensus yet exists, however, as to the meaning of the Holocaust for Christian history.

A number of Christian theologians now maintain that the Holocaust was a 'watershed event' also in the history of Christianity, perhaps the definitive event in the history of European Christendom. The demand for a radical change in Christian preaching and teaching appears in a growing volume of lectures, essays and books.

The context of this demand must be held firmly in mind, for modern demands that Christian doctrine and utterance be changed come from several directions. Item: since the Enlightenment, Christian dogmas and teachings – the 'intellectual discipline' of the Christian movement – have come under heavy 'scientific' attack. Many well-meaning people think 'divisive' teachings and 'sectarian' moral positions should be relaxed for the sake of the general society. Item: with the rise in awareness of other world religions, some visionaries have affirmed a hidden unity of 'the religious spirit' beneath all 'outward differences', and some intellectuals have come forward with plans to blend 'the great religious truth systems' into one harmonious whole.

Bosnia, Sarajevo. A UN soldier and civilians take shelter behind an APC in central Sarajevo. June 8, 1995.

The argument of this essay takes another tack, namely that an imperative case for radical change in Christian preaching and teaching issues directly from an historical event: the murder of circa six million Jews, primarily during the years 1939-1945, by baptized Christians in the heart of Christendom. It is this historical event, in its precise context of verifiable facts, which puts the credibility of contemporary Christianity to the question.

The earthiness of this context removes the Holocaust from mystification: the crime was not committed under unknown circumstances by unknown perpetrators surrounded by bodies of unknown spectators. We know the names.

The precise context defines the uniqueness of the Holocaust. The facts that created and still surround it give the event universal meaning. Two issues of primary significance for Christians emerge from the event in its unique and universal aspects. The first is purging the body of Christian preaching and teaching, liturgies and world views, of antisemitism. The second is relating the Nazi genocide of the Jews to other genocides of modernity, giving energy to the identification and punishment of the crime.

Antisemitism in Christendom

Although the word itself was invented by Wilhelm Marr in Hamburg, Germany in the late 19th Century, *antisemitismus* (correctly translated 'antisemitism') has corrupted Christianity since the family quarrel split the followers of Jesus from those who followed the founding teachers of rabbinical Judaism. As in most family alienations, the arguments to justify the division were far more bitter than any used in ordinary quarrels. The arguments against the Christians from the side of the rabbinical schools were just as sweeping as the Christian apologetics against Judaism, but they are not the appropriate subject for a post-Auschwitz Christian writer. His role is to help clean up the Christian act.

Antisemitism in Christendom may be discerned at three levels – theological, cultural and political – marking three periods of alienation between Christians and Jews. As Christian antisemitism went along, through the centuries it appropriated and assimilated convergent anti-Jewish prejudices.

At its first level, controversial apologetics prevailed. The argument was that the Christians inherited the promise: those who stayed with rabbinical Judaism – which took form after the destruction of the Second Temple – missed the turn in the road.

The message of dismissal was well rounded: with the coming of the Messiah, the Christ, the Hebraic gift to mankind was accomplished. Now 'the new Israel,' gathered in the Christian churches, carried history. God was through with the Jews. When the puzzle of their survival became pressing, a great Christian theologian, St. Augustine, explained that God allowed them to survive as a negative lesson, to model the fate of a reprobate people.

The initial quarrels were unpleasant, but not fatal. They became dangerous when two things happened. First, the Christian missionaries to the gentiles were astonishingly successful: within a few decades what began as a Jewish sect among many others swelled to a membership consisting overwhelmingly of non-Jewish converts throughout the Mediterranean basin. Second, with the conversion of Constantine the Great (Roman Emperor 306-37), Christianity became the privileged, legally established, and persecuting religion.

During the Middle Ages, Christian antisemitism assumed its cultural shape. Depending upon the level of literacy of the tribes converted, and also on the intellectual training of their clergy, 'the Jew' was the satanic adversary of Christian mythology. He was the preachers' foil in sermons, and the rulers' excuse for failure in politics. Paintings were seen by few, but with the invention of printing, the defamatory pictures of 'the Jew' were widely disseminated.

During the ages of theological and cultural antisemitism, the Christian teachers managed to keep

'. . . Between the forces of terror and the forces of dialogue, a great unequal battle has begun. I have nothing but reasonable illusions as to the outcome of that battle. But I believe it must be fought, and I know that certain men at least have resolved to do so. I merely fear that they will occasionally feel somewhat alone, that they are in fact alone . . . What I know – which sometimes creates a deep longing in me – is that if Christians made up their minds to it, millions of voices – millions, I say – throughout the world would be added to the appeal of a handful of isolated individuals who, without any sort of affliction, today intercede almost everywhere and ceaselessly for children and for men.'

Albert Camus. *Resistance, Rebellion, and Death,*

the connection of the 'New Testament' to the 'Old Testament,' although there were gentile churches lasting into the 7th Century that rejected the Old Testament. The canon of Christian scripture was fixed in the 4th Century, with 80 percent of the Christian Bible consisting of Hebrew scriptures. Nevertheless, until the rise of modern biblical studies, Christian realities were read back into the 'Old Testament', and until the Holocaust there were scholars of eminence in great theological faculties who denigrated the significance of the Old Testament. Where the Old Testament was treasured in the churches, its connection with 'the Jews' was not part of the story.

In the modern period antisemitism was transformed into a weapon of ambitious politicians, and finally into a genocidal program. In a society with the level of literacy of France or Germany or Holland, it assimilated to itself some of the ideas of social Darwinism, *völkisch* nationalism, economic determinism. As a finished ideology, genocidal antisemitism comprised a number of energies not attributable to Christianity alone.

Nevertheless, no professing Christian can avoid the substantial Christian input in the Holocaust – both in laying part of the theoretical groundwork and in providing the personnel that committed the crime – baptised Christians, never rebuked let alone excommunicated by the church officials. The Annual Scholars' Conference on the Holocaust and the Churches, for example, has done important pioneering work in confronting the churches with this harsh truth. Without such spiritual surgery there can be no reconciliation between the Jewish people and the Christians, and no ring of truth in the preaching and teaching of the churches.

'The highest principles for our aspirations and judgments are given to us in the Jewish-Christian religious tradition. It is a very high goal which, with our weak powers, we can reach only very inadequately, but which gives a sure foundation to our aspirations and valuations.'

Albert Einstein

Dealing with Genocide

Although mass murders by rulers – like duelling, feuding, polygamy, infanticide, etc. – were widespread in past centuries, the realization that genocide is a crime came out of the Holocaust. Even at the Nuremberg trials, 'genocide' was not yet a concept in international law; those who committed the Holocaust were tried for 'crimes against humanity' (a classical concept of Roman Law) and breach of 'the rules of land warfare' (defined by Francis Lieber and issued by President Lincoln during the American Civil War, modified and entered into International Law by the Hague Convention, 1907.) The man who invented the word 'genocide' and pushed the concept beyond public moral statements by statesmen of legal standing in the International Genocide Convention of 1957 was a refugee from Hitler's Europe: Raphaol Lemkin (1901-59).

Rwandan refugees run towards a food distribution site in Kibumba refugee camp north of Goma Zaire, South Africa.

As with all advance in the government of human society by law, there are stages in awareness and effectiveness. First there are prophets who condemn the sin. There is an increase in public

For Further Reading

Richard L. Rubenstein. *The Cunning of History: The Holocaust and the American Future.* New York: Harper & Row, 1987.

Lyman H. Legters. *Western Society After the Holocaust.* Colorado: Westview Press, 1983.

Steven T Katz. *The Holocaust in Historical Context.* Oxford: Oxford University Press, 1994.

Franklin Littell is Professor Emeritus at Temple University and from 1972-92 was Adjunct at the Institute of Contemporary Jewry, Hebrew University .
He is the only Christian member of the International Council of Yad Vashem. He is also co-founder of the Annual Scholars' Conference on the Holocaust and the Churches, and President of the Philadelphia Center on the Holocaust, Genocide and Human Rights.

uneasiness about continuation of the wrong practice. Next, the custom is recognized as a crime, no longer an unavoidable disaster like a flood or an earthquake. Next, the crime and its penalties are defined at law. Finally, those who commit the crime are apprehended and punished.

Today in civilized societies crimes such as human sacrifice, gladiatorial combat, infanticide and chattel slavery are punished. With genocide, we are moving slowly along the path between the point when the crime is defined at law and the time when criminals are apprehended and punished. Nevertheless, for the first time in history a ruler has been identified as a genocide criminal; although not yet apprehended he cannot safely leave the small country he rules. And, again for the first time, there are several dozen persons in custody, in The Hague and elsewhere, charged with the crime of genocide.

Maintaining the memory and memorialization of the Holocaust is imperative for Christians as well as Jews. There is also a religious obligation vigorously to move the public conscience to the point where genocide no longer goes unpunished anywhere in the world. This is also a fitting tribute too, to those who perished in the Holocaust, victims in an age when national and racial violence was not yet checked in the law of nations.

In Conclusion

After Auschwitz, churchly condemnation of antisemitism is widespread, although the specific implications in such sectors as home missions, seminary education and church discipline have yet to be worked out.

Confronting the crime of genocide is still at a more elementary level. The Christian churches are frequently still captive to political powers, as the general record of the churches during Hitler's domination of Europe plainly documents. In now confronting the crime of genocide, the task of the churches is to create and cultivate a culture of resistance to nationalist and ethnic prejudice and a stance of conscientious objection to immoral – and now illegal – genocidal actions of government.

Whether in Europe – with its churches still too often servile before those in political power, or in the United States – where old-fashioned nationalists led by the Chairman of the Senate Foreign Relations Committee still strive to cripple American participation in effective international action against genocide, the responsibility of post-Auschwitz Christians seems plain to read: to help build up a strong public consensus calling for inhibition of the crime of genocide, and to demand the efficient punishment of the criminals when and where they are identified.

This requires a willingness on the part of the churches' leaders to confront criminal governments and publicly to condemn criminal acts by legitimate governments. This may be the simple most important lesson to be mastered by post-Holocaust Christians.

IS THERE A FUTURE FOR CHRISTIANITY?

Stephen D. Smith

A Parable

There was once a man going about his business, trying to live out his life peacefully and without offence to those around him. One day as he went about his life, a group of men set upon him. They robbed him and they stripped him and they left him on the side of the road for dead. Presently, along came an educated, God-fearing and good man; a man known for his generosity and charity. He saw the man who had been beaten and robbed, but he crossed over the road and carried on his way. Shortly, along came a priest, a well-respected man of wisdom and of learning. Seeing his neighbor in distress, he too crossed over to the other side; after all, he would not be seen helping a Jew. And so the Jew lay in the gutter waiting for the good Samaritan.

But there was no good Samaritan.

Not this time.

The Challenge of the Holocaust to Christian Belief and Practice

Two thousand years of teaching love for one's neighbors and care for the oppressed. Two thousand years preaching mercy for those that suffer, the giving of charity, and compassion for the dying. Two thousand years of mission, in which to believe in Christ meant redemption from a world embittered with hatred and violence and the consequences of the abuse of power. Two thousand years of existence, and everything that Christianity said it stood for was about to be put to the test. It was not the Christian Churches that designed the gas chambers, dug the mass graves or ordered the mass murder of the Jews of Europe. Those images of our age came from an altogether more evil force. What was required of Christians was to reply to this evil with the principles of Christian practice. What Christians had to do was to demonstrate compassion, to uphold the value of human life, and to lead by example. What Christians had to do was to love their neighbors, to care for the oppressed, have mercy on the suffering, and to shun hatred, violence and the abuse of power. In all of this and more, when the test finally came, all too often, Christians were found wanting.

Criticism is clearly due. But I find criticism is more difficult to arrive at than you might think. Not

> *'I am convinced that – with all the implications involved for theology and Church history – the crucifixion and resurrection of the Jewish people are the most important events for Christian history in centuries.'*
>
> Franklin H. Littell, *Crucifixion of the Jews.*

'The Lord assigned me a role to speak and write during the war, when – as it seemed to me – it might help. It did not. Furthermore, when the war came to its end, I learned that the governments, the leaders, the scholars, the writers did not know what had been happening to the Jews. They were taken by surprise. The murder of six million innocents was a secret…

Then I became a Jew.

Like the family of my wife – all of them perished in the ghettos, in the concentration camps, in the gas chambers – so all murdered Jews became my family.

But I am a Christian Jew.

I am a practicing Catholic.

Although I am not a heretic, still my faith tells me the second Original Sin has been committed by humanity: through commission, or omission, or self-imposed ignorance, or insensitivity, or self-interest, or hypocrisy, or heartless rationalization.

This sin will haunt humanity to the end of time.

It does haunt me.

And I want it to be so.'

Jan Karski in *How One Man Tried to Stop the Holocaust*

because what happened was right, on the contrary; but I fear I might have reacted similarly myself. Criticism is warranted and indeed necessary; but always with an equal measure of self-reflection, as such relection should cause us to consider the way in which we confront this past in the present and make it part of our future. Can the religion, theology and institutions of Christianity guarantee in future that Christians will be christian in their practice as well as in their stated belief?

Doubtless, the Righteous Among the Nations come to mind; those brave souls who in some cases, out of true conviction of their belief, risked everything to save Jewish souls. Their heroic acts of hiding, moving, and protecting Jewish neighbors, friends or even complete strangers were among the greatest acts of bravery and demonstrated true christian values. One might conclude it proves that Christianity can produce real heroes and martyrs. This might be true, but it could equally demonstrate that in the vast majority of cases it will not.

Facing these realities, the Holocaust is not only a tragedy for all time for the Jews, it is also a disaster for Christianity. Two generations later, our institutions, our Christian identity and personal faith have only just begun to face these challenges and all that they entail.

The Challenge to the Institutions of Christianity

The essays in this volume clearly, accurately and informatively demonstrate the enormous pressure that the institutional bodies of Christendom found themselves under during the Nazi period and the consequent mass murder of European Jewry. These institutions were there to provide leadership for the faithful, but they were also, by nature, political institutions. Each had their own constituencies, that is, the professing Christian membership of their churches, and each had 'political' interests to protect. The leadership of the respective bodies usually fulfilled their direct obligations adequately on both counts, but to quite tragic ends. They *did* represent the interests of their constituencies by providing a means for the continuity of religious practice (of a kind), and by working within the system to keep the churches open. They also protected the political interests of the church through accepting the imposition of Nazi ideology or assuming a form of 'political neutrality'. However, in view of the nature of Nazism, 'neutrality' was not an option, as neutrality in itself became a political statement of non-intervention and was tantamount to collusion.

Many questions remain for Christian institutions today in the wake of this history. I would like to ask just two. Firstly, are Christian institutions confident that its stated political position always defers priority and dignity to the value of human life – even in preference to the survival of the Church itself? Secondly, has the institution of Christianity sufficiently altered its theological (and ecclesiastical) structures to encompass a relationship of trust between Judaism and Christianity and perhaps more importantly, between Jews and Christians?

The Challenge to the Identity of Christianity

Christianity as a religion and Christians as its adherents have long prided themselves upon specific statements of moral certitude. To be a Christian is to profess and maintain a specific moral code and ethical identity. Christians have convinced themselves that Christian belief results in christian behavior.

The Holocaust demonstrated that you can no longer presume with any certainty that Christians will be christian when called upon so to be. We now know that it is possible for Christians to believe in the eternal life offered through faith in Jesus, and simultaneously assist in, or condone the murder of Jews. History has sadly demonstrated that for some this is not a contradiction of faith, but even its affirmation.

Christianity has also prided itself upon the authority of the New Testament as a more recent revelation, fulfilling many of the prophecies of the Hebrew scriptures, and endorsing its superior nature. This has led to the damaging assumption of Christian supercessionism, in which Christian revelation is believed to have superceded the Jewish tradition and, by extension, that Christians are superior to Jews. For Christians to avoid the same repetition of contempt in future, acknowledging the priority and validity of the Jewish tradition is fundamental to establishing and maintaining a relationship of trust.

The Challenge to Personal Faith

Where Christianity happens in practice, is in the hearts and homes of individuals of faith. Here too, there are difficult questions to ask ourselves. Imagine for a moment, pious and secular Jews who arrived at the death camps or stood on the edge of mass graves awaiting their untimely deaths. Some were staunch in their belief in an al-powerful and all-loving God who was still in control of all that was happening to them. Others questioned the very nature of divinity and lost their belief altogether. The vast majority died their deaths and took their prayers of belief or protest with them. Among the survivors, a variety of reactions ensued after the liberation. Some could not make sense of mass murder in the presence of an all-powerful God who either could not or would not intervene to protect the Jews. Others blamed human free will for the evil of the Holocaust and maintained a belief in the power and presence of God.

Whatever the conclusions, Jews have had to grapple with the possibility that the Holocaust creates a break between old assumptions and current thinking. It creates the possibility that God is

> '*Jews find in the Holocaust no new definition of Jewish identity because we need none. Nothing has changed. The tradition lives on.*'
>
> Jacob Neusner, 'The Implications of the Holocaust' in Journal of Religion, 1973, p.308

> '*. . . all kinds of Jews, regardless of their identities and even religions found themselves in the gas chambers at Auschwitz - that is the only fixed reality that Jews know or ought to know, about themselves.*'
>
> J. Webber. 'Modern Jewish Identities' in Jewish Identities in the New Europe. p.85

> *Jews have had to grapple with the possibility that the Holocaust creates a break between old assumptions and current thinking. Christians, however, have only addressed their concerns about the actions (or inaction) of the Christian Churches'*

For Further Reading

Helen P. Fry ed. *Christian-Jewish Dialogue*. Exeter: University of Exeter Press, 1996.

Douglas K Huneke. *The Stones Will Cry Out: pastoral reflections on the Shoah (with liturgical responses)*. Westport: Greenwood Press, 1995.

Alice L Eckardt and A Roy Eckardt. *Long Night's Journey into Day: a revised retrospective on the Holocaust*. Detroit: Wayne State University Press, 1988.

Paul M. van Buren. *A Theology of the Jewish-Christian Reality, Part 1: Discerning the Way*. Cambridge: Harper & Row, 1987.

Stephen D. Smith (UK) is co-founder and director of the Beth Shalom Holocaust Memorial Centre, UK. He is a member of the Intergovernmental Task Force for Holocaust Remembrance, Research and Education. His publications include *Making Memory: Creating Britains' First Holocaust Centre* and he is also editor of *The Witness Collection*. Among his forthcoming publications is *Forgotten Places: The Holocaust and the Remnants of Destruction*.

not all that Jews have professed for the last six millennia. Christians, however, have only addressed their concerns about the actions (or inaction) of the Christian churches and are yet to consider the question of the presence or absence of God: that is questioning faith itself. Clearly, if the God of the Jews was absent, so was the God of the Christians. If God cannot intervene on behalf of the Jews, neither can He intervene for Christians; unless you hold the outdated and never-valid belief that God is no longer obliged to the Jews – in which case you have just wasted your time reading this book.

Christians have yet to confront the tough reality that the Holocaust challenges and touches almost everything and everyone within the Christian faith. For example, how can you maintain that faith is more important than deeds after the Holocaust? You cannot, unless you are content to go to Church and run the risk of inadvertently condoning genocide. How can we as believing Christians go blithely on, when survivors live with the intolerable burden of doubt, thrust upon them through circumstances created in the context of a so-called Christian civilization?

The Demand for Change

'Why does thy brother's blood cry out from the ground?' God asked Cain, presumably knowing the answer, but awaiting an honest reply. The answer never came. 'Am I my brother's keeper?' he replied, which of course was not to answer at all. Cain was punished and made a 'restless wanderer' on the face of the earth. Today, the churches face the same question; 'Why does your brother's blood cry out from the ground?' What should our answer be? Can we find one? How honest can we be?

As we contemplate the future of a third millennium of Christianity, a new demand is placed upon those who choose to profess Christianity after the Holocaust. The bravery of a few and the exemplary leadership of even fewer, does not offset the terrible and unavoidable challenge of the *Shoah*. The murdered and forgotten Jews of Europe make a new demand on all Christians everywhere.

After the *Shoah*, it is no longer acceptable just to call yourself a Christian. Now you must prove it.

> 'If men cannot always make history have a meaning, they can always act so that their own lives have.'
>
> Albert Camus

AFTERWORD

And so this part of your journey confronting "the Holocaust and the Christian world" comes to an end, but it is not over. There will always be more to learn, more to ponder, more to discuss, which is why we hope you will continue your interest in the topic, embracing the questions at ever deeper levels. We also hope you will reflect on what you have learned about the Holocaust and about what those who professed to be Christian did, and failed to do, in the heart of Europe - "Christian" for more than fifteen hundred years - more than half a century ago, during Nazi Germany's Third Reich and the Shoah (1933-1945). What can we learn for today? What should we learn?

In compiling this volume, we have tried to put together an interesting and challenging set of short essays focusing on various aspects of what we know is a complex, sensitive, even volatile topic, "The Holocaust and the Christian World." From the beginning, we wanted to challenge and engage you, our readers, to encourage you to think about questions you may not have thought about before. At times, you may have found this daunting, as all of us do who confront the Holocaust and discover how we Christians - individually and institutionally - for the most part, failed our Jewish brothers and sisters during those years of terror and horror. Our intention was not to discourage readers, but to challenge and encourage them to do things differently now - and in the future.

It is one thing to recognize and be scandalized by the action or inaction of those who were un-responsive to the cries of the Jews - and other victims of the Nazis - during World War II and the Holocaust, easy enough to condemn the un-responsiveness of individuals and institutions who called themselves Christian, easy enough to condemn the "power political realism" that motivated action or inaction, care and concern or neutrality and indifference toward Jews during the Shoah, but what about today? Have we learned anything from history, or are we condemned to repeat it?

You personally may not be in a position to change the way Christian institutions are structured, or the way Christian theology is taught in schools, churches, and seminaries, nor may you be in a position to influence those who do change such things, but you are in a position to examine how you live your life, how you relate to others, how you respond when others need your help. The question, "Who is part of my universe of obligation" is an important one, not just for the last millennium but for this one as well. How you answer that question today is a good indication for you about how you would have answered that question during the Holocaust.

The Holocaust and the Christian World: Reflections on the Past, Challenges for the Future is a great title, but it has to be more than that. It must be a spur to incite us to action on behalf of others. If your confrontation with The Holocaust and the Christian World provokes you to do something today about trying to make the future more humane for all people, then our efforts in putting this volume together will have been worthwhile, for we believe that it will contribute to *tikkun olam* - the healing and repair of the world - and so will yours.

The Editors

FOR FURTHER STUDY

This section has been compiled to help you further your interest in the Holocaust and the Christian World. Throughout the book, we have provided suggestions for further reading as well as thoughts for reflection. Hopefully, you have found these useful. In the coming pages you will find a selection of useful historical documents, Church statements, as well as useful video and internet resources.

DOCUMENTS RELATED TO CHURCH ISSUES DURING THE HOLOCAUST

In this section, we have provided texts of selected documents (letters, statements, and other comments) related to issues faced by the Churches during the Holocaust. We also have included selected documents issued by various Churches - Catholic and Protestant - since 1945 that show a developing understanding within the Churches about antisemtism, Judaism, and the impact of the Holocaust on Christianity. In some instances we have provided complete texts; in others, excerpts from longer documents.

1 Norway:

Protests Against Discrimination or Deportation of Jews

On November 11, 1943, the Lutheran bishops, in co-operation with clergy from several other Protestant sects, sent a letter of protest to Vidkun Quisling, Head of the Nazi puppet government of Norway; in December it was twice read from the pulpit, and it was also published as the New Year's message for 1943. This proclamation was circulated in Norway and Sweden but was read over the Norwegian-language and other broadcasts of the BBC. After noting the arrest of all Jewish males over the age of fifteen and the order confiscating Jewish property, the protest states:

For 91 years Jews have had a legal right to reside and to earn a livelihood in our country. Now they are being deprived of their property without warning . . . Jews have not been charged with transgression of the country's laws, much less convicted of such transgressions by judicial procedure. Nevertheless, they are being punished as severely as the worst criminals are punished. They are being punished because of their racial background, wholly and solely because they are Jews . . . Thus, according to God's Word, all people have, in the first instance, the same human worth and thereby the same human rights. Our state authorities are by law obliged to respect this basic view . . . To remain silent about this legalized injustice against the Jews would render ourselves co-guilty in this injustice.

Leni Yahil. *The Holocaust: The Fate of European Jewry, 1932-1945:* New York: Oxford University Press. 1990, p396.

2 Greece:

The Archbishop of Athens protested to the German Foreign Office and to the Greek Prime Minister against the deportation of the Jews of Salonika. The Greek protestors included school and university rectors and representatives of business and professional associations, and continually stressed the innocence of Greek Jews, while acknowledging that Jews of other nations might have given the Germans reason for recrimination. The petition of Greek leaders of March 24, 1943 noted:

'We must add that the above mentioned Jews have never acted against our interests, even in the smallest matters; on the contrary, they have always felt a sense of responsibility towards the Greek majority. Most of them belong to the poorer of the Jews living in Germany and have no knowledge whatsoever of the language of Poland where they are being sent to live.

In addition to the above facts, we wish to add that during the long course of our history, ever since the era of Alexander the Great and his descendants, and through all the centuries of Greek Orthodoxy down to the present time, our relations with the Jewish people have always been harmonious. We believe, therefore, that, in your high office as ruler of our country during the present war, you will not hesitate to accept our present request and decide, even if provisionally, to suspend the expulsion of Greek Jews from Greece until the Jewish question can be examined in the light of a special and detailed investigation.

Our present request is based upon the recent historical fact that during the surrender of Salonika and, later, that of the whole of Greece, among the clauses of the protocol, the following is included: 'The Occupation forces promise to protect the life, the honor and the properties of the population.' Certainly this clause implies that no persecution would be made against Greek subjects, on account of religion and race, and that consequently the theory relating to racial or religious discrimination would not be applied in Greece.'

Helen Fein. *Accounting for Genocide: National Responses and Jewish Victimization during the Holocaust.* p.117

3 France:
The protest of the French assembly of cardinals and archbishops, July 22, 1942.
The assembly declared to Marshal Pétain:

'Profoundly moved by what is reported to us of the massive arrests of the Jews carried out last week and of the harsh treatment which has been inflicted upon them, notably at the Winter Sports Stadium, we cannot stifle the cry of our conscience.

It is in the name of humanity and of Christian principles that our voice is raised in protest in favor of the improscribable rights of human beings. It is also an anguished call to mercy for the immense sufferings, especially those which befall so many mothers and children.

We ask . . . that you please take account of this in order, that the requirements of justice and the rights of charity be respected.'

Helen Fein. *Accounting for Genocide: National Responses and Jewish Victimization during the Holocaust.* p.118

4 France:
Letter from Léon Bérard, French Ambassador to the Vatican, to Marshal Phillipe Pétain:
Vatican City
September 2, 1941

Monsieur le Marechal [Pétain]:

In your letter of August 7, 1941, you required certain information as to the problems and difficulties which could arise from the Roman Catholic point of view in connection with the measures your government has taken with respect to the Jews. I had the honor of sending you a first reply in which I stated that at the Vatican I have never been told anything which – from the standpoint of the Holy See – implied criticism and disapproval of the legislative and administrative acts in question . . . The subject is complex . . . On July 29, 1938, in a speech addressed to students of the College of Propaganda, Pius XI said: 'We forget that the human species, the whole human species is one single, grand, universal, human race. At any rate, we cannot deny that in the universal race there is place for special races' . . . However, the teaching of the Church on racial theories does not necessarily mean that it condemns any particular measure of any state against the so-called Jewish race . . .The Church recognizes that among the distinctive features of the Israelitic community there are particular, not racial but ethnical, qualities. The Church has always clearly seen this fact and has always reckoned with it. History tells us that the Church often protected Jews against the violence and injustice of their persecutors and that at the same time it has consigned them to the ghettos . . . While proscribing any policy of oppression towards the Jews, Saint Thomas recommends, nevertheless, to take measures designed to limit their action in society and to check their influence. It would be unreasonable, in a Christian state, to permit them to exercise the functions of government and thus to submit the Catholics to their authority. Consequently it is legitimate to bar them from public functions, legitimate also to admit but a fixed proportion of them to the universities (*numerous clauses*) and to the liberal professions . . . As I was told by an authority spokesman at the Vatican: we shall not in the least be reprimanded for this statute on the Jews.

Helen Fein. *Accounting for Genocide: National Responses and Jewish Victimization during the Holocaust.* pp.111-112

5 Demark:

Denmark's Lutheran State Church also condemned the Germans' plans for the Jews. The Bishop of Copenhagen, Dr. Hans Fuglsang-Damgaard (1890-1979) prepared a written statement which he signed on behalf of all the Danish Lutheran Bishops. It was sent to the German occupation officials and was dispatched, via theological students, on Saturday, October 2, 1943 to churches in Bishop Fuglsang-Damgaard's diocese. On Sunday, October 3, the written protest was read in Lutheran State Churches:

Whenever persecutions are undertaken for racial or religious reasons against the Jews, it is the duty of the Christian Church to raise a protest against it for the following reasons:

1.   Because we shall never be able to forget that the Lord of the Church, Jesus Christ, was born in Bethlehem, of the Virgin Mary into Israel, the people of his possession, according to the promise of God. The history of the Jewish people up to the birth of Christ includes the preparation for the salvation which God has prepared in Christ for all men. This is also expressed in the fact that the Old Testament is part of our Bible.

2.   Because the persecution of the Jews is irreconcilable with the humanitarian concept of love of neighbors which follows from the message which the Church of Jesus Christ is commissioned to proclaim. With Christ there is no respect of persons, and he has taught us that every man is precious in the eyes of God. 'There is neither Jew nor Greek, there is neither bond nor free, there is neither male nor female: for ye are all one in Christ Jesus.' (Gal. 3, 28.)

3.   Because it contradicts the sense of justice, inherent during centuries in our Danish civilization and which lives in the Danish people. In accordance with the above principles, all Danish citizens have equal rights and duties before the law and freedom of religion assured to them by the constitution.

We understand by freedom of religion the right to exercise our faith in God according to vocation and conscience, in such a way that race and religion can never be in themselves a reason for depriving a man of his rights, freedom, or property. Despite different religious views we shall therefore struggle to ensure the continued guarantee to our Jewish brothers and sisters [of] the same freedom which we ourselves treasure more than life.

The leaders of the Danish Church are conscious of our responsibility to be law abiding citizens; we do not needlessly revolt against those who exercise the functions of authority over us; but at the same time, we are obliged by our conscience to maintain the law and to protest against any violation of human rights. Therefore we desire to declare unambiguously our allegiance to the word, *we must obey God rather than man*.

Johan M. Snoek, *The Grey Book*. New York: Humanities Press, 1970, p.168

POST-HOLOCAUST STATEMENTS FROM THE CHURCHES

An Address To The Churches, Seeligsberg (Switzerland), 1947

We have recently witnessed an outburst of antisemitism which has led to the persecution and extermination of millions of Jews. In spite of the catastrophe which has overtaken both the persecuted and the persecutors, and which has revealed the extent of the Jewish problem in all its alarming gravity and urgency, antisemitism has lost none of its force, but threatens to extend to other regions, to poison the minds of Christians and to involve humanity more and more in a grave guilt with disastrous consequences.

The Christian Churches have indeed always affirmed the un-Christian character of antisemitism, as of all forms of racial hatred, but this has not sufficed to prevent the manifestation among Christians, in various forms, of an undiscriminating racial hatred of the Jews as a people. This would have been impossible if all Christians had been true to the teaching of Jesus Christ on the mercy of God and love of one's neighbour. But this faithfulness should also involve clear-sighted willingness to avoid any presentation and conception of the Christian message which would support antisemitism under whatever form. We must recognize, unfortunately, that this vigilant willingness has often been lacking.

We therefore address ourselves to the Churches to draw their attention to this alarming situation. We have the firm hope that they will be concerned to show their members how to prevent any animosity towards the Jews which might arise from false, inadequate or mistaken presentations or conceptions of the teaching and preaching of the Christian doctrine, and how on the other hand to promote brotherly love towards the sorely-tried people of the old covenant.

Nothing would seem more calculated to contribute to this happy result than the following:

TEN POINTS

1. Remember that One God speaks to us all through the Old and the New Testaments.

2. Remember that Jesus was born of a Jewish mother of the seed of David and the people of Israel, and that His everlasting love and forgiveness embraces His own people and the whole world.

3. Remember that the first disciples, the apostles and the first martyrs were Jews.

4. Remember that the fundamental commandment of Christianity, to love God and one's neighbor, proclaimed already in the Old Testament and confirmed by Jesus, is binding upon both Christians and Jews in all human relationships, without any exception.

5. Avoid distorting or misrepresenting biblical or post-biblical Judaism with the object of extolling Christianity.

6. Avoid using the word Jews in the exclusive sense of the enemies of Jesus, and the words 'the enemies of Jesus' to designate the whole Jewish people.

7. Avoid presenting the Passion in such a way as to bring the odium of the killing of Jesus upon all Jews or upon Jews alone. It was only a section of the Jews in Jerusalem who demanded the death of Jesus, and the Christian message has always been that it was the sins of mankind which were exemplified by those Jews and the sins in which all men share that brought Christ to the Cross.

8. Avoid referring to the scriptural curses, or the cry of a raging mob: 'His blood be upon us and our children,' with out remembering that this cry should not count against the infinitely more weighty words of our Lord: 'Father forgive them for they know not what they do.'

9. Avoid promoting the superstitious notion that the Jewish people are reprobate, accursed, reserved for a destiny of suffering.

10. Avoid speaking of the Jews as if the first members of the Church had not been Jews.

*   *   *   *

Excerpt from the Declaration on The Relationships of the [Roman Catholic] Church to Non-Christian Religions, *Nostra Aetate* (In Our Time), October 28, 1965

4. Judaism

As the sacred synod searches into the mystery of the Church, it remembers the bond that spiritually ties the people of the New Covenant to Abraham's stock.

Thus the Church of Christ acknowledges that, according to God's saving design, the beginnings of her faith and her election are found already among the Patriarchs, Moses and the Prophets. She professes that all who believe in Christ - Abraham's sons according to faith[6]- are included in the same Patriarch's call, and likewise that the salvation of the Church is mysteriously foreshadowed by the chosen people's exodus from the land of bondage. The Church, therefore, cannot forget that she received the revelation of the Old Testament through the people with whom God in His inexpressible mercy concluded the Ancient Covenant. Nor can she forget that she draws sustenance from the root of that well-cultivated olive tree onto which have been grafted the wild shoots, the Gentiles.[7] Indeed, the Church believes that by His cross Christ, Our Peace, reconciled Jews and Gentiles. making both one in Himself.[8]

The Church keeps ever in mind the words of the Apostle about his kinsmen: "theirs is the sonship and the glory and the covenants and the law and the worship and the promises; theirs are the fathers and from them is the Christ according to the flesh" (Rom. 9:4-5), the Son of the Virgin Mary. She also recalls that the Apostles, the Church's main-stay and pillars, as well as most of the early disciples who proclaimed Christ's Gospel to the world, sprang from the Jewish people.

As Holy Scripture testifies, Jerusalem did not recognize the time of her visitation,[9] nor did the Jews in large number, accept the Gospel; indeed not a few opposed its spreading.[10] Nevertheless, God holds the Jews most dear for the sake of their Fathers; He does not repent of the gifts He makes or of the calls He issues - such is the witness of the Apostle.[11] In company with the Prophets and the same Apostle, the Church awaits that day, known to God alone, on which all peoples will address the Lord in a single voice and "serve him shoulder to shoulder" (Soph. 3:9).[12]

Since the spiritual patrimony common to Christians and Jews is thus so great, this sacred synod wants to foster and recommend that mutual understanding and respect which is the fruit, above all, of biblical and theological studies as well as of fraternal dialogues.

True, the Jewish authorities and those who followed their lead pressed for the death of Christ;[13] still, what happened in His passion cannot be charged against all the Jews, without distinction, then alive, nor against the Jews of today. Although the Church is the new people of God, the Jews should not be presented as rejected or accursed by God, as if this followed from the Holy Scriptures. All should see to it, then, that in catechetical work or in the preaching of the word of God they do not teach anything that does not conform to the truth of the Gospel and the spirit of Christ.

Furthermore, in her rejection of every persecution against any man, the Church, mindful of the patrimony she shares with the Jews and moved by the spiritual love of the Gospel and not by political reasons, decries hatred, persecutions, manifestations of anti-Semitism, directed against Jews at any time and by anyone.

Besides, as the Church has always held and holds now, Christ underwent His passion and death freely, because of the sins of men and out of infinite love, in order that all may reach salvation. It is, therefore, the burden of the Church's preaching to proclaim the cross of Christ as the sign of God's all-embracing love and as the fountain from which every grace flows.

5. The Brotherhood of Man

We cannot truly call on God, the Father of all, if we refuse to treat in a brotherly way any man, created as he is in the image of God. Man's relation to God the Father and his relation to men his brothers are so linked together that Scripture says: "He who does not love does not know God" (1 John 4:8).

No foundation therefore remains for any theory or practice that leads to discrimination between man and man or people and people, so far as their human dignity and the rights flowing from it are concerned.

The Church reproves, as foreign to the mind of Christ, any discrimination against men or harassment of them because of their race, color, condition of life, or religion. On the contrary, following in the footsteps of the holy Apostles

Peter and Paul, this sacred synod ardently implores the Christian faithful to "maintain good fellowship among the nations" (1 Peter 2:12), and, if possible, to live for their part in peace with all men,[14] so that they may truly be sons of the Father who is in heaven.[15]

Notes

6. cf. Gal. 3:7

7. cf. Rom. 11:17-24

8. cf. Eph. 2:14-16

9. cf. Lk. 19:44

10. cf. Rom. 11:28

11. cf. Rom. 11:28-29; cf. Dogmatic Constitution, Lumen Gentium (Light of Nations) AAS, 57 (1965), p. 20

12. cf. Is. 66:23; Ps. 65:4; Rom. 11:11-32

13. cf. John. 19:6

14. cf. Rom. 12:18

15. cf. Matt. 5:45

Catholic Jewish Relations: Documents from the Holy See (London: Catholic Truth Society, 1999), pp. 18-21. With Permission

★   ★   ★   ★

Evangelical Lutheran Church in America
Statement on Lutheran-Jewish Relations Church Council of the
Adopted, April 18, 1994

In the long history of Christianity there exists no more tragic development than the treatment accorded the Jewish people on the part of Christian believers. Very few Christian communities of faith were able to escape the contagion of anti-Judaism and its modern successor, anti-Semitism. Lutherans belonging to the Lutheran World Federation and the Evangelical Lutheran Church in America feel a special burden in this regard because of certain elements in the legacy of the reformer Martin Luther and the catastrophes, including the Holocaust of the twentieth century, suffered by Jews in places where the Lutheran churches were strongly represented.

The Lutheran communion of faith is linked by name and heritage to the memory of Martin Luther, teacher and reformer. Honoring his name in our own, we recall his bold stand for truth, his earthy and sublime words of wisdom, and above all his witness to God's saving Word. Luther proclaimed a gospel for people as we really are, bidding us to trust a grace sufficient to reach our deepest shames and address the most tragic truths.

In the spirit of that truth-telling, we who bear his name and heritage must with pain acknowledge also Luther's anti-Judaic diatribes and the violent recommendations of his later writings against the Jews. As did many of Luther's own companions in the sixteenth century, we reject this violent invective, and yet more do we express our deep and abiding sorrow over its tragic effects on subsequent generations. In concert with the Lutheran World Federation, we particularly deplore the appropriation of Luther's words by modern anti-Semites for the teaching of hatred toward Judaism or toward the Jewish people in our day.

Grieving the complicity of our own tradition within this history of hatred, moreover, we express our urgent desire to live out our faith in Jesus Christ with love and respect for the Jewish people. We recognize in anti-Semitism a contradiction and an affront to the Gospel, a violation of our hope and calling, and we pledge this Church to oppose the deadly working of such bigotry, both within our own circles and in the society around us. Finally, we pray for the continued blessing of the Blessed One upon the increasing cooperation and understanding between Lutheran Christians and the Jewish community.

Retrieved from the World Wide Web: http://www.jcrelations.com

Joint Statement: Hungarian Bishops and the Ecumenical Council of Churches in Hungary, November 1994

The bishops of the Hungarian Catholic Church as well as the bishops and leading pastors of the member churches of the Ecumenical Council of Churches in Hungary and the communities they are here representing commemorate in piety the tragic events of fifty years ago, when Jews living in Hungary were dragged off to concentration camps and slaughtered in cold blood. We consider it as the greatest shame of our twentieth century that hundreds of thousands of lives were extinguished merely because of their origin.

On the anniversary of these painful events we pay the tribute of respect to the memory of the victims. Conforming to the message of the Scripture we all consider the Holocaust as an unpardonable sin. This crime burdens our history as well as our communities and reminds us of the obligation of propitiation, apart from pious commemoration.

On the occasion of the anniversary we have to state that not only the perpetrators of this insane crime are responsible for it but all those who, although they declared themselves members of our churches, through fear, cowardice, or opportunism, failed to raise their voices against the mass humiliation, deportation, and murder of their Jewish neighbors. Before God we now ask forgiveness for this failure committed in the time of disaster fifty years ago.

We look at those, who in that dehumanized age, rescued lives at the cost of their own, or endangering it, and surmounting denominational considerations, protested with universal and general effect against the diabolical plots.

It is a task of conscience for us all to strengthen the service of reconciliation in our communities, for this is the only way for all persons to be equally respected and live in mutual understanding and love.

We have to aim at developing true humaneness, so that there will be no more antisemitism or any kind of discrimination, and so that the crimes of the past will never happen again.

Catholics Remember the Holocaust (Washington, DC: United States Catholic Conference, 1998), pp. 7-8. With Permission

Opportunity to Re-examine Relationships with the Jews: German Bishops, January 23, 1995

On January 27, 1945 the concentration camps of Auschwitz and Auschwitz-Birkenau were liberated. Numerous people were murdered there in a terrible manner: Poles, Russians, Roma and Sinti people (Gypsies) as well as members of other nations. The overwhelming majority of prisoners and victims in this camp consisted of Jews.

Therefore Auschwitz has become the symbol of the extermination of European Jewry which is called Holocaust, or - using the Hebrew term - Shoah.

The crime against the Jews was planned and put into action by the National Socialist rulers in Germany. The "unprecedented crime" which was the Shoah (Pope John Paul II, June 9, 1991) still raises many questions which we must not evade. The commemoration of the 50th anniversary of the liberation of Auschwitz gives German Catholics the opportunity to re-examine their relationship with the Jews.

At the same time this day recalls the fact that Auschwitz is also part of the Polish history of suffering and burdens the relationship between Poles and Germans.

Already during earlier centuries, Jews were exposed to persecution, oppression, expulsion and even to mortal danger. Many looked for and found refuge in Poland. However, there were also places and regions in Germany where Jews could live relatively untroubled. Since the eighteenth century, there was a new chance of a peaceful coexistence in Germany. Jews decisively contributed towards the development of German science and culture. Nevertheless, an anti-Jewish attitude remained, also within the Church.

This was one of the reasons why during the years of the Third Reich, Christians did not offer due resistance to racial antisemitism. Many times there was failure and guilt among Catholics. Not a few of them got involved in the ideology of National Socialism and remained unmoved in the face of the crimes committed against Jewish-owned property and the life of Jews. Others paved the way for crimes or even became criminals themselves.

It is unknown how many people were horrified at the disappearance of their Jewish neighbors and yet were not strong enough to raise their voices in protest. Those who rendered aid to others, thereby risking their own lives, frequently did not receive support.

Today the fact is weighing heavy on our minds that there were but individual initiatives to help persecuted Jews, and that even the pogroms of November 1938 were not followed by public and express protest - i.e., when hundreds of synagogues were set on fire and vandalised, cemeteries were desecrated, thousands of Jewish-owned shops were demolished, innumerable dwellings of Jewish families were damaged and looted, people were ridiculed, ill-treated and even killed.

The retrospect on the events of November 1938 and on the terror regime of the National Socialists during twelve years visualizes the heavy burden of history. It recalls "that the Church, which we proclaim as holy and which we honor as a mystery, is also a sinful Church and in need of conversion" (statement by the German and Austrian bishops' conferences on the fiftieth anniversary of the November 1938 pogroms).

The failure and guilt of that time have also a church dimension. We are reminded of that fact when quoting the witness given by the joint synod of dioceses in the Federal Republic of Germany:

We are that country whose recent political history was darkened by the attempt to systematically exterminate the Jewish people. And in this period of National Socialism - despite the exemplary behavior of some individuals and groups - we were nevertheless, as a whole, a church community who kept on living our lives while turning our backs too often on the fate of this persecuted Jewish people. We looked too fixedly at the threat to our own institutions and remained silent about the crimes committed against the Jews and Judaism. . . . The practical sincerity of our will of renewal is also linked to the confession of this guilt and the willingness to painfully learn from this history of guilt of our country and of our Church as well. ("Our Hope" Resolution of November 2, 1975).

We request the Jewish people to hear this word of conversion and will of renewal.

Auschwitz faces us Christians with the question of what relationship we have with the Jews and whether this relationship corresponds to the spirit of Jesus Christ. Antisemitism is "a sin against God and humanity," as Pope John Paul II has said many times. In the Church there must not be any room for or consent to hostility towards Jews. Christians must not harbor aversion, dislike, and even less, feelings of hatred for Jews and Judaism. Wherever such an attitude comes to light, they have the duty to offer public and outspoken resistance.

The Church respects the autonomy of Judaism. Simultaneously she has to learn anew that she is descended from Israel and remains linked to its patrimony concerning faith, ethos and liturgy. Wherever it is possible, Christian and Jewish communities should cultivate mutual contacts. We have to do everything in our power to enable Jews and Christians in our country to live together as good neighbors. In this way they will make their own distinctive contribution to a Europe whose past was darkened by the Shoah and which, in the future, is to become a continent of solidarity.

Catholics Remember the Holocaust (Washington, DC: United States Catholic Conference, 1998), pp. 9-11. With Permission

The Victims of Nazi Ideology: Polish Bishops, January 1995

Half a century has passed since the liberation of the Auschwitz-Birkenau concentration camp on January 27, 1945. Once again our attention is drawn to the painful reality and symbolism of this camp, where more than 1 million Jews, Poles (70,000-75,000), Gypsies (21,000), Russians (15,000), and other nationalities (10,000-15,000) found an atrocious death.

Only a few months into the war, in the spring of 1940, the Nazi Germans created the Auschwitz concentration camp on occupied Polish territory annexed to the Third Reich. At the beginning of its existence, the first prisoners and victims were thousands of Poles, mainly intelligentsia, members of the resistance movement as well as clergy and people representing almost all walks of life. There probably isn't a Polish family that hasn't lost someone close at Auschwitz or at another camp. With great respect we bow our heads before the infinite suffering which was often accepted in a deep Christian spirit. An eloquent example is the heroic figure of Fr. Maximilian Kolbe, who sacrificed his life for a fellow prisoner in August 1941. He was beatified by Pope Paul VI and canonized by Pope John Paul II. His victory, motivated by the Gospel of Jesus Christ, bears witness to the power of love and goodness in a world of outrage and violence.

Almost from the beginning, Polish Jews were sent to this camp, as part of Polish society, to be destroyed. Since 1942, the Auschwitz-Birkenau complex, as well as other camps in occupied Poland, as a result of the Wannsee Conference became extermination camps to realize the criminal ideology of the "final solution," in other words, the plan to murder all European Jews. The Nazis transported to the death camps Jews from all European countries occupied by Hitler. Not only Auschwitz, but also Majdanek, Treblinka, Belzec, Chelmno, and others were located in occupied Poland by the Germans as places to exterminate Jews, because this was where the majority of European Jews lived and, therefore, such a Nazi crime could be better hidden from world public opinion in a country totally occupied and even partly annexed to the Third Reich.

It is estimated today that more than 1 million Jews died at Auschwitz-Birkenau alone. Consequently, even though members of other nations also perished at this camp, nevertheless, Jews consider this camp a symbol of the total extermination of their nation. "The very people who received from God the commandment "Thou shalt not kill," itself experienced in a particular way what is meant by killing" (John Paul II, homily at Auschwitz-Birkenau death camp, June 7, 1979).

Extermination, called Shoah, has weighed painfully not only in relations between Germans and Jews, but also to a great extent in relations between Jews and Poles, who together, though not to the same degree, were the victims of Nazi ideology. Because they lived in close proximity, they became involuntary witnesses to the extermination of Jews. Regretfully, it has to be stated that for many years Auschwitz-Birkenau was treated by the communist regime almost entirely in terms of an anti-fascist struggle that did not help to convey the extent of the extermination of Jews.

It must be underlined that Poles and Jews have lived in this country for centuries, and although now and again conflicts did arise, they considered it their homeland. Driven out of western Europe, Jews found refuge in Poland. Consequently, Poland often had the reputation of being paradisus Judaerorum ("a Jewish paradise"), because here they could live according to their customs, religion, and culture. Contrary to many European countries, until the time of World War II, Jews were never driven out of Poland. About 80 percent of Jews living in the world today can trace their descent through their parents and/or grandparents to roots in Poland.

The loss of Polish independence and Poland's partition by Russia, Austria, and Prussia -which lasted more than 120 years - brought about, in the midst of other dramatic consequences, a deterioration in Polish Jewish relations. In the period of time between World War I and World War II, when Poland, after regaining her independence in 1918, sought to find forms of her own identity, new conflicts arose. Their underlying factors were of psychological, economic, political and religious nature but never racist. Despite the antisemitism of some circles, shortly before the outbreak of World War II, when Hitler's repressions intensified, it was Poland that accepted thousands of Jews from Germany.

Seeing the Nazi extermination of Jews, many Poles reacted with heroic courage and sacrifice, risking their lives and that of their families. The virtues of the Gospel and solidarity with the suffering and the persecuted motivated almost every convent in the general government to give Jewish children refuge. Many Poles lost their lives, in defiance of threats of the death penalty with regard to themselves and their family members, because they dared to shelter Jews. It should be mentioned that, as a consequence of giving refuge to Jews, the rule of common responsibility was applied to Poles. Often whole families, from children to grandparents, were killed for harboring Jews. In acknowledgment of this, thousands were awarded with medals "righteous among the nations of the world." Nameless others also brought help.

Unfortunately, there were also those who were capable of actions unworthy of being called Christian. There were those who not only blackmailed, but also gave away Jews in hiding into German hands. Nothing can justify such an attitude, though the inhumane time of war and the cruelty of the Nazis led to Jews, themselves tormented by the occupier, being forced to hand over their brothers into the hands of the Germans. Once again, we recall the words of the Polish bishops' pastoral letter that was read at all Catholic churches and chapels on January 20, 1991, which stated: "In spite of numerous heroic examples of Polish Christians, there were those who remained indifferent to that inconceivable tragedy. In particular, we mourn the fact that there were also those among Catholics who in some way had contributed to the death of Jews. They will forever remain a source of remorse in the social dimension."

The creators of Auschwitz were the Nazi Germans, not Poles. Everything that symbolizes this death camp is a result of a National Socialist ideology that was not born in Poland. Another totalitarian system, similar to the Nazi, which was communism, gathered many millions in a harvest of death. Nazism also meant trampling on the dignity of the human being as an image of God. There existed a dramatic community of fate between Poles and Jews in constraint and ruthless extermination. However, it was the Jews who became the victims of the Nazi plan of systematic and total liquidation. "An insane ideology decided on this plan in the name of a wretched form of racism and carried it out mercilessly" (John Paul II, beatification of Edith Stein, Cologne, Germany, May 1, 1987).

The world in which the cruelties of Auschwitz were carried out was also a world redeemed and at the same time a world of challenge, even after the Shoah, from where arises the message to all Christians that they should reveal God in their actions and not contribute to the questioning of his presence. God was and continues to be everywhere. What is satanic and represents hatred never originates from God but from man, who submits himself to the influence of the Evil One and doesn't respect the dignity of the human being or God's commandments.

The half century that has passed since the liberation of Auschwitz-Birkenau obliges us to express a clear objection to all signs of disregard for human dignity such as racism, antisemitism, xenophobia, and anti-Polish attitudes. Living in a country marked with the burden of a horrible event called Shoah, with Edith Stein, who died at Auschwitz because she was a Jew, with faith and total confidence in God, the Father of all humanity, we emphatically repeat: Hatred will never have the last word in this world (John Paul II's message prior to visiting the Federal Republic of Germany, April 25, 1987).

The only guarantee of this is to educate future generations in the spirit of mutual respect, tolerance, and love according to the recommendations contained in the Holy See's Notes on the Correct Way to Present the Jews and Judaism in Preaching and Catechesis in the Catholic Church (June 24, 1985).

Catholics Remember the Holocaust (Washington, DC: United States Catholic Conference, 1998), pp. 12-15. With Permission

Excerpt from the Declaration of Repentance: French Bishops, Drancy, September 1997

As one of the major events of the twentieth century, the planned extermination of the Jewish people by the Nazis raises particularly challenging questions of conscience which no human being can ignore. The Catholic Church, far from wanting it to be forgotten, knows full well that conscience is formed in remembering, and that, just as no individual person can live in peace with himself, neither can society live in peace with a repressed or untruthful memory.

The Church of France questions itself. It, like the other churches, has been called to do so by Pope John Paul II as the third millennium draws near: "It is good that the Church should cross this threshold fully conscious of what she has lived through. . . . Recognizing the failings of yesteryear is an act of loyalty and courage which helps us strengthen our faith, which makes us face up to the temptations and difficulties of today and prepares us to confront them."[1] . . .

The time has come for the Church to submit her own history, especially that of this period, to critical examination and to recognize without hesitation the sins committed by members of the Church, and to beg forgiveness of God and humankind.

In France, the violent persecution did not begin immediately. But very soon, in the months that followed the 1940 defeat, antisemitism was sown at the state level, depriving French Jews of their rights and foreign Jews of their freedom. All of our national institutions were drawn into the application of these legal measures. By February 1941, some 40,000 Jews were in French internment camps. At this point, in a country which had been beaten, lay prostrate, and was partially occupied, the hierarchy saw the protection of its own faithful as its first priority, assuring as much as possible its own institutions. The absolute priority which was given to these objectives, in themselves legitimate, had the unhappy effect of casting a shadow over the biblical demand of respect for every human being created in the image of God.

This retreat into a narrow vision of the Church's mission was compounded by a lack of appreciation on the part of the hierarchy of the immense global tragedy which was being played out and which was a threat to Christianity's future. Yet many members of the Church and many non-Catholics yearned for the church to speak out at a time of such spiritual confusion and to recall the message of Jesus Christ.

For the most part, those in authority in the Church, caught up in a loyalism and docility which went far beyond the obedience traditionally accorded civil authorities, remained stuck in conformity, prudence and abstention. This was dictated in part by their fear of reprisals against the church's activities and youth movements. They failed to realize that the Church, called at that moment to play the role of defender within a social body that was falling apart, did in fact have considerable power and influence, and that in the face of the silence of other institutions, its voice could have echoed loudly by taking a definitive stand against the irreparable. . . .

So it is that, given the antisemitic legislation enacted by the French government - beginning with the October 1940 law on Jews and that of June 1941, which deprived a whole sector of the French people of their rights as citizens, which hounded them out and treated them as inferior beings within the nation - and given the decision to put into internment camps foreign Jews who had thought they could rely on the right of asylum and hospitality in France, we are obliged to admit that the bishops of France made no public statements, thereby acquiescing by their silence in the flagrant violation of human rights and leaving the way open to a death-bearing chain of events.

We pass no judgement either on the consciences or on the people of that era; we are not ourselves guilty of what took place in the past; but we must be fully aware of the cost of such behavior and such actions. It is our Church, and we are obliged to acknowledge objectively today that ecclesiastical interests, understood in an overly restrictive sense, took priority over the demands of conscience - and we must ask ourselves why.

Over and above the historical circumstances which we already have recalled, we need to pay special attention to the religious reasons for this blindness. To what extent did secular antisemitism have an influence? Why is it, in the debates which we know took place, that the Church did not listen to the better claims of its members' voices? . . .

In the process which led to the Shoah, we are obliged to admit the role, indirect if not direct, played by commonly held anti-Jewish prejudices, which Christians were guilty of maintaining. In fact, in spite of (and to some extent because of) the Jewish roots of Christianity, and because of the Jewish people's fidelity throughout its history to the one God, the "original separation" dating back to the first century became a divorce, then an animosity, and ultimately a centuries-long hostility between Christians and Jews. . . .

In the judgement of historians, it is a well-proven fact that for centuries, up until Vatican Council II, an anti-Jewish tradition stamped its mark in differing ways on Christian doctrine and teaching, in theology, apologetics, preaching and in the liturgy. It was on such ground that the venomous plant of hatred for the Jews was able to flourish. Hence, the heavy inheritance we still bear in our century, with all its consequences which are so difficult to wipe out. Hence our still open wounds.

To the extent that the pastors and those in authority in the Church let such a teaching of disdain develop for so long, along with an underlying basic religious culture among Christian communities which shaped and deformed people's attitudes, they bear a grave responsibility. Even if they condemned antisemitic theories as being pagan in origin, they did not enlighten people's minds as they ought because they failed to call into question these centuries-old ideas and attitudes. This had a soporific effect on people's consciences, reducing their capacity to resist when the full violence of National Socialist antisemitism rose up, the diabolical and ultimate expression of hatred of the Jews, based on the categories of race and blood, and which was explicitly directed to the physical annihilation of the Jewish people. As Pope John Paul II put it, "an unconditional extermination . . . undertaken with premeditation."

Subsequently, when the persecution became worse and the genocidal policy of the Third Reich was unleashed within France itself, shared by the Vichy government, which put its own police force at the disposition of the occupier, some brave bishops[2] raised their voices in a clarion call, in the name of human rights, against the rounding up of the Jewish population. These public statement, though few in number, were heard by many Christians. . . .

Nevertheless while it may be true that some Christians - priest, religious and lay people - were not lacking in acts of courage in defense of fellow human beings, we must recognize that indifference won the day over indignation in the face of the persecution of the Jews and that, in particular, silence was the rule in face of the multifarious laws enacted by the Vichy government, whereas speaking out in favor of the victims was the exception.

As Franáois Mauriac wrote, "A crime of such proportions falls for no small part on the shoulders of all those witnesses who failed to cry out, and this whatever the reason for their silence.[3] . . .

Today we confess that such a silence was a sin. In so doing, we recognize that the Church of France failed in her mission as a teacher of conscience and that therefore she carries along with the Christian people the responsibility for failing to lend their aid, from the very first moment, when protest and protection were sill possible as well as necessary, even if, subsequently, a great many acts of courage were performed.

This is the fact that we acknowledge today. For this failing of the Church of France and of her responsibility toward the Jewish people are part of our history. We confess this sin. We beg God's pardon, and we call upon the Jewish people to hear our words of repentance.

This act of remembering calls us to an ever keener vigilance on behalf of humankind today and in the future.

Notes:

1 John Paul II, On the Coming of the Third Millennium (Tertio Millennio Adveniente) no. 33.
2 In 1942, five archbishops and bishops in the southern (unoccupied) part of France protested against the violation of human rights caused by the rounding up of the Jews. They were Archbishop Saliege of Toulouse; Bishop Theas of Montauban; Cardinal Gerlier of Lyons; Archbishop Moussaron of Albi and Bishop Daly of Marseilles. Within the occupied zone, Bishop Vansteenberghe of Bayonne published a protest on the front page of his diocesan newsletter Sept. 20, 1942
3 From the Preface to Leon Poliakov's book, Brèviare de la haine (Breviary of Hate) 1951, p.3.

N.B.

- The German bishops and the Polish bishops each published a declaration on the attitude of their churches during the war on the occasion of the fiftieth anniversary of the liberation of Auschwitz.
- The legislation passed by the Vichy government, and particularly the Jewish statutes of 1940 and 1941, can be found in Les Juifs sous l'Occupation. Recueil des textes officiels francáis et allemands 1940-1944, published by the FFDJF (1982) as well as in Michael R. Marrus and Robert O. Paxton, Vichy France and the Jews (New York: Schocken Books, 1983).
- The main stances taken by Protestants can be found in Spiritualitè, Thèologie et Rèsistance (Presses Universitairs de Grenoble, 1987), pp.151-182

Catholics Remember the Holocaust (Washington, DC: United States Catholic Conference, 1998), pp. 31-37. With Permission

★   ★   ★   ★

Letter of Pope John Paul II

To my venerable brother, Cardinal Edward Idris Cassidy:

On numerous occasions during my Pontificate I have recalled with a sense of deep sorrow the sufferings of the Jewish people during the Second World War. The crime which has become known as the Shoah remains an indelible stain on the history of the century that is coming to a close.

As we prepare for the beginning of the Third Millennium of Christianity, the Church is aware that the joy of a jubilee is above all the joy that is based on the forgiveness of sins and reconciliation with God and neighbor. Therefore she encourages her sons and daughters to purify their hearts through repentance of past errors and infidelities. She calls them to place themselves humbly before the Lord and examine themselves on the responsibility which they too have for the evils of our time.

It is my fervent hope that the document "We Remember: A Reflection on the Shoah", which the Commission for Religious Relations with the Jews has prepared under your direction, will indeed help to heal the wounds of past misunderstandings and injustices. May it enable memory to play its necessary part in the process of shaping a future in which the unspeakable iniquity of the Shoah will never again be possible. May the Lord of history guide the efforts of Catholics and Jews and all men and women of good will as they work together for a world of true respect for the life and dignity of every human being, for all have been created in the image and likeness of God.

March 12, 1998

Catholics Remember the Holocaust Washington, DC: United States Catholic Conference, 1998), p43. With Permission

We Remember: A Reflection on the Shoah
Holy See's Commission for Religious Relations with the Jews
March 1998

I. The Tragedy of the Shoah and the Duty of Remembrance

The twentieth century is fast coming to a close and a new Millennium of the Christian era is about to dawn. The 2000th anniversary of the Birth of Jesus Christ calls all Christians, and indeed invites all men and women, to seek to discern in the passage of history the signs of divine Providence at work, as well as the ways in which the image of the Creator in man has been offended and disfigured.

This reflection concerns one of the main areas in which Catholics can seriously take to heart the summons which Pope John Paul II has addressed to them in his Apostolic Letter Tertio Millennio Adveniente:

It is appropriate that as the Second Millennium of Christianity draws to a close the Church should become more fully conscious of the sinfulness of her children, recalling all those times in history when they departed from the spirit of Christ and his Gospel and, instead of offering to the world the witness of a life inspired by the values of faith, indulged in ways of thinking and acting which were truly forms of counter-witness and scandal.[1]

This century has witnessed an unspeakable tragedy, which can never be forgotten: the attempt by the Nazi regime to exterminate the Jewish people, with the consequent killing of millions of Jews. Women and men, old and young, children and infants, for the sole reason of their Jewish origin, were persecuted and deported. Some were killed immediately, while others were degraded, ill-treated, tortured and utterly robbed of their human dignity, and then murdered. Very few of those who entered the camps survived, and those who did remained scarred for life. This was the Shoah. It is a major fact of the history of this century, a fact which still concerns us today.

Before this horrible genocide, which the leaders of nations and Jewish communities themselves found hard to believe at the very moment when it was mercilessly being put into effect, no one can remain indifferent, least of all the Church, by reason of her very close bonds of spiritual kinship with the Jewish people and her remembrance of the injustices of the past. The Church's relationship to the Jewish people is unlike the one she shares with any other religion.[2] However, it is not only a question of recalling the past. The common future of Jews and Christians demands that we remember, for "there is no future without memory."[3] History itself is memoria futuri.

In addressing this reflection to our brothers and sisters of the Catholic Church throughout the world, we ask all Christians to join us in meditating on the catastrophe which befell the Jewish people and on the moral imperative to ensure that never again will selfishness and hatred grow to the point of sowing such suffering and death.[4] Most especially, we ask our Jewish friends, "whose terrible fate has become a symbol of the aberrations of which man is capable when he turns against God,"[5] to hear us with open hearts.

II. What We Must Remember

While bearing their unique witness to the Holy One of Israel and to the Torah, the Jewish people have suffered much at different times and in many places. But the Shoah was certainly the worst suffering of all. The inhumanity with which the Jews were persecuted and massacred during this century is beyond the capacity of words to convey. All this was done to them for the sole reason that they were Jews.

The very magnitude of the crime raises many questions. Historians, sociologists, political philosophers, psychologists and theologians are all trying to learn more about the reality of the Shoah and its causes. Much scholarly study still remains to be done. But such an event cannot be fully measured by the ordinary criteria of historical research alone. It calls more for a "moral and religious memory" and, particularly among Christians, a very serious reflection on what gave rise to it.

The fact that the Shoah took place in Europe, that is, in countries of long-standing Christian civilization, raises the question of the relation between the Nazi persecution and the attitudes down the centuries of Christians towards Jews.

III. Relations Between Jews and Christians

The history of relations between Jews and Christians is a tormented one. His Holiness Pope John Paul II has recognized this fact in his repeated appeals to Catholics to see where we stand with regard to our relations with the Jewish people.[6] In effect, the balance of these relations over two thousand years has been quite negative.[7]

At the dawn of Christianity, after the crucifixion of Jesus, there arose disputes between the early Church and the Jewish leaders and people who, in their devotion to the law, on occasion violently opposed the preachers of the Gospel and the first Christians. In the pagan Roman Empire, Jews were legally protected by the privileges granted by the emperor and the authorities at first made no distinction between Jewish and Christian communities. Soon, however, Christians incurred the persecution of the State. Later, when the Emperors themselves converted to Christianity, they at first continued to guarantee Jewish privileges. But Christian mobs who attacked pagan temples sometimes did the same to synagogues, not without being influenced by certain interpretations of the New Testament regarding the Jewish people as a whole. "In the Christian world - I do not say on the part of the Church as such - erroneous and unjust interpretations of the New Testament regarding the Jewish people and their alleged culpability have circulated for too long, engendering feelings of hostility towards this people."[8] Such interpretations of the New Testament have been totally and definitively rejected by the Second Vatican Council.[9]

Despite the Christian preaching of love for all, even for one's enemies, the prevailing mentality down the centuries penalized minorities and those who were in any way "different". Sentiments of anti-Judaism in some Christian quarters, and the gap which existed between the Church and the Jewish people, led to a generalized discrimination, which ended at times in expulsions or attempts at forced conversions. In a large part of the "Christian" world, at the end of the eighteenth century, those who were not Christian did not always enjoy a fully guaranteed juridical status. Despite that fact, Jews throughout Christendom held on to their religious traditions and communal customs. They were therefore looked upon with a certain suspicion and mistrust. In times of crisis such as famine, war, pestilence or social tensions, the Jewish minority was sometimes taken as a scapegoat and became the victim of violence, looting, even massacres.

By the end of the eighteenth century and the beginning of the nineteenth century, Jews generally had achieved an equal standing with other citizens in most States and a certain number of them held influential positions in society. But in that same historical context, notably in the nineteenth century, a false and exacerbated nationalism took hold. In a climate of eventful social change, Jews were often accused of exercising an influence disproportionate to their numbers. Thus there began to spread in varying degrees throughout most of Europe an anti-Judaism that was essentially more sociological and political than religious.

At the same time, theories began to appear which denied the unity of the human race, affirming an original diversity of races. In the twentieth century, National Socialism in Germany used these ideas as a pseudo-scientific basis for a distinction between so called Nordic-Aryan races and supposedly inferior races. Furthermore, an extremist form of nationalism was heightened in Germany by the defeat of 1918 and the demanding conditions imposed by the victors, with the consequence that many saw in National Socialism a solution to their country's problems and cooperated politically with this movement.

The Church in Germany replied by condemning racism. The condemnation first appeared in the preaching of some of the clergy, in the public teaching of the Catholic bishops, and in the writings of lay Catholic journalists. Already in February and March 1931, Cardinal Bertram of Breslau, Cardinal Faulhaber and the Bishops of Bavaria, the bishops of the Province of Cologne and those of the province of Freiburg published pastoral letters condemning National Socialism, with its idolatry of race and of the state.[10] The well-known Advent sermons of Cardinal Faulhaber in 1933, the very year in which National Socialism came to power, at which not just Catholics but also Protestants and Jews were present, clearly expressed rejection of the Nazi anti-Semitic propaganda.[11] In the wake of the Kristallnacht, Bernard Lichtenberg, Provost of a Berlin Cathedral, offered public prayers for the Jews. He was later to die at Dachau and has been declared blessed.

Pope Pius XI too condemned Nazi racism in a solemn way in his encyclical letter Mit brennender Sorge,[12] which was read in German churches on Passion Sunday 1937, a step which resulted in attacks and sanctions against members of the clergy. Addressing a group of Belgian pilgrims on 6 September 1938, Pius XI asserted: "Anti-Semitism is unacceptable. Spiritually, we are all Semites".[13] Pius XII, in his very first encyclical, Summi Pontificatus, of October 20, 1939,[14] warned against theories which denied the unity of the human race and against the deification of the State, all of which he saw as leading to a real "hour of darkness."[15]

IV. Nazi anti-Semitism and the Shoah

Thus we cannot ignore the difference which exists between antisemitism, based on theories contrary to the constant teaching of the Church on the unity of the human race and on the equal dignity of all races and peoples, and the long-standing sentiments of mistrust and hostility that we call anti-Judaism, of which, unfortunately, Christians also have been guilty.

The National Socialist ideology went even further, in the sense that it refused to acknowledge any transcendent reality as the source of life and the criterion of moral good. Consequently, a human group, and the state with which it was identified, arrogated to itself an absolute status and determined to remove the very existence of the Jewish people, a people called to witness to the one God and the law of the covenant. At the level of theological reflection we cannot ignore the fact that not a few in the Nazi party not only showed aversion to the idea of divine Providence at work in human affairs, but gave proof of a definite hatred directed at God himself. Logically, such an attitude also led to a rejection of Christianity and a desire to see the Church destroyed or at least subjected to the interests of the Nazi state.

It was this extreme ideology which became the basis of the measures taken first to drive the Jews from their homes and then to exterminate them. The Shoah was the work of a thoroughly modern neo-pagan regime. Its antisemitism had its roots outside of Christianit, and in pursuing its aims, it did not hesitate to oppose the Church and persecute her members also.

But it may be asked whether the Nazi persecution of the Jews was not made easier by the anti-Jewish prejudices imbedded in some Christian minds and hearts. Did anti-Jewish sentiment among Christians make them less sensitive, or even indifferent, to the persecution launched against the Jews by National Socialism when it reached power?

Any response to this question must take into account that we are dealing with the history of people's attitudes and ways of thinking, subject to multiple influences. Moreover, many people were altogether unaware of the "final solution" that was being put into effect against a whole people; others were afraid for themselves and those near to them; some took advantage of the situation; and still others were moved by envy. A response would need to be given case by case. To do this, however, it is necessary to know what precisely motivated people in a particular situation.

At first the leaders of the Third Reich sought to expel the Jews. Unfortunately, the governments of some Western countries of Christian tradition, including some in North and South America, were more than hesitant to open their borders to the persecuted Jews. Although they could not foresee how far the Nazi hierarchs would go in their criminal intentions, the leaders of those nations were aware of the hardships and dangers to which Jews living in the territories of the Third Reich were exposed. The closing of borders to Jewish emigration in those circumstances, whether due to any anti-Jewish hostility or suspicion, political cowardice, or shortsightedness, or national selfishness, lays a heavy burden of conscience on the authorities in question.

In the lands where the Nazis undertook mass deportations, the brutality which surrounded these forced movements of helpless people should have led to suspect the worst. Did Christians give every possible assistance to those being persecuted and, in particular, to the persecuted Jews?

Many did, but others did not. Those who did help to save Jewish lives as much as was in their power, even to the point of placing their own lives in danger, must not be forgotten. During and after the war, Jewish communities and Jewish leaders expressed their thanks for all that had been done for them, including what Pope Pius XII did personally or through his representatives to save hundreds of thousands of Jewish lives.[16] Many Catholic bishops, priests, religious, and laity have been honored for this reason by the State of Israel.

Nevertheless, as Pope John Paul II has recognized, alongside such courageous men and women, the spiritual resistance and concrete action of other Christians was not that which might have been expected from Christ's followers. We cannot know how many Christians in countries occupied or ruled by the Nazi powers or their allies were horrified at the disappearance of their Jewish neighbors and yet were not strong enough to raise their voices in protest. For Christians, this heavy burden of conscience of their brothers and sisters during the Second World War must be a call to penitence.[17]

We deeply regret the errors and failures of those sons and daughters of the Church. We make our own what is said in the Second Vatican Council's Declaration Nostra Aetate, which unequivocally affirms: "The Church . . . mindful of her common patrimony with the Jews, and motivated by the Gospel's spiritual love and by no political considerations, deplores the hatred, persecutions and displays of antisemitism directed against the Jews at any time and in any form and from any source."[18]

We recall and abide by what Pope John Paul II, addressing the leaders of the Jewish community in Strasbourg in 1988, stated: "I repeat again with you the strongest condemnation of antisemitism and racism, which are opposed to the principles of Christianity."[19] The Catholic Church therefore repudiates every persecution against a people or human group anywhere, at any time. She absolutely condemns all forms of genocide as well as the racist ideologies that give rise to them. Looking back over this century, we are deeply saddened by the violence that has enveloped whole groups of peoples and nations. We recall in particular the massacre of the Armenians, the countless victims in Ukraine in the 1930's, the genocide of the Gypsies, which was also the result of racist ideas, and similar tragedies which have occurred in America, Africa and the Balkans. Nor do we forget the millions of victims of totalitarian ideology in the Soviet Union, in China, Cambodia and elsewhere. Nor can we forget the drama of the Middle East, the elements of which are well known. Even as we make this reflection, "many human beings are still their brothers' victims."[20]

V. Looking Together to a Common Future

Looking to the future of relations between Jews and Christians, in the first place we appeal to our Catholic brothers and sisters to renew the awareness of the Hebrew roots of their faith. We ask them to keep in mind that Jesus was a descendant of David; that the Virgin Mary and the Apostles belonged to the Jewish people; that the Church draws sustenance from the root of that good olive tree on to which have been grafted the wild olive branches of the gentiles (cf. Romans 11:17-24); that the Jews are our dearly beloved brothers, indeed in a certain sense they are "our elder brothers."[21]

At the end of this Millennium the Catholic Church desires to express her deep sorrow for the failures of her sons and daughters in every age. This is an act of repentance (teshuvah), since, as members of the Church, we are linked to the sins as well as the merits of all her children. The Church approaches with deep respect and great compassion the experience of extermination, the Shoah, suffered by the Jewish people during World War II. It is not a matter of mere words, but indeed of binding commitment. "We would risk causing the victims of the most atrocious deaths to die again if we do not have an ardent desire for justice, if we do not commit ourselves to ensure that evil does not prevail over good as it did for millions of children of the

Jewish people. . . . Humanity cannot permit all that to happen again."[22]

We pray that our sorrow for the tragedy which the Jewish people has suffered in our century will lead to a new relationship with the Jewish people. We wish to turn awareness of past sins into a firm resolve to build a new future in which there will be no more anti-Judaism among Christians or anti-Christian sentiment among Jews, but rather a shared mutual respect, as befits those who adore the one Creator and Lord and have a common father in faith, Abraham.

Finally, we invite all men and women of good will to reflect deeply on the significance of the Shoah. The victims from their graves and the survivors through the vivid testimony of what they have suffered, have become a loud voice calling the attention of all of humanity. To remember this terrible experience is to become fully conscious of the salutary warning it entails: The spoiled seeds of anti-Judaism and antisemitism must never again be allowed to take root in any human heart.

March 16, 1998.

Cardinal Edward Idris Cassidy President,

Bishop Pierre Duprey Vice-President,

Rev. Remi Hoeckman, OP, Secretary

Notes

1. John Paul II, apostolic letter Tertio Millennio Adveniente Sedis (AAS) 87 (1995): 25, no. 33.
2. Cf. John Paul II, speech at the Rome synagogue, April 13, 1986. AAS 78 (1986): 1120, no. 4.
3. John Paul II, Angelus prayer, June 11, 1995. Insegnamenti 18/1 (1995): 1712.
4. Cf. John Paul II, address to Jewish leaders in Budapest, August 18, 1991. Insegnamenti 14/7 (1991): 349, no. 4.
5. John Paul II, encyclical Centesimus Annus. AAS 83 (1991) 814-815, no. 17.
6. Cf. John Paul II address to episcopal conferences'delegates for Catholic-Jewish relations, March 6, 1982. Insegnamenti 5/1 (1982): 743-747.
7. Cf. Holy See's Commission for Religious Relations with the Jews, Notes on the Correct Way to Present the Jews and Judaism in Preaching and Catechesis in the Roman Catholic Church, June 24, 1985, VI, 1. Enchiridion Vaticanum 9, 1656.
8. Cf. John Paul II, speech to symposium on the roots of Anti-Judaism, October 31, 1997. L'Osservatore Romano (November 1, 1997): 6, no. 1.
9. Cf. Vatican Council II, Nostra Aetate, no. 4.
10. Cf.B. Statiewski, ed., Akten Deutscher Bisch^fe ‹ber die Lage der Kirche, 1933-1945, Vol. I, 1933-1934 (Mainz, 1968), Appendix.
11. Cf. L. Volk, Der Bayerische Episkopat und der Nationalsozialismus 1930-1934 (Mainz, 1966), 170-174.
12. The encyclical is dated March 14, 1937. AAS 29 (1937): 145-167.
13. La Documentation Catholique, 29 (1938): col. 1460.
14. AAS 31 (1939): 413-453.
15. Ibid., 449.
16. The wisdom of Pope Pius XII's diplomacy was publically acknowledged on a number of occasions by representative Jewish organizations and personalities.
17. Cf. John Paul II, address to the Federal German Republic's new ambassador to the Holy See, November 8, 1990. AAS 83 (1991): 587-588, no. 2.
18. Nostra Aetate, no. 4. Translation by Walter M. Abbott, SJ, in The Documents of Vatican II.
19. John Paul II, address to Jewish leaders in Strasbourg, October 9, 1988. Insegnamenti 11/3 (1988): 1134, no. 8.
20. John Paul II, address to the diplomatic corps, January 15, 1994. AAS 86 (1994): 816, no. 9.
21. John Paul II, Rome synagogue speech, no. 4.
22. John Paul II, address at a commemoration of the Shoah, April 7, 1994. Insegnamenti 17/1 (1994): 897 and 893, no. 3.

Catholics Remember the Holocaust (Washington, DC: United States Catholic Conference, 1998), pp. 47-56. With Permission

Excerpt from the Declaration of the General Synod of the Evangelical Church A.B. and H.B.[Augsburg and Helvetian Confessions] in Austria: Vienna, Austria, October 28, 1998

November 9th [1998] will see the 60th anniversary of the 1938 pogrom against Jews. This event prompts us Protestant Christians and churches in Austria to again grapple with this century's dreadful history of the deliberate attempt to annihilate Europe's Jews. The part played by Christians and churches and their shared responsibility for the suffering and misery of Jews can no longer be denied. . . .

We realize with shame that our churches showed themselves inured by the fate of the Jews and countless other victims of persecution. This is all the more incomprehensible because Protestant Christians in their own history, especially in the Counter-Reformation, were themselves discriminated against and persecuted. The churches did not protest against visible injustice; they were silent and looked away; they did not "throw themselves into the spokes of the wheel" (Bonhoeffer).

Therefore, not only individual Christians but also our churches share in the guilt of the Holocaust/Shoah.

We remember with grief all victims of persecution who were divested of their civil rights and their human dignity, abandoned to an unrelenting pursuit and murdered in concentration camps.

The General Synod asks the Jewish congregations [Israelitische Kultusgemeinden] and the Jews in Austria to receive the following assurance:

* The Evangelical Churches know themselves obliged to always keep alive the memory of the Jewish people's history of suffering and of the Shoah.
* The Evangelical Churches know themselves obliged to check the teaching, sermons, instruction, liturgy and practice of the church for any antisemitism and to also, through its media, stand up against prejudices.
* The Evangelical Churches know themselves obliged to fight every social and personal antisemitism.
* The Evangelical Churches want, in their relations to Jews and Jewish congregations, to walk a common way into a new future.

Therefore, we make an effort to reconsider and shape the relationship of Protestant Christians and Jews accordingly.

The evolution of antisemitism into the Shoah represents for us as Protestant churches and Protestant Christians a challenge that reaches down into the roots of our faith. The God of Christians is no other than the God of Israel who called Abraham to faith and chose the enslaved Israelites to be his people. We profess to the permanent election of Israel as God's people. "God did not terminate this covenant" (Martin Buber). It exists to the end of time. . . .

. . . we as Protestant Christians are burdened by the late writings of Luther and their demand for expulsion and persecution of the Jews. We reject the contents of these writings.

The biological and political racism of the 19th and 20th centuries was able to make use of Christian anti-Judaism for its religious-ideological confirmation. Against this there was hardly any resistance in our churches. Rather, Protestant Christians and pastors also involved themselves in antisemitic propaganda. If the churches looked after persecuted Jews, it looked mainly after those who were baptized.

This, our burdened past, demands an about-turn which comprises the church's interpretation of the Holy Scriptures, its theology, teaching and practice. . . .

Excerpt retrieved from the World Wide Web: http://www.jcrelations.com

VIDEOGRAPHY

Carol Rittner   Stephen Smith
With the Assistance of Amy Kettler and Henry Klos

Act of Faith
28 min'ts / ADL of B'nai B'rith, New York, NY

The dramatic story of the heroic Danish resistance movement against Hitler. Filmed in Denmark, it is a first hand account of the role played by the Danish people in saving their Jewish countrymen from Nazi extermination.

The American Expression: Radio Priest
58 min'ts / PBS Video, Alexandria, VA

During the Depression, Father Charles Coughlin was almost as popular as Franklin Delano Roosevelt. Millions of Americans listened every Sunday to the 'Radio Priest.' Coughlin eventually began allying himself with the fascists who were gaining control of Europe.

As If It Were Yesterday
85 min'ts / 1980 Almi Home Video Corp., New York, NY

Film documents the heroism of the Belgian people who, during the Nazi occupation, hid or helped more than 4,000 Jewish children escape deportation and extermination.

The Assisi Underground
115 min'ts / 1985 Social Studies School Service, Culver City, CA

Film sheds light on the work done by the Catholic Church and the people of Assisi to rescue several hundred Italian Jews from Nazi execution following the German occupation of Italy in 1943.

Au Revoir Les Enfants (In French with English Subtitles)
103 min'ts / 1987 Social Studies School Service, Culver City, CA

During the German occupation of France, a Catholic school headmaster tries to hide the identification of some Jewish pupils. One of them befriends a Catholic boy with tragic results.

The Avenue of the Just
58 min'ts / 1983 ADL of B'nai B'rith, New York, NY

The title refers to the tree-lined walk at Yad Vashem honoring righteous Gentiles who saved the lives of Jews. There are interviews with men and women who sacrificed for others, and with some of the people they saved.

The Boat is Full
104 min'ts / Social Studies School Service, Culver City, CA

The haunting story of a group of Jewish refugees who escape from Nazi Germany and seek asylum in Switzerland. When their true identity becomes known, they are forced back to the German border by ordinary Swiss civilians who are indifferent to the plight of refugees.

Conspiracy of the Heart: Nuns Smuggling Jews
110 min'ts

Film about nuns in Nazi Germany who, at risk of their lives, assisted Jews.

Courage to Care
28 min'ts / 1986 PBS Video, Alexandria, VA

An unforgettable encounter with ordinary people who refused to succumb to Nazi tyranny. These people followed their conscience while others ' followed orders.'

The Cross and the Star
55 min'ts / First Run Icarus Films, New York, NY

This video boldly examines the Christian anti-Semitism that may have paved the way for the Holocaust. It argues that the ideological seeds which developed into the Nuremberg laws and then the death camps may have been sown into Christian dogma many centuries prior to the rise of the Third Reich.

Diamonds in the Snow

55 min'ts / Cinema Guild, New York, NY

Three women born in Bendzin, Poland recall a childhood of hiding from the Nazis, and reflect on the Polish-Christian rescuers who saved their lives.

Dietrich Bonhoeffer: Memories and Perspectives

60 min'ts / First Run Icarus Films, New York, NY

This documentary film explores Bonhoeffer's life and times in a chronological fashion: the American experience, the early years of the Church struggle, Bonhoeffer's peace sermon at Fano, the underground seminary at Finkenwald, the flight to America in 1939, his return to Germany, work in the resistance movement, and, finally, prison and death.

Drancy: A Concentration Camp in Paris, 1941-1944

55 min'ts / Filmmakers Library, New York, NY

The film details the complicity of the French authorities during the Nazi occupation in arresting and interning over 74,000 Jews in France prior to their transport to Auschwitz.

Genocide, 1941-1945 (World At War Series)

50 min'ts / 1982 Zenger Video, Culver City, CA

The story of the destruction of European Jewry is told using archival footage and testimonies of victims, perpetrators, and bystanders.

The Hangman

12 min'ts / 1964 McGraw-Hill Training System, Heightstown, NJ

Animation is used to illustrate the poem by Maurice Odgen about a town in which the people are hanged one by one by a mysterious hangman while the town stands by rationalizing each victimization.

The Hiding Place

145 min'ts / 1975 World Wide Pictures, Inc.

Filmed in Holland and other authentic European locations, the film traces the lives of Corrie ten Boom, her father, and sister Betsie, from the quiet years before World War II, to their work with the 'underground' in helping to save the lives of countless Jewish families.

History Undercover: Pope Pius XII and the Holocaust

46 min'ts / 1997 A&E Home Video

The same year that Hitler unleashed WWII, Eugenio Pacelli, Bishop of Padua, became Pope Pius XII and an opponent to totalitarian regimes. Then how do we explain his silence against the persecution of Jews by Hitler? The film searches for possible answers.

The Holocaust in a Catholic Educational Setting

28 min'ts / CSE-TV Productions, Morristown, NJ

Three faculty members discuss why and how they incorporate Holocaust studies into the curriculum at the College of Saint Elizabeth.

John Paul II: The Millennial Pope

150 min'ts / 1999 PBS Home Video, Alexandria, VA

This film is a journey through the twentieth century to the sources of his character and his beliefs, and a journey into our passionate reaction to him.

Jehovah's Witnesses Stand Firm Against Nazi Assault

78 min'ts / 1996 Watch Tower Bible and Tract Society of Pennsylvania, Brooklyn, NY

Historians from Europe and North America, and more than 20 Witness Survivors, relate the story of the thousands of Jehovah's Witnesses who suffered brutal persecution at the hands of the Nazis, but still stood firm in their beliefs.

Jewish Community of Salonika

11 min'ts / The National Center for Jewish Film, Waltham, MA

This film is based on historical photos from the period preceding the Second World War and describes the Jewish community of Salonika.

The Longest Hatred: The History of Anti-Semitism

180 min'ts / 1993 Films for the Humanities and Sciences, Princeton, NJ

Drawing on interviews with Jews and antisemites as well as prominent scholars in Europe, America, and the Middle East, this excellent video traces antisemitism from its earliest manifestations to recent outbreaks in Germany and Eastern Europe.

Miracle at Moreaux

58 min'ts / 1986 Social Studies School Services, Culver City, CA

In December 1943, three Jewish children fleeing Nazi-occupied France find refuge in a Catholic school run by Sister Gabrielle.

My Brother's Keeper

25 min'ts

Israel Birnbaum, an artist, tells the story of the Holocaust, in a series of dramatic paintings.

The Nazis: A Warning From History

300 min'ts / 1998 BBC/A&E Entertainment

Tells the story of the Nazis through the functioning of the Nazi state. Includes interviews and documentary footage.

Of Pure Blood

100 min'ts / 1972 Filmic Archives, Botsford, CT

Film chronicles the Nazis' attempts to create a 'master race.'

The Papal Concert to Commemorate the Holocaust

90 min'ts / 1994 Rhino Home Video

Conceived and organized by Pope John Paul II and American conductor Gilbert Levine, this remarkable musical event commemorates the Holocaust and celebrates the Vatican's recognition of the State of Israel.

Persecuted and Forgotten (The Gypsies of Auschwitz)

54 min'ts / 1989EBS Productions, San Francisco, CA

This video follows a group of German Gypsies as they return to Auschwitz after World War II.

Purple Triangles

25 min'ts / 1991 Watchtower Bible and Tract Society of New York, Inc., Brooklyn, NY

Documentary video detailing the persecution of Jehovah's Witnesses by the Nazi regime.

Religious Implications of the Holocaust

30 min'ts / Emory University, Atlanta, GA

Three religion and theology professors discuss the meaning of the Holocaust for today.

Rescue in Scandinavia

55 min'ts / Documentaries International, Washington, DC

This video focuses on the courageous acts Christian rescuers performed in order to guide thousands of Jews to safety in Sweden.

The Righteous Enemy

84 min'ts / The National Center for Jewish Film, Waltham, MA

A documentary that reveals the active protection given by Italian military and government officials to 40,000 Jews in Italian-occupied France, Greece, and Yugoslavia.

Shadow on the Cross

52 min'ts / 1990 Landmark Films Inc., Falls Church, VA

Film looks at the tragic story of Jewish-Christian relations over the past 2000 years and explores the influences of historic Christian antisemitism on the Third Reich.

The Star, The Castle & The Butterfly

25 min'ts / Shooting Stars Film and Video Distribution, London, UK

This film both celebrates and remembers a world and a time that is no more and which has left a lasting legacy of spirituality and beauty.

Triumph of Memory

30 min'ts / 1972 PBS Video, Alexandria, VA

Non-Jewish resistance fighters sent to Nazi concentration camps bear witness to the atrocities that took place in Mauthausen, Buchenwald, and Auschwitz-Birkenau.

So Many Miracles

58 min'ts / National Center for Jewish Film, Waltham, MA

This docudrama tells the story of how Zofia and Ludwig Banya and their son, Maniek, hid two Jews in their home in the Polish village of Pinczow.

The Sorrow and the Pity

242 min'ts / Prestige Film Corp., New York, NY

Film is an account of the German occupation of France, the French collaboration with the Nazis, and the subsequent rejection by the French of what they had done.

Teaching the Holocaust for Today's World

21 min'ts / Washington State Holocaust Education Resource Center, Seattle, WA

This video serves as a guide on how to teach the Holocaust.

They Risked Their Lives: Rescuers of the Holocaust

24 min'ts / Gay Block – Vendor

Righteous Gentiles, who have been honored at Yad Vashem for saving Jewish lives during the Holocaust, tell their stories.

Varian Fry : The Artist's Schindler

51 min'ts / 1997 A BBC/RM Arts Co-Production

An improbable pimpernel who rescued some 2,000 Europeans from the Nazis, Varian Fry was the United States' answer to Germany's Oskar Schindler.

Weapons of the Spirit

90 min'ts / 1990 Friends of Le Chambon, Los Angles, CA

(Also available in a 35 min'te classroom version distributed by ADL of B'nai B'rith, New York, NY)

Film tells the true story of a small French village that managed to save five thousand Jews from the Holocaust.

Where Shall We Go?

56 min'ts / 1991 Swingbridge Video, Newcastle upon Tyne, UK

This film makes it clear that not all Germans were Nazis, some non-Jews risked their lives to save Jews and Jewish people were not the only victims of the Holocaust.

The White Rose (German with English subtitles)

108 min'ts / Zenger Video, Culver City, CA

This film dramatizes the true story of a group of German students, the White Rose, who printed and distributed thousands of anti-Nazi leaflets during WWII.

Witnesses: Anti-Semitism in Poland – 1946

26 min'ts / Filmmakers Library, Inc., New York, NY

This films details the events of July 4, 1946, when Jewish survivors returned to the town of Kielce, Poland to reclaim their lives, but were attacked. Forty-two Jews were killed, and many more wounded because of a rumor that Jews were killing Christian children for their blood.

Zegota – A Time To Remember

52 min'ts / Documentaries International, Washington, DC

This video is the story of moral courage evidenced by Polish Christians on behalf of Polish Jewish victims during the Holocaust period.

ON-LINE RESOURCES

Carol Rittner   Stephen Smith
With the Assistance of Henry Klos

Every day new websites about the Holocaust appear on the world wide web (www). Some sites prove to be excellent; others are deceptive, fraudulent, and filled with falsehoods and lies about the Holocaust. The websites we have selected are historically accurate, educational, filled with useful information, and historically reliable. At the time of publication, they were up and running and easily accessible using a standard web browser. While we had to be selective because of space limitations, we tried to select sites that were informational as well as challenging.

The American Jewish Committee
http://www.ajc.org

Site of the AJC, an organization that works to strengthen principles of pluralism as a defense against antisemitism. Information about Jewish life, international issues, search engine, links.

Anne Frank Educational Trust
http://www.annefrank.org.uk/

General information about the Holocaust; Holocaust testimonies, eyewitness accounts, exhibition, links to other websites.

Anti-Defamation League
http://www.adl.org

Site for the ADL, an organization that works to investigate the roots of hatred against Jews. Serves as a public resource for the government, media, law enforcement agencies and the general public.

Beth Shalom Holocaust Memorial & Educational Centre
http://www.bethshalom.com/

General information about the Holocaust; eye witness accounts, documents, photographs, a range of useful links to other sites.

The Centre for Jewish-Christian Relations
http://www.jcrelations.com/cjcr

Information on the CJRC which offers a forum for Jews and Christians to study and work together. CJRC's goal is to improve relations between Judaism and Christianity through education.

The Council of Christians and Jews
http://www.ccj.org.uk

Site of CCJ, an organization that works to bring together Christians and Jewish communities in Britain to fight prejudice, intolerance, and discrimination between people of different religions, races, and colors. Offers a listing of publications, events, and articles.

Cybrary of the Holocaust
http://remember.org

Contains a wealth of facts about the Holocaust; uses art, discussion groups, photos, and other resources to educate about the Holocaust. Links to other sites.

Danish Center for Holocaust and Genocide Studies
http://www.holocaust-history.org/

A free archive of documents, photographs, recordings, and essays about the Holocaust. Includes information about Holocaust-denial.

The Holocaust Teacher Resource Center
http://www.holocaust-trc.org

Contains numerous resources and materials to assist teachers with Holocaust education. Particular link – http://www.holocaust-trc.org/Jehovah.htm – contains the full text of a Untied States Holocaust Memorial Museum booklet on Jehovah's Witnesses.

Ghetto Fighters' House
http://www.gfh.org.il/english/

Library and archives, exhibitions, educational resources and events, links to other sites.

International Coalition for Religious Freedom
http://www.religiousfreedom.com/

Offers access to world reports, articles on religious freedom, and conference proceedings. Examines the status of religious freedom throughout the world.

International Council of Christians and Jews (ICCJ)
http://www.iccj.org

Site offers informatin on various councils, conferences, publications and web links dealing with the ICCJ's goal of promoting mutual understanding among Jews and Christians to combat antisemitism.

International Interfaith Centre
http://www.interfaith-center.org/aims.htm

Provides access to Interfaith resources, events, and publications in an attempt to further peaceful relations, respect and understanding between people of different faith beliefs.

Institute for Christian and Jewish Studies
http://www.icjs.org/intro.html

Site for ICJS, a non-profit organization that concentrates its educational expertise on disarming religious hatred and establishing interfaith understanding.

Jewish Holocaust Museum and Research Centre of Melbourne, Australia
http://www.arts.monash.edu.au/affiliates/hlc/

General information about the Holocaust, lecture transcripts, material for schools.

Jewish-Christian Relations Links
http://www.jcreations.com/link.htm

Provides links to web sites related to Jewish-Christian relations, Jewish-Christian dialogue, theology, interfaith issues, Judaism, the Holocaust and antisemitism, and world and international organizations.

Jewish-Christian Relations Page
http://member.tripod.com/JCRelations/main.html

Compiles extracts from articles, quotes, and other information promoting a dialogue between Judaism and Christianity in order to combat hatred and ignorance.

Mechelen Museum of Deportation and the Resistance in Belgium
http://www.cicb.be/shoah/welcome.html

General information about the Holocaust in Belgium; resistance fighters, photographs.

National Conference of Catholic Bishops/United States Catholic Conference (NCCB/USCC)
http://www.nccbuscc.org

Addresses the goals of the NCCB/USCC – which cover an array of Catholic concerns ranging from worship and prayer and revitalizing parishes, to averting nuclear war.

Nizkor Project
http://www1.us.nizkor.org

General and specialized information about the Holocaust; includes topical research guides, information about Holocaust deniers, Nuremberg Trials, people (from A to Z), concentration and death camps, organizations in various countries, and an archive resource. Links to other sites.

Norges Hjemmefrontmuseum (Norway's Resistance Museum)
http://www.nhm.mil.no/index_eng.html

On-line exhibit about resistance in Norway during WW II; information about the Holocaust.

The Simon Wiesenthal Center
http://www.wiesenthal.com

General information about the Holocaust; teaching resources, visual exhibits, links to other websites.

Sweden: International Forum on the Holocaust
www.holocaustforum.gov.se

Swedish government sponsored website highlighting January 26-28, 2000 International Conference on Education, Remembrance and Research about the Holocaust. Updated continuously. Links to other sites.

The United States Holocaust Memorial Museum
http://www.ushmm.org

General information about the Holocaust; teaching resources; archival resources; maps and photographs; on-line exhibits; links to other sites.

The Vatican

http://www.vatican.va/

Web site of the Vatican. Provides on-line search and the latest news relating to the Vatican.

Watchtower: Official Website of Jehovah's Witnesses

www.watchtower.org

Site provides information about Jehovah's Witnesses. Particular link –

www.watchtower.org/library/g/1995/8/22/one_voice.htm – contains the full text of an Awake issue on the Holocaust (based on a lecture given at the United States Holocaust Memorial Museum).

White Rose International

www.WhiteRoseInternational.org

In the spirit of the Nazi-era 'White Rose' resistance movement, this site seeks to reclaim and promote authentic Christian response to totalitarianism – principled resistance – information about rescuers and resisters. Links to other sites.

World Council of Churches

http://www.wcc-coe.org/

International Christian organization built upon the foundation of ecumenical collaboration.

World Jewish Congress

http://www.virtual.co.il/orgs/orgs/wjc/

Site of the WJC, the representative body of Jewish communities worldwide. Contains information about current events, newsletters, policies that affect the Jewish community.

Yad Vashem

http://www.yad-vashem.org.il

General information about the Holocaust; teacher resources, on-line exhibits, information about the Righteous Among the Nations, links to other sites.

INDEX

THE EDITORS

Dr. Carol Rittner, R.S.M. (USA) is Distinguished Professor of Holocaust Studies at The Richard Stockton College of New Jersey. Her activities include involvement in Christian-Jewish Relations, scholarly work on the Holocaust, and community work in Northern Ireland where she serves as a consultant to Holywell Trust, Derry.

Dr. Rittner is the author or editor of numerous essays and books, including *The Courage to Care: Rescuers of Jews During the Holocaust, Different Voices: Women During the Holocaust, Beyond Hate: Living with Our Deepest Differences,* and *Anne Frank in the World: Essays and Reflections.* She is the co-editor (with John K. Roth) of the series, *Christianity and the Holocaust: Core Issues* (Greenwood Publications, USA). Among her forthcoming publications are *Men, Women and War* and *What's the 'Good News' After Auschwitz?*

Stephen Smith, MBE (UK) is co-founder and Director of Britain's first Holocaust Memorial, Beth Shalom in Nottinghamshire. He writes and lectures frequently on Holocaust and Genocide Studies and is the editor of the *Witness Collection* series. Among his forthcoming publications is *Forgotten Places: The Holocaust and the Remnants of Destruction.* A member of the International Task Force on Holocaust Education (Sweden), he works closely with Holocaust projects in Lithuania, Sweden and the USA and is Consultant to South Africa's Cape Town Holocaust Memorial Museum.

Irena Steinfeldt (Israel) is a member of the Education Development Department at Yad Vashem International School for Holocaust Studies in Jerusalem. She teaches students and professionals from both European and Israeli backgrounds and is a regular contributor to international colloquia on teaching about the Holocaust.